lonely planet

Danny Palmerlee
Beth Kohn

YOSEMITE, SEQUOIA & KINGS CANYON
NATIONAL PARKS

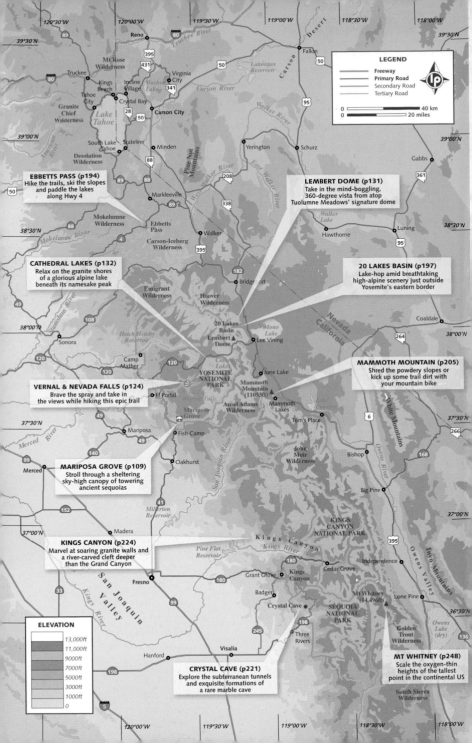

LEGEND

	Freeway
	Primary Road
	Secondary Road
	Tertiary Road

0 ──────── 40 km
0 ──────── 20 miles

EBBETTS PASS (p194)
Hike the trails, ski the slopes
and paddle the lakes
along Hwy 4

LEMBERT DOME (p131)
Take in the mind-boggling,
360-degree vista from atop
Tuolumne Meadows' signature dome

CATHEDRAL LAKES (p132)
Relax on the granite shores
of a glorious alpine lake
beneath its namesake peak

20 LAKES BASIN (p197)
Lake-hop amid breathtaking
high-alpine scenery just outside
Yosemite's eastern border

MAMMOTH MOUNTAIN (p205)
Shred the powdery slopes or
kick up some trail dirt with
your mountain bike

VERNAL & NEVADA FALLS (p124)
Brave the spray and take in
the views while hiking this epic trail

MARIPOSA GROVE (p109)
Stroll through a sheltering
sky-high canopy of towering
ancient sequoias

KINGS CANYON (p224)
Marvel at soaring granite walls and
a river-carved cleft deeper
than the Grand Canyon

CRYSTAL CAVE (p221)
Explore the subterranean tunnels
and exquisite formations of
a rare marble cave

MT WHITNEY (p248)
Scale the oxygen-thin
heights of the tallest
point in the continental US

ELEVATION

	13,000ft
	11,000ft
	9000ft
	7000ft
	5000ft
	3000ft
	1000ft
	0

YOSEMITE, SEQUOIA & KINGS CANYON NATIONAL PARKS

Yosemite and neighboring Sequoia & Kings Canyon occupy the most spectacular region of one of the most spectacular mountain ranges on the planet. With wild rock formations, astonishing waterfalls, unimaginably vast swaths of granite, humbling peaks and a four-season climate that consistently delivers the perfect setting, the area is no less than – hell, we'll say it – perfect. Whether you have the family in tow or you're heading out for some solitude on the trail, you'll find the nature experience you're after – guaranteed. It would take a lifetime to explore this region in its entirety, and this book only scratches the surface. Strike out on your own and you'll find more mountain paradise than you could ever dream up.

Falls Fanatic

Lakes are fun. Rivers? Love 'em. But nothing can strike you speechless like water plunging off a cliff. Standing at the base of a massive waterfall, hearing its roar and reveling in its drenching spray, is simultaneously invigorating and humbling. This region of the Sierra Nevada – especially Yosemite – undoubtedly holds the world's greatest collection of waterfalls. Not one or two but *dozens* of them wait to astound you. The highlights here are simply the ones you shouldn't skip.

Author Tip

It's a no-brainer: if you want waterfalls, visit in late spring/early summer when the runoff from snowmelt makes all the falls pump. The difference between a quiet wisp and a raging torrent is night and day. (You also miss the summer crowds and catch the dogwoods in bloom.) Always toss a rain shell in the pack; some of the falls can literally drench you – fine when it's hot, not when it's not.

❶ Vernal & Nevada Falls

Pack a lunch and climb through the rainbow-filled mist of Vernal Fall (p125) and finally top out above mighty Nevada Fall (p125), where views over the 'Giant Staircase' will boggle your brain.

❷ Bridalveil Fall

Cycle or walk to the base of Yosemite's most graceful waterfall (p102) and watch it career 620ft in uninterrupted perfection to the valley floor. The access trail is an easy stroll.

❸ Yosemite Falls

Sit anywhere you can see it and Yosemite's most iconic waterfall (p101) – actually three falls in one – will entrance you for hours as it dances and shifts in the wind.

❹ Wapama Falls

Wanna get wet? Take a springtime hike to the base of these often-missed waterfalls (p135) that plummet forcefully into Hetch Hetchy Reservoir (and imagine what they were like before the dam!).

❺ Waterwheel Falls

Shoulder your pack for an overnight hike to this strange waterfall (p148) in Yosemite's high country. You'll pass numerous falls, but only one lives up to the name Waterwheel. You'll see why...

❻ Mist Falls

Hike out to this magnificent cascade (p229) in Kings Canyon in early summer and you'll find out why it got its name – and get a wee bit wet in the process.

Peak Season

Whether you climb to the summit of these glorious peaks or simply sit beneath them and stare in wonder, there's no denying their ability to hold a human in awe. From below, these great behemoths tower over the surrounding scenery, at once inspiring the imagination and quieting the mind. From their summits, they offer not only views (which are invariably mind-blowing), but also the combined euphoria of achievement and an astonishment at one's surroundings. Either way, the experience is awesome.

Author Tip

If you're going to attempt a summit, spend at least a day acclimatizing; not only does it increase your odds of reaching the top, but also guarantees a much more enjoyable hike. Do your research and always hike (or climb) within the ability of the least-skilled person in your party. To take your hiking skills further, grab a copy of *Mountaineering: The Freedom of the Hills,* published by the Mountaineers.

① Mt Dana (13,053ft)

Hiking to the top of Yosemite's second-highest peak (p135) affords fantastic vistas of Mono Lake, the Grand Canyon of the Tuolumne and Yosemite's spectacular high country.

② Cathedral Peak (10,911ft)

Whether from the shores of Cathedral Lakes (p132) or from behind a field of purple lupines on Cathedral Pass, the views of spiky Cathedral Peak are simply heart-stopping.

③ Mt Whitney (14,496ft)

Summiting the highest peak (p248) in the contiguous USA, dominating the eastern border of Sequoia National Park, requires utter physical fitness and acclimatization. But oh, what a feeling.

④ Mt Lyell (13,114ft)

Sure, you could strap on crampons and traverse the Lyell Glacier to the summit of Yosemite's highest peak, but the view from Lyell Canyon (p143) below is arguably just as spectacular.

⑤ Mt Hoffmann (10,850ft)

Smack in the geographical center of Yosemite, Mt Hoffmann (p128) affords endless views over the park's high country. Can't hack the Class 2 scramble to the top? View it from May Lake below.

⑥ Clouds Rest (9926ft)

Skip the overcrowded hike up Half Dome and make for nearby Clouds Rest (p129), an equally epic hike that arguably boasts the finest views of Yosemite Valley.

Tip-Top Time Warps

Sure, the timeless beauty of the mountains is what you're *really* up here for. But a trip down memory lane – especially when it means wandering through a ghost town or knocking back pints of ice-cold beer in an old-time saloon – is just as much a part of the Sierra Nevada experience. So forget the present, at least for now, and plunge head-long into the past by visiting one of these classic time warps.

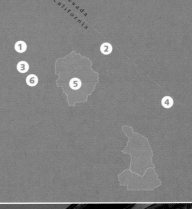

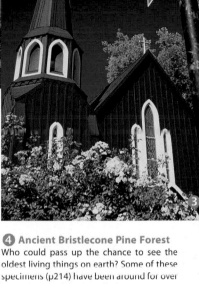

Author Tip

In historic tourist towns outside the parks, businesses often close on Tuesday and/or Wednesday, which means that special museum or wine-tasting room might be closed. When you're reserving a room in a historic hotel, check for the air-con icon ( ) in this book. No air-con? Ask which rooms stay the coolest in summer; those on the shadier side can be markedly fresher than those on the south or sunnier side.

❶ Murphys
With community theater, good restaurants, wine-tasting galore and three blocks of fabulously preserved gold rush–era buildings, this historic foothills town (p190) on Hwy 4 is a must-see.

❷ Bodie State Historic Park
Whoa, who stopped the clock? Journey down a back road to this beautifully preserved ghost town (p200), among the best in California. It's hard to believe it once had 10,000 people living here!

❸ Sonora
Head up to Hwy 108 and see why over 50 films and TV shows were shot in this historic gold-mining town (p189), deemed the 'Queen of the Sierra Mines.'

❹ Ancient Bristlecone Pine Forest
Who could pass up the chance to see the oldest living things on earth? Some of these specimens (p214) have been around for over 4000 years *and they're still alive!*

❺ Miwok-Paiute Baskets
Hit the Yosemite Museum (p98) for a glimpse of these astonishing baskets, hand-woven by indigenous Miwok and Paiute basket weavers, mostly during the 1920s and '30s.

❻ Iron Door Saloon
Mosey up and order a whiskey (neat, of course) at the bar (p182) that claims to the be the oldest in California. Whether it is or not, the atmosphere is unbeatable.

Backcountry Bonanza

Something about spending time in the wilderness resets the brain. You step back, assess situations with fresh eyes and put things into perspective. Maybe it has something to do with the timelessness of the landscape – the ancient glaciers or the glow of the lakes at dusk and dawn. It could be the trail camaraderie, when everyone sweats and swears but makes it into camp in time for dinner. In an age of immediacy, what a luxury to be unreachable.

Author Tip

Even if you're first in line when the wilderness office opens, you can't necessarily scoop up a hiking permit and hit the trail. A certain percentage of permits are reserved for walk-ups, but they're released the day *before* the hike begins. You might luck out and snag a same-day permit, but for popular trailheads, lines form the day before. Sometimes you can still hike a loop by reversing your direction.

❶ Rancheria Falls

Dodge bear scat during a spring hike (p149) past raging Wapama Falls, Hetch Hetchy Dome and Kolana Rock, to this tumbling cascade that spills into the Hetch Hetchy Reservoir.

❷ Lyell Canyon

Give those muscles a break and try some level ground for a change. With a modest elevation gain of 200ft, this flat hike (p143) feels like a cakewalk.

❸ High Sierra Camps

Lighten the load and give in to soft beds and real showers (p165). Feel a spring in your step as you trek in without the weight of a tent or food.

❹ Ansel Adams Wilderness

To the south of Yosemite, ascend to sparkling alpine lakes surrounded by razor-sharp ridges. This stunning high country (p210) is easy to access, and the trails are incomparable.

❺ Rae Lakes Loop

Get acquainted with the Kings Canyon backcountry on a jaunt (p233) between a chain of sparkling lakes, and find out why this is the most popular loop hike in the park.

❻ Whitney Backdoor Route

Sneak up on Mt Whitney (p231) from Sequoia and forgo the lottery system. The very hard-to-get Whitney permits don't apply to hikers summiting from the peak's west side.

Winter Wonderland

For solitude and serenity, winter rules. Summer may be high season in the parks, but after seeing snow in the Sierras you might well question why. Snow paints the trees and splatters the mountains, and your breath turns into moist, puffy clouds. Go swooshing across the backcountry, barreling down some powdery slopes or just stay inside and warm your toes by a roaring wood fire. Whatever your energy level, there are fun activities to fill your days.

Author Tip

Winter in the Sierras means the possibility of snow at any time. Don't even think about driving to the mountains without packing a set of snow chains. During snow storms, the Highway Patrol will turn around vehicles without them. If you've never used chains before, make sure you figure 'em out before you hit the road. If you have front-wheel drive, they'll go on the front tires.

① Mammoth Mountain

Steel yourself for a gondola ride to 11,053ft and some of the most effortless views in the Sierras. This mountain (p205) is tall and the season practically lasts until summer begins.

② Curry Village Ice Skating

A favorite Yosemite tradition where you can practice those rusty pirouettes alfresco under the gaze of Glacier Point. Twirl around the ice (p157), and watch the Zamboni tidy it up.

③ Yosemite Valley

Wake up and watch the flakes fall on a hushed snow-swaddled Valley (p157), with no crowds and few cars. Start a snowball fight, make snow angels and fuel up on hot chocolate.

④ Badger Pass

California's oldest ski resort (p157) is still a charmer. Learn to ski, prepare to fall, and then start all over again. Beginners will love the gentle hill.

⑤ Snowshoe Walks

Plod through the parks (p158 and p237) when the trails go white and wintry. Suit up in those funny-looking waffle shoes and head out on a ranger-led walk.

⑥ Ski Huts

Strap on the skins and set out over snowy cross-country hills and valleys. At the end of the journey, snuggle down in a rustic stone cabin in Yosemite (p158) or Sequoia (p240).

Go Get Wet

Daytime in summer can be sweltering, yet high-altitude nights can chill the bones. Chock-full of deep lakes, careening rivers and veins of gentle streams, there are endless watery adventures to choose from here. You can swan dive into pools, paddleboat pristine lakes, sink a fishing line or raft through tempestuous snow-melt rapids. Alternatively, simmer in boiling liquid and then plunge into an icy pond. However you like your swim spots and boating speed, there's something that will tickle your fancy.

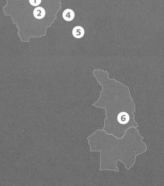

Author Tip

Sorry to say, but the best swimming holes never make it to print. Understandably, the locals jealously guard the locations of their favorite swimming spots. But if you ask around enough, you'll get the skinny on a remote backcountry hot spring or a serpentining flume that flows like a water ride. Some places are too fragile to handle an onslaught of visitors, and others are best discovered through serendipity.

❶ Tenaya Lake

Build sand castles on the beach (p156) and coax those toes into the chilly water. At these altitudes, it's never going to feel balmy, so jump in quickly.

❷ Merced River

Suit up and wander down to Yosemite's best summer splashing. Rent a raft and paddle the wild and scenic waterway (p156), or sit on boulders and just soak up some sun.

❸ Mono Lake

A little salty for swimming, but get an eyeful of all that crazy tufa! Canoe through this beautiful blue bowl (p199) and discover why locals refused to let it die.

❹ June Lake Loop

Choose from four lovely lakes (p202) punctuated by two awesome peaks, and get a boat ready. The trout are out there, just waiting for the line to hit the water.

❺ Eastern Sierra Hot Springs

Toe-test that tub before jumping in – it could be a doozy! Prowl around for a solitary soaking spot (p207) with a mountain view and then strip down to your birthday suit.

❻ Muir Rock

Cannonball off John Muir's lecture site (p224) and do laps from shore to shore in the lazy summer sunshine. The current's gentle and you can float the day away.

El Capitan (p102), one of the world's largest granite monoliths

Contents

Regional Map Contents

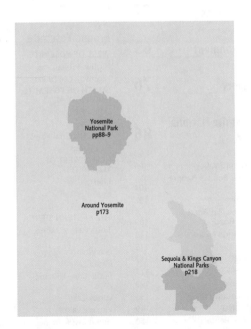

Yosemite National Park pp88–9

Around Yosemite p173

Sequoia & Kings Canyon National Parks p218

The Authors

DANNY PALMERLEE

Our Man in South America for years, writer and photographer Danny Palmerlee recently relocated to his home turf in California in order to cover the park where he hiked and fished throughout his childhood and teenage years. His return to the Yosemite region has reignited his love for California (despite the developers) and reminded him, once again, that nothing soothes the soul like a trip to the Sierras. Danny is the main author of numerous Lonely Planet books, including *Argentina, Best of Buenos Aires, South America on a Shoestring, Ecuador* and *Baja California & Los Cabos*. His work has appeared in the *Los Angeles Times,* the *Miami Herald, San Francisco Chronicle* and the *Dallas Morning News,* as well as other publications throughout the USA and the world. During research for this book, he became obsessed with dehydrated backpacker food, trading in his long-held belief that 'eating that overpriced crap is like chewing corks' for the ease of having no dishes to wash.

My Yosemite National Park

Rolling into Yosemite Valley (p96) in the spring, when the dogwoods are in bloom and the waterfalls are pumping, is simply amazing. Of all the hikes out of Yosemite Valley, the semiloop up to Vernal & Nevada Falls (p124) is probably my favorite. If you have kids, take them on one of the ranger-led 'Starry Skies' walks (p52) and sign them up for a rock-climbing class at the Yosemite Mountaineering School (p155); it'll give you some time alone (wink, wink), and your kids will be eternally grateful. The spectacular high country around Saddlebag Lake (p197) is incredible. If I could be anywhere right now, it would likely be the southern end of Lyell Canyon (p143) or somewhere around Green Creek (p201).

BETH KOHN

A lucky long-time resident of San Francisco, Beth spends months of every year fantasizing about warm-weather backpacking trips in the Sierras – poring over Tom Harrison topo maps, piecing together lake-to-lake loop hikes and wheedling potential cohorts. The opportunity to spend most of a summer traipsing through the mountains and sleeping under the stars felt too good to be true. For this book, she finally conquered her anxiety about trailside bear encounters, tallying nine uneventful sightings before she returned home. Along the way, she did laps in freezing lakes, waded into tepid rivers and soaked in every geothermal puddle she could locate. An author of Lonely Planet's *Venezuela* and *USA* guides, you can see more of her work at www.bethkohn.com.

My Sequoia & Kings Canyon National Parks

My favorite five-star viewpoints are Junction View (p224) – the 'oh wow!' overlook on the drive to Cedar Grove – and Moro Rock (p220), a 360-degree altitude rush atop a steep granite knob. For leisurely hikes, Crescent Meadow (p226) has cool historic cabins and excellent bear-spotting – I saw three there in one day. I love natural soaking and swimming spots. My two faves are a series of small granite pools on Mineral King Rd (p235), about nine miles in, and, of course, all the Eastern Sierra hot springs (p207) with fantastic mountain views. And Manzanar National Historic Site (p246) is the best museum in eastern California, bar none, with a beautiful location and a haunting history.

CONTRIBUTING AUTHOR

David Lukas wrote the Environment chapter. A professional naturalist who lives only minutes from Yosemite National Park, David has contributed environment and wildlife chapters to more than a dozen Lonely Planet guides.

Destination Yosemite, Sequoia & Kings Canyon National Parks

The Sierra Nevada Mountain Range spans 400 miles roughly north to south across Central California, rising up like a vast wrinkled wall from the floor of the Great Central Valley. One can almost imagine the Spanish explorers of the 18th century looking west from the Central Valley, their hands shielding their eyes from the blinding sun, wondering from a distance what those mountains beheld. More than a century later, famed naturalist John Muir gazed at the Sierras from across the same valley and described the range as 'so gloriously colored and so radiant, it seemed not clothed with light, but wholly composed of it, like the wall of some celestial city.'

If Muir had it his way, the Sierra Nevada would be called the Range of Light, as he deemed it, rather than the 'range of snow,' as the Spanish named it in the 18th century. But the Spaniards were hardly wrong – it is indeed a *sierra nevada*. The peaks of the mountain range are some of the highest in the United States, regularly rising above 11,000ft and blanketed by snow for much of the year. Glaciers, although receding, still gnaw at their shoulders as they have for millennia.

Between the Sierras' towering peaks lie saddles, which, for those who knew the way, provided summertime passage across the otherwise impassible mountains. To this day, trails mark the routes taken by indigenous Californians – the Sierra Miwok, the Paiute and others – who traded between the western foothills and the Eastern Sierra. Perhaps the most fortunate of them were the Ahwahneechee, a subtribe of the Sierra Miwok that inhabited a majestic valley near the center of the range, where waterfalls plunged thousands of feet from granite ledges into a sheltered land, which, throughout most of the year, resembled nothing less than paradise. Today, it's known as Yosemite Valley (Yosemite being a mispronunciation of the Miwok word *Oo-hoo'-ma-te* or *uzumate*, meaning 'grizzly bear'), and it's visited by an astounding 3.3 million people every year.

Yet Yosemite Valley, so famous throughout the world and so utterly incapable of losing its power over the soul, is only a small slice of the epic landscape that surrounds it. By all means, visit 'the Valley.' It will blow your mind, guaranteed. But save as much time as you can to explore the country surrounding it.

Each summer, in the high country around Tuolumne Meadows, the Sierra Nevada's largest meadow bursts into life as wildflowers bloom beneath the jagged peaks of the Cathedral Range. The northern sector of the park is home to the Sierra's largest wilderness area, beckoning intrepid backpackers into its hidden folds. The rarely visited Hetch Hetchy Reservoir fills a glacial valley whose beauty rivaled Yosemite's until the completion of the O'Shaughnessy Dam in 1923. But waterfalls still rage from its cliffs, and massive granite domes tower above its shores. In southern Yosemite, Wawona is home to swimming holes, waterfalls and the Mariposa Grove of Giant Sequoias.

'Yosemite [is] a mispronunciation of the Miwok word Oo-hoo'-ma-te or uzumate, meaning "grizzly bear"'

South of Yosemite lie Sequoia & Kings Canyon National Parks, two glorious, adjacent parks that are effectively managed as one. No trip to the Sierras is complete without visiting them. Sequoia National Park is home to the world's largest living thing – a giant sequoia named General Sherman. It's also home to the Giant Forest, Mt Whitney (the highest mountain in the contiguous United States), a spectacular network of hidden caves and a roadless wilderness of incomparable beauty. The park's northern extension is Kings Canyon, where you'll find a stunning glacial valley with a fraction of the crowds found in Yosemite.

North of Yosemite, two high-mountain passes – Ebbetts Pass on Hwy 4 and Sonora Pass along Hwy 108 – cross the sierras, providing access to less-visited areas of the range and to a slew of activities that you won't find within the parks, including mountain biking and the state's best rafting. Then there's the Eastern Sierra, a region east of the Sierra Crest peppered with hot springs, shimmering subalpine lakes and, at Mammoth Lakes, outstanding mountain biking, skiing and snowboarding. The Eastern Sierra is also home to Mono Lake, whose bizarre mineral tufas, which rise like drip-castles from the surface of the lake, are one of the country's strangest sights.

'Sequoia National Park is home to the world's largest living thing – a giant sequoia named General Sherman'

Along with its endless natural wonders, the Sierras also possess an array of fascinating cultural and historic marvels. Gold Country towns like Groveland, Murphys and Sonora hark back to California's gold-rush years during the mid-1800s. Rather than hardware stores and brothels, their creaky wooden buildings now hold art galleries, boutiques and wine-tasting rooms. For the purist, saloons still offer what they did a century ago: cold beer, booze and company. Then there are the more surreal places: the ghost town of Bodie (north of Mono Lake), the long-abandoned mining settlement of Bennettville (near Tuolumne) and the old mining shacks near Mono Pass.

Of course, history is as much in the making as it is in the past. As you tool around the region, you'll turn up issues that the national parks and forests face as they struggle with everything from global warming, to forest fires, to the impact of millions of visitors every year. The importance of *leaving no trace* when you do whatever you do up here is paramount. When you drive into Yosemite Valley, remember it's a privilege that may one day be revoked.

Climate change is a biggie. Glaciers such as the Lyell Glacier are rapidly receding as temperatures rise. Small, upper-elevation mammals such as the beloved little pika (a tiny relative of the rabbit) have moved to higher, previously uninhabitable elevations and abandoned their lower stomping grounds. Hand in hand with climate change, fire suppression has transformed the natural world throughout the Sierras, and the park service continues to educate visitors about controlled burning and preventing fires. Cliché as it sounds, the future of the parks lies in public hands – the more time you spend up here, the more obvious that becomes. Which is exactly why you should bag the daily grind and head for the hills. Consider it…the right thing to do.

Planning Your Trip

Let's face it, planning is half the fun. It's also the best way to ensure you'll pull off your trip without a hitch – or at least without one that matters much. This chapter is designed to point you to the best resources out there (books, websites, maps); to give you some pointers on when to go ('C'mon, do the waterfalls really dry up?'); and to help you figure out what things might cost (Fill up the tank *before* you get to the parks!). For more tourist information sources, see p257.

WHEN TO GO
The easy answer is: 'Whenever you can!' And it's highly unlikely you'll be disappointed. But if you have particular interests (such as waterfalls, wildflowers or river rafting) or dislikes (crowds or hot weather), you'll need to look a little more closely at the when-to-go question.

Although most people visit the parks in summer (June through early September, but especially July and August), it's not necessarily the best time to visit. First of all, everything is crowded. (Sequoia & Kings Canyon gets a fraction of the visitors Yosemite gets, so crowds are a lesser concern there.) In Yosemite, there's also the waterfall factor: after the springtime snowmelt, the waterfalls – including Yosemite Falls – slowly wither to trickles and, by late summer, sometimes dry up entirely. That said, summer is the only time *everything* (save Badger Pass Ski Area) is open, including campgrounds, trails and facilities along Tioga Rd (which includes Tuolumne Meadows), Glacier Point Rd and other high-country locales. Temperatures in Yosemite Valley and lower areas of Sequoia & Kings Canyon regularly soar into the 90s, but summer weather at higher altitudes is sublime.

Spring – particularly April, May and the first half of June – is a splendid time to visit both parks. In Yosemite Valley, the dogwoods are in bloom (a magnificent sight), temperatures are mild and, except on weekends, crowds are practically nonexistent. Most importantly, spring is waterfall season, when Yosemite's falls are at their most spectacular. The high country, however, (including all passes over the Sierras) is usually inaccessible until summer.

For more on weather patterns throughout the region, see the climate charts on p252.

Fall can be a great time to visit, especially from early September (the end of the school summer break) until the temperatures drop, usually near the end of October. Fall foliage in Yosemite may never match New England's technicolor displays, but leaves do create that vibrant autumnal mood, especially in Yosemite Valley and Wawona. Winter snows close the high-elevation roads, and most facilities shut down in and around both parks. But crowds disappear entirely, and snow brings a silent magic to Yosemite Valley well worth experiencing.

For information on the best time to practice certain activities, see p38. For a list of holidays that make the parks crowded, see p255. For festivals and events that you might want to catch, see p254.

COSTS & MONEY
Entrance Fees & Passes
Both Yosemite and Sequoia & Kings Canyon charge a $20 entrance fee. In 2007 there was talk of raising the Yosemite fee to $25, but enough people raised hell over the matter to keep the fee at $20, at least for the near future. Anyone entering by foot, bicycle, motorcycle or charter bus pays $10 per

PLANNING YOUR TRIP

QUICK PLANNER

The weather and your interests will determine the best time to make for the mountains. So...

If you want to:	Then visit:	And be sure to:
avoid mosquitoes in the high country	late Jul–Aug	pack bug repellent anyway
avoid the crowds in Yosemite	mid-Sep–mid-Jun	make a reservation anyway
backpack in Mineral King	Jun-Oct	marmot-proof your car
backpack in the High Sierras	Jul–mid-Sep	reserve a wilderness permit
be wowed by Yosemite's waterfalls	Apr–Jun	hike to Vernal and Nevada Falls
day hike in Hetch Hetchy	mid-Apr–Jun	book a room at the Evergreen Lodge
drive Hwys 120, 108 or 4 over the Sierras	Jul–mid-Sep	check road conditions (www.dot.ca.gov /hq/roadinfo) before heading out
experience Yosemite Valley blanketed in snow	Dec-Feb	bring warm bedding for the tent cabins
hike the Mt Whitney Trail	May-Oct	apply for the lottery in Feb
ice skate at the rink in Yosemite Valley	Dec-Feb	pack a flask and your sense of humor
raft or kayak on the Tuolumne or Merced Rivers	Apr-early Jun	bring straps for your sunglasses
ski at Badger Pass or Bear Valley	Dec-Feb	pack the tire chains
spelunk in Crystal Cave	mid-May–Oct	bring warm clothes
swim in the Merced, Stanislaus or Tuolumne Rivers	Jul-Aug	swim where you know the currents aren't strong
witness the Pacific dogwoods in bloom	Apr-May	bring the camera

---

person – there is no charge for passengers on the Yosemite Area Regional Transportation System (YARTS) buses into Yosemite. An annual pass for Sequoia & Kings Canyon costs $30, while the same for Yosemite costs $40. For updated fee information see the **Yosemite National Park** (www.nps.gov/yose) and **Sequoia & Kings Canyon National Park** (www.nps.gov/seki) websites.

The National Park Service (NPS) offers a series of annual discount passes that cover all national parks and federal recreation areas. The standard Annual Pass costs $80 and grants the holder (and everyone in his or her vehicle) entrance to any national park or federal recreation area for one year. It can be purchased at any park entrance or through the **US Geological Survey** (USGS; ☎ 1-888-275 8747; http://store.usgs.gov/pass).

American citizens and permanent residents who are over 62 years old can purchase the 'America the Beautiful' Senior Pass, which at $10 must be one of the country's last great perks for seniors. The Access Pass is a free lifetime pass available to any US citizen or permanent resident with a permanent disability. Both the Senior Pass and the Access Pass are available at park entrances only. Also see Discount Cards, p254.

Expenses

Once you've coughed up your entrance fee, all your sightseeing, hiking and ranger-led programs are free. Visitors who camp and cook all their own food (purchased *outside* of the park, of course) can easily keep costs to a minimum. Campsites run anywhere from $5 at a walk-in campground to $20 for a standard site in Yosemite. So with food being your only other required expense, there's no reason a party of two can't get by on about $20 to $30 per day, all in.

Staying at a hotel in either park, especially in Yosemite, is when things start getting expensive. For example, the cost for two adults to share a hotel room in Yosemite Lodge and dine exclusively at park restaurants can exceed $250 a day. You can opt to stay in a motel outside the park,

The National Parks are largely surrounded by National Forests, and the National Forests have a vast network of mostly public dirt roads. You can camp for free along many of them – great news when official campgrounds are full.

but even budget places run at least $60 to $70 a night in summer – many are even higher. Couple that with the $25 to $30 per day to eat at park restaurants, and you can see how things add up quickly. Tent cabins in both parks bring the cost down, but even they start at around $75, and you still have to pay for your food. Cooking your own meals and packing a picnic lunch help to lower costs. Only the tent cabins at Yosemite's Housekeeping Camp (p165) allow cooking.

Extracurricular activities such as renting bikes, rafting or hiring a guide will increase your costs. For information on public-transportation costs, see p266.

For some classic fireside literature make sure you dip your toes into John Muir's *The Mountains of California*.

BOOKS

You'll find loads of other book recommendations interspersed throughout this book (see their related chapters), but these must-reads should start you off.

No one more passionately nor more lyrically evokes the wonders of Yosemite and the Sierras than John Muir. His descriptions and meanderings on everything from the Douglas squirrel to Yosemite Falls takes you deeper into the natural world than you likely ever dreamed possible. You can follow Muir into the Sierras in his eloquent *My First Summer in the Sierra* (1911), in which he describes his first venture into the region as a sheepherder in 1869.

FESTIVALS & EVENTS

Whether it's a writers conference at 8150ft or a music festival out in a sun-beaten field, there's something uniquely special about festivals (and events) in the Sierras. Folks are friendly, spirits are high and there's always someone wearing a funny hat. Festivals and events of predominantly local significance are covered within their respective destination sections throughout this book. For events with a literary bent, see the boxed text, p26.

- **Chefs' Holidays** (☎ 559-253-2001; www.yosemitepark.com) Top American chefs lead cooking demonstrations, offer kitchen tours and cook a sumptuous gala dinner in January and February at the Ahwahnee Hotel. Reservations are required.

- **Yosemite Springfest** (☎ 209-372-8430) Badger Pass Ski Area hosts this winter carnival on the last weekend of each ski season (usually in March or April). Events include slalom racing, costume contests, obstacle courses, a barbecue and snow-sculpting.

- **Strawberry Music Festival** (☎ 209-984-8630; www.strawberrymusic.com) Twice a year (each Labor Day and Memorial Day weekend), lovers of country and folk music beeline to this wildly popular music festival held in a meadow at Camp Mather, about 10 miles northwest of Yosemite's Big Oak Flat Entrance. Children's programs constitute half the fun, and organized camping is allowed. Tickets sell out fast.

- **Picnic in the Park** (www.mineralking.org) Each July, residents tell stories and celebrate the Mineral King community during this family event sponsored by the Mineral King Preservation Society.

- **Vintners' Holidays** (☎ 559-253-2001; www.yosemitepark.com) Wine-lovers descend upon the Ahwahnee each November and December for this annual wine- and food-tasting extravaganza. Reservations are required.

- **Bracebridge Dinner** (☎ 559-252-4848; www.bracebridgedinners.com) Held at the Ahwahnee Hotel, Yosemite's best-known seasonal event is a traditional Christmas pageant that's part grand feast and part Renaissance fair. Guests indulge in a multicourse meal while being entertained by more than 100 actors in 17th-century costume. Tickets cost around $375 and sell out a year in advance.

The *Yosemite* (1912), also by Muir, is less narrative in style than *My First Summer in the Sierra,* but it conjures the spirit of Yosemite in a way that will surely set your feet to itching. It's worth picking up if only for the chapter titled 'How Best to Spend One's Time in Yosemite': Muir's suggestions on what to do while you're there.

If you're heading to Yosemite, there's no better way to brush up on the area's history than by reading Margaret Sanborn's excellent book, *Yosemite: Its Discovery, Its Wonders & Its People* (1981). For the Sequoia & Kings Canyon side of the story, check out Douglas Strong's *From Pioneers to Preservationists* (1990), or the dry but comprehensive *Challenge of the Big Trees* (1990), by Lary M Dilsaver & William C Tweed. Both are published by the Sequoia Natural History Association.

When you need a break from the classics, pick up a copy of Michael Ghiglieri and Butch Farabee's *Off the Wall: Death in Yosemite* (2007), a tome of a work detailing the morbid side of Yosemite. With a subtle sense of humor and unembellished prose, the book even boasts a little suspense: not everyone who suffers dies.

John W Simpson's *Dam!* (2005) offers an extremely readable history of Hetch Hetchy Reservoir without getting too bogged down in political nitty-gritty.

For in-depth detail on hiking and backpacking in Yosemite and the surrounding mountains, seek out Lonely Planet's *Hiking in the Sierra Nevada* by John Mock and Kimberley O'Neil. You can find broader statewide coverage in Lonely Planet's *California* guide.

MAPS

National Geographic (www.ngmapstore.com) publishes five outstanding Yosemite hiking maps under its Trails Illustrated series: the 1:80:000 *Yosemite* map ($10), which covers the whole park; and the more detailed 1:40,000 *Yosemite NW, Yosemite SW, Yosemite NE* and *Yosemite SE* maps ($9). A 1:80,000 *Sequoia/Kings Canyon* map ($10) is also available. All are waterproof, tear-resistant, color topographical maps with well-marked trails and geographic features.

The *Topographic Map of Yosemite National Park and Vicinity* ($10), published by **Wilderness Press** (☎ 800-443-7227; www.wildernesspress.com) is an excellent map for hikers and more serious sightseers.

THE LITERARY JUKEBOX

Those who live and love the literary life will find these Yosemite National Park events well worth attending:

- **Mariposa Storytelling Festival** (☎ 209-966-3155, 800-903-9936; www.arts-mariposa.org/storytelling .html) The town of Mariposa (p176) hosts this internationally recognized storytelling event each year in late February or early March.

- **Tuolumne Meadows Poetry Festival** (☎ 209-379-2646) A poetry festival on the grass in Tuolumne Meadows? How can you beat that? Sponsored by the Yosemite Association, the festival happens each August.

- **Yosemite Winter Literary Conference** (☎ 209-379-2646) Each February the Ahwahnee Hotel and the Yosemite Association host a series of seminars and discussions featuring an impressive selection of writers and poets.

- **Yosemite Writers Conference** (www.yosemitewriters.com) Tenaya Lodge (p188) hosts an annual writers conference around the end of August, and tickets are reasonable (about $55).

You can create your own custom USGS topographical map at **Adventure station.com** (☎ 775-787-6777; www.adventurestation.com). The website will bring up a USGS 7.5-minute topo map based around any geographic feature or coordinate you type in. You can then order that map in standard, waterproof or laminated paper in a variety of sizes. For map-lovers, it's no less than amazing.

Mapping software and GPS receivers open a whole world of navigational possibilities. Check out National Geographic's *Yosemite National Park Explorer 3D*, which allows you to view topographic and 3D maps of the entire park, create routes, download waypoints to your GPS and print maps. If you plan to hit both parks or just Sequoia & Kings Canyon, get the *National Parks Explorer 3D* version, which covers all US national parks.

For drivers, nothing beats the *California Road and Recreation Atlas*, published by **Benchmark Maps** (www.benchmarkmaps.com). If you're a member of the **American Automobile Association** (AAA; www.aaa.com), be sure to pick up free maps of the region; they're just about the easiest way to map and drive at the same time.

INTERNET RESOURCES

There's no need to expound on the internet's limitless information. In fact, there's often *too* much information out there. With that in mind, we've rounded up the best general websites on Yosemite, Sequoia & Kings Canyon and the Sierra Nevada we could find (and threw in an extra one we're particularly fond of). Other websites are listed in the chapters to which they're related.

High Sierra Topix (www.highsierratopix.com) Sections of this easily navigated website cover everything from packing lists and food storage to fishing and backpacking (all in the Sierras, of course), but the forums are what really make it shine. Organize rides, get weather reports, offer tips on gear and much more.

Lonely Planet (www.lonelyplanet.com) Check in for succinct summaries on traveling to most places on earth; postcards from other travelers; and the Thorn Tree bulletin board, where you can ask questions before you go and dispense advice when you get back.

Sequoia & Kings Canyon National Park (www.nps.gov/seki) The Sequoia & Kings Canyon official website, providing indispensable advice for planning any trip to the park.

Yosemite Blog (www.yosemiteblog.com) A park just isn't a park without its blog, now is it?

Yosemite National Park (www.nps.gov/yose) The official Yosemite National Park website contains the most in-depth information about almost everything you need to know, from bear updates to wilderness permit requirements. You can download current and archived issues of Yosemite Today for a rundown of daily park programs and schedules.

Yosemite Online (www.yosemite.ca.us) This site provides direct answers to your questions. Though not much to look at, it's worth checking out if you'd like to pose queries to those who know Yosemite.

YosemiteFun.com (www.yosemitefun.com) Although it's no feat of website design, this is a comprehensive and sometimes humorous resource packed with info on Yosemite offered by Fresno-based photographer Phil Hawkins. Lots of photos, discussions of local politics and insider tips.

USEFUL ORGANIZATIONS

The nonprofit **Yosemite Association** (YA; ☎ 209-379-2646; www.yosemite.org) is an educational organization founded in 1923 with the specific purpose of supporting Yosemite National Park. Through membership dues, book sales, seminar fees and donations, YA offers financial assistance directly to the park. YA also aids with visitor services, organizes volunteer work crews, supports scientific and educational research projects, publishes its own series of books and operates the Ostrander Ski Hut (see the

At 9945ft, Tioga Pass (Hwy 120, east of Yosemite) is the highest paved road over the Sierras. The next highest is Sonora Pass (Hwy 108) at 9624ft, followed by Ebbetts Pass (Hwy 4) at 8730ft.

PLANNING YOUR TRIP

boxed text, p158) and the wilderness permit reservation system. Pick up YA information at kiosks throughout the park or at the visitor center bookstores.

Founded by John Muir in 1892, the **Sierra Club** (☎ 415-977-5500; www .sierraclub.org; 85 Second St, San Francisco, CA 94105) today boasts more than 700,000 members and remains an active and important environmental advocate, both for Yosemite and Sequoia & Kings Canyon. Outings, mostly led by informed volunteers, are a vital part of club activities.

Other extremely helpful organizations include the **Mono Lake Committee** (☎ 760-647-6595; www.monolake.org) and the **Sequoia Natural History Association** (☎ 559-565-3759; www.sequoiahistory.org).

Itineraries

THE GRAND TOUR
Two to Four Weeks/Sequoia to Ebbetts Pass

- Kick off the trip with three to four days in **Sequoia & Kings Canyon National Parks** (p215)
- Head up Hwy 41, camp at **Wawona** (p107) and explore the southern reaches of the park
- Spend *at least* three days exploring the miraculous falls and granite monoliths of **Yosemite Valley** (p96)
- Hike the trails of Yosemite's high country while camped out at spectacular **Tuolumne Meadows** (p113)
- Explore the shimmering alpine lakes dotting the surreal countryside in the **20 Lakes Basin** (p197)
- Journey down to Hwy 395 and detour south to the bizarre **Devils Postpile National Monument** (p211)
- Drive north to Hwy 108 and head up to **Scenic Sonora Pass** (p189) for more superb hiking
- Loop around Hwy 4 to **Ebbetts Pass** (p194) for outstanding river swimming, hiking, bouldering and biking

Finagle extra holiday time for this epic 510-mile road trip between Sequoia National Park in the south and Hwy 4's spectacular Ebbetts Pass to the north.

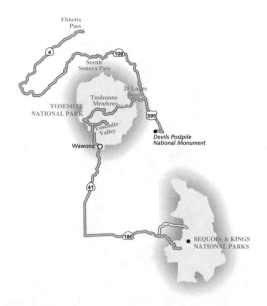

YOSEMITE NATIONAL PARK   Seven to 10 Days

Spend a busy week or a relaxed 10 days following this 150-mile route through the park, visiting each of its four main areas: Yosemite Valley, Hetch Hetchy, Wawona and Tuolumne Meadows.

- Get acquainted with Yosemite Valley's natural and human history by strolling the **Yosemite Valley loop trails** (p118)
- Experience mind-altering views hiking the Mist Trail to **Vernal and Nevada Falls** (p124)
- Be a lazy toad and float the **Merced River** (p155) – the best views from a raft you'll ever have
- Hike the Four-Mile Trail to **Glacier Point** (p124) for vistas from the park's most famous viewpoint
- Go climb a rock: take a climbing class at the **Yosemite Mountaineering School** (p155)
- Drive out to Hetch Hetchy and hike to **Tueeulala and Wapama Falls** (p135)
- Gobble down a giant breakfast in style at the historic **Wawona Hotel** (p167)
- After breakfast at the Wawona, humble yourself exploring the **Mariposa Grove of Giant Sequoias** (p109)
- Pack a lunch and hike to thundering **Chilnualna Falls** (p126), near Wawona
- Sun your buns while taking in the dazzling views from the sandy shores of **Tenaya Lake** (p141)
- Wander around the Sierra Nevada's biggest alpine meadow while camped at **Tuolumne Meadows** (p113)

HIGH COUNTRY HIGH

One to Two Weeks

- Hike into **Lyell Canyon** (p143) for fishing, dipping and views like you won't believe
- Climb up to **Cathedral Lakes** (p132), possibly the most spectacular lakes in the entire Sierra Nevada
- Carry a bottle of wine to the top of **Pothole Dome** (p114) for a fabulous sunset treat
- Scramble to the top of **Lembert Dome** (p131) for jaw-dropping views over Tuolumne Meadows
- Hike in style to **Vogelsang High Sierra Camp** (p165), and leave the cooking to the pros
- Giggle at wildflowers and soak up the scenery beside the lazy **Tuolumne River** (p113)
- Wolf down a burger, fries and ice cream at the **Tuolumne Meadows Grill** (p170) while people-watching out front
- Follow an ancient Miwok/Piute trade route past Dana Meadows and over **Mono Pass** (p134)
- Explore the alpine lakes and endless vistas of the **20 Lakes Basin** (p197)
- Spend a cozy night at the rustic **Tioga Pass Resort** (p195), and wake up with a huge breakfast
- Get *really* high: hike to the top of **Mt Dana** (p135), Yosemite's second-highest peak

Driving time is kept to a minimum during this wander through the spectacular high-country around Tuolumne Meadows and Tioga Pass, the region John Muir deemed the most 'delightful high pleasure-ground' he'd ever seen.

ITINERARIES

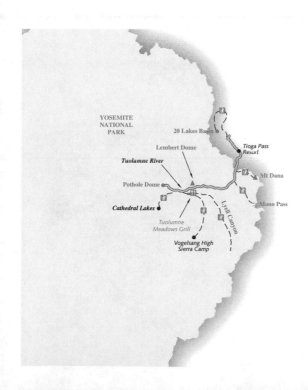

YOSEMITE NATIONAL PARK

20 Lakes Basin

Lembert Dome

Tioga Pass Resort

Tuolumne River

Mt Dana

Pothole Dome

Cathedral Lakes

Mono Pass

Tuolumne Meadows Grill

Lyell Canyon

Vogelsang High Sierra Camp

THE NORTHERN LOOP

Two to Three Weeks

After exploring the best Yosemite has to offer, this 270-mile journey will take you over Tioga Pass to the Eastern Sierras, up beautiful Hwy 395 and back over the Sierra crest via Ebbetts Pass.

- Start with three days exploring Yosemite Valley, being certain to see **Vernal and Nevada Falls** (p124)
- Journey the rough road down to **Yosemite Creek Campground** (p164) for a quiet night
- Spend two days in Tuolumne Meadows and don't miss **Cathedral Lakes** (p132)
- Camp near Saddlebag Lake and explore the **20 Lakes Basin** (p197)
- Drive down the Lee Vining Scenic Byway (Hwy 120 E) to **Mono Lake** (p199)
- Spend a day fishing and smelling the wildflowers at uncrowded **Lundy Lake** (p201)
- Camp out at **Green Creek Campground** (p201) and hike through beautiful aspen groves
- Head out to surreal **Bodie** (p200), California's most stunningly preserved ghost town
- Spend two days exploring the lakes and trails, and mountain biking around **Ebbetts Pass** (p194) on Hwy 4
- While away a day wine tasting in the delightful gold-rush town of **Murphys** (p190)
- Transport yourself back to the Wild West with a visit to historic **Sonora** (p189)

YOSEMITE VALLEY IN A DAY   **15 Hours**

■ 7am–1:30pm: hike the Mist Trail (quickly) to **Vernal and Nevada Falls** (p124); picnic en route

■ 2pm: rent a **beach cruiser** (p150) at the Yosemite Lodge for your ride around the Valley floor

■ 2:20pm: park the bike at **Lower Yosemite Falls** (p101) and walk to the viewing area

■ 2:50–3:30pm: Pedal west on Northside Dr to the base of **El Capitan** (p102) for views of the park's biggest rock

■ 3:30–4pm: ride across Pohono Bridge and double around to the base of **Bridalveil Fall** (p102)

■ 4–4:30pm: continue east on Southside Dr to Sentinel Bridge for the view of **Half Dome** (p101)

■ 4:30–5:15pm: ride up to **Mirror Lake** (p118) and snap a photo of the glorious reflection therein

■ 5:15–6:30pm: zip over to the historic **Ahwahnee Hotel** (p102) for a well-deserved cocktail

■ 6:30–7:30pm: return the bike then indulge in food *and* views at the **Mountain Room Restaurant** (p169)

■ 8–9:30pm (entertainment option A): relax to a Yosemite-related flick at the **West Auditorium** (p98)

■ 9–10pm (entertainment option B): take a ranger-led **Starry Skies over Yosemite Valley walk** (p52)

Also known as the Manic Rock & Waterfall tour, this itinerary – designed for those with little time or lots of Attention Deficit Disorder – gets you to the best stuff fast.

ITINERARIES

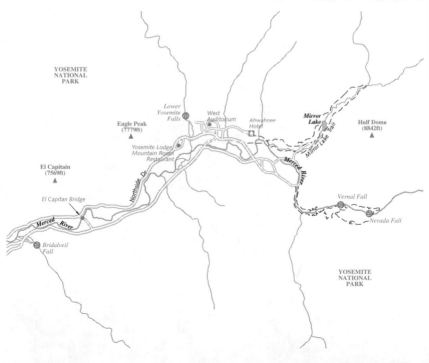

SEQUOIA NATIONAL PARK

One Day

Focus your attention on the sights of Sequoia, and take the free shuttle bus from the Giant Forest Museum to many of these highlights. Total driving distance will be 68.6 miles.

- Stop by the **Foothills Visitor Center** (p221) to reserve tour tickets for Crystal Cave
- Hit the brakes at **Tunnel Rock** (p221) and visualize squeezing through with a monster car
- Scale the crazy stairs up to **Moro Rock** (p220) for bird's-eye canyon and peak views
- Snap a time-lapse photo of your car streaming through the **Tunnel Log** (p235) archway
- Steady yourself for a possible face-to-face with a black bear at **Crescent Meadow** (p226)
- Feel dwarfed by the majestic **General Sherman Tree** (p220), the largest tree in the world
- Picnic at Lodgepole, with gourmet sandwiches and fresh salads from the **Watchtower Deli** (p242)
- Revel in the delicate marble formations and new scientific discoveries at **Crystal Cave** (p221)
- Let the kids play with fake poop at the **Beetle Rock Education Center** (p220)
- Stand inside a replica of a mature giant sequoia at the **Giant Forest Museum** (p220)
- Slip away from the pack and bed down at the cozy **Stony Creek Lodge** (p241)

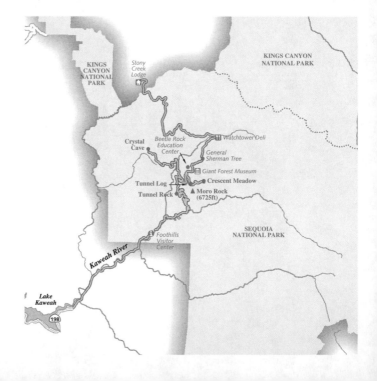

MAMMOTH HIKE & BIKE   **Four Days**

- Get a taste of the high country with a stunning day trip to **Shadow Lake** (p210) on the Thousand Island Lake trail
- Rinse off the trail dust at the **hot spring showers** (p210) at Reds Meadow campground
- Camp by the riverside and hike to the cascade at **Minaret Falls** (p210)
- Wonder at the bizarre basalt columns and hexagonal-patterned ridge of **Devils Postpile** (p211)
- Hike out to see the corona mist of **Rainbow Falls** (p212), passing through rejuvenating forest
- Gear up and fly down the trails at the high-altitude **Mammoth Mountain Bike Park** (p206)
- Soak in the natural **Hot Tub** (p207), just a few miles south of town, and soothe your aching muscles
- Ricochet off the undulating cement walls at the **Volcom Brothers Skate Park** (p209)
- Sample a smorgasbord of fine beers at the basement digs of the **Clocktower Cellar** (p209)
- Survey the heavenly spires and peaks of the Ansel Adams Wilderness from **Minaret Vista** (p210)
- Toil your way up and effortlessly belay down the Mammoth Mountain **Climbing Rock** (p208)

There's a mandatory shuttle to Devils Postpile and the Ansel Adams Wilderness, so the only real driving involved is the 23-mile round-trip to the hot spring.

ITINERARIES

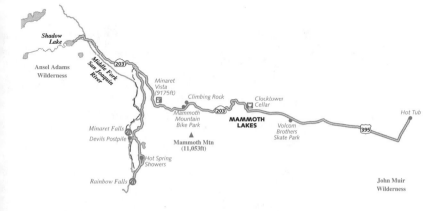

SEQUOIA & KINGS CANYON   **One Week**

Traverse the length
of the park via
the Kings Canyon
Scenic Byway and
the Generals Hwy.
Expect a dirt road
to the lookout and
rough patches to
Mineral King.

▪ Survey the canyon depths and distant peaks from the shoulder of lofty **Junction View** (p224)

▪ Get your first glimpse of the local caves with a tour at **Boyden Cavern** (p224)

▪ Spend a sunny day perfecting your backstroke at the placid waters of **Muir Rock** (p224)

▪ Saunter around lush green **Zumwalt Meadow** (p227) and admire the striking granite canyon views

▪ Swim some more, try your luck fishing and then camp at **Hume Lake** (p225)

▪ Mourn the senseless deaths of the many giant sequoias near the **Boole Tree** (p225)

▪ Traipse through a hollowed-out tree in **General Grant Grove** (p223) that once housed a hotel

▪ Conquer vertigo and ascend to the panoramic pinnacle of the **Buck Rock Lookout** (p222)

▪ Ease through eerie passageways of **Crystal Cave** (p221), sucking it in on the tight corners

▪ Admire the largest tree in the world in the shady grove of **Giant Forest** (p220)

▪ Steady your steering wheel and wind into the quiet valley of remote **Mineral King** (p222)

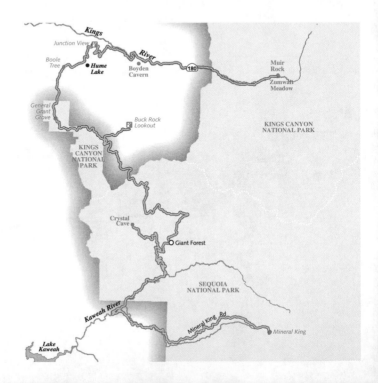

AWESOME EASTERN SIERRA　　　　　　Two to Three Weeks

- Swoon at the tufa formations as you hike the shore of **Mono Lake** (p199)
- Hopscotch between campgrounds and lakes, fishing every few miles along the **June Lake Loop** (p202)
- Saddle up for a day-long **horseback ride** (p208) heading out from Mammoth Lakes
- Pack your camera for a multiday hike through the justly named **Ansel Adams Wilderness** (p210)
- Surrender to the myriad **natural hot springs** (p207) off Benton Crossing Rd near Mammoth
- Chalk up your fingertips while sizing up the blissful bouldering spots outside **Bishop** (p213)
- Rejuvenate sore muscles with a swim in the pools at **Keough's Hot Springs** (p213)
- Go up, up and away to the **Ancient Bristlecone Pine Forest** (p214), where twisted trees thrive
- Learn about the troubling wartime internment of Japanese-Americans during a half-day at **Manzanar** (p246)
- Bask in the evening alpenglow as you camp in the **Alabama Hills** (p247)
- Summit the tantalizing peak of **Mt Whitney** (p248), spending three days on the main trail

A drive through the Hwy 395 corridor is a sight to behold. Rack up 188 miles sampling some of the best hikes and natural attractions the Eastern Sierra has to offer.

ITINERARIES

YOSEMITE NATIONAL PARK

Mono Lake

June Lake Loop

395

Natural Hot Springs

Ansel Adams Wilderness

Mammoth Lakes

Ancient Bristlecone Pine Forest

168

Bishop

Keough's Hot Springs

KINGS CANYON NATIONAL PARK

395

Manzanar National Historic Site

Alabama Hills

SEQUOIA NATIONAL PARK

Mt Whitney (14,496ft)

38

Activities

We met a guy on the trail in Yosemite who'd been hiking for seven hours with a full pack *after* driving five hours to Tuolumne Meadows – from sea level – the same day. The plan: hike until dark, eat, sleep, get up at the crack of dawn, summit Lyell Peak *and* neighboring Mt McLure and then hike out and drive home. 'I've done this approach four times,' he said, 'and every time I swear I'll never do it again. But I can't stop.'

Fanatical. Some might say insane. But that's what these hills can do to you. Every time you get home from a trip to Yosemite or Sequoia & Kings Canyon, all you can think about for weeks is the *next* trip. Maybe it's the granite. Or the big, big trees. Whatever it is, it's not just the reserve of maniacal mountaineers. Hikers, fly casters, cross-country skiers, even the kids skating around Yosemite Valley's ice-skating rink have that same look in their eye. It's as if everyone up here knows you can do this stuff anywhere in the world, but the setting anywhere else could never match up. And that's why this is paradise when it comes to active pursuits in the great outdoors. Few places compare.

As far as summer activities go, the region is a dream: few mountain ranges anywhere can boast the same perpetually beautiful and gloriously mild summer weather. As for winter, the snow gets thick and the Sierras offer everything from world-class downhill skiing and snowboarding (think Mammoth) to phenomenal cross-country skiing in Yosemite National Park. And if you can work around the wet weather, spring and fall are sublime.

HIKING

Whether strolling leisurely along the floor of Yosemite Valley or schlepping a 60lb pack over a High Sierra pass, hiking is the way most people experience Yosemite and Sequoia & Kings Canyon. And it's no wonder: Between the three parks, over 1600 miles of trails traverse a diverse and spectacular landscape that is, as a whole, one of the greatest hiking destinations in the world.

ACTIVITIES

WHERE TO GEAR UP

Whatever it is that you're kicking yourself for forgetting, you can probably get it at one of the many sport shops throughout the region.

- **Bear Valley Adventure Company** (Bear Valley, Hwy 4) Cross-country skiing, paddling, hiking, maps and clothing. See p193.
- **Curry Village Mountain Shop** (Curry Village, Yosemite Valley) Climbing, hiking, clothing, maps and books; it's excellent. See p101.
- **Mammoth Mountaineering Supply** (Mammoth Lakes) Topos, equipment rentals, hiking, backpacking, shoes and snow sports. See p207.
- **Mountain Sage** (Groveland, Hwy 120) Minimal clothing, gear and maps. See p182.
- **Sierra Nevada Adventure Company** (Arnold, Hwy 4; Sonora, Hwy 108) Paddling, hiking, maps, gear and clothing. See p192 and p189.
- **Sport Shop** (Yosemite Village, Yosemite Valley) Clothing and some gear. See p97.
- **Tuolumne Meadows Sport Shop** (Tuolumne Meadows, Yosemite) Climbing, hiking and maps. See p113.

> **DEFINING THE HIKES**
>
> Yosemite and Sequoia & Kings Canyon (not to mention the areas around the parks) together offer a vast range of hikes suitable for everyone from the novice to the pro. The hikes in this book are organized into three levels of difficulty to help you gauge which is right for you.
>
> - **Easy** Manageable for nearly all walkers, an easy hike is under 4 miles, with fairly even (possibly paved) terrain and no significant elevation gain or loss.
> - **Moderate** Fine for fit hikers and active, capable children, moderate hikes have a modest elevation gain in the range of 500ft to 1000ft and are usually under 7 miles long.
> - **Demanding** Hikes falling into the 'demanding' category have elevation gains of over 1000ft, are mostly steep, may have tricky footing and are often over 8 miles long. Being physically fit is paramount.
>
> All the hikes included in this book – from day hikes to backcountry treks – follow marked, established trails and the distance listed in each hike description is for a *round-trip* journey unless it says otherwise. The estimated duration listed in each hike description will vary a bit depending on the hiker's ability.

Easy Trails

Some of the region's most spectacular sights are accessible to even the most inexperienced walker. Trails around Grant Grove (p226) and along Zumwalt Meadow (p227), both in Kings Canyon, are gentle and divinely scenic. The loop trails of Yosemite Valley (p118), mostly flat and partly paved, offer a delightful escape from the Valley's crowds, with views of Half Dome, Yosemite Falls, Bridalveil Fall and more. In Sequoia National Park, both the paved Congress Trail (p220) and the longer Trail of the Sequoias (p220) immerse walkers in the majestic sequoia groves of the Giant Forest and require very little leg expenditure.

The highest concentration of Yosemite hikes lie in and around the subalpine high country of Tuolumne Meadows (p113). This part of the park is only fully open three to four months every summer, but when the snow melts the place jumps to life, with green meadows growing at the base of craggy peaks and colorful wildflowers poking up wherever they can. It's a magnificent destination no hiking enthusiast should miss, even beginners. Hikes such as those to Dog Lake (p131) and down Lyell Canyon (p143) make fine choices for families and stone-cold novices.

Moderate & Demanding Trails

Many of the most famous hikes in Yosemite are day hikes, but they involve steep ascents and, in summer, often blistering heat that combine to make them strenuous hikes. Yet they're not to be missed. Trails to the top of Yosemite Falls (p123), Glacier Point (p124) and Vernal and Nevada Falls (p124) take you through some of the most mind-blowing scenery on the planet. To avoid the crowds and the afternoon heat, be sure to hit the trail early if you're tackling these in summer.

Moderate hikes in Tuolumne Meadows include such outstanding tramps as Glen Aulin (p133), the glorious Cathedral Lakes (p132), Young Lakes (p144) and Mono Pass (p134). You can find excellent hikes in every other corner of the park, too, leading to such premier sights as the often-overlooked Chilnualna Falls (p126) in Wawona; the gushing torrent of Wapama Falls in Hetch Hetchy (p135); the awe-inspiring 360-degree views from the easily reached summit of Sentinel Dome (p120), off

Stay abreast of current issues related to hiking in the Sierra Nevada by logging onto and/or joining the High Sierra Hikers Association (www.highsierrahikers.org).

Whatever you do when you take to the hills, remember to adhere to the principles of Leave No Trace (www.lnt.org).

ACTIVITIES

LEAVING NO TRACE

Hitting the backcountry is all about escaping the constraints of civilization, but a set of widely accepted ethics and rules exist in order to minimize human impact on the natural environment. These guidelines also make the trails more pleasant for everyone. And remember: planning ahead, researching your destination and preparing thoroughly for your trip is the best way to minimize your impact. Before you hit the trail, check out **Leave No Trace** (www.lnt.org).

Food

- Store food in a bear-resistant canister (p279) – hanging food bags in trees rarely works anymore.
- Never feed the wildlife and avoid leaving food scraps behind. Animals can become dependent on hand-outs, contributing to unbalanced populations and to disease.

Waste

- Don't put any soap in the water (even biodegradable soap pollutes).
- Discard all grey-water 100ft (about 80 paces) from water sources.
- Carry out all trash, including toilet paper. Toilet paper burns poorly and animals will dig up anything scented. Take minimal packaging to minimize waste.
- Relieve yourself at least 200ft from any water source; when making offerings of the solid sort, do so in a hole 4in to 6in deep or carry it out in a poop tube. In snow, dig down to the soil.

Fires

- Don't start any campfires over 9600ft or above the tree line.
- Below the tree line, collect only dead and downed wood. Better yet, avoid campfires altogether. The cutting of wood for fires in popular trekking areas can cause rapid deforestation. Dead wood contributes to a healthy forest. Use only sticks that can be broken by hand.
- If you do have a fire, do so in existing fire rings.
- Don't depend on open fires for cooking. Cook on a light-weight backpacking stove; avoid those powered by disposable butane gas canisters.

Walking & Camping

- Stay on the trail – making and taking shortcuts contributes to erosion.
- Camp at least 100ft from water and, if possible, the trail.
- Be considerate of other visitors and yield to stock animals.
- Always camp in existing sites or on durable surfaces and keep campsites small.

Glacier Point Rd; and the gorgeous, wide-screen look at classic Yosemite scenery on the Panorama Trail (p125), as you meander from Glacier Point to the top of Nevada Fall.

From Road's End in Kings Canyon, trails leave the valley behind and ascend into the high country. Hikes such as the Rae Lakes Loop (p233) offer incomparable scenery and outstanding backpacking opportunities. Sequoia's Mineral King Valley (p222), set at 7500ft, is both a backpackers mecca and a day hiker's dream, with beautiful subalpine scenery, cooler temperatures and steep ascents that demand physical fitness, so keep crowds somewhat minimal.

And then there are the hikes for the lovers of extremes: Yosemite's most famous (and popular) hike is the 17-mile roundtrip trek from

Happy Isles to the top of Half Dome (p138), a journey that thousands attempt every summer – often as a day hike – despite its grueling nature. Experienced and physically fit climbers can tackle Mount Lyell (p143), Yosemite's highest peak; Mt Dana (p135), the park's second-highest peak; and, on the Eastern border of Sequoia National Park, 14,496ft Mt Whitney (p248), the highest point in the continental USA.

For spectacular hikes beyond the parks' borders, head to the 20 Lakes Basin (p197), east of Tioga Pass near Saddlebag Lake; Hite Cove (see the boxed text, p178), along Hwy 140, known for its awesome wildflower displays each spring; and The Minarets (p210) in the Ansel Adams Wilderness. The entire Eastern Sierra (p195) is a fun-ground for adventurous hikers.

Long-Distance Trails

Several long-distance trails pass through Yosemite, including the John Muir Trail, which follows the Sierra Crest between Yosemite and Sequoia National Parks, and the daunting Pacific Crest National Scenic Trail, which extends from Canada to Mexico. The province of experts, these trails can be a lifetime achievement for those who manage to hike their entire distance; many people choose to hike them in smaller, more manageable sections. You'll cross parts of them while hiking shorter local trails in several areas of Yosemite.

For more information on both trails, contact the **Pacific Crest Trail Association** (☎ 916-349-2109; www.pcta.org). For toll-free trail conditions, call ☎ 888-728-7245.

Planning to hike your way around the Sierra Nevada? If so, pick up a copy of the Lonely Planet's award-winning *Hiking in the Sierra Nevada* by John Mock and Kimberley O'Neil.

JOHN MUIR TRAIL

Linking Yosemite with Sequoia & Kings Canyon, the John Muir Trail runs from Yosemite Valley to Mt Whitney (14,496ft). Between the parks, it passes through the Ansel Adams Wilderness, the John Muir Wilderness and Devil's Postpile National Monument. The grand total: a 211-mile trail coughing up what many consider the very best mountain hiking in the United States.

Uncrossed by any roads, the trail is a spectacular and pristine route through continual wilderness. It crosses 11 mountain passes, half of which are higher than 12,000ft and all but one are above 10,000ft. As it traverses the timberline country of the High Sierra, the trail passes thousands of lakes and numerous granite peaks between 13,000ft and 14,000ft and takes in the Sierra's highest peak. The trail frequently descends from the Sierra Crest into forested areas of the Western Sierra, with 5000ft-deep canyons.

Assuming a north-to-south hike, the trail begins at Happy Isles (4035ft) in Yosemite Valley and climbs over Cathedral Pass (9700ft) to Tuolumne Meadows (8600ft). Traveling along the Lyell Fork of the Tuolumne River, it then climbs out of the national park and into the Ansel Adams Wilderness at Donohue Pass (11,056ft) before covering the wilderness areas, entering Sequoia & Kings Canyon and topping out at Mt Whitney. You then must descend about 11 miles to Whitney Portal in order to complete the hike.

An average hiker covering 12 miles per day needs 19 or 20 days to complete the trail. Faster backpackers might take as few as 12 days.

PACIFIC CREST TRAIL

The Pacific Crest National Scenic Trail (PCT) stretches 2650 miles from Campo, California, on the Mexican border to Manning Provincial Park

ACTIVITIES

NATIONAL PARK

	Region	Round-trip distance	Duration	Difficulty	Elevation change
	Tuolumne Meadows	8 miles	4-7hr	moderate	+1000ft
	Wawona	8.6 miles	4-5hr	moderate-demanding	+2240ft
Clouds Rest	day	Crane Flat & Tioga Rd	14.4 miles	6-7hr	demanding	+2205ft
Elizabeth Lake	day	Tuolumne Meadows	5.2 miles	2½-4hr	moderate	+800ft
Four-Mile Trail to Glacier Point	day	Yosemite Valley	9.2 miles	4-8hr	demanding	+3200ft
Gaylor Lakes	day	Tuolumne Meadows	3 miles	2-3hr	moderate	+560ft
Glen Aulin	day	Tuolumne Meadows	11 miles	6-8hr	moderate	-600ft
Half Dome	backcountry	Yosemite Valley	17 miles	10-12hr	demanding	+4800ft
Inspiration Point	day	Yosemite Valley	2.6 miles	1½-2½hr	moderate-demanding	+1000ft
Lembert Dome	day	Tuolumne Meadows	2.4 miles	2-3hr	moderate	+850ft
Lukens Lake	easy	Crane Flat & Tioga Rd	1.6 miles	1hr	easy	+200ft
Lyell Canyon	backcountry	Tuolumne Meadows	17.6 miles	2 days	easy-moderate	+200ft
Mariposa Grove to Wawona	easy	Wawona	6.5 miles (one way)	2-3hr	easy-moderate	-2000ft
May Lake & Mt Hoffmann	day	Crane Flat & Tioga Rd	6 miles	4-5hr	moderate-demanding	+2004ft
McGurk Meadow	easy	Glacier Point & Badger Pass	1.6 miles	1hr	easy	+150ft
Merced Grove	easy	Crane Flat & Tioga Rd	3 miles	1½-2hr	easy-moderate	+600ft
Mirror Lake & Tenaya Canyon Loop	easy	Yosemite Valley	4.8 miles	1-2hr	easy	+100ft
Mono Pass	day	Tuolumne Meadows	7.4 miles	4hr	moderate-demanding	+915ft
Mt Dana	day	Tuolumne Meadows	5.8 miles	6-7hr	demanding	+3108ft
North Dome	day	Crane Flat & Tioga Rd	8.5 miles	4½-5hr	moderate	-1000/+422ft
Panorama Trail	day	Glacier Point & Badger Pass	8.5 miles (one way)	5hr	moderate-demanding	-3200/+760ft
Pohono Trail	day	Glacier Point & Badger Pass	13.8 miles (one way)	7-9hr	moderate-demanding	-2800ft
Sentinel Dome	easy	Glacier Point & Badger Pass	2.2 miles	1hr	easy-moderate	+370ft
Taft Point & the Fissures	easy	Glacier Point & Badger Pass	2.2 miles	1hr	easy	+250ft
Tenaya Lake to Yosemite Valley	backcountry	Crane Flat & Tioga Rd	17.2 miles (one way)	2 days	demanding	+2205ft

Wildlife Watching   View   Great for Families   Waterfall   Restrooms   Drinking Water

ACTIVITIES

Features	Facilities	Description	Page
		Easily one of Yosemite's most spectacular hikes with incredible views of Cathedral Lakes and Peak	132
		Uncrowded trail along cascading creek to top of waterfalls over Wawona Dome's shoulder	126
		Yosemite's largest expanse of granite; arguably its finest panoramic viewpoint	129
		Great short jaunt for acclimatizing on your first day in Tuolumne; superb views; lots to explore	132
		One of the grandest viewpoints in the entire country; also accessible by car or bus	124
		This short, steep hike rewards with epic scenery of the high country and lakes above Tioga Pass	134
		Follow the Tuolumne River past numerous waterfalls to one of the High Sierra Camps	133
		The park's most difficult day hike is a strenuous push to the top of Yosemite's iconic dome	138
		Offers some of the finest views of Yosemite Valley; easily extended to include other viewpoints	122
		One of the best places to watch the sunset in Yosemite is atop this granite dome	131
		Quick hike to small but attractive lake; lots of wildflowers	122
		One of the flattest trails in the Sierras offers superb views of Mt Lyell and its eponymous glacier	143
		Woodsy, downhill alternative to shuttle bus	121
		Short easy hike to May Lake High Sierra Camp, with the option to summit nearby peak	128
		Short, flat walk to a lush meadow; lots of wildflowers and an old log cabin	119
		The park's least-visited sequoia grove; the hike is downhill with a stiff ascent on the return	121
		Best in spring, this short walk offers a relaxed stroll to the lovely sight of reflective Mirror Lake and beyond	118
		Outstanding, moderately paced day hike into high country above Tioga Pass	134
		Lung-busting, thigh-burning hike to the top of the park's second-highest peak	135
		Astounding views of Yosemite Valley, Half Dome and Tenaya Canyon; includes 1000ft descent	130
		Includes 3200ft descent from Glacier Point to Valley floor, with postcard views the whole way down	125
		Passes numerous Valley viewpoints; requires car shuttle	126
		Easiest hike to top of a dome with amazing 360-degree views	120
		Major Valley viewpoint with interesting geological features	119
		Includes 6321ft descent from Tioga Rd to Yosemite Valley, with the option to summit Clouds Rest	141

 Backcountry Campsite   Swimming

HIKING IN YOSEMITE NATIONAL PARK *continued*

Name	Hike type	Region	Round-trip distance	Duration	Difficulty	Elevation change
Tueeulala & Wapama Falls	day	Hetch Hetchy	5.4 miles	2½-3hr	easy-moderate	+400ft
Tuolumne Grove	easy	Crane Flat & Tioga Rd	2 miles	1½hr	easy-moderate	+500ft
Vernal & Nevada Falls	day	Yosemite Valley	6.5 miles	4-7hr	moderate-demanding	+1900ft
Vogelsang	backcountry	Tuolumne Meadows	27 miles	3 days	moderate-demanding	+3852ft
Waterwheel Falls	backcountry	Tuolumne Meadows	18 miles	2 days	demanding	+2260ft
Wawona Meadow Loop	easy	Wawona	3.5 miles	1-1½hr	easy	+200ft
Yosemite Falls	day	Yosemite Valley	6.8 miles	5-6hr	demanding	+2400ft
Yosemite Valley Loops	easy	Yosemite Valley	varies	varies	easy	+330ft

HIKING IN SEQUOIA & KINGS CANYON NATIONAL PARKS

Name	Hike type	Region	Round-trip distance	Duration	Difficulty	Elevation change
Big Trees Trail	easy	Giant Forest	1.2 miles	1hr	easy	+80ft
Crescent Meadow to Bearpaw Meadow	backcountry	Giant Forest	22 miles	2 days	moderate-demanding	+1100ft
Crescent Meadow Loop	easy	Giant Forest	1 miles	½hr	easy	+75ft
General Grant Tree Trail	easy	Grant Grove	0.5 miles	½hr	easy	+30ft
General Sherman Tree to Moro Rock	day	Giant Forest	6 miles (one way)	2½-4hr	moderate	+3000ft
Marble Falls	day	Foothills	7.8 miles	3-4hr	moderate-demanding	+2000ft
Mist Falls	day	Cedar Grove	9.5 miles	3-5hr	moderate	+600ft
Monarch Lakes	backcountry	Mineral King	8.4 miles	2 days	moderate-demanding	+2580ft
Moro Rock	easy	Giant Forest	0.5 miles	½hr	easy-moderate	+300ft
Rae Lakes Loop	backcountry	Cedar Grove	41.5 miles	5 days	demanding	+6943ft
Tokopah Falls	easy	Lodgepole	3.4 miles	2hr	easy	+500ft
Zumwalt Meadow	easy	Cedar Grove	1.5 miles	1hr	easy	+50ft

 Wildlife Watching   View   Great for Families   Waterfall   Restrooms   Drinking Water

Features	Facilities	Description	Page
🦌👓👫▨		Undulating trail to the base of Hetch Hetchy's roaring waterfalls boasts views aplenty	135
👫	🚻	Descend along a portion of Old Big Oak Flat Rd to a small but less-crowded sequoia grove	121
🏔👫👫▨	🚻🚰	Justifiably popular hike to two of Yosemite's finest falls; mind-blowing scenery too	124
🦌🏔▨	🚻🚰▲	Exceptional, multiday, high-country backpack trip with astounding views of the Cathedral Range	146
🦌🏔▨	🚰▲	Splendid series of waterfalls at head of Grand Canyon of the Tuolumne River	148
🦌	🚻🚰	Loop around meadow is shaded and flat, but has lots of horse manure	120
🏔👫▨	🚻🚰🏊	Sweat yourself silly and enjoy the views hiking to the top of Yosemite's highest falls	123
👫▨	🚻🚰🏊	Meander quietly around the Valley along these surprisingly uncrowded trails that pass all the major sights	118

Features	Facilities	Description	Page
👫	🚻🚰	Paved interpretive trail circling a sequoia-bordered meadow	226
🏔	🚻🚰▲	Gorgeous sequoia grove and canyon-view hike	231
🦌🏔👫	🚻🚰	Beautiful subalpine meadow ringed by firs and sequoias; summer wildflowers	226
👫	🚻🚰	Paved interpretive loop through a giant sequoia grove	223
🦌🏔	🚻🚰	Huge sequoias, gorgeous green meadows and the pinnacle of Moro Rock	229
▨	🚻🚰	Lower elevation hike parallels a river canyon to a thundering cascade	227
🏔▨	🚻🚰🏊	Longish walk to falls highlights the beauty of Kings Canyon	229
🦌👓👫▨	🚻🚰▲🏊	Out-and-back high-country hike to two alpine lakes at base of Sawtooth Peak	230
🏔👫		Steep ascent to the top of a stunning panoramic dome	226
🦌🏔▨	🚻🚰▲🏊	Loop hike passes a chain of jewel-like lakes in the heart of the high country	233
🦌👓👫▨	🚻🚰	One of parks' largest and most scenic waterfalls; starts from campground	225
🏔👫		Flat loop around a lush meadow traces the Kings River; canyon wall views	227

▲ Backcountry Campsite   🏊 Swimming

ACTIVITIES

WORDS FROM THE PACIFIC CREST TRAIL

When we ran into Amanda Schuler on the Pacific Crest Trail (PCT) and learned that she was hiking it solo (and donning a sombrero), we knew she'd be able to shed some light on the subject of the country's greatest long-distance trail.

What's the time frame? I started hiking April 29 [2007], and I'm hoping to finish by October 2. On average, people take 5½ to six months.

How many miles per day? The miles fluctuate. In Southern California, I was hiking about 23 miles a day. Along the John Muir Trail, I hiked about 17 miles a day. Now, in Northern California, I'm doing about 25 miles a day.

How has it been hiking solo as a woman? I love it. I generally find groups of people to hike with, but it is very casual and you're not obligated to stay with the same people. I love having independence out here and making my own decisions. People worry it's scary, but it is actually very comforting with this kind of community. It is amazing to see how other people look out for and care for each other. I'm not sure if I would experience that to the same depth if I were hiking with someone else.

Do you need to be an expert at wilderness navigation? No. The trail is easy to follow, with a few exceptions, and you get used to how it's set up. You become more in tune with your instincts. Many people have traveled the trail before you, so there are foot prints or sticks and rocks set up by others, guiding you through the confusing times. I only got off the trail once and quickly recognized my mistake.

What about shoes? I buy new shoes about every 500 to 600 miles. I've used trail running shoes and regular running shoes. Boots are heavy and hot.

Anything you'd recommend people bring? Admittedly, music. I did not want to bring my MP3 player at first because I didn't want to mix 'the world' with the trail, but it really helps on days I'm not feeling motivated. It changes my attitude dramatically!

Greatest challenges? The most difficult part is finding the energy or motivation to hike on days when you just don't feel like it. Hike 20 or more miles at that! The day-to-day things are sometimes very difficult. It becomes a bit monotonous, but there is always some great motivation: beautiful views, good people, knowing you are getting good exercise. Also, battling with blisters: it is so hard to hike with blisters, let alone 20 to 25 miles a day. But you truly build character and strength. It's amazing what a person is capable of.

Any advice for would-be hikers? Do adequate research. Talk to other people who have done the trail. There is nothing to be worried about. But do be cautious about hitchhiking solo. I've had no bad experiences hitchhiking, but I've also never done it alone. I would really encourage more women to hike the PCT or any long-distance hike. It is quite the confidence booster, and my self-esteem has increased greatly. It is an amazing feeling knowing you can be so independent.

Tell us about the sombrero. I found it at a thrift store for $1. It's so fun to wear. Great sun protection, and it is light. It's only hard when the wind picks up which forces me to take it off. Everyone recognizes me, and it can really lift spirits. I love it!

in British Columbia, Canada. It hugs the crest of the glacially carved Sierra Nevada range in California and the volcanic Cascade Range in northern California, Oregon and Washington, crossing seven national parks: three in the Sierra Nevada and four in the Cascades. Most of this mountainous terrain lies within 24 national forests and 33 roadless wilderness areas, with the longest unbroken stretch extending more than 200 miles. The wilderness of the High Sierra is crossed by only five roads.

The trail skirts the Mojave Desert along the Tehachapi Range and then enters the southern Sierra, where it joins the John Muir Trail in Sequoia National Park, just west of Mt Whitney. Leaving the park via Forester Pass (13,120ft), the trail's highest point, it continues through

Kings Canyon National Park, where imposing peaks rise above the deep canyons of the Kings River. After passing Devils Postpile National Monument, the path enters Yosemite National Park at Donohue Pass and diverges from the John Muir Trail at Tuolumne Meadows. It crosses Dorothy Lake Pass as it exits Yosemite, then travels over Sonora Pass, Ebbetts Pass, Carson Pass and Echo Summit. Entering the popular Desolation Wilderness Area west of Lake Tahoe, the trail passes Alpine Meadows and Squaw Valley ski resorts en route to Donner Summit. It undulates through deep river valleys in the northern Sierra and continues to Lassen Volcanic National Park, marking the southern extent of the Cascade Range.

Most hikers take five to six months to complete the trail, averaging about 20 miles per day (actual hiking days).

Guided Hikes & Courses

Folks who wish to learn more about hiking or about the environment through which they're hiking, or who simply would like to hike with a group, have several options. Several organizations – including the Yosemite Institute, the Yosemite Association and the Sequoia Natural History Association – offer educational programs based around day hikes or multiday backpacking trips. For more information, see p27.

If you'd rather have someone guide you through the backcountry or if you simply wish to bone up on your backcountry skills, consider taking a class with the highly regarded **Yosemite Mountaineering School** (☎ 209-372-8344; www.yosemitemountaineering.com), which has a year-round location in Yosemite Valley and a summer location in Tuolumne Meadows. Long in the business, **Southern Yosemite Mountain Guides** (☎ 800-231-4575; www.symg .com) is another outfitter offering guided hiking and backpacking trips as well as backcountry skills courses.

CYCLING

Yosemite and Sequoia & Kings Canyon both make for excellent but challenging bicycle touring destinations. For those peddling to the latter, the highlight is undoubtedly the Kings Canyon Hwy (aka the Kings Canyon Scenic Byway or Hwy 180), which drops over 2000ft in 36 miles as it winds its way into the Kings Canyon from Grant Grove Village. Of course, you have to turn around and climb back up it in order to get out. Aside from that, Sequoia & Kings Canyon is devoid of great cycling routes.

As for Yosemite, there's plenty of tooling around to do in Yosemite Valley, where bicycles are an excellent means of transportation for exploring the Valley floor: 12 miles of mostly flat paved bike trails weave past nearly all of Yosemite's most famous sights and up to Mirror Lake. Just be sure to ride defensively – the path is not always clearly marked, and there are lots of people paying more attention to gawking than steering. You can even rent beach cruisers in Yosemite Valley if you didn't bring (or ride in on) your own. See p150 for more information.

Yosemite offers greater challenges for more serious cyclists. Tioga Rd/ Hwy 120 (p111) is a grueling route, climbing over 4000ft from Yosemite Valley to Tioga Pass at a lung-busting 9945ft. The road then drops dramatically – make that *frighteningly* – down the Lee Vining Canyon until, after 3500ft of descent, it ends at Hwy 395 and Mono Lake. If you head south on Hwy 395, you can pick up Hwy 120 west again and knock out a spectacular Eastern Sierras loop by taking Benton Crossing Rd back out to Hwy 395. This is the route of the annual, open-registration **High**

Planning the six-month hike along the Pacific Crest Trail is one hell of a task, which is why Craig's PCT Planning Program (as in *computer* program) comes in very handy. Check it out at www .pctplanner.com.

Some of Yosemite's more interestingly named climbs include: Satanic Mechanic, Sherrie's Crack, A Boy and His Knob, The Gerbil Launcher, Crotch Cricket, Renus Wrinkle, Realm of the Flying Monkeys and Stroke My Erect Ear Tufts.

ACTIVITIES

Sierra Fall Century (www.fallcentury.org), which at only $50 (less for the shorter routes) makes for a great group ride. Further south, the June Lake Loop (p202) offers more outstanding cycling.

For more information on safe cycling, see p274. Also see Bicycle, p265.

MOUNTAIN BIKING

Mountain bikes are not allowed on any dirt trails within any of the national parks. They are, however, allowed on most National Forest trails outside of designated wilderness areas. In other words, there are heaps of terrific rides in recreation areas surrounding the park. In the Stanislaus National Forest, Bear Valley (p193) is an excellent mountain-biking destination, boasting copious amounts of single-track and even a fair amount of granite slab upon which to toast your knobbies. Although there are plans to adapt the chairlifts for mountain bikers (check back around 2010), there is currently no lift-assisted biking in Bear Valley. As an employee of the **Bear Valley Adventure Company** (☎ 209-753-2834; www .bearvalleyxc.com) put it, 'You still gotta earn it.' But you don't *really* have to: loads of trails snake their way from the resort to the town of Bear Valley, and car shuttling is generally an easy way to give you and your buddies well over 10 miles of downhill in one shot. If you're interested in mountain biking in the area, contact the Bear Valley Adventure Company, which can provide you with maps, shuttle service, repairs, rentals and friendly advice.

The region's most renowned mountain-biking destination, however, is Mammoth Mountain (see p205) in the Eastern Sierra. When the snow melts, Mammoth spits up over 90 miles of single-track, downhill rides of all difficulty levels, several free-ride trails and shuttles, gondolas and chairlifts to get you to the top of them all. Instructional camps, lessons and bike rentals are all available.

SWIMMING

Few sensations top the joy of jumping into a river or swimming in an icy mountain lake, and you'll find plenty of opportunity to do both up here. In Yosemite, however, you'd best be able to tolerate cold water. Midsummer you'll find the warmest waters (and air temperatures) in the Valley, where there are plenty of swimming holes fringed with sandy beaches along the Merced River (p156). For something a little nippier, dip into Tenaya Lake (p122), where a long horseshoe beach with spectacular views rings the lake's east side. Harden Lake (p128), near Tioga Rd, is a bit of a rarity if only because it's fairly warm. The South Fork Merced River, which runs through Wawona, has some great swimming holes (see p156). In Kings Canyon, people congregate atop Muir Rock (p230) and goad each other into jumping off into the South Fork Kings River. Just outside the park, you'll find good lake swimming (be you Christian or heathen) at Hume Lake (p225), which is also home to several Christian camps.

Beyond the park, there's no shortage of places for a quick cold plunge, a lakeside lounge or even a hot-tub soak. Off Hwy 4, the Stanislaus River, particularly upstream from the bridge inside Calaveras Big Trees State Park, offers excellent swimming holes, rock-jumping and plenty of sun-baked granite. Further up Hwy 4, Lake Alpine (p194) is a chilly but fun spot for a swim. Just outside Yosemite's northwest border, Cherry Lake (p188) is a favorite local swimming area. Along the Eastern Sierra, there's June Lake (p202), Lundy Lake (p201), and Lake Sabrina (p213), near Bishop. Thanks to major underground runoff

---

SNORKELING, IN SEQUOIA?

Carey Goldstein, Crystal Cave Manager, Sequoia Natural History Association, gives us the rundown on Crystal Cave, and snorkeling and hiking in Sequoia National Park.

What about Crystal Cave most inspires you? The amount and variety of cave formations. There are sparkling beautiful crystals all over the place, and the public usually gets to see some sort of wildlife – typically millipedes – and sometime cave-adapted millipedes, cave crickets, spiders or bats.

What are some of your favorite things to do in the park? This may be a little odd, but I really love snorkeling. In the summer here it's so darn hot and the water's clear at the larger lakes and pools. I've never seen anybody else doing it.

Where do you snorkel? Starting down in the Foothills at the Research Pools, all the way up to Twin Lakes, Heather Lake – some of those places that you can get to on a day hike but that still are quite a chug. Twin Lakes is almost 2800ft of vertical. I go up there and the water's crystal clear and there's fish – I feel like I'm in Hawaii, but at about 9000ft. If the lake is shallow enough, it's warm by August.

Where do you like to go hiking? I like the Twin Lakes hike and Pear Lake. Also Little Baldy, Big Baldy and Tokopah Falls – when there's water. And I love just walking around Crescent Meadow and Giant Forest. With the shuttle system it's really easy to do a point-to-point hike. And down in the Foothills in the winter, it's green and there's lots of water. The Mineral King power flume is also awesome for hiking. If you hike from Mineral King downstream to where it ends, there are fantastic views and you're hanging off the edge of a cliff. You walk on top of the flume by taking one of the fire roads up to it. By the time you get to the terminus you've got big views of the Middle Fork and Three Rivers.

---

from the Sierra Crest, the east side is also full of hot springs (see the boxed text, p207).

Whenever swimming in a river, always swim where others are swimming unless you're absolutely certain about the nature of the current. People drown every year in rivers up here. For those who'd simply avoid that risk altogether, there are public swimming pools with lifeguards at Curry Village (p100) and Yosemite Lodge (p103).

HORSEBACK RIDING & PACKING

If you're hankering to put ass to saddle (or simply have a beast of burden carry your gear), there's ample opportunity within all three national parks. But refrain from imagining yourself galloping across a High Sierra meadow with the wind at your back: stock animals must stick to the trails. Also keep in mind that, unless you're bringing your own horses, any 'horseback rides' offered within the parks are actually mule-back rides. Anyone who knows their horses, however, also knows this is a good thing; mules are the toughest, most patient and most surefooted breed out there. And darn, they're cute!

In Yosemite, three different stables (p153) offer daily two-hour to full-day trips from late spring through midfall. In Kings Canyon, Grant Grove Stables offers one-and two-hour guided trail rides, while Cedar Grove Pack Station (in Kings Canyon) and Horse Corral Pack Station (in Sequoia) both offer half- and full-day trips that get you further afield. For more information see p236.

If you really want to get out into the wilderness, and do it in style, a multiday pack trip is the way to go. Both Cedar Grove Pack Station and Horse Corral offer a variety of trips into the wilderness that allow you to bring just about anything you want (meaning stock up on beer,

The mule is the most highly valued pack animal. It possesses the stamina, patience and sure-footedness of the donkey, the strength and courage of the horse, and hard skin that is resistant to rain and sun.

GO CLIMB A ROCK

Classic Rock

If there's one activity that's synonymous with Yosemite, it's rock climbing. With 3000ft granite monoliths, sheer spires, near-vertical walls and a temperate climate, Yosemite is no less than the world's holy grail of rock. Camp 4, Yosemite Valley's cheap, no-reservations walk-in campground, has for decades been the hangout for some of climbing's legendary stars. In 2003 it was placed on the National Register of Historic Places as the 'birthplace of modern rock climbing.'

Indeed, Yosemite's granite, most of it deemed impossible until the 1940s, necessitated entirely new techniques, equipment and climbing styles. In 1947, using hand-forged steel pitons, Swiss climber John Salathé became the first to climb the Lost Arrow Chimney, regarded as the most difficult climb of the day. Following Salathé's path came a team of illustrious climbers who changed the sport forever, including Royal Robbins, a pioneer of clean climbing techniques, and Yvon Chouinard, founder of Chouinard Equipment (which later became Black Diamond) and Patagonia.

Attacking the world's greatest single slab of granite in stages between July 1957 and November 1958, big-wall pioneer Warren Harding took 16 months to climb the now world-famous Nose route on El Capitan. In 1994 Lynn Hill free-climbed the route (meaning she used no protection) in less than 24 hours. Eleven years later, Tommy Caldwell 'freed' it in under 12 hours. Needless to say, climbing has come a long way.

Modern Rock

While first ascents and new routes are mostly a thing of the past in Yosemite, the climbing spirit soars as high as ever. During spring and fall, climbers flock to Yosemite Valley, and boulder-strewn Camp 4 (p162) remains ground zero. Need a climbing partner? Check the Camp 4 bulletin board. Looking for used climbing equipment? Camp 4. Want route information from fellow climbers? You guessed it.

---

wine and steaks!). In Yosemite, pack trips go to the park's High Sierra Camps (p146), a hugely popular excursion requiring reservations far in advance.

Beyond the park, the Eastern Sierra is particularly well suited for horseback adventuring, with its Sierra Crest vistas, lakes, sweeping valleys and easily accessible wilderness. Numerous outfitters run trips for all levels out of Mammoth (p203) and Bishop (p212), where riders are within easy reach of the gorgeous terrain of the Ansel Adams and John Muir Wilderness Areas.

WHITE-WATER RAFTING & KAYAKING

Two rivers descend from Yosemite – the Merced and the **Tuolumne** (www .tuolumne.org) – but with the exception of gentle river floating, all the real white-water action happens outside the park's boundaries, where runoff from typical early-season snowmelt creates massive flows and lots of rapids (Class II to IV+). Later in the season, lower flows and river levels often result in more technical white water. During the summer months, floating the Merced inside the park (see p155) simply offers a fun way to beat the heat.

Usually, the runoff starts sometime in mid-March. The Tuolumne runs into September, while the Merced usually wraps up by mid-July, and both are well suited for beginner to intermediate rafters. For experts, there's renowned Cherry Creek, a section of the upper Tuolumne about 15 miles west of Hetch Hetchy. Cherry Creek weighs in with a 9-mile stretch of nearly nonstop Class V and V+ rapids marked by narrow shoots, huge

Cherry Creek, on the Upper Tuolumne River, is widely considered the most challenging run in the entire country.

Come summer, many climbers relocate to the gentler and quieter Tuolumne Meadows, where temperatures tend to be a good 15°F to 20°F cooler than in the Valley and where there's an abundance of glacially polished granite domes. Bulletin boards at the Tuolumne Meadows Store (p113) and the campground become information hubs.

With so much glacial debris scattered about, Yosemite is also an outstanding place for bouldering, the sport of climbing without a rope at short distances above the ground. Because the only equipment necessary is shoes and a chalk bag (and maybe a bouldering mat if you can't use your friend's), it's also a great way to enter the sport of climbing. Camp 4 is home to some of the world's most famous boulders, but there are plenty of other places throughout the park.

Rock Around Yosemite

Yosemite doesn't have a *complete* monopoly on rock climbing. Sequoia & Kings Canyon (p236) has some outstanding climbing with a fraction of the crowds. North of Yosemite, there's good bouldering near Bear Valley (p193) and Sonora Pass (p189). Beyond the park's east boundary, near Bishop, the Owens River Gorge (p213) and the Buttermilks (p213) are top climbing areas. There's also plenty of high-altitude climbing between Saddlebag Lake (p197) and the Yosemite border.

Schools of Rock

Folks who are new to climbing or who want to add techniques and knowledge to their old back of tricks should head to the **Yosemite Mountaineering School** (☎ 209-372-8344; www.yosemitemountaineering.com), regarded as the country's best. The school maintains offices at the Curry Village Mountain Shop (p101) and, during summer, the Tuolumne Meadows Sport Shop (p113).

For climbing courses and guides in the Eastern Sierra, check out **Sierra Rock Climbing School** (☎ 877-686-7625; www.sierrarockclimbingschool.com), based in Mammoth Lakes. Up north, check out **Mountain Adventure Seminars** (☎ 209-753-6556; www.mtadventure.com), based in Bear Valley.

boulders, sheer drops, precarious ledges and vertical holes. The 15 named rapids have a gradient average of 110ft per mile (as opposed to 40ft per mile elsewhere on the Tuolumne). It's one of the country's best.

The **North Fork Stanislaus River** (www.stanislaus-river.com), between the town of Dorrington and Calaveras Big Trees State Park, offers five nonstop miles of technical Class IV rapids guaranteed to knock your adrenaline into the upper notches. Rafting season on the 'North Stan' runs May to September. In Sierra National Forest, the Kings River offers a scenic 10-mile stretch of exciting, mostly Class III rapids with a season that runs roughly from late April to mid-July. It's a good river for beginners. With its headwaters in Sequoia National Park, the Kaweah River kicks out challenging Class IV+ rapids west of the park. Dependant entirely on snowmelt, its season runs April and May.

The stretch of the Eastern Sierras covered in this book has very little white-water rafting, with the nearest boatable river being East Fork Carson River, which offers gentle floats on Class II to III rapids with one added bonus of riverside hot springs.

Permits

You can run any of these rivers on your own or with a rafting outfitter. Parties wishing to raft the Tuolumne or Cherry Creek on their own must obtain river permits through the **Groveland Ranger District** (☎ 209-962-7825; www.fs.fed.us/r5/stanislaus/groveland/river.shtml; 24545 Hwy 120) in Groveland. A quota system exists for the Tuolumne, and reservations can be made starting January 1 of the year you wish to raft. You can

---

GREETINGS, STARGAZERS

On many summer Saturday nights, the Glacier Point amphitheater hosts various astronomy clubs, which set up telescopes and let the public take a closer-than-usual look at what's deep in the night sky – from the moon's mottled surface to fuzzy, faraway star clusters. These programs are accompanied by 'Stars Over Yosemite' discussions, during which rangers point out constellations in the sky above Glacier Point. Bring the kids.

Throughout the summer, astronomy walks are also regularly hosted by amateur astronomers in Tuolumne Meadows, Yosemite Valley and Wawona. In Tuolumne you get to walk out into the meadow, lay on granite still warm from the afternoon sun and gaze up at star-blazoned sky.

Check *Yosemite Today* for a current schedule. They're great fun.

---

also drop in (beginning one day before you raft) to get a permit, provided there are any left; odds are best midweek. Cherry Creek permits are available on a drop-in basis only (either the day before or day of your trip); the only quota system on Cherry Creek is the rapids – their insanity keeps numbers to a minimum. Cherry Creek rafters must be at least 18 years old.

Stever Roper's Camp 4: Recollections of a Yosemite Rockclimber, an insider's history of rock climbing in Yosemite Valley, reads like good climbing: it's packed with suspense and hard to put down, despite the rough spots.

Guided Trips

Several outfitters offer one- to three-day excursions during rafting season, with prices that vary by season and day of the week. Generally, rafters must be at least 12 years old. Most operators listed here offer additional trips on rivers outside the region; we've listed only those trips within the areas covered by this book. For more information and outfitters, check out www.stanislaus-river.com.

All-Outdoors Whitewater Rafting (☎ 800-247-2387, 925-932-8993; www.aorafting.com) One of two companies that runs Cherry Creek. Also does North Fork Stanislaus, Merced, Tuolumne and the Kaweah. Based in Walnut Creek, CA.

ARTA River Trips (☎ 209-962-7873, 800-323-2782; www.arta.org) Runs one-day and multiday Tuolumne trips departing from Groveland, as well as day trips on the Merced that leave from El Portal.

OARS (☎ 800-346-6277; www.oars.com) Worldwide rafting operator with a solid reputation and an admirable environmental ethic. Offers trips on the North Fork Stanislaus and the Tuolumne. Based in Angel's Camp.

Sierra Mac (☎ 800-457-2580; www.sierramac.com) One of two outfitters offering trips on hairy Cherry Creek. Also does the Tuolumne. Based in Groveland.

Whitewater Voyages (☎ 800-400-7238, 510-222-5994; www.whitewatervoyages.com) Offers trips on the Tuolumne, Merced, Kaweah and Kings River. Based in El Sobrante, CA.

Zephyr Rafting (☎ 209-533-1401, 209-532-6249, 800-431-3636; www.zrafting.com) Large, reputable outfitter offering trips on the Merced, Tuolumne and Kings Rivers. Based in Columbia, CA.

LAKE CANOEING & KAYAKING

Within the national parks, Yosemite's sapphire Tenaya Lake (p111) offers the best canoeing and kayaking. Outside the parks, lake-paddling options grow exponentially. To the north, off Hwy 4, Lake Alpine and Spicer Reservoir (p194) offer great paddling and have campgrounds. But the best reservoirs and lakes in **Stanislaus National Forest** (www.fs.fed.us/r5/stanislaus) lie along the (sometimes dirt) roads that leave Hwy 4; for suggestions and more information, check out the national forest website.

In the Eastern Sierras, Tioga Lake (p195) and Saddlebag Lake (p197) lie immediately outside the Yosemite border, have easy put-ins and are both resplendent. Beyond, there are many other fine places to paddle, including Mono Lake (p199), Lundy Lake (p201), June Lake (p202) and the several small lakes around Mammoth (p203). There are no real accessible lakes for kayaking or canoeing in Sequoia & Kings Canyon.

You can rent canoes and kayaks through the **Sierra Nevada Adventure Company** (www.snacattack.com), which has locations in Arnold and Sonora. In Bear Valley (p193), the **Bear Valley Adventure Company** (www.bearvalleyxc.com) rents single and double kayaks. Rates at both places run $35 to $50 per day (depending on the boat) and drop for each additional day. Be sure to make reservations.

FISHING

While the parks are hardly big fish country, fishing can certainly be fun and fruitful. The Kings River has some outstanding fishing, as does the Tuolumne immediately above Hetch Hetchy Reservoir. The South Fork of the Merced, and the Lyell and Dana Forks of the Tuolumne (in Tuolumne Meadows), offer some of the best stream fishing in Yosemite. There are loads of trout in the lakes and streams throughout the high country and, although the fish aren't whoppers, they're certainly fun to catch, especially if you're fly casting.

The best waters for big trout, however, lie beyond the parks' boundaries. The Carson River and the numerous lakes and hundreds of miles of streams along the Eastern Sierra offer some of the best fishing in the state. Anglers have long been lured by a list of legendary trout-filled waters, including Virginia Lakes (p201), Twin Lakes (p202) and June Lake (p202). To the north, Lake Alpine (p194), Mosquito Lake (p194) and the other lakes off of Hwy 4 hold some big fish and are easily accessible.

Stocking in Yosemite officially ended in 1991, but anglers can still find five types of trout in several of the streams and lakes in and around all three parks: native rainbow, brook, brown, golden and cutthroat. The fishing season for streams and rivers runs from the last Saturday in April through mid-November, except for Frog Creek (near Lake Eleanor), which opens in mid-June; fishing is permitted year-round on the reservoirs and lakes.

To fish anywhere in the region, you must get a valid California fishing license if you're over the age of 16. One-day, two-day and annual licenses cost $12.10, $18.65 and $37.30 respectively (nonresidents pay more). These can be purchased at sporting good and general stores within the parks and throughout the region. You must obey all California state fishing laws as prescribed by the **California Department of Fish & Game** (☎ 559-243-4005; www.dfg.ca.gov), which includes wearing your license in a visible spot whenever you're fishing. There are also park-specific regulations: in Yosemite, fishing from bridges is prohibited, and there's a strict catch-and-release policy for rainbows, as well as a five-fish-per-day limit on brown trout caught between Happy Isles and Pohono Bridge. You can pick up a list of regulations from any park visitor center.

Hank Johnson's *Yosemite Trout* offers some good tips. If you're staying in Yosemite, the regular 'How to Catch a Fish in Yosemite' interpretive talk is fun and informative (check *Yosemite Today* for a schedule). Online, you'll find some interesting tidbits at www.yosemitefun.com/fishing.htm. For current water levels throughout the region call the information system at the **Department of Water Resources** (☎ 800-952-5530).

Guided fly-fishing excursions are offered by several operators. Expect to pay around $400 for a day trip for two people.

Sierra Fly Fisher Tours (☎ 559-683-7664; www.sierraflyfisher.com)
Southern Yosemite Mountain Guides (☎ 800-231-4575; www.symg.com)
Yosemite Fly Fishing (☎ 209-379-2746; www.yosemiteflyfishing.net)

Most of the fish in Yosemite's rivers and streams were introduced by Europeans. Only the lower Merced and Tuolumne Rivers had native fish populations.

ACTIVITIES

DOWNHILL SKIING & SNOWBOARDING

When it comes to downhill skiing and snowboarding in the central Sierra, Mammoth Mountain (p205) reigns supreme. A top-rate mountain with excellent terrain for all levels of ability, Mammoth is known for its sunny skies, vertical chutes, airy snow and laid-back atmosphere. For these reasons it attracts skiers from around the world. For a much more local vibe, hit Bear Valley (p193), north of Yosemite, or June Mountain Ski Area (p203), near Mammoth. The Bear Valley Mountain Resort boasts some surprisingly good runs, good rates and it is currently expanding its slopes. While it is low on the list when it comes to adrenaline, Yosemite's Badger Pass (p157) is nonetheless a historical spot: it was California's first ski resort. It is a long-adored mountain, where multiple generations have learned the sport at the excellent ski school. Gentle slopes and consistent snow make it a good spot for beginners.

Backcountry skiers and snowboarders determined to carve up the Sierra peaks without the help of ski lifts should pick up a copy of Paul Richin Jr's *50 Classic Backcountry Ski & Snowboard Summits in California: Mount Shasta to Mount Whitney.*

CROSS-COUNTRY SKIING

Outstanding cross-country skiing is found throughout the Sierras. Yosemite is a fantastic spot for skiers of all levels, with options ranging from scenic half-mile loops to challenging 20-mile trails. Nordic skiers can take their pick from more than 350 miles of trails, many accessed from Badger Pass; from there, you can ski out to the Clark Range Vista and Glacier Point, an invigorating 21-mile round trip. Those who'd like to spend the night on the trail, but doubt their ability to build a snow cave, should head to the cozy and incredibly scenic Glacier Point Hut, the Ostrander Lake Ski Hut or, if you're up for the 16 mile ski-in from Lee Vining, the Ski Hut at Tuolumne Meadows. For more on all three, see the boxed text, p158. There are also good trails at Crane Flat and the Mariposa Grove. Most trails are well marked and easy to follow, and you can pick up ski and topo maps at the visitor centers and ranger stations.

In Sequoia & Kings Canyon, some 50 miles of marked but ungroomed trails crisscross Grant Grove and Giant Forest areas, and winter road closures offer excellent groomed skiing. For more, see p237.

In the Eastern Sierra, the Ansel Adams Wilderness, the Saddlebag Lake basin and the peaks encircling Mt Dana offer endless exploring opportunities for backcountry skiers. Mammoth has some top-rate cross-country skiing, particularly in the areas accessed by Lake Mary Rd and around Devils Postpile. Mammoth's Tamarack Cross Country Ski Center (p206) is an excellent base. To the north, Bear Valley (p193) boasts a cross-country ski school as well as a vast network of trails, ski workshops and even a telemark festival (skiing using the telemark turn, also called free-heel skiing). Hwy 4 offers numerous opportunities for cross-country skiing. Another great base for cross-country skiing is the Evergreen Lodge (p167), located near Hetch Hetchy, just outside the western boundaries of Yosemite.

Rentals & Ski Schools

In Yosemite, the **Badger Pass Cross-Country Center & Ski School** (☎ 209-372-8444; www.yosemitepark.com) is a highly regarded cross-country ski school operated by the Yosemite Mountaineering School. It offers a wide range of instruction (including snow camping and backcountry skiing education), packages and tours, as well as guided overnight ski trips to Yosemite's two backcountry huts. In Sequoia & Kings Canyon, you can rent cross-country skis at several locations (see p237).

WINTER IN THE WILDERNESS

Anyone heading into the backcountry in winter by ski or snowshoe generally must abide by the same backcountry regulations that apply in summer. If you're organizing a trip for yourself, make sure you have plenty of backcountry experience – ill-prepared travel in the wilderness can always be dicey, but it can be downright deadly in winter. If you're uncertain of your skills, take a course at the Badger Pass Cross-Country Ski School or at Mountain Adventure Seminars, where you can gain the know-how needed to survive in winter conditions. Wilderness permits are still required to spend the night in the backcountry, but reservations are not required.

In Bear Valley, the **Bear Valley Adventure Company** (www.bearvalleyxc.com) offers beginning cross-country ski lessons and rents skis and snowshoes (see p193). The store will also provide you with loads of information on where to go in the Hwy 4 area. Also based in Bear Valley, **Mountain Adventure Seminars** (☎ 209-753-6556; www.mtadventure.com) offers courses in backcountry skiing, telemarking, snowboarding and snowshoeing, as well as avalanche education and mountaineering courses. In Mammoth, the **Tamarack Lodge & Resort** (www.tamaracklodge.com) operates its Cross Country Ski Center, with lessons, rentals and over 19 miles of trails accessible from the lodge. See p206.

SNOWSHOEING

One of the easiest ways to explore the winter wilderness is to step into a pair of snowshoes and head out on any of the hiking or cross-country skiing trails – for good karma's sake, just don't tramp directly in ski tracks themselves. Provided there's adequate snow, you can snowshoe anywhere. Some excellent choices in Yosemite include the John Muir Trail (p41) and Mariposa Grove (p109). You can rent snowshoes at Badger Pass and explore on your own or join one of the park's popular and fun ranger-led excursions. Near Hetch Hetchy, the Evergreen Lodge (p167) rents out snowshoes and offers guided snowshoe hikes inside and outside the park. In Sequoia & Kings Canyon, ranger-led snowshoe walks depart from the Wuksachi Lodge (p219); these fill up fast, so reserve a spot by calling the location or by stopping by one of the park visitor centers. All of the cross-country ski centers mentioned earlier also offer snowshoe rentals and lessons.

ICE SKATING, SLEDDING & SNOW TUBING

One of the more delightful – and certainly most popular – winter activities in Yosemite is skating on Curry Village's open-air rink (p157), which is open daily from mid-November through March. If you prefer less control and higher speeds, climb aboard a snow tube and send yourself rocketing downhill at Yosemite's Badger Pass (p158). Sledding and tubing are also popular at Crane Flat, but you must bring your own vessel. In Mammoth, there's even a park specifically for sledding and tubing (see p206).

GOLF

If you find the need to smack the ol' tiny white ball around, head to Yosemite's nine-hole, par-35 **Wawona Golf Course** (☎ 209-375-6572; www.yosemitepark.com; green fees for 9/18 holes $18.50/29.50, cart rentals $15/24.50), which was built in 1917. The course hails itself as the country's only 'organic' golf course, meaning no pesticides are used on the lawn and everything is

Yvon Chouinard, founder of Patagonia, got his start making climbing equipment (hand-forged pitons, to be exact), which he sold from the trunk of his car in Yosemite Valley. His company, Chouinard Equipment, later became Black Diamond

ACTIVITIES

irrigated with gray water. What's more, green fees are phenomenally low. For more of a challenge, head to Mammoth's Sierra Star Golf Course (p208), an 18-hole, par 75 championship course where the main claim to fame is altitude: at 8000ft, it's California's highest.

VOLUNTEERING

Some choose to see the Sierras from the saddle, some from the bicycle seat and some from the seat of a canoe. Why not see it from an entirely different perspective? Beside helping support understaffed parks and organizations, volunteering provides a unique lens through which to see the national parks. It's also a great way to meet locals and fellow volunteers – contacts that can last a lifetime. As a volunteer you can do everything from weeding and sweeping to working on restoration projects, monitoring bears and leading educational walks. Most volunteer positions require advanced application and background checks.

There are several resources to explore when researching volunteer opportunities. A great place to start is calling the **Yosemite Park Volunteer Coordinator** (☎ 209-379-1850; www.nps.gov/yose) or the **Sequoia & Kings Canyon Park Volunteer Coordinator** (☎ 559-565-313; www.nps.gov/seki). Both park websites maintain updated information on volunteering in their respective 'Support Your Park' sections. The **Volunteer.gov/gov** (www.volunteer.gov/gov) website maintains a comprehensive database on positions available at all national parks and federal recreation areas, allowing you to browse openings by category: backcountry, fish and wildlife, historical preservation etc.

The **Yosemite Association** (☎ 209-379-2317; www.yosemite.org) runs an established volunteer program for its members that includes restoration and revegetation projects, as well as staffing information stations. Long-term volunteers receive free camping, a small stipend and bookstore discounts. Earth Day (April 22) celebrations in Yosemite feature chances to help out the park – including cleanup projects, tree planting etc – as well as kids' educational events, a vendors' fair, and live music and poetry. Also in Yosemite, the **Sierra Club's LeConte Memorial Lodge** (☎ volunteer info winter 209-372-4542, summer 209-403-6676; www.sierraclub.org/education/leconte) puts Sierra Club members to work as volunteers who assist in the operation of the lodge for one-week stints between May 1 and September 30.

Kids & Pets

When we leave home and head for the parks, of course we want to bring our loved ones – all of them! Traveling with children and with pets requires more advance planning, though the rewards are immeasurable. Kids love the parks, and bringing them along is a no-brainer. There's loads for them to do – the hard part is choosing what to do first.

You could spend your days swimming, rafting, biking or hiking. How about spying on the wildlife, marveling at sky-diving waterfalls, peering over tall cliffs or exploring some crazy-cool caves? For many kids, just sleeping in a tent for the first time – and listening to all the strange noises of the night – can be the biggest adventure of all. In addition, the parks organize lots of activities and programs geared specifically to children for all age groups and interests. To find kid-friendly or kid-oriented events, check listings in the park newspapers and look at daily calendars posted at some ranger stations and visitor centers.

That said, travel with kids always requires some extra planning and safety measures. As you're planning your trip, ask yourself some scheduling and safety questions. Will you need to factor in some daily down time or nap time? Do your kids know what to do if they see a bear?

If you want to experience the outdoors with your pets, it's paramount to make sure that you keep them comfortable and safe. Considerations include the availability of overnight quarters, possible interactions with other animals and trail restrictions. As part of trip planning, you'll want to check the regulations governing the area you plan to visit. There's no sense bringing your dog for a good romp, and then finding out that dogs must be leashed where you're staying.

BRINGING THE KIDS

When planning what to do and see, try not to overdo things as packing too much into your trip can cause frustration and spoil the adventure. When choosing activities, make sure they appeal to your kids as well. Balance a morning at the Yosemite Museum (p98), for instance, with a swim in the Merced River (p156). Or spend time at a place both adults and children might enjoy, such as Sequoia's Crystal Cave (p221) or the LeConte Memorial Lodge (p104) and the Nature Center at Happy Isles (p104) in Yosemite. Even better, include the kids in the trip planning from the get-go. If they have a hand in choosing activities, they'll be much more interested and excited when you arrive. For more information, advice, and anecdotes, pick up a copy of Lonely Planet's *Travel with Children* by Cathy Lanigan.

Active, adventurous, and environmentally aware parents are often eager to share those interests with their kids. Take care, though, not to turn a

---

FIVE KID-FRIENDLY HIKES IN YOSEMITE

- Yosemite Valley Loop (p118)
- Lukens Lake (p122)
- Mariposa Grove (p121)
- Vernal Falls (footbridge below the falls; p124)
- Soda Springs (p114)

diversion into a chore. For example, don't make your kids memorize 80 different kinds of rocks – that's no fun for anyone (adults included). Kids may be curious and eager to learn, but they also need time to play. Consider participating in organized activities, such as ranger programs and nature walks, or visiting kid-friendly spots like the Happy Isles Nature Center – great ways to spark kids who seem lackluster about the whole 'nature thing.' Kids also usually like it when there are other kids around.

The parks and the nearby towns do a lot to cater to families. Kids under 12 usually can sleep for free in the same room as their parents, and most restaurants have kids' menus with smaller portions and significantly lower prices. Parents can also expect discounts of to 30% to 50% on transportation and many activities (note that the cutoff age is almost always 12 years). In addition, kid-sized recreational equipment like skis, bikes or ice skates is almost always available for rent. Sequoia & Kings Canyon even has a newspaper just for kids called *Sequoia Seeds*. Also see the boxed text, p209, for some things to do at Mammoth Lakes.

Give kids some responsibility for your trip, and let them carry a backpack of some kind. Just don't overfill it, or they may never want to strap one on again. *Backpacking with Babies & Small Children* by Goldie Silverman is a useful resource for anyone planning a hike with the kids.

In Yosemite Valley, keep the free shuttle bus in mind when you're out and about. That way, if your kids get tired you can simply hop the bus and head back to your car, campsite or lodge.

> The website www.nps
> .gov/seki/forkids/index
> .htm is the main page for
> kid-related activities and
> educational programs in
> Sequoia & Kings Canyon,
> and includes a link to
> the *Sequoia Seeds* kids'
> newspaper.

Fun Stuff for Families
Peruse *Yosemite Today* for more children's programs in Yosemite, including an hour of nature stories, a photo walk geared just for kids and a 'Wee Wild Ones' program of stories and activities for those six and under. Other events such as the evening campfires and the 'Stars Over Yosemite' astronomy talk at Glacier Point (see p159) are great for kids and families, too.

BIKING
Rent bikes in Yosemite Valley or bring your own. The bike path is quite level, looping around gorgeous meadows with views of domes and waterfalls. Outside the parks, older kids will go bananas over the enormous summer mountain-bike park (p206) at Mammoth Lakes. For more on mountain biking, see p48.

CLASSES
Park partner organizations offer all types of classes where kids can learn about ecology and wilderness skills. In Yosemite, take a rock-climbing class from the Yosemite Mountaineering School (ages 10 and up; see p155) or draw or paint at the Art Activity Center (p100). In Sequoia, the

---

KIDS & PETS

FIVE KID-FRIENDLY HIKES IN SEKI

- Zumwalt Meadow (p227)
- Crescent Meadow Loop (p226)
- Tokopah Falls (p225)
- General Grant Tree Trail (p226)
- Monarch Lakes (older children; p230)

Sequoia Natural History Association has field classes and talks on insects and animals that are usually open to kids over 12. For more information on courses, see p253.

JUNIOR RANGER PROGRAM

Make sure you ask about getting a Junior Ranger booklet when you arrive. It's a park-specific activity book of fun games, and it helps children of different ages learn about local wildlife, park history and resource preservation. All in all, it's one of the best bundles of things for kids to do in the parks. The booklets have scavenger hunts, crossword puzzles and assignments like picking up a bag of trash on the trail or interviewing a real ranger. Upon completion, kids get a badge. It's an educational and very neat way to experience the parks, and it's open to adults too! The booklets are free from Sequoia & Kings Canyon visitor centers, and cost $3.50 in Yosemite bookstores. Yosemite also has a similar program – called Little Cubs – that's designed for children three to six; accompanying activity booklets are $3.

Every summer, Phil Frank's *Farley* comic strip goes on vacation in Yosemite. The books *Fur and Loafing in Yosemite* and *Eat, Drink & Be Hairy* are compilations of these hysterical, bear-filled Yosemite adventures.

HIKING

Hiking is great exercise for kids, though parents should gauge their children's abilities and choose hikes that won't overwhelm them. If you're unsure, try hikes that don't require much elevation gain, like Mirror Lake (p118) or Lukens Lake (p122) in Yosemite, or the Big Trees Trail (p226) in Sequoia National Park. If the little ones handle that fine, work your way up from there. Kids often thrill at Yosemite viewpoints such as Sentinel Dome (p120), Lembert Dome (p131) and Taft Point (p119), which are all reachable via short, easy trails. For magical strolls of any length, take a walk around a giant sequoia grove.

HISTORY

The Yosemite Museum (p98) and the Indian Village out back are worth a look, as are the great old buildings, stagecoaches and the covered bridge at the Pioneer Yosemite History Center (p108) in Wawona. You can even take a 10-minute stagecoach ride. And at the Yosemite Valley Visitor Center (p97), you can rent the equipment to take a **GPS walking tour** (☎ 877-477-8687; www.lowerfallsloop.com; tour adult/child $9.95/7.95, headset rental $1) of the valley. Narrated in part by muppet Ranger Bill, the hand-held device tells stories about the locations visited, and has fun games.

HORSEBACK RIDING

A multitude of stables offer trail rides at the parks. In Yosemite, head for the Valley, Wawona, Hetch Hetchy or Tuolomne Meadows (see p153), and in Sequoia & Kings Canyon, you can hitch up at Cedar Grove, Grant Grove or the Giant Forest National Monument (see p236). Also see Horseback Riding & Packing (p49).

NATURE & EDUCATION CENTERS

Help the kids put the parks in context while interacting with creative displays and playing goofy games. Yosemite's Nature Center at Happy Isles (p104) has great hands-on exhibits and dioramas depicting various natural environments and including numerous stuffed animals. You may not encounter a porcupine, owl or coyote in the wild during your trip, but kids can get a close-up view of what they look like here. They can also learn about pine cones, rub their hands across some granite, check out different animal tracks and even snicker a bit at the display on animal scat. Out back is an

---

RAINY DAYS IN THE PARKS

It's raining, it's pouring – will the kids think it's superboring? A little weather doesn't have to spoil your trip. In fact, it might prod you to explore some of the cool indoor activities you might not have noticed.

In Yosemite, the cozy children's corner at the **LeConte Memorial Lodge** (p104) has green-friendly projects where kids can lean about natural resources and the environment, or they can just browse the books and bugs. The **Nature Center at Happy Isles** (p104) has hands-on animal displays and identification activities that are interesting for adults, too. But don't overlook the creative opportunities at the **Art Activity Center** (p100). If you just need somewhere to sit through the storm, head to the **Camp Curry Lounge** (p101), where the kids can play games by the fire (bring the cards!) and make all the noise they want.

In Sequoia & Kings Canyon, even a deluge won't stop you from spelunking the area's underground labyrinths at **Boyden Cavern** and **Crystal Cave** (p236). The top-notch **Beetle Rock Education Center** (p220) is a blast – rain or shine – with activity stations throughout the building and large tents to play in.

Outside the parks, one of the best options is the **Children's Museum of the Sierra** (p183) in Oakhurst, where kids can lose themselves in educational games and crafts. The re-created mine and weird rocks at Mariposa's **California State Mining & Mineral Museum** (p176) make a cool excursion, and to the west of Yosemite, aspiring cowpokes can whoop it up at the **Oakdale Cowboy Museum** (p180).

---

exhibit explaining the 1996 rockfall that happened nearby, which some kids find mighty cool. In Sequoia, the Beetle Rock Education Center contains even more stuff to touch, play with and explore. And at the Discovery Room in the back of the Grant Grove visitor center, kids can do pine cone identification and a spot-the-species game with the surrounding murals.

'Yosemite's Interactive Classroom' (www.nps.gov/archive/yose/education) is an educational site with handy bite-sized facts and figures to answer questions that kids may have about the park.

TRAINS

Lots of kids (and adults) are fascinated by old trains, and a few places outside the park are good destinations for train buffs. The best by far is the Yosemite Mountain Sugar Pine Railroad (p187) in Fish Camp, where you can ride historic trains into the forest and take part in a reenacted train robbery. Other interesting whistle stops include the Laws Railroad Museum (p212) in Bishop and the Yosemite Valley Railroad exhibit (p178) in El Portal.

WATER SPORTS

If your kids love to get wet, summertime options abound. In Yosemite, go rafting (p155) on the Merced River or just splash around by the shore. Construct sand castles at the Lake Tenaya beach, and swim at the Curry Village pool (see p156). In Sequoia & Kings Canyon, Hume Lake and Muir Rock (see p236) are great swimming spots as well. For more on swimming, see p48.

WINTER SPORTS

When the temperature drops, winter sports at the parks include ice skating, snowshoeing, downhill and cross-country skiing, and tubing at snow-play areas. The gentle slopes at Yosemite's Badger Pass (p157) are excellent for learning to ski, and the Badger Pups kids downhill program offers lessons for little skiers and boarders from four to six years old. It also has babysitting so adults can head out for some of the trickier stuff.

Outside the parks, the June Mountain resort (p203) and Mammoth (p205) have superb skiing and snowboarding as well.

Keeping It Safe

When hiking, be sure your kids stay within earshot (if not sight) of the adults. They may want to rush ahead, but it's very easy to miss a necessary junction or take a wrong turn. As a precaution, dress them in brightly colored clothes, and have each one carry a flashlight and safety whistle. Make sure they know what to do if they get lost (for instance, stay put and periodically blow the whistle).

Whether you're hiking or just plain sightseeing, dress kids (and yourself) in layers, so they can peel off or pull on clothing when needed. And bring along lots of high-energy snacks and drinks, even on short outings.

If you're traveling in the high country such as Tuolumne Meadows or Mineral King, keep in mind that kids are just as vulnerable as adults to altitude sickness. They may not know what it is they're feeling, and they may not let you know. Familiarize yourself with the symptoms (headaches and nausea are common) and watch for them, especially during physical activities. If your child shows symptoms, descend to lower elevations.

Be extra cautious around viewpoints such as Yosemite's Taft Point, which has a railing at the cliff's edge but none around the periphery (including around the Fissures – giant cracks in the granite that plunge thousands of feet to the Valley floor). The same goes for the summits of any peaks or domes.

A cute resource for taking kids to the park, www .visitsequoia.com/Just ForKids.aspx includes an *I Spy* checklist, download-able coloring pages and information on bears and park trees.

BRINGING THE PETS

Pets are allowed in the national parks, though the restrictions are pretty limiting. They are permitted on roads and paved trails, but you can't bring your dog (we assume you're not even *thinking* of bringing the cat) on nonpaved hiking trails or into any wilderness areas. However, note that service animals (eg guide dogs) *are* welcome in the parks. To prevent misunderstandings with park rangers, service animals should always wear their vests.

The rules protect wildlife from your dog, and vice versa, and keep your dog from disturbing other hikers. Do not try to sneak dogs into back-country or expect to leave them at campgrounds during the day, because you will be cited. In the National Forests, dogs are usually permitted on trails, with the possible exception of designated wilderness areas.

Fun with Fido

In Yosemite there are a few exceptions to the nonpaved trail rule, including walks on Wawona Meadow Loop and parts of Old Big Oak Flat Rd south of Hodgdon Meadow. Except for service animals, dogs are not allowed on shuttle buses or inside lodge rooms. In Sequoia & Kings Canyon, dogs are allowed in all campgrounds, and in Yosemite, you can

---

AGE-APPROPRIATE FUN

The parks offer a wealth of kid-friendly activities, but some outdoor endeavors are easier for kids to master than others. Youngsters can learn paddling skills and begin cross-country skiing fairly early, around age three or four. Children four and up can enroll in downhill skiing lessons at Badger Pass, a popular wintertime option. Horseback riding and bicycling are good summer-time choices, and there are plenty of pleasant hikes easy enough for little legs. Climbing and rafting, on the other hand, require a higher level of dexterity and endurance and are best left to teens and adults.

KIDS & PETS

bring pets into most except for Tamarack Flat, Porcupine Flat and any of the walk-in campgrounds. Some Yosemite campgrounds allot special sections for pet owners, so look for signs. At both parks, dogs must be on leashes (6ft or less) at all times and never left unattended. And surprise, surprise – you must always clean up the pooch poop.

> Pets are extremely susceptible to overheating. If left in a hot car, dogs can experience brain and organ damage after only 15 minutes.

These park regulations aim to ensure your furry one's health and happiness. If your dog is running around off-leash, there's more of an opportunity for it to roll around in poison oak or get in a tussle with another animal. Keep your dog healthy by periodically checking for ticks and being prepared for weather extremes, whether it's plenty of water on hot days or extra blankets for chilly evenings. And never leave your dog in a hot car.

In the Sequoia National Forest, leashed dogs are permitted on trails, but they must sleep inside a tent or vehicle, and they are not permitted at developed swimming areas.

Yosemite has a **dog kennel** (☎ 372-8348; fax 372-8351; ✆ May-Sep) at the Valley stables, though it's quite bare bones. Small shaded outdoor cages are tucked away from the main buildings in an apple orchard that's frequented by grazing bears. The dogs are safe behind fencing, but stay unattended. Board runs $8 for the day, and another $8 if your dog stays overnight. Dogs must be at least six months old and over 10lb. You must fax or provide a copy of vet immunization records, and reservations are accepted.

For up-to-date pet policies, check these websites:
Sequoia & Kings Canyon National Parks (www.nps.gov/seki/planyourvisit/pets.htm)
Sequoia National Forest (www.fs.fed.us/r5/sequoia/faq/)
Yosemite National Park (www.nps.gov/yose/planyourvisit/pets.htm)

Horse Trails & Equestrian Facilities

Bringing a horse or a pack animal for a backcountry trip requires even more advance planning. Without adequate precautions, animals can die from injuries, wildlife attacks, frostbite, heat exhaustion, dehydration or malnutrition. And you cannot just show up at a park and expect to tie up somewhere, or ask if you can use ranger corrals (which is strictly forbidden). In Yosemite, there are a number of campgrounds with facilities for stock (see p155), and the **Yosemite concessionaire** (☎ 372-1000) has some overnight board facilities by advance reservation. In the Sequoia & Kings Canyon area, there is a dedicated Horse Camp in the Sequoia National Forest, not too far from the Generals Hwy. There are also a number of horse camps outside the parks, such as the well-positioned Agnew Meadows in the Ansel Adams Wilderness near Mammoth Lakes.

In the backcountry, stock users must follow strict guidelines on group size, grazing and dispersal of manure, as well as feed restrictions to prevent the introduction of invasive plant species. Trails are generally horse-friendly unless posted otherwise. If you don't have your own animals, there are a number of pack outfits in and around the parks (see p49).

Sequoia & Kings Canyon have a number of trails popular with horse groups. They include the Garfield Grove Trail in South Fork, the Woods Creek Trail from Roads End, and the Atwell-Hockett Trail, Franklin Pass Trail, Timber Gap Trail and Tar Gap Trail in Mineral King. In Yosemite, a number of popular trails depart from trailheads on Tioga Rd.

For the most recent stock use and grazing regulations, visit these sites:
Sequoia & Kings Canyon National Parks (www.nps.gov/seki/planyourvisit/stockreg.htm)
Sequoia National Forest (www.fs.fed.us/r5/sequoia/maps/brochures/horse_sense.html)
Yosemite National Park (www.nps.gov/archive/yose/wilderness/stock.htm)

Environment

The Sierra Nevada, which takes in Yosemite & Kings Canyon National Parks, is a 400-mile-long range of 14,000ft peaks that gives California much of its astonishing biological and geological diversity. Half of the state's 7000 plant species grow in the Sierra Nevada, while more than 400 animal species find permanent or temporary homes here.

A mountain range on the scale of the Sierra Nevada profoundly shapes the environment of California. When the range reached its current height two million years ago, it created a towering wall that captures clouds and douses the western slope in water while shutting off the supply of rain to the eastern slope and the entire Great Basin desert further east. Surprisingly, the wall also protects California from bitter winter storms blowing west out of the interior states, giving the state a mild and pleasant climate. Relict plant species (the last of otherwise extinct lineages) have managed to survive in California because of the Sierra Nevada's influence.

THE LAND

Geologists call the Sierra Nevada a tilted fault block range – and it's a particularly impressive example at that, running more than 400 miles long and 40 to 60 miles wide, with 500 peaks over 10,000ft. Picture a tilted fault block as an iceberg listing to one side while floating in the earth's crust. The Sierra Nevada is an immense body of granite known as a batholith (meaning 'deep rock') that formed deep within the crust, then 'floated' up and became exposed over millions of years. Today we see the tip of this batholith, though it is obscured in places where older rocks (mostly metamorphic) still cling, like pieces of a torn cloak, or where newer rocks (mostly volcanic) have been added on top, like icing.

Want to learn more about the Sierra? Check out *A Sierra Club Naturalist's Guide*, by Stephen Whitney for an explanation of everything.

The Lay of the Land over Time

Around 225 million years ago, the area that is now the Sierra Nevada was a shallow sea lying off the coast of a young North American continent. Material from offshore island volcanoes, plus debris eroding from the continental landmass, was gradually filling this sea with layers of sediment at the same time the North American (continental) plate started drifting westward and riding over the leading edge of the Pacific (ocean) plate. This movement forced the edge of the Pacific plate down to depths where it melted into magma that later cooled to form the Sierra Nevada batholith. Today's Sierra Nevada and Cascade mountain chains mark the edge of this submerged, melting plate. The force of two plates colliding and crushing together also generated such enormous heat and pressure that old sedimentary and volcanic rocks turned into the metamorphic rocks now found throughout the Sierra Nevada.

As it pushed over the Pacific plate, the North American plate buckled so strongly that it formed a proto–Sierra Nevada of folded rock that may have reached as high as 15,000ft. This building phase ceased about 130 million years ago, and the old mountains began a long erosional phase that reduced them to gently rolling uplands by 50 million years ago and left the batholith exposed on the earth's surface.

The Sierra Nevada batholith formed between 80 and 210 million years ago, as magma deep in the earth's crust cooled and formed giant blocks of rock over one hundred different times. Each magma event formed a discrete body of granitic rock known as a pluton (from Pluto, the Roman

ENVIRONMENT

god of the underworld), each with a characteristic composition and appearance. Hikers can today trace these well-mapped plutons by examining the mix of minerals and the size of crystals within the rock matrix.

Ten million years ago, the granite batholith began to lift and bulge upward between parallel sets of faults (cracks in the earth's crust). Regions of much older rocks were uplifted on the newly forming crest. Remnants of old rocks perched on top of granite ridges are called roof pendants, of which Mt Dana and the Ritter Range are fine examples. The batholith has continued to lift, reaching its current height an estimated two million years ago; since then, the counterbalancing forces of uplift and erosion have created an equilibrium that keeps the Sierra at more or less the same size.

From two million years ago until about 10,000 years ago, Ice Age glaciers covered portions of the Sierra Nevada with snow and ice. The largest ice field was a giant cap of ice that covered an area 275 miles long and 40 miles wide between Lake Tahoe and Yosemite. From high-elevation ice fields, rivers of ice (glaciers) flowed down and scoured out rugged river canyons, simply enlarging some or beautifully sculpting others like Yosemite Valley or the upper portions of Kings Canyon.

After the Ice Age came a warm period when there were no glaciers in the Sierra, but within the last 1000 years about 99 glaciers and 398 glacierets (small glaciers or pockets of ice) have reformed during the Little Ice Age. The largest remaining glaciers are on Mt Lyell and Mt Maclure in the Yosemite region, and on the Palisades further south. However, due to global warming these are melting rapidly and are in imminent danger of disappearing within years.

The Forces at Work

The fascinating tale of how these rocks first formed is only the beginning of the geologic story – as soon as the rocks were exposed on the earth's surface a host of new forces shaped them into what you see before you today. Hugely powerful Ice Age glaciers have played a dramatic role, but erosion and weathering have also done their part, as have lava and ash eruptions.

GLACIERS

Most of the Sierra Nevada's landscape has been substantially shaped by glaciers. In fact, of all the forces that have contributed to the landscape, none have had greater impact than the relentless grinding caused by millions of tons of ice over two million years. Evidence of grinding is often

---

SHAKY GROUND

Uplift of the Sierra's batholith continues to occur along its eastern face, where a zone of geologic activity keeps life exciting for folks living between Mammoth Lakes and Lone Pine. In 1872 the Eastern Sierra jerked upward 13ft in a single earthquake, while over the past two decades Mammoth has endured a nerve-wracking series of minor earthquakes and tremors. The Sierra crest is estimated to lift as much as 1.5in per century and as a result of this skewed tilting the eastern face of the Sierra is now an abrupt wall rising up to 11,000ft high while the western face is a long gentle incline.

Due to uplift along the eastern face, rivers flowing down the west slope have picked up speed and cut progressively deeper canyons into the formerly flat, rolling landscape. Today, a total of 17 major river canyons mark the west slope, and the rock that formerly filled those canyons now buries the Central Valley under 9.5 miles of sediment.

JOHN MUIR

Arriving in San Francisco in the spring of 1868, John Muir started out to walk across California's Central Valley to the then scarcely known landmark of Yosemite Valley, where his wanderings and writings earned him lasting worldwide fame. This Scotsman's many treks led him into the highest realms of the Yosemite backcountry, where he took little more than a wool overcoat, dry crusts of bread and a bit of tea. Though not a scientist by training, Muir looked at the natural world with a keen curiosity, investigating glaciers, trees, earthquakes, bees and even the most plain-coated of the Sierra birds, recording them in great detail. His musings on glaciation led him to argue with Josiah Whitney, the head of the California Geological Survey, who disbelieved Muir's contention that glaciers had helped to shape Yosemite Valley's realm of polished granite.

Not only did his prolific and florid writings span the gap between poetic literature and his growing conservation awareness, but Muir's articles and lobbying efforts became the foundation of the campaign that established Yosemite as a national park in 1890. But despite his success with Yosemite National Park and his accomplishments with the Sierra Club, Muir was unable to save Hetch Hetchy Valley, which he believed rivaled Yosemite Valley in beauty and grandeur. He lost the battle in 1913, when Hetch Hetchy Valley was sacrificed to the water and power needs of a growing San Francisco. Despondent and outraged, Muir likened the damming of Hetch Hetchy to the desecration of a holy temple. He died in 1914, before the dreaded building of the O'Shaughnessy Dam in 1923 and the subsequent flooding of Hetch Hetchy Valley.

right at your feet in areas where glaciers have worn granite surfaces down to a smooth, shiny finish. Along the road at Tenaya Lake, for example, flat granite shelves are so polished they glisten in the early morning light. In contrast, hikers to high alpine nunataks (peaks and plateaus that were too high to be glaciated) such as Mt Conness find rough-textured, sharp-edged and jagged granite formations.

Glaciers arise in regions where snowfields fail to melt completely by summer's end. Over time, delicate snow crystals dissolve into tiny spheres that connect and fuse into solid ice. True glacial ice forms after hundreds of years, with the original snowflakes becoming nine times heavier and 500 times stronger in the process. These ice fields develop in high mountain valleys where snowdrifts readily accumulate, and from there they flow downhill at the rate of inches or yards per day. The longest known glacier in the Sierra Nevada was a 60-mile tongue that flowed down the Tuolumne River Canyon about 20,000 years ago. In some valleys, the Sierra ice field reached up to 4000ft thick.

Hundreds or thousands of feet of ice created an unbelievable amount of pressure and shearing strength that completely altered the landscape. Massive boulders were plucked up and dragged along like giant rasping teeth on a file's edge. Smaller rocks and sand carried along the glacier's bottom acted like sandpaper that polished underlying bedrock. Every rock that was loose or could be pried loose was caught up and transported for miles.

Glaciers have the funny effect of rounding out landscape features that lie below the ice while sharpening features that rise above the ice. The same grinding force that smoothes out valleys also quarries rocks from the base of peaks, resulting in undercutting that forms towering spikes. In Tuolumne Meadows this effect is particularly dramatic – compare the smooth domes on the valley floor, like Lembert and Pothole, with the sheer spires of Cathedral and Unicorn Peaks.

ROCK ACTIVITY

The Sierra's granite owes its appearance not only to the tremendous sculpting power of glaciers but also to something far more subtle – its own internal properties. Granite tends to crack and separate along regular planes, often parallel to the surface. Everywhere you travel in the High Sierra, you'll find evidence of this process at work.

At Olmsted Point along the Tioga Pass Rd, visitors can see a surrealistic view of vast granite walls peeling off like onion layers below Clouds Rest. This exfoliation is the result of massive rock formations expanding and cracking in shell-like layers as the pressure of overlying materials erodes away. Over time, sharp angles and corners give way to increasingly rounded curves that leave us with distinctive landmarks like Half Dome and Moro Rock.

Weathering breaks granite down through a different process than glacial erosion or internal cracking, yet its effects are equally profound. Joints in the granite allow water to seep into deep cracks where the liquid expands during winter's freezing temperatures. This pushes open cracks with pressures up to a thousand pounds per square inch and eventually forces square-angled blocks to break off from the parent formation. Edges and corners are further weathered over time to create rounded boulders. Finally, rain and exposure wear down granite's weaker minerals, leaving an unstable matrix of hard pale minerals (quartz and feldspar) that crumble into fine-grained rubble called grus. Hikers walking on granite slabs might experience the unnerving sensation of slipping on tiny pebbles of grus that roll underfoot like ball bearings. Grus finally breaks down into soil in the presence of water.

In the Western Sierra Nevada, granites are mostly fine-grained, with joints spaced fairly widely. As a result, rock formations tend to be massive structures shaped by exfoliation. In the Eastern Sierra Nevada, granites are more likely to be coarse-grained and to have closely spaced

Located in the stunning terrain of the southern Sierra, the Sequoia Natural History Association (www.sequoiahistory .org) has one of the best classrooms in the world.

ROCKS: A PRIMER

The Sierra Nevada is one of the world's premier granite landscapes, yet the range includes more than just granite. To make things simple, we can divide the region's rocks into metamorphic, granitic and volcanic rocks.

Metamorphic rocks are older volcanic and sedimentary rocks whose structure has been dramatically altered by intense heat and pressure deep within the earth's crust. These rocks pre-date the Sierra Nevada batholith. Fine examples of metamorphic rocks line Tioga Pass Rd between Tioga and Ellery Lakes, where seafloor sediments 500 million years old have been pushed up by the rising batholith and are now cast along the Sierra crest. These reddish, purplish or greenish rocks are a distinctive change from the speckled grays of granite just to the west.

Granite is the popular label for a broad category of rocks that form when molten magma cools within the earth's crust (this same molten rock is called lava when it erupts or flows onto the earth's surface). Sierra Nevada granite actually consists of five separate minerals occurring in complex combinations that produce a characteristic salt-and-pepper appearance. With practice, hikers can learn to recognize these five minerals: quartz, which is a clear gray color; potassium feldspar and plagioclase feldspar, both clear gray when freshly exposed but chalky white after weathering; biotite, which consists of blackish hexagonal crystals that flake off in thin plates; and hornblende, which occurs in long, rod-shaped crystals of a dark green hue. Easily, the most striking set of granite examples can be found in Yosemite Valley itself.

Chemically identical to rocks that form deep within the crust, volcanic rocks change as they erupt on the surface as lava; this process injects gases into the liquid rock, giving it a pockmarked or bubbled appearance when it hardens, and forcing it to cool quickly. Rocks that have cooled deep underground (such as granite) do so very slowly, which leads to the formation of large, visible crystals; liquid rock exposed to air cools so quickly that crystals aren't able to form. Most of the Sierra's volcanic rocks have weathered away except for high, uplifted pockets.

joints. Here the process of water seeping into cracks and pushing rocks apart (called frost riving) results in characteristically jagged, sawtooth ridges such as those that form the Cathedral Range near Tuolumne Meadows.

VOLCANOES

Between five and 20 million years ago, a series of lava and mud flows covered about 12,000 square miles of the Sierra Nevada north of Yosemite, with some volcanic activity extending south to the area now enclosed by the park. While much of this history has since eroded away, caps of old volcanic material still exist at Sonora Pass, an otherworldly landscape of eroding volcanic debris easily explored on several short hikes. Perhaps the most dramatic volcanic feature is the Dardanelles Cones, a resistant volcanic plug that towers like a foreboding castle over Hwy 108.

About three million years ago, the zone of volcanic activity shifted from the region north of Yosemite to the slopes east of the Sierra crest. Massive eruptions between Mammoth Lakes and Mono Lake created a series of calderas and volcanic mountains, including Mammoth Mountain itself. Mono Lake gained two islands and a small chain of hills on its southern side during this period of activity, which is still ongoing; the landscape at Mono Lake has undergone dramatic volcanic changes as recently as 640 years ago.

The most familiar and popular landmark to form in the 'current' era of volcanic activity is Devils Postpile, located west of Mammoth Lakes. Here a 600ft- to 700ft-deep lava flow filled a river canyon about 600,000 years ago, cooling so quickly that it formed one of the world's most spectacular examples of columnar basalt. The four-, five-, six- and seven-sided columns are virtually perfect in their symmetry, evoking awe in all who view the formation.

The rawness and newness of these volcanic formations remind us how active and ongoing the Sierra Nevada's evolution is. Visitors only have to consider that Ice Age glaciers retreated a mere 10,000 years ago, not even enough time for soil to develop in most places. This is a remarkably young range, still jagged and sharp, still rising, still shaking!

The Yosemite Association (www.yosemite.org) is a nonprofit support group that publishes books and teaches a wide variety of fascinating classes about the Sierra Nevada.

WILDLIFE

Wildlife ranges from lumbering bears and soaring birds to scampering lizards and fleeting butterflies, all scattered across a vast and wild region. In only a few places do animals congregate in large or conspicuous numbers. If you remain patient and alert, these virtues might indeed be rewarded with lifelong memories, but remember not to feed or disturb animals at any time.

Large Mammals
MULE DEER

The most common large mammals in the Sierra Nevada, mule deer dwell in all forest habitats below the timberline. In parks, they have become remarkably unconcerned about human observers and tend to frequent meadows from late afternoon until sunset. White-spotted fawns first appear in mid- to late July, while tannish adults with big floppy ears become numerous in early winter, when deep snows push them out of the high country and they congregate below 5500ft. At all times, deer favor leaves and young twigs as a source of food, with Ceanothus shrubs being a perennial favorite. In late fall, deer feed heavily on acorns.

ENVIRONMENT

BLACK BEARS

Arguably the animal people would most like to see (or most like to avoid) is the black bear. Weighing in at around 350lb (or in exceptional cases almost double that), bears can be formidable animals, especially since they can act fearless around people. Nothing compares with the anxiety you'll feel when encountering a bear on a remote trail or in your campsite at night, but you can take comfort from the fact that bears generally shy away from human contact. Whether climbing trees, poking under logs and rocks or swimming in water, bears are basically big noses in search of food – and they'll eat almost anything. Bears often spend a considerable amount of time grazing like cows on meadow plants. Later in the summer, they switch over to berries and acorns, with insects (including yellowjackets) making up about 10% of their diet.

For tips on how to avoid confrontations with bears, see p269.

'Whether climbing trees or swimming in water, bears are basically big noses in search of food'

BIG CATS

Lucky and rare is the visitor who glimpses a mountain lion bounding off into the woods. Reaching up to 9ft from nose to tail tip and weighing as much as 190lb, this solitary and highly elusive creature makes a formidable predator; in the Sierra, mountain lions roam all forested habitats below the timberline in search of mule deer. Humans are rarely more than a curiosity or nuisance to be avoided, although a few attacks have occurred in regions where encroachment by humans has pushed lions to their limits (mainly around rapidly growing suburban areas).

Hikers are more likely to see the handsome bobcat, which looks like a scaled-up version of the domestic tabby, with a brown-spotted, yellowish-tan coat and a cropped tail.

COYOTES & FOXES

Wild members of the dog family include the ubiquitous coyote and its much smaller cousin, the gray fox. Both share the same grayish-brown coat and both have adapted to human habitats, becoming increasingly comfortable around roads, houses and (of course) food left unguarded. You stand a good chance of seeing a coyote during the daytime, especially around meadows, where they hunt for rodents. Foxes mainly come out at night; you might spy one crossing trails or roads.

Small Mammals

SQUIRRELS

The golden-mantled ground squirrel is often mistaken for a chubby chipmunk, though it differs in numerous physical and behavioral ways. For one thing, ground squirrels have no stripes on their heads and shoulders (chipmunks are striped all the way to the tip of their noses). For another, ground squirrels spend the winter hibernating – so starting in late summer they become extremely focused on gaining weight. These bulging beggars will badger you relentlessly for food. However tempting, it is strictly forbidden to feed animals in national parks and strongly discouraged elsewhere.

A large cousin of the chipmunk, the bold western gray squirrel never hesitates to stamp its feet angrily on branches and scold human intruders. These pale gray rodents, with a long, fluffy tail trailing behind, tend to live in black oak forests at low to mid-elevations on the west slope. Above the zone of black oak, the smaller Douglas squirrel, or chickaree, recognized by its slender tail and rusty tone, makes its home in dark conifer forests up to the timberline.

MARMOTS

Among the largest rodents in the region, the yellow-bellied marmot inhabits rock outcrops and boulder fields above 7500ft. Sprawled lazily on sun-warmed rocks, marmots scarcely bear notice until closely approached, when they jolt upright and send out shrieks of alarm to the entire marmot neighborhood. Marmots have a great appetite – they spend four to five months putting on weight (an incredible 50% of their body weight is fat) before descending into a long, deep hibernation until the following spring.

PIKAS

If you come across a pika you're likely to hear its odd little 'bleating' call coming from jumbles of rocks and boulders. A careful search will reveal the hamsterlike vocalist peering from under a rock with small beady eyes. Pikas typically live on talus slopes above 7700ft, especially in the realm of mountain hemlock, whitebark pine and heather plants. If you're hiking up that high, you're bound to make the acquaintance of these unforgettable characters.

Birds

Whether you enjoy the aerial acrobatics of swifts and falcons over Yosemite Valley waterfalls, the flash of brilliant warblers in oak woodlands, or the bright inviting lives of more than 300 other bird species found in the region, it goes without question that birds are one of the Sierra Nevada's wildlife highlights.

The highest single-tier waterfall in North America is not Yosemite Falls – it's Ribbon Fall, which plummets 1612ft from a precipice west of El Capitan. With three distinct falls, Yosemite Falls gets disqualified.

SMALL BIRDS

No other bird commands attention quite like the Steller's jay, found in virtually every forested habitat but most abundant around campgrounds, trailheads and other human destinations. Flashing a shimmering cloak of blue feathers and an equally jaunty attitude, these noisy birds wander fearlessly among picnic tables and parked cars in pursuit of overlooked crumbs.

Another conspicuous bird, the small mountain chickadee, with its distinctive black cap, is a perennial favorite with children because its merry song sounds like 'cheese-bur-ger.' You'll hear this song often in all forested areas above 4000ft.

In the highest mountain forests, campers and hikers can expect greetings from the raucous and inquisitive Clark's nutcracker, a hardy resident of subalpine forests recognized by its black wings and white tail. A flock of nutcrackers will survive the winter by gathering and storing up to four million pine nuts each fall, burying the nuts in thousands of small caches that they memorize and dig up later for food.

John Muir greatly favored the American dipper (formerly known as a water ouzel) above all other birds for its ceaseless energy and good cheer even in the depths of winter. This 'singularly joyous and lovable little fellow' rarely leaves the cascading torrents of cold, clear mountain streams, where it dives to capture underwater insects and larvae.

BIRDS OF PREY

While 11 species of owls live in the Yosemite region, no other owl evokes the mystery of the nocturnal realm quite like that rare phantom, the great gray owl. Easily the most famous and sought-after bird in Yosemite, this distinctive owl stands 2.5ft tall. A small population (about 50 individuals) of these birds survive in the park. These majestic owls have been spotted at Ackerson Meadow and Crane Flat, where they hunt around large meadows in the late afternoon.

You'll be fortunate if you see the peregrine falcon, a species that has climbed back from the brink of extinction and now is present in healthy numbers. This streamlined, fierce hunter with long, pointed wings and a black 'moustache' mark on its cheek sometimes hangs out around remote cliffs.

Amphibians & Reptiles
FROGS & TOADS
The Yosemite region is home to several unique amphibians, including its namesake Yosemite toad. This endemic, high-elevation toad used to abound in an area spanning 6000ft to 12,000ft, but in recent years it has mysteriously disappeared from many of its former haunts. At lower elevations, its close relative, the western toad, is still quite common and often observed moving along trails or through campgrounds at night. To identify a toad, look for a slow, plodding walk and dry, warty skin, which easily distinguishes them from smooth-skinned, quickly hopping frogs.

Another amphibian of the High Sierra is the scarce mountain yellow-legged frog, whose numbers have declined sharply in alpine lakes stocked with trout. This strong jumping and diving frog resides on lake margins. The abundant Pacific treefrog, by contrast, is a weak hopper that usually floats languidly on the water surface. Extremely widespread and diverse in their habitat preferences, treefrogs have the familiar 'ri-bet' call that nearly everyone associates with singing frogs (thanks to Hollywood movies that use this frog in their soundtracks).

SALAMANDERS
Oddest among amphibians is the Mt Lyell salamander, first discovered in Yosemite in 1915 when accidentally captured in a mousetrap. A member of the web-toed salamander family, this granite-colored salamander resides on granite domes and talus slopes from 4000ft to 12,000ft, where it uses its toes and strong tail to climb sheer cliffs and boulders in search of food.

LIZARDS
The most abundant and widespread reptile is the western fence lizard, a 5in- to 6in-long creature you're likely to see perched on rocks and logs or scampering across the forest floor. During the breeding season, dark-gray males bob energetically while conspicuously displaying their shiny blue throats and bellies.

Found in forest floor debris, southern alligator lizards wiggle off noisily like clumsy snakes when disturbed. These 8in- to 10in-long yellow-tan lizards reside from the lower foothills up into the mixed conifer zone.

SNAKES
Among the region's 10 or so snake species, garter snakes live in the widest diversity of habitats and are the snakes you're most likely to see. Two kinds of garter snake sport mainly black skin, with yellow or orange stripes running the length of their bodies. A third species, restricted to low to mid-elevation rivers, features a black checkerboard pattern on an olive-gray body.

No other snake elicits as much fear and curiosity as the western rattlesnake. Even if they're not rattling, you can quickly recognize rattlers by their bluntly triangular heads perched on remarkably slender necks. Rocky or brushy areas below 8000ft are the preferred haunts of this venomous though generally docile snake.

Could this be the ultimate field guide? You'll be amazed by the dazzling coverage found in *The Laws Field Guide to the Sierra Nevada*, by John Muir Laws.

Fish

The most widely distributed fish in the Western Sierra is the rainbow trout. Formerly limited to the lower reaches of streams below insurmountable barriers (such as waterfalls), rainbow trout have been introduced into countless alpine and eastern creeks and lakes for sportfishing. In addition, three spectacular subspecies collectively called 'golden trout' are found in the Kern River drainage of Sequoia & Kings Canyon National Park.

Further complicating the natural order of things, four nonnative trout (brook trout, lake trout, brown trout and kokanee) have been successfully introduced throughout the Sierra Nevada. Introduced fish have had a devastating impact on aquatic ecosystems, especially in formerly fishless alpine areas, where fragile nutrient cycles and invertebrate populations have changed dramatically as a result.

Insects

Most visitors won't notice the amazing variety of insects in the Sierra Nevada, except for a handful of conspicuous butterflies and other charismatic insects. Foremost among the large, showy butterflies are the six or so swallowtails. The Western tiger swallowtail, yellow in color with bold black bars and beautiful blue and orange patches near its 'tail,' follows stream banks from the lower foothills to subalpine forest. Restricted to the foothill zone, the stunning, iridescent-blue pipevine swallowtail flits in large numbers along foothill canyons and slopes almost year-round.

The moth known as the lodgepole needle miner appears every two years in late July or August. Swirling around lodgepole pine forests, these moths lay eggs that hatch into caterpillars that bore into the tips of pine needles. With a two-year life cycle, and millions of caterpillars occurring during a single outbreak, this species might kill 90% of the needles in an infected area and cause entire hillsides to turn orange with dying trees. While this event seems like something of a tragedy, the caterpillars serve as a critical winter food supply for small songbirds and the dying trees are ecologically important.

Plants

The Sierra Nevada boasts one of the richest selections of plants found anywhere in North America. Encompassing less than 1% of the state's land area, Yosemite National Park alone is home to 23% of the state's plant species. Richest of all is the Dana Plateau, which towers over Tioga Pass, where one square mile hosts 50% of all the alpine plant species in the entire range. It's possible to find flowering plants from late March until the end of August, and taking time out to smell the flowers will definitely enrich your park experience.

TREES

While flowers rise and fade with ephemeral beauty, trees hold their majesty for centuries and, thus, make an ideal study for the beginning nature enthusiast. Given a few simple tips, you can identify many of the region's prominent species and appreciate the full sweep of trees cloaking the landscape.

Pines are conifers whose needles appear in tight clusters, with two, three or five needles per cluster. Named for its straight, slender trunk, the abundant lodgepole pine has two-needled clusters, and globular cones that are less than 2in long. This is the most common tree around mountain meadows because the species has adapted to survive in waterlogged soils or in basins where cold air sits at night (so-called frost pockets).

'Foremost among the large, showy butterflies are the six or so swallowtails'

The ponderosa pine, with some examples of the Jeffrey pine mixed in, covers vast tracts of low to mid-elevation slopes. Three-needled clusters characterize both trees. Virtually identical in appearance, the two species do have distinct cones; on ponderosa cones the spines curve outward, and on Jeffrey pines they curve inward. If you're unsure of the identification, simply hold a cone in your hand and remember the adage: 'Gentle Jeffrey, prickly ponderosa.'

The wide variety of deciduous trees in the region includes the quaking aspen, with its smooth, white bark and circular leaves. Every brief gust sets these leaves quivering on their flattened stems, an adaptation for shaking off sudden snowfalls that would otherwise damage fragile leaves. Aspens consist of genetically identical trunks arising from a single root system that may grow to be more than a hundred acres in size. By sprouting repeatedly from this root system, aspens have what has been called 'theoretical immortality,' and some aspens are thought to be over a million years old.

Magnificent black oaks up to 80ft high and 4.5ft in diameter grow between 2000ft and 6000ft, where their immense crops of acorns serve as the main food source for many animals, including mice, pigeons, bears and deer. Large, deeply indented leaves with spine-tipped lobes distinguish black oaks from other species.

SHRUBS

At higher elevations, huckleberry oak and greenleaf manzanita form a dense, nearly impenetrable habitat known as montane chaparral that carpets the high country around granite boulders and outcrops. Here bears, deer, rabbits and many other animals find food and shelter not provided in nearby forests.

At lower elevations, montane chaparral gives way to foothill chaparral, which is characterized by whiteleaf manzanita and a number of ecologically important Ceanothus shrubs. The two manzanitas feature the same smooth,

GIANTS' REALM

The giant sequoia is the Sierra Nevada's most famous tree and also the source of much legend and ballyhoo. Even information as basic as the trees' maximum height and width remains uncertain because loggers and claim-seekers who cut down many of the original giants found it beneficial to exaggerate record trees. The General Sherman tree of Sequoia National Park, 275ft tall and more than 100ft in circumference, is recognized as the largest known living specimen. Sequoias cluster in fairly discrete groves on the western slopes of the Sierra Nevada. You can recognize them by their spongy, cinnamon-red bark and juniperlike needles (reduced to small overlapping scales lying along the stem). Despite claims that these are the world's oldest trees, it's now thought that the longest they can live is 3300 years, far short of the age reached by bristlecone pines.

Although giant sequoias grow only on the west slope of the Sierra Nevada today, this was not always the case. Between five and 25 million years ago, their ancestors covered a vast area between the Sierra Nevada and the Rocky Mountains. Migrating westward, possibly through low mountain passes, these trees got a foothold on the west slope of the Sierra Nevada just as the range began to achieve its current height. The formation of the Sierra Nevada isolated those sequoias on the west slope while at the same time creating a rain shadow that killed off the main population to the east. Giant sequoias survive today in 67 scattered patches or groves.

In Yosemite National Park the Tuolumne Grove and Merced Grove along Hwy 120 and the Mariposa Grove along Hwy 41 are relatively small groves, while the 20-plus groves in Sequoia & Kings Canyon National Parks are generally more extensive because the soils are deeper and better developed in areas that weren't covered by glaciers. There are also large groves in Calaveras Big Trees State Park (p192), north of Yosemite.

reddish bark and small, red, applelike berries (manzanita is Spanish for 'little apple'), but they differ in the color of their leaves. During late summer, the scat of animals like black bears, coyotes and foxes is chock-full of partly digested manzanita berries.

Ceanothus is a broad category of eight or more shrubs that provide a primary food source for mule deer and other animals. Deer favor the succulent young twigs while birds and rodents feast on the plants' seeds. Thriving between 1500ft and 6000ft, the tall Ceanothus known as deer brush puts out large displays of creamy white flowers. You can also recognize it by its leaves, which have three veins arising from the base.

No other shrub is as worthy of note as the maligned poison oak, which triggers an inflammatory skin reaction in many people who touch any part of the plant. If you'll be exploring the western slopes below 4500ft, learn how to identify – and avoid – this common trailside plant. The shrub is distinguished by its shiny, oaklike leaves that occur in groups of three. These leaves often take on various red and orange hues. Clusters of white berries appear by late summer and make a good meal for birds and rodents throughout the winter.

WILDFLOWERS
At low elevations in early spring, when wildflowers carpet low-elevation hillsides, you can't miss the brilliant orange of the California poppy, with its four large, floppy petals and finely indented leaves. At night and on cloudy days, poppy petals fold up and become inconspicuous.

At least 13 species of Indian paintbrush of varying colors and shapes can be found in the region. Most are red or orange in color and seem somewhat hairy. Surprisingly, the flowers themselves are hidden and accessible only to hummingbirds (the plants' pollinators), while a set of specialized colored leaves take on the appearance of petals. Paintbrushes are semiparasitic, often tapping into the roots of their neighbors to draw nourishment.

Mountaineers climb into a rarified realm rich in unique flowers, and if you need a single target flower to hunt for, one that's rare and mysterious like a distant peak, you couldn't make a better choice than the Sierra primrose. Confined to a handful of high subalpine slopes and peaks, this brilliant magenta beauty is a real find for the lucky hiker. Arising from clumps of toothed, succulent leaves, primroses sometimes grow in large patches sprawling across rocky slopes.

Highest and showiest of all is the aptly named sky pilot. Found only on summits over 11,000ft, this plant erupts into flagrant displays of blue flowers arranged in dense, ball-like clusters. After a long and grueling ascent, hikers to the highest peaks will better understand the name 'sky pilot,' a slang term for a person (eg missionary) said to lead others to heaven.

ENVIRONMENTAL ISSUES
The Gold Rush
With the discovery of gold in 1848, the natural world of the Sierra Nevada was forever altered by a rush of new settlers. Within a year, the number of ships entering San Francisco Bay jumped from four to 700 per year, and an estimated 150,000 to 175,000 people poured into the Sierra Nevada over the following decade. The stampede to find gold and profit at any cost had a devastating impact on both the Native Americans of the region and the landscape. In the gold-bearing region north of Yosemite, rivers were diverted, rocks moved and entire hillsides washed away to reveal gold deposits. More than 1.5 billion tons of debris flowed downstream, with harsh consequences for aquatic ecosystems and watershed health.

'During late summer, the scat of animals like black bears, coyotes and foxes is chock-full of partly digested manzanita berries'

ENVIRONMENT

Hoofed Locusts to Chainsaws

Although the Yosemite, Sequoia and Kings Canyon regions escaped largely unscathed, they were hit hard by a subsequent stampede that particularly appalled John Muir. This time, scores of sheep wreaked havoc – every year, ranchers drove six million sheep upslope to lush mountain meadows. In this profit-driven free-for-all, grazing rights went to whoever could get the most sheep to a meadow first. And the result? Sheep turned meadows into choking dustbowls by chowing down on fragile plants before they could flower and produce seeds. For a period in the late 1800s, the greatest danger to a 'tourist' traveling in the Sierra Nevada was that his pack animals might starve to death because not a single blade of grass could be found. Even now, over a hundred years later, the pattern of vegetation in the high mountains largely reflects this grazing history, with many hillsides still dry and barren or choked with species the 'hoofed locusts' didn't like. Fortunately, the mountain environment is so extreme that few weed species took hold. However, the opposite is true of foothill slopes, where weed species introduced by the influx of sheep and humans now utterly dominate and choke out native plants.

John Muir's concern over destructive logging practices, especially those that felled his beloved giant sequoias, played an important part in the establishment of Yosemite National Park, but Muir didn't live long enough to see the worst of what could happen. Industrial-scale logging took off after WWII, when gasoline-powered chainsaws, logging trucks and heavy equipment were systematically brought into the hills with an intent to take everything that was profitable. Decades later, the debate over logging practices and their consequences remains far from resolved, though the scale of logging has been reduced in recent years. By now there's little disagreement that logging activities have been responsible for many forest fires or the conditions that lead to forest fires, that heavy equipment compacts soils and causes lasting damage, and that logging roads create long-term harm to watersheds – the question now is what level of destruction society is willing to tolerate – for the sake of affordable wood products.

Started by John Muir, the Sierra Club (www.sierra club.org) has a reputation as North America's oldest, largest and most effective environmental organization.

Water

Without doubt, the greatest benefit the Sierra Nevada provides to the state of California is an abundant supply of fresh, clean water, and ironically the greatest harm to the Sierra Nevada has come from managing and collecting this precious water. Some have said that the building of Hetch Hetchy Dam in Yosemite broke John Muir's heart just before he died, and since then the damming of the Sierra's waters has only increased in pace and scale. In the last century, a virtual curtain of dams has been drawn across the face of the Sierra Nevada, severely altering aquatic habitats and eliminating spawning habitat for fish such as salmon, the population of which previously numbered more than a million.

Now near extinction in the Sierra Nevada, salmon number only in the dozens or low hundreds during their spawning runs. Out of 40 species of fish native to the Sierra Nevada, only a few still boast healthy populations, while 22 have landed on the threatened and endangered species list or are under review for a place on the list. Native fish populations and aquatic ecosystems have been further decimated by the introduction (mostly for fishing) of 30 nonnative fish species that have come to dominate countless aquatic habitats.

ENVIRONMENT

Air

Perhaps the most pernicious contemporary issue is air pollution, which can spoil the visual landscape all summer long. In 2004 Yosemite joined a growing list of national parks that violate federal smog standards, and the situation in Sequoia and Kings Canyon is much worse. Even though monitoring stations in Yosemite detect high ozone levels only one dozen to two dozen times a year, it is not uncommon for Valley views to be obscured by a bluish haze. On the other hand, Sequoia and Kings Canyon experience more than twice as many air-quality violations as any other national park. A great deal of this pollution comes from large cities outside the park. It is claimed that tighter regulations are making California's air cleaner, but it is hard to believe it when you see how much smog drifts up from the Central Valley into the parks.

Benign though they may seem, recreation and tourism have a detrimental effect on the landscape. Each visitor inevitably contributes to the overall impact, whether through car exhaust and traffic jams, through campfire smoke and wood use, or through heavy foot traffic on popular trails – and in parks where thousands of acres are dedicated to visitor use, the cumulative effect can be significant. From backpacking to tour-bus sightseeing, each type of tourist experience has its own consequences, but together they reshape a region that's being punished by too much love. Meanwhile, park personnel do all they can to preserve the experience of wilderness and nature for all visitors. Do your part to minimize your impact as much as possible – stay on trails, avoid trampling fragile areas, and respect other park regulations. For advice on minimizing your impact, see the boxed text, p40.

SUSTAINABILITY

Doing your part to help the parks during your visit may be as simple as leaving your car behind and riding the parks' shuttle-bus systems while visiting. Yosemite, in particular, has an impressive fleet of new hybrid buses that visit nearly every important stop in Yosemite Valley. If you are driving your own car or riding on a tour bus, turn the engine off or ask that the engine be turned off rather than letting the vehicle idle at stops. Consider how exciting it would be to bring or rent a bike and tour the park under your own power.

Increasingly, the parks and their concessionaires are promoting and facilitating recycling efforts at every stop (see some of the concessionaires' award-winning results at www.yosemitepark.com/Destination_Environment_GreenPath.aspx). Be conscious of recycling and do your part to recycle as much of your waste as possible. All of this stuff has to be hauled out of the parks so reduce and reuse as much as you can.

Finally, keep your eyes open and see what else you can do. Inquire whether concessionaires are using paper rather than plastic products, and let the parks know if you see wasteful practices that could be improved upon. And wherever possible, comment favorably upon ecologically sustainable practices already in place. Let Yosemite know that you like their hybrid buses, learn more about the remarkable, environmentally friendly Ground Source Heat Pump System that they installed in their new employee housing complex, or give the folks at the recycling center behind the Village Store a cheerful smile when you drop off your recyclables. See the inside front cover for a list of organizations that support the national parks.

Known as the little organization that triumphed over Los Angeles, the Mono Lake Committee (www .monolake.org) has matured into a highly successful environmental powerhouse.

History

History emanates from every corner of Yosemite and Sequoia & Kings Canyon National Parks. The names you'll encounter as you explore them – Tenaya, Whitney, Ahwahnee, Muir – tell the story of their peopled past, just as the rocks, plants and wildlife tell the story of their souls.

INDIGENOUS CULTURES

Europeans occupy but a blink in the 8000 years of human history in the Sierra Nevada. That's how long archeologists believe Native Americans had been present in the region before Spaniards, traveling up from the south, and Americans, traveling from the east, arrived in the territory.

Artifacts found in the Sierra Nevada suggest that the Native Americans' way of life here did not change dramatically over those years. Most Sierra tribes migrated with the seasons and, although they established warm-weather hunting sites in the High Sierra, they generally kept to the lower elevations. Heavy snow cover on the western slopes discouraged year-round habitation above 5000ft, but the oak forests of the lower western foothills, and the piñon-juniper forests on the eastern escarpments, were hospitable year-round.

First published in 1965, Francis P Farquhar's excellent *History of the Sierra Nevada* is still one of the region's definitive books on the subject and continues to be an extremely enjoyable read.

At the time American explorers were making their way across the Sierra Nevada, the regions on both sides of the mountain range were occupied by distinct linguistic groups. The western slopes of today's Yosemite region were home to the Sierra Miwok. To the south, two Shoshonean speaking tribes – the Western Mono (or Monache) and the Tubatulabal – inhabited the western slopes of what is today Sequoia & Kings Canyon National Parks. The Eastern Sierra was home to the Mono Lake Paiute to the north and the Owens Valley Paiute to the south.

While most of these groups traveled only when migrating or when hunting and gathering, trading parties regularly crossed the Sierra on foot to exchange goods. Obsidian and pine nuts from the Eastern Sierra were in great demand by western slope and coastal peoples, who traded them for acorns and seashells. Early Euro-American explorers making their way over the Sierra often found themselves on these ancient trade routes – as do hikers today. The Mono Pass trail (p134) was one of many trade routes over the Sierras.

TIMELINE

4000 BC	AD 1542	1804	1827	1833
The Ahwahneechee, a subtribe of the Sierra Miwok, settle in Yosemite Valley and become the first known permanent residents in the Valley	Representing Spain, Portuguese-born explorer Juan Rodríguez Cabrillo lands at San Diego and becomes the first European to explore California.	The province of California, then part of the Spanish colony of New Spain, is divided into Alta California and California, today known as Baja California	Hunter and trapper Jedediah Smith becomes the first European to cross the Sierra Nevada – doing so from west to east – after Mexican authorities order him out of Alta California	American fur trapper and trader Joseph Reddeford Walker and his party become the first Europeans to cross the Sierra Nevada from east to west

> **PEOPLE OF THE GAPING MOUTH**
>
> Thanks to its abundance of natural resources, Yosemite Valley was a permanent home to Native Americans for thousands of years. For centuries before Europeans arrived, the Sierra Miwok referred to Yosemite Valley as Ahwahnee (or Awahni), meaning 'valley of the gaping mouth.' The people who lived there were known as the Ahwahneechee. At some point before the arrival of Europeans to the area, a fatal illness decimated their numbers and the surviving Ahwahneechee dispersed and joined other tribes. Some time before 1851, Chief Tenaya, an Ahwahneechee chief who was born and raised with the Mono Lake Paiute, gathered other Ahwahneechee descendants and reestablished his people's home in Yosemite Valley.

ENTER THE EUROPEANS

The first nonindigenous people to explore California were the Spanish, who worked their way north from Mexico. Known as Alta California, the region was part of the Mexican Republic until it was ceded to the United States following the Mexican–American War (1846–48). Long before the war, Spanish explorers had described a great *sierra nevada* – a serrated, snow-covered mountain range – that they first saw from the San Joaquin valley in the 18th century. But not until the mid-19th century did anyone of European decent enter that range, and those who first did weren't from Spain.

Even before California became a US state in 1850, American trappers and explorers were making incursions into Alta California from the east. In 1827 a man named Jedediah Smith made his way to San Gabriel Mission (in present-day Los Angeles County), then wandered north to become the first European to cross the Sierra Nevada, doing so from west to east.

Six years later, a frontiersman named Joseph Reddeford Walker led the first party across the range from east to west, making his way out of the foothills just south of today's Sequoia National Park. During their trek, they stared down into Yosemite Valley from its northern rim, but were too exhausted to appreciate the extraordinary sight.

The next decade saw a remarkable shift in the patterns of westward expansion, as rumors of rich farmlands in Alta California (still held by Mexico) reached emigrants on the Oregon Trail. Several groups made the difficult trans-Sierra trek, which inevitably ended at the region's only nonindigenous settlement: Sutter's Fort, a nascent utopian community on the Sacramento River created by Swiss immigrant John Sutter.

As Sutter saw his community growing, he sent his foreman, James Marshall, up into the conifer forests to build a sawmill on the South Fork of the American River. Marshall went, but his labors were destined to have an outcome quite different from what he and Sutter had envisioned.

Written between 1860 and 1864, William Brewer's entertaining journal *Up and Down California* makes scaling a mountain sound like a Sunday picnic. The book tops any good Sierra reading list.

1848	1851	1853	1855	1858
Mexico cedes California to the US under the Treaty of Guadalupe Hidalgo. Gold is discovered at Sutter's Mill, starting the great California gold rush	Members of the Mariposa Battalion, led by James Savage in pursuit of Native Americans, become the first white men to enter Yosemite Valley	Chief Tenaya, the last chief of the Ahwahneechee, is killed under still-mysterious circumstances, and the last of his people disperse from Yosemite Valley	In Yosemite's first summer as a 'tourist destination,' 42 people visit the Valley; one of them is Galen Clark, who later became its first (nonindigenous) caretaker	Homesteader Hale Tharp becomes the first white man to enter the grove of giant sequoias that would later be named the Giant Forest in Sequoia National Park

THE RUSH IS ON

In February 1848, during construction of the sawmill, Marshall found flecks of gold in the water. News of Marshall's discovery immediately spread around the world, setting off a stunning reconfiguration of the Sierra Nevada's physical and demographic landscapes. Men (and a few women) eventually made their way to the Sierra mines from northern Europe and the eastern US, but in the early gold-rush years, many of the miners were Chinese, South American and Mexican. In a bitterly ironic coincidence, the Treaty of Guadalupe Hidalgo was signed in February 1848, ending the Mexican War and ceding the entire Southwest, including Alta California, to the US. The Spanish-speaking *Californios*, some of whom could trace their lineage to the conquistadors, suddenly became foreigners in US territory. Along with the Chinese and South Americans, they were systematically divested of their rights to a share of the gold.

The Native Americans of the Sierra faced an even grimmer fate. The genocide that began with diseases (introduced in the earlier Spanish missionary period) progressed to enslavement and outright slaughter under the Americans. Native Californians were not prone to war, but eventually self-defense prompted them to rise up against the gold rush incursion. As their raids upon settlers increased, the state sanctioned the creation of militias to settle any problems the new arrivals had with the native inhabitants.

The gold rush never reached as far south as present-day Sequoia & Kings Canyon National Parks. Despite a flurry of claims that were filed in the optimistically named Mineral King area, the region failed to turn up anything of value. Those who ventured south from Gold Country did so to ranch or farm. It was the former that brought the region's first homesteader, Hale Tharp, to the area. In 1858 Tharp became the first white man to enter the Giant Forest, where he famously fashioned a cabin inside a fallen giant sequoia.

Robert Wilson's The Explorer King (2007) is a fascinating glimpse into the adventurers of Clarence King (1842–1901), the geologist, explorer and writer who traversed the Sierras and became famous for exposing the Great Diamond Hoax of 1872.

THE MARIPOSA BATTALION

It was in the gold-rush era of state-sanctioned militias that the prospector James D Savage began mining on the Merced River in an area the Spanish called Mariposa. After clashes with local tribes culminated in the burning of his trading post, Savage sought revenge by creating a militia called the Mariposa Battalion.

When Savage learned that the raiding Indians might belong to a hold-out group of Sierra Miwok from a valley further up the Merced, the militia hastened upriver to root them out. On March 27, 1851, after a

1863–64	1864	1865	1868	1873
During the Whitney Survey, California State geologist Josiah D Whitney and his team conduct scientific expeditions in Yosemite, Kings Canyon and the Mt Whitney region	President Lincoln signs the Yosemite Grant, establishing Yosemite Valley and Mariposa Grove as a state park, the first such park in the world	The last of the indigenous Monache leave Sequoia's Hospital Rock, an important milling site and an area that still is home to superb pictographs	Hired to watch over a flock of sheep and its wayward herder, naturalist John Muir makes his first visit to the Sierras and Yosemite Valley	After small amounts of silver are discovered, miners converge on Mineral King Valley in present-day Sequoia National Park

brief encounter with Ahwahneechee Chief Tenaya (who was returning to Yosemite), the Mariposa Battalion entered Yosemite Valley. Among the battalion was a young recruit named Lafayette Bunnell. Apparently the only one among the men who was moved by the scenery, Bunnell proceeded to name the features he saw. Bunnell gave the valley the name 'Yosemity,' a corruption of the Miwok word *Oo-hoo'-ma-te*, or *uzumate*, meaning 'grizzly bear.'

In continuation of their gruesome pursuit, the Mariposa Battalion made several forays into the Yosemite region that spring and moved Tenaya and most of his people from their Yosemite Valley home to a reservation. During one melee with a group of Miwok, the battalion killed Tenaya's son. The following winter, the chief and some of his people were finally allowed to return to Yosemite. But hostilities continued in the following years, and in circumstances that are still a matter of debate, Chief Tenaya was killed in Yosemite Valley, apparently by Mono Lake Paiute angered over the theft of some horses. Tenaya Lake bears his name.

THE SECRET IS OUT

Tales of cascading waterfalls and towering stone columns followed the Mariposa Battalion out of Yosemite and soon spread into the public awareness. In 1855 an entrepreneurial Englishman named James M Hutchings made the journey to Yosemite Valley to see if the rumors were true. The party's enthusiastic reports spurred three other groups to visit that summer, and the proto-park received a grand total of 42 visitors.

Among the summer of '55 visitors was the ailing, 42-year-old Galen Clark, who returned the following year to establish a homestead near the Mariposa Grove of giant sequoias to live out his final years. The environment, however, seemed to agree with him, and he lived on in the park until his death at the ripe old age of 95. From the start, Clark's camp served as a lodge and artists camp. Clark himself took on the role of Yosemite guardian, a title that became official when the park became public land in 1864; he continued on in his role as guardian until 1896.

As word got around, entrepreneurs and homesteaders began arriving to divvy up the real estate of Yosemite Valley, creating ramshackle residences and roads, cutting down forests and planting the meadows with gardens and orchards. They brought in livestock, and started running sheep into the high mountain meadows where the trampling hooves destroyed wildflowers and delicate grasses.

Carl Russell's *100 years in Yosemite* is widely considered the definitive book on Yosemite history. It's a bit drier than other history reads out there, but well worth the read for Yosemite history buffs.

1875	1879	1878	1889	1890
John Muir visits a grove of giant sequoias inside present-day Sequoia National Park and calls it 'the Giant Forest'; the name sticks	Despite consistently unproductive mining claims in Mineral King Valley, Mineral King Rd is built, creating the first wagon access to the area	San Franciscan Aaron Harris opens Harris Campground, Yosemite's first public campground. The site was near where the Ahwahnee Hotel sits today	During a camping trip in Tuolumne Meadows, John Muir and publisher Robert Underwood Johnson devise a plan to preserve the watersheds of the Tuolumne and Merced Rivers	In September, President Harrison authorizes the creation of Sequoia National Park; two months later Congress passes the *Yosemite Act*, establishing Yosemite National Park

HISTORY

THE ROAD TO PROTECTION

As if by divine intervention, the Reverend Thomas Starr King, a Unitarian minister, orator and respected nature writer, arrived to help rescue Yosemite from runaway commercialism. After his visit in 1860, King wrote a series of widely read letters to the *Boston Evening Transcript* describing his trip.

Shortly after the publication of King's articles, an exhibition opened in New York featuring photographs of Yosemite by photographer Carleton E Watkins. The exhibition was a critical success, and Watkins' work caught the attention of California Senator John Conness.

Meanwhile, Frederick Law Olmsted, the landscape architect who designed New York's Central Park, brought his ideals to bear on Yosemite. He believed that government should play a role in preserving natural spaces that nourished the human spirit. Olmsted met with San Francisco businessman Israel Ward Raymond, who had become concerned about the fate of Yosemite's giant sequoias. In February 1864 Raymond wrote a letter to Senator Conness, proposing a bill that would grant Yosemite Valley and the Mariposa Grove to the State of California. Conness presented the bill to Congress, and on June 30, 1864, in the midst of the Civil War, President Abraham Lincoln signed the Yosemite Grant into law. This marked the first time that government had mandated the preservation and protection of a natural area for public use. Yosemite became the first state park in the world, and the foundation of what is now the national park system.

WHITNEY & MUIR

As Yosemite neared park-hood and the gold rush waned, interest in California's natural resources and landscapes grew. In 1860 the newly appointed California State geologist, Josiah D Whitney, assembled a crew of scientists, surveyors and cartographers to map out those resources. Officially deemed the California State Geological Survey, the Whitney Survey toured Yosemite in the summer of 1863, and the Kings Canyon and Mt Whitney regions the following year. During their expeditions, the team surveyed and named lakes, passes and peaks throughout the region. Mt Dana, Mt Hoffman and Mt Lyell in Yosemite, and Mt Whitney, Mt Tyndall and Mt Brewer in Sequoia & Kings Canyon, are just a few examples.

As the survey cobbled together its theories on Yosemite's formation (none of which had anything to do with glaciers) a naturalist and 'amateur' geologist named John Muir, who first visited the Valley in 1869, began to put forth his own ideas. Muir attributed the Valley's formation to glaciers, a theory Whitney himself vehemently shot down, but that would later prove correct. Muir, of course, would soon become the park's most adamant and successful defender (see p65).

The Sierra Club's online John Muir Exhibit (www.sierraclub.org /john_muir_exhibit) is a storehouse of everything Muir, featuring the author's complete books, as well as photos, essays and historical pieces.

1892	1898	1899	1900	1903
The Sierra Club is founded with 182 charter members, and John Muir is elected its first president; its first task is to defeat proposed reductions in Yosemite's boundaries	Ranchers John Broder and Ralph Hopping start a packing service to bring tourists to Sequoia National Park's Giant Forest, where they established the park's first lodging	David and Jennie Curry establish Camp Curry, offering food and board in canvas tents for $2 – half of the Valley's going hotel rate	The first automobile sputters into Yosemite Valley; a ban on cars inside the park is immediately established	San Francisco is denied after applying for water rights in Hetch Hetchy Valley. The US Army finishes the Colony Mill Rd into the Giant Forest

THE NEW NATIONAL PARKS
Yosemite National Park

In 1889 John Muir took Robert Underwood Johnson, the publisher of *Century* magazine, on a camping trip to Tuolumne Meadows (see p115), and the two hammered out a plan to save the larger watersheds of the Tuolumne and Merced Rivers from the 'hoofed locusts' (as Muir famously deemed sheep) and commercial interests. The plan drew upon the precedent set by Yellowstone, which was established as the country's first national park in 1872. Muir agreed to write some articles promoting the concept, which were published in *Century* the following summer, while Johnson wielded his considerable influence in Washington.

On October 1, 1890, Congress passed the *Yosemite Act* of 1890, creating Yosemite National Park, which encompassed both watersheds, though Yosemite Valley and Mariposa Grove remained under state jurisdiction, as had been established in the earlier grant.

Johnson realized that the creation of the national park might not be enough to protect Yosemite from the large and vocal contingent that saw the whole idea of public land as an affront to the Western ethic of free enterprise. He encouraged Muir to organize an advocacy association, which became the Sierra Club (see p28), chartered in 1892 with Muir as its first president.

Sequoia National Park

Around the same time, the sequoia groves to the south of Yosemite were falling at an alarming rate beneath the saws of lumber companies, which were acquiring enormous tracts of old-growth forest through government loopholes. A visionary Visalia newspaper editor named George Stewart began pushing for the protection of the remaining groves. Stewart looked to Yosemite and Yellowstone, and, arguing that the former was fraught with problems under state protection, pushed for federal protection of a sequoia grove known as the Giant Forest. Shortly afterwards, John Muir, Robert Underwood Johnson and others joined the fight.

Finally, on September 25, 1890, President Benjamin Harrison signed a bill into law that protected the Giant Forest, thus creating Sequoia National Park, California's first national park (and the country's second). A week later, Harrison signed into law the bill that created Yosemite National Park *and* General Grant National Park, which encompassed Grant Grove and would later be incorporated into Kings Canyon National Park.

Thousands of pages of online books fill the digital Yosemite Online Library (www.yosemite.ca.us/library), including the complete texts of numerous authors, century-old newspaper articles and more. Despite the title, it's great for Sierra history in general.

HISTORY

1903	1904	1906	1908	1916
Led by Colonel Charles Young, a regiment of the 'Buffalo Soldiers,' the so-called all-black regiments of the US Army, arrive for duty in Sequoia National Park	Sequoia National Park receives its first automobile, which was driven into the park by a couple from Vallejo, California	The State of California cedes Yosemite Valley and Mariposa Grove to Yosemite National Park; the San Francisco Earthquake cripples the city's water supply	The Department of Interior grants the city of San Francisco water rights to Hetch Hetchy Valley after the city successfully petitions for the reopening of its application	Congress authorizes establishment of the National Park Service, and Stephen T Mather becomes its first director; Tioga Rd and the John Muir Trail open

ENTER THE ARMY

'The pack that walks like a man,' Norman Clyde carried likely the Sierras' most famous backpack, with of a skillet, fishing gear, books, axe, firearm, boots and cameras.

With the parks designated federal land in 1890, the Department of the Interior now had the responsibility of protecting the wilderness from its new owners – the public! During the army's tenure at Yosemite, highly skilled trackers blazed most of the current trails through the backcountry (while chasing cattlemen and sheepherders) and created maps with far more detail than those made by the Whitney Survey, 30 years earlier. They planted trout in the streams and lakes, educated visitors about trash disposal and forest fires, and stood up against poachers and elite hunting parties.

In 1906, after lobbying by John Muir and the Sierra Club, the State of California finally ceded Yosemite Valley and the Mariposa Grove to the national park, and the Army promptly moved its headquarters from Wawona to Yosemite Valley. There it faced the challenge of bringing the nearly 10,000 annual visitors in line with its conservation policies. But the army was not destined to stay. In 1916 Congress established the National Park Service, which relieved the Fourth Cavalry of its cherished Yosemite assignment.

THE LOVERS WERE FIGHTERS

Tourist hordes have sometimes ridden roughshod over the park, but throughout Yosemite's history certain groups of visitors have proved essential in the fight to preserve the park's resources, most notably the Sierra Club. Founder John Muir was the first in a long line of well-known members who advocated through the organization for all three national parks.

The journals and photographs of Sierra Club cofounder Joseph N LeConte's epic expeditions revealed some of the most forbidding terrain of the High Sierra to the outside world (also see p104). Charter member Theodore S Solomons kindled the idea of the John Muir Trail (p41), and nature photographer and mountaineer Norman Clyde was famous for his mountain rescues and for bagging over 100 first ascents in the Sierras.

THE BUFFALO SOLDIERS

When the parks were created in 1890, the US Army was called in to safeguard these new natural resources. In the summer of 1903, troops from the 9th Cavalry – one of four well-respected though segregated African-American regiments known as the 'Buffalo Soldiers' – were sent to patrol Sequoia and Yosemite. In Sequoia and what was then General Grant National Park, the troops had an impressively productive summer, building roads, creating a trail system and setting a high precedent as stewards of the land. The troops were commanded by Captain (later Colonel) Charles Young, who at the time was the only African-American captain in the Army; his post as Acting Superintendent made him the first black superintendent of a national park.

1918	1922	1923	1926	1927
Park construction employees AL Medley and CM Webster discover Crystal Cave in Sequoia National Park	Total annual visitation to Yosemite surpasses 100,000; General Grant National Park gets 50,456 visitors and Sequoia National park lags behind with 27,514	Construction of O'Shaughnessy Dam is completed, costing $100 million and 68 lives, and damming the Tuolumne River in Hetch Hetchy Valley	After four years of construction, the Generals Hwy finally opens in Sequoia National Park, linking Ash Mountain and the Giant Forest	Yosemite's luxurious Ahwahnee Hotel, which was initiated by park service director Stephen Mather, opens on the site of a former Miwok village

Francis P Farquhar, a contemporary of Clyde's and a longtime Sierra Club president, wrote the delightful and definitive *History of the Sierra Nevada* (1965) and his successor, activist David Brower, was the club's first advocate of low-impact wilderness use and a staunch opponent to the construction of more dams.

Artists also played a key political role in Yosemite's history by bringing the fragile spirit of the wilderness to the public's awareness. The works of Thomas Ayres, who drew the first illustration of Yosemite Valley in 1855, painter Albert Bierstadt and Yosemite's first photographer, Carleton Watkins, played a crucial role in the bid to establish Yosemite as a national park. Their legacy was continued by artists such as painters Thomas Hill and Chiura Obata, and photographers Ansel Adams and Galen Rowell.

THE CANVAS & CLAPBOARD DAYS

Hotels came and went in Yosemite Valley's early years. At one point near the end of the 19th century there were nine hotels in operation throughout the Valley. Hastily erected of wood and canvas to house the ever-increasing hoards of tourists, many of the early hotels met their demise when sparks escaped from stoves, or when lanterns got too close to curtains.

Some visitors found 'camping' to be a pleasant alternative – especially given the typically large and well-equipped tents that were common in the era. In 1899, when a night in the popular Sentinel Hotel cost $4, David and Jennie Curry established a camp with seven tents at the base of Glacier Point. At Camp Curry, for a mere $2 a day, campers were provided with a comfortable bed in a tent, bath and restroom facilities and meals. The camp became immensely popular as families discovered that camping, Curry-style, made for an affordable summer vacation. What's more, Camp Curry offered an evening program of music, stunts, educational talks and the nightly Firefall (see the boxed text, p106).

Tourism remained insignificant in Sequoia National Park until 1898, when two Tulare County ranchers set up a packing service to bring visitors to see the big trees of the Giant Forest, housing them in a tent hotel. In 1903 the Army finally finished the Colony Mill Road into the Giant Forest, which essentially opened up the grove to tourists for the first time.

THE AUTO COMETH

The first automobile sputtered into Yosemite Valley in the summer of 1900, but cars were quickly prohibited from the park. The ban was lifted in 1913, and three years later a serviceable dirt road opened through Tioga Pass. Annual visitation spiked to more than 30,000 that year, and by 1922 it had surpassed 100,000.

Ansel Adams' photographs aren't his only legacy in the Sierras. Adams organized, wrote the script for and performed in the first Bracebridge Dinner (p25) at the Ahwahnee Hotel.

1935	1940	1943	1954	1970
After years of work, the General's Hwy is extended to General Grant National Park (now Kings Canyon); it's immediately declared one of the nation's most scenic roads	Congress passes a law creating Kings Canyon National Park, which absorbs General Grant National Park into its much larger boundaries	To conserve funds during the war effort, Sequoia National Park and Kings Canyon National park are merged under a single administrative body	Annual visitation at Yosemite National Park surpasses one million. Kings Canyon National Park gets 551,541 visitors, and neighboring Sequoia National Park receives 484,563	On July 4, the Stoneman Meadow Riot rocks Yosemite Valley as mounted rangers forcibly remove people partying in Stoneman Meadow

In Sequoia National Park, the first automobile didn't arrive until 1904, and in 1926 the General's Hwy finally opened between Ash Mountain and the Giant Forest. It took another nine years, however, to push that road through to General Grant National Park, finally connecting the two parks that would become Sequoia & Kings Canyon. Although the road was one of the country's most scenic (and expensive), the park received a quarter of the number of the visitors Yosemite did.

GROWTH SPURTS & WAR

Although the automobile certainly contributed to increased visitation, it was the enthusiastic – and sometimes extreme – policies of the National Park Service's first director, Stephen T Mather, that really sent the numbers climbing. During his tenure between 1917 and 1929, Mather oversaw the development of the Wawona Golf Course, the Yosemite Museum, the Ahwahnee Hotel and the ice rink at Camp Curry, and he initiated nature walks and interpretive programs at all three parks.

In 1940, just before the US entered WWII, Congress passed a law creating Kings Canyon National Park, which absorbed General Grant National Park into its much larger boundaries. As the war effort gobbled up funds, Sequoia & Kings Canyon National Parks were merged into a single administrative body in 1943.

In Yosemite, the Ahwahnee Hotel became a naval hospital and the US Army set up camps at Wawona and Badger Pass. The California National Guard was stationed at Hetch Hetchy, and 90,000 troops trained in Yosemite Valley. Needless to say, public visitation dropped significantly.

THE POSTWAR YEARS

After the war, the American art of the summer vacation blossomed, and campers started rolling into the Valley in record numbers. Even the backcountry began to see crowds as the San Francisco Beat culture discovered backpacking. By the 1970s, Yosemite Valley in summer had become an unsavory place for the average tourist, as 'hippies and freaks' swarmed into the Valley, and theft, drug abuse and noise pollution rose. The tension between youth and park rangers came to a head on July 4, 1970, during the Stoneman Meadow Riot, when rangers on horseback forcefully removed partying youth from Stoneman Meadow. Revelers were beaten, rangers were pulled from their horses and, by morning, 135 people were arrested and 30 were hospitalized.

The 1970s were much quieter for Sequoia & Kings Canyon. The biggest event of the decade occurred in 1978, when Mineral King was added to Sequoia National Park.

Part history and part adventure writing, Clarence King's *Mountaineering in the Sierra Nevada* (1902) is a dramatic account of his exploits in the Sierras and a gripping read to boot.

1978	1980	1984	1996	1997
Mineral King Valley, a glacially formed canyon of vast natural beauty, is added to Sequoia National Park	As annual visitation in Yosemite reaches 2.5 million, the park creates its first General Management Plan to assess and confront overuse of the park	Unesco declares Yosemite National Park a World Heritage site; Congress passes the *California Wilderness Act*, giving most of Yosemite wilderness status	Annual visitation to Yosemite peaks at 4.2 million visitors	Massive flooding on the Merced River washes out sections of Hwy 140 and damages campgrounds, employee camps and more; Yosemite National Park closes for several months

THE PLAN

In Yosemite, spikes in visitation and the Stoneman Meadow Riot prompted the park service to introduce one-way roads and free shuttle service, as well as a quota system for backcountry use. Still, with visitor numbers hitting 2.5 million in 1980 and more than one million vehicles driving into the Valley annually, the National Park Service decided it was time for a plan.

In 1980 the park service drew up its first General Management Plan, calling for restrictions on private cars, increases in public transportation, changes to campgrounds within the Merced River plain, and relocation of many commercial services outside the park. Mired in political and public opposition, however, the plan foundered and underwent many changes over the years. Finally, in 1997, when a major flood in Yosemite Valley forced the plan into another state of revision, the park service drew up the Final Yosemite Valley Plan, which was officially adopted on December 29, 2000.

Since then, some projects put forth by the plan have been addressed, including the restoration of meadows and the riparian ecosystem along the Merced River, as well as major improvements to the impacted area around Lower Yosemite Fall. Other plans are still in the works, including rerouted roads, increased shuttle bus use and a reduction of parking spaces in Yosemite Valley. This last item, which is intended to reduce the number of cars in the Valley, has fueled the greatest uproar (many argue it will decrease the park's accessibility, especially for day-trippers) and continues to be one of Yosemite's most contentious issues.

THE PARKS TODAY

Although Yosemite's visitation numbers have fallen since its 4.2 million peak in 1996, the debate about capping visitor use continues to gobble up resources and, subsequently, bog down certain aspects of the Yosemite Valley Plan. But visitor numbers might just take care of themselves. In 2006, fewer visitors entered Yosemite than any year since 1990, and the park service projected numbers would continue to fall.

Of course, there's plenty of speculation on the reasons behind the decline: the 1997 flood; negative press about overcrowding; the murders of four women by Cary Stayner in 1999 (Stayner today sits on Death Row); the 2006 rockslide that closed Hwy 140 to buses; and high gas prices have all been singled out.

Visitation at Sequoia & Kings Canyon (and, for that matter, all national parks) has been falling steadily over the last decade, so Yosemite is hardly alone. Americans are taking shorter vacations and staying closer to home. It's all bad news for the park service purse strings, but hey, it's good for the rest of us!

Just exactly how much is planned in that Yosemite Valley Plan anyway? Find out on the National Park Service Website (www.nps.gov/archive/yose/planning/), which details all the current plans for the park.

1998	2000	2006	2006	2007
As part of an ongoing project to return the Giant Forest to a more natural state, the park service permanently closes Giant Forest Village	The final Yosemite Valley Plan is completed and adopted, proposing $441 million in work to Yosemite Valley with the objective of minimizing human impact	A major rockslide closes Hwy 140 west of the town of El Portal in May, temporarily closing access to the park via Arch Rock	In August, four cave researchers discover the Ursa Minor cave in Sequoia National Park, said to be one of the most significant cave discoveries in recent history	The Yosemite Valley Visitor Center opens the doors to the new $1.3 million exhibit hall, which hadn't been upgraded in 40 years

Yosemite National Park

Yosemite has a way with humans. Its beauty – which is utterly overwhelming – inspired writers and artists like John Muir and Ansel Adams to produce their finest work. It gave birth to the idea of setting aside land as a protected park. To the indigenous Miwok who inhabited Yosemite and Hetch Hetchy Valleys before Europeans arrived, it was a land of natural abundance, of forest and river spirits and of thousands of years of ancestral history. Today it's a very different place, and some visitors find themselves quickly embittered by the commercialism in Yosemite Valley and the sheer number of people in the park.

But don't let the numbers get you down – not only would that be ignoring the fact that most people visit in summertime and then stick to the Valley, but it would be missing the point of Yosemite entirely. Look instead to the core of people: the park rangers who have been here for years, the artists, the historians, the climbers, the mountaineers and the volunteers who are all actively engaged in protecting – and thoroughly enjoying – the park. Their inspiration is truly infectious. Then, should you remain skeptical in the least, look to Half Dome at sundown. Hike to Nevada Fall in springtime or wander through the Mariposa Grove of giant sequoias. Head up to Tuolumne Meadows and take in the view from the top of Lembert Dome, or hike up to Cathedral Lake. Wander into the backcountry for a few days. Hell, you could even join the families on the shores of the Merced River in the middle of summer – simply swimming in that cold emerald water beneath the backdrop of Yosemite Falls will soothe the mind of any sentient earthling.

HIGHLIGHTS

- Hiking to **Vernal and Nevada Falls** (p124) via the Mist and John Muir Trails
- Basking in the summer sun on the shore of Tuolumne's **Cathedral Lake** (p132)
- Standing beneath Hetch Hetchy's roaring **Wapama Falls** (p135) in spring
- Soaking up epic views while swimming in **Tenaya Lake** (p111)
- Heading out to scenic **Chilnualna Falls** (p126) in Wawona

---

FAST FACTS

▪ **Total Area** 1169 sq miles

▪ **Yosemite Valley elevation** 3955ft

▪ **Average high/low temperature in Yosemite Valley in July** 90/54°F (32/12°C)

When You Arrive

The park is open 24 hours, every day of the year. If you arrive at night and the gate is unattended, simply pay the entrance fee when you leave. Keep your receipt, as you must show it every time you leave or re-enter the park. For information on entry fees, senior passes and discounts for disabled travelers, see p23.

Upon entering the park, you'll receive an illustrated National Park Service (NPS) map and copies of the *Yosemite Guide* (a biannual newspaper with park news, sightseeing tips and useful background information) and the biweekly *Yosemite Today* (with current ranger programs, park activities, opening hours of visitor services, and a shuttle bus map and schedule). Save both – they'll come in handy.

Orientation

Though the park encompasses nearly 1200 sq miles of land (about the size of Rhode Island), more than 94% of it is designated wilderness and, therefore, inaccessible by car. Elevations range from below 3000ft at Hetch Hetchy to 13,114ft atop Mt Lyell, the park's tallest peak.

The most popular (and crowded) region is Yosemite Valley, a relatively small sliver of the park at the heart of Yosemite. Along with spectacular scenery, you'll find the largest concentration of visitor services, including lodges, campgrounds, stores and restaurants.

About 55 miles northeast of the Valley, near the east end of Tioga Rd, is Tuolumne Meadows (elevation 8600ft), the focal point of Yosemite's high country and summertime home to a small hub of visitor services.

Crane Flat sits at the junction of Tioga and Big Oak Flat Rds. You'll find limited visitor services here and to the north at the park's Big Oak Flat Entrance. Between Crane Flat and Tuolumne Meadows is a stretch we've labeled 'Along Tioga Rd,' which covers camping, hiking and other activities along this section of Hwy 120. North of Tioga Rd lies the park's vast northern wilderness, accessible only by serious backpackers. To the west, a short drive from the Big Oak Flat Entrance, is Hetch Hetchy Reservoir.

Perched 3200ft above Yosemite Valley, Glacier Point is the park's prime viewpoint, reachable during summer via a trail from the Valley or by car along Glacier Point Rd. Also on Glacier Point Rd is the Badger Pass Ski Area, which is open in winter only.

Thirty-six miles south of Yosemite Valley is Wawona, home to a historic hotel and other services for those visiting the giant sequoias of nearby Mariposa Grove. The southeastern corner of the park harbors another large wilderness area.

ENTRANCES

The park has four main gates: Big Oak Flat Entrance (Hwy 120) and Arch Rock Entrance (Hwy 140) from the west, Tioga Pass Entrance (Hwy 120) from the east, and South Entrance (Hwy 41) near Wawona. The only one open year-round is Arch Rock, though Big Oak Flat and Wawona are open when weather permits. Tioga Pass (9945ft) is the highest roadway across the Sierra, usually open between early June and mid-November, though the dates vary every year. The **Hetch Hetchy Entrance Station** (☎ 209-379-1922; ◷ 7am-9pm summer, 8am-5pm winter) is open only during daylight hours, and anyone not spending the night in the wilderness must be out by the time the entrance closes.

GATEWAY ROUTES

Hwy 140 runs from the west directly into Yosemite Valley and offers access to the park year-round. Hwy 120 also enters the park from the west, where it becomes Big Oak Flat Rd. The only road that crosses the park is Tioga Rd, running from Crane Flat to Tioga Pass. Hwy 41 enters from the south, passing Wawona and the turnoff for Glacier Point before meeting Hwy 140. Glacier Point Rd runs east from Hwy 41 to Glacier Point. For information on services along these roads, see the Around Yosemite chapter, p172.

Yosemite National Park

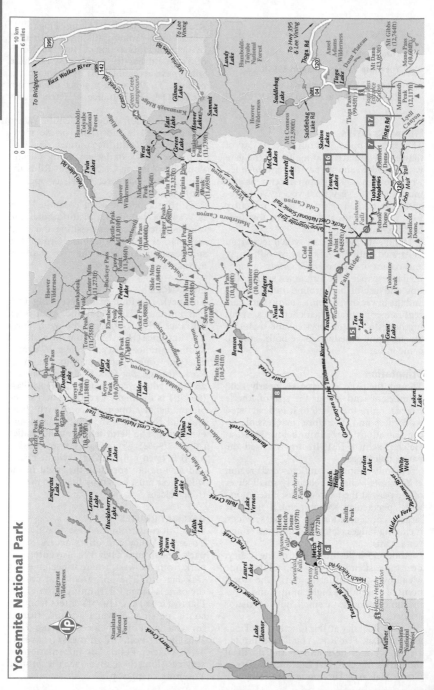

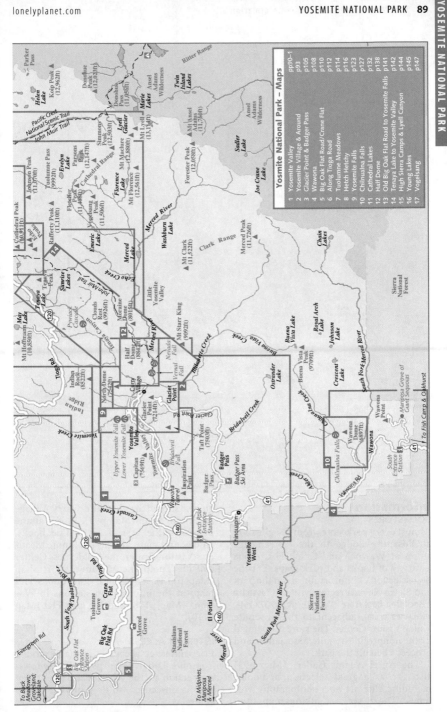

Yosemite National Park – Maps

Yosemite Valley

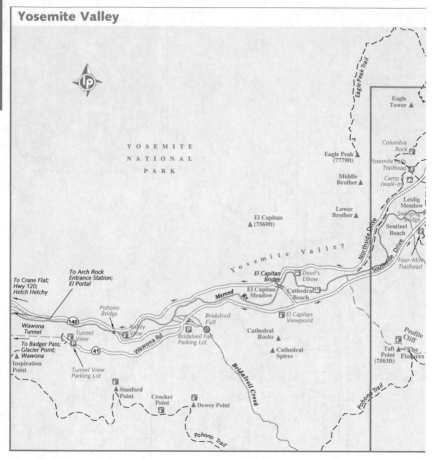

Information

BOOKSTORES

Almost every park store, from the gift shop at Yosemite Lodge to the convenience stores at Wawona and Crane Flat, offers a variety of books and park maps. For the best selection of information about the park and Sierra Nevada region, visit the **Yosemite Association Bookstore** (Map p93; ☎ 209-379-2648; www.yosemite.org), adjacent to the Yosemite Valley Visitor Center. The store is operated by the nonprofit Yosemite Association, and proceeds benefit the park.

The Ansel Adams Gallery (Map p93) also carries a great selection of books, including fine-art and photography volumes. Those seeking hiking maps and

guides should head to the Curry Village Mountain Shop (Map p93). In Tuolumne Meadows, the best places to find books, guides, and maps are the Tuolumne Meadows Visitor Center, the Wilderness Center and the Tuolumne Meadows Sport Shop (Map p114). You'll also find books and maps at the information stations in Wawona (Map p108) and Big Oak Flat (Map p110).

INTERNET ACCESS

Pricy internet access is available at the Yosemite Lodge (Map p93). The wireless connection in the Ahwahnee Hotel (Map p93) is unsecured, so drag in your laptop and relax.

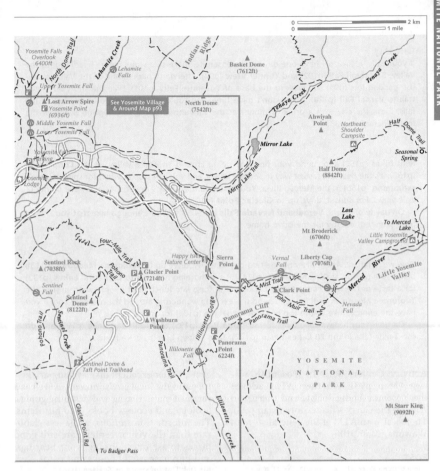

For free internet access, head to the **public library** (Map p93; ☎ 209-372-4552; ☉ 8:30-11:30am Mon, 10am-2pm Tue, 8:30am-12:30pm Wed, 4-7pm Thu) in Yosemite Valley, or the **Bassett Memorial Library** (Map p108; ☎ 209-375-6510; 7971 Chilnualna Falls Rd; ☉ noon-5pm Wed-Fri, 10am-3pm Sat) in Wawona. Sessions at both are limited to 30 minutes (unless no one is waiting), and they generally cut off use 15 minutes before closing.

INTERNET RESOURCES

Though it's hard to tell who's at the helm, the regularly updated **Yosemite Forum** (www .yosemite.ca.us/forum) features discussion boards on a wide range of subjects, from trip planning to rock climbing. The **Yosemite Blog**

(www.yosemiteblog.com) always makes for an interesting browse. For more useful websites (including park service sites), see p27.

MEDIA

For newspapers in Yosemite Valley, hit the coin-operated boxes outside Degnan's Deli (Map p93), in front of the stores at Curry Village (Map p93) and at Housekeeping Camp (Map p93). In Tuolumne Meadows (Map p114), they're sold in front of the store and at the Tuolumne Meadows Lodge.

MONEY

There are no banks in the park. There's a no-name ATM in the Village Store and a Bank of America ATM outside the Art

YOSEMITE NATIONAL PARK

YOSEMITE IN...

One Day
If you really, *really* only have one day to see Yosemite, make two stops before heading into the Valley: **Bridalveil Fall** (p102) and **Tunnel View** (p97). Afterward, park in one of the Valley's day-use parking lots (p95) and walk to the base of **Yosemite Falls** (p101). Hike the short but steep trail to **Vernal Fall** (p124); if you don't have time, you could stop at the footbridge below the falls. Close the day with a drink or dinner at the **Ahwahnee Bar** (p169). Option B: follow the mad itinerary on p33.

Two Days
Rent **bikes** (p150) and spend your first day riding around Yosemite Valley on the **Loop Trails** (p150). It's the best and fastest way to see the Valley, and you can stop anytime for some leisurely **swimming** (p156) in the Merced River. You'll pass all the Valley's major sites and have plenty of epic views. For sunset, drive up to **Glacier Point** (p105).

On day two, hike to **Vernal and Nevada Falls** (p124). It's a short enough hike that you should have plenty of energy for the drive home.

Four Days
Now we're talkin'. After following the two-day itinerary, drive up to **Tuolumne Meadows** (p113), being sure to stop at **Olmsted Point** (p111). In the morning head off to **Cathedral Lakes** (p132) for a taste of the high country. Get back in time for a late lunch (and people-watching) at the **Tuolumne Meadows Grill** (p170). Spend the evening wandering around the meadow and, if you have the energy, hike to the top of **Lembert Dome** (p131) for sunset.

On your fourth day, drive over scenic **Tioga Pass** (p195) to **Saddlebag Lake** (p197) and do the 5-mile hike in the **20 Lakes Basin** (p197). Take a deep breath. Drive home.

Activity Center, both in Yosemite Village (Map p93). Another ATM adorns the Yosemite Lodge lobby, and there's an ATM at the Curry Village Store (Map p93). There's also an ATM at the general store in Wawona (Map p108).

POST
Curry Village Post Office (Map p93; 🕙 11:30am-2:30pm Mon-Fri, closed approx mid-Sep–mid-Jun)
Tuolumne Meadows (Map p114; 🕙 9am-4pm Mon-Fri, to noon Sat, closed mid-Sep–mid-Jun) Inside the Tuolumne Meadows Store.
Wawona (Map p108; 🕙 9am-5pm Mon-Fri, to 1pm Sat) At Wawona Store.
Yosemite Lodge (Map p93; 🕙 11:30am-2:45pm Mon-Thu, to 4:30pm Fri) Inside the lodge.
Yosemite Village Post Office (Map p93; 🕙 8:30am-5pm Mon-Fri, 10am-noon Sat) To the right (east) of the Wilderness Center.

VISITOR CENTERS
Rangers staff the park visitor centers and smaller information stations, and can answer questions and suggest suitable hiking trails, activities and sights. The visitor centers offer excellent displays on park history and the local environment, as well as a range of maps, hiking and climbing guides, geology and ecology books, and gift items. The information *stations*, while less elaborate than the visitor centers, are still good places to ask questions, get your bearings, and purchase useful books and maps.
Big Oak Flat Information Station (Map p110; ☎ 209-379-1899; 🕙 8am-5pm Apr-Oct, to 6pm midsummer) Also see p109.
Tuolumne Meadows Visitor Center (Map p114; ☎ 209-372-0263; 🕙 9am-6pm Jul-Aug, to 5pm spring & fall) Also see p113.
Wawona Information Station (Map p108; ☎ 209-375-9531; 🕙 8:30am-5pm May-early Oct) Located inside the Hill's Studio building next to the Wawona Hotel. Also see p108.
Yosemite Valley Visitor Center (Map p93; ☎ 209-372-0299; 🕙 8am-6pm in summer, reduced hours off-season) The park's main visitor center; also see p97.

WILDERNESS CENTERS
Yosemite has two main wilderness centers: the **Yosemite Valley Wilderness Center** (Map p93; ☎ 209-372-0745; 🕙 7:30am-6pm summer, 9am-5pm

fall & spring, closed winter) and the **Tuolumne Meadows Wilderness Center** (Map p114; ☎ 209-372-0309; 7:30am-6pm midsummer, 8am-5pm late spring & early fall, closed Oct-May). At both, hikers can buy maps and guidebooks, check current weather and trail conditions, get helpful tips on planning and packing, and – perhaps most importantly – obtain wilderness permits. You can also rent the all-important bear-proof food canisters ($5; see p279). Permits and canisters can also be obtained at the **Big Oak Flat Wilderness Center** (Map p110; ☎ 209-379-1967), inside the Big Oak Flat Information Station, at the Wawona Information Station (Map p108), and at the Hetch Hetchy Entrance Station (Map p116).

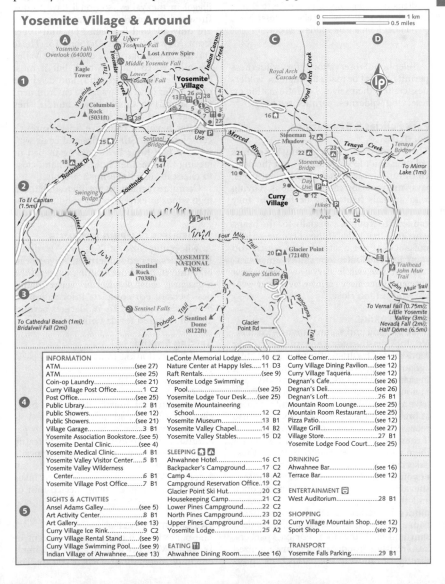

Yosemite Village & Around

0 ——— 1 km
0 ——— 0.5 miles

INFORMATION		LeConte Memorial Lodge.............10 C2	Coffee Corner.............................(see 12)
ATM..(see 27)		Nature Center at Happy Isles.....11 D3	Curry Village Dining Pavilion....(see 12)
ATM..(see 25)		Raft Rentals................................(see 9)	Curry Village Taqueria..............(see 12)
Coin-op Laundry.......................(see 21)		Yosemite Lodge Swimming	Degnan's Cafe............................(see 26)
Curry Village Post Office............1 C2		Pool......................................(see 25)	Degnan's Deli.............................(see 26)
Post Office................................(see 25)		Yosemite Lodge Tour Desk......(see 25)	Degnan's Loft.............................26 B1
Public Library...............................2 B1		Yosemite Mountaineering	Mountain Room Lounge..........(see 25)
Public Showers..........................(see 25)		School....................................12 C2	Mountain Room Restaurant....(see 25)
Public Showers..........................(see 21)		Yosemite Museum.......................13 B1	Pizza Patio.................................(see 12)
Village Garage..............................3 B1		Yosemite Valley Chapel...............14 B2	Village Grill................................(see 27)
Yosemite Association Bookstore..(see 5)		Yosemite Valley Stables...............15 D2	Village Store................................27 B1
Yosemite Dental Clinic...............(see 4)			Yosemite Lodge Food Court....(see 25)
Yosemite Medical Clinic...............4 B1		SLEEPING	
Yosemite Valley Visitor Center.....5 B1		Ahwahnee Hotel..........................16 C1	DRINKING
Yosemite Valley Wilderness		Backpacker's Campground..........17 C2	Ahwahnee Bar............................(see 16)
Center..6 B1		Camp 4..18 A2	Terrace Bar.................................(see 12)
Yosemite Village Post Office.........7 B1		Campground Reservation Office..19 C2	
		Glacier Point Ski Hut...................20 C3	ENTERTAINMENT
SIGHTS & ACTIVITIES		Housekeeping Camp....................21 C2	West Auditorium.........................28 B1
Ansel Adams Galley...................(see 5)		Lower Pines Campground............22 C2	
Art Activity Center........................8 B1		North Pines Campground............23 D2	SHOPPING
Art Gallery.................................(see 13)		Upper Pines Campground............24 D2	Curry Village Mountain Shop...(see 12)
Curry Village Ice Rink..................9 C2		Yosemite Lodge...........................25 A2	Sport Shop.................................(see 27)
Curry Village Rental Stand.........(see 9)			
Curry Village Swimming Pool.....(see 9)		EATING	TRANSPORT
Indian Village of Ahwahnee......(see 13)		Ahwahnee Dining Room...........(see 16)	Yosemite Falls Parking...............29 B1

YOSEMITE TELEPHONE NUMBERS

The area code for all telephone numbers within Yosemite National Park is ☎ 209. All numbers contain the prefix 379 (ie, ☎ 209-379-2648), so you only really have to remember the last four digits. Locals often give telephone numbers by their last four digits only. Finally, you only have to dial the last four digits when calling a Yosemite number from a park courtesy phone.

Telephone reservations for wilderness permits cannot be made through the wilderness centers themselves. For information on reserving wilderness permits, see p137.

Park Policies & Regulations

WILDLIFE

There's one main rule regarding Yosemite's wildlife: don't feed the bears…nor the deer, chipmunks, raccoons, skunks, squirrels, jays, marmots or mountain lions. Giving wild animals treats may be fun, but they learn to associate humans with food. That can lead to trouble, especially for the bears, who are often killed if they become serious nuisances – not a situation to which you want to contribute. Remember, small critters can bite, while deer (no matter how cute and tame they seem) may charge people who get too close.

FOOD STORAGE

Store all food and scented items – cosmetics, toothpaste, soda cans and any other food-related trash – in the bear-proof storage lockers provided at each campsite and in major parking lots. Never leave anything in your car, including canned goods. Bears have a powerful sense of smell and are adept at breaking into locked vehicles. They also recognize coolers and grocery bags, so even if these are empty and clean, at least cover them with a blanket. Failure to follow these rules can lead to a citation (or the trashing of your car). When cooking at your campsite, avoid leaving the locker hanging open and the food spread out. That's an open dinner invitation. Treat the locker like a fridge – pull out only what you need, then shut and latch the door. For backpackers, bear-resistant food canisters are required throughout most of the park's back country. For more on bears, including what to do if you encounter one, see p269.

CAMPFIRES

Everyone loves a campfire, but take note of a few rules. Fires in Yosemite campgrounds are allowed only within established fire rings or barbecue pits. Wood gathering is illegal in the Valley, so you'll have to buy firewood. To improve air quality, campfires are only allowed between 5pm and 10pm from May 1 through October 15. Those staying in campgrounds outside the Valley are allowed to gather wood, but it must be downed (on the ground) and dead. It's often easier (and always more environmentally sound) to simply buy a bundle; they average about $7 per box.

After having a campfire, make sure it's completely out. Stir the fire and coals with water a half-hour before going to bed or leaving the site, then hold your hand close to check for any lingering hot spots.

Campfire regulations are often stiffened in high winds or extremely dry conditions. For more on backcountry regulations, see p137.

WILDERNESS CAMPING & PERMITS

A whopping 94% of Yosemite National Park is designated wilderness. Anyone can hike into it, but those wishing to spend the night in it must obtain the proper wilderness permit. For complete information on how to do so, see p137. Wilderness permits are not required for day hikes.

Getting Around

For information on tours within the park, see p257.

BICYCLE

Twelve miles of mostly flat, paved bicycle trails run up and down Yosemite Valley, making biking a fantastic way to get around. If you've ever sat in Valley traffic on a summer day, you know the merits of strapping a couple of bikes to the car. Since the Valley is flat, single-speed bikes are great. For a good two-wheeled tour of the Valley, see p150.

CAR & MOTORCYCLE

The park speed limit is 45mph, except in Yosemite Valley, where it drops to 25mph or 35mph, depending on where you are. The truth is that you'll mostly be driving slower than that due to traffic.

You'll find gas stations in Crane Flat, Wawona and (in summer) Tuolumne Meadows. The stations generally close after dark, but you can gas up anytime by paying at the pump with a credit card. Gas is not available in Yosemite Valley; the closest gas station to the Valley is in El Portal (p178).

If you're in Yosemite and happen upon the unfortunate need for automotive repairs, you can call the **Village Garage** (Map p93; ☎ 209-372-8320; ☺ 8am-5pm), which is across the street from the Village Store. It also offers 24-hour roadside service.

Most trailheads have free parking areas where you can leave your vehicle for several days. Make sure to put all food and scented items in a bear box. In Yosemite Valley, backpackers must park in the hikers' parking area between Curry Village and Happy Isles. Day-use visitors can use the day-use parking lots either at Curry Village or near Yosemite Village, and take the free shuttle bus around the Valley.

You'll find a number of parking areas in Tuolumne Meadows, White Wolf, Crane Flat, Hetch Hetchy, Glacier Point and Wawona. Overnight parking is not permitted on Tioga or Glacier Point Rds after October 15.

FREE SHUTTLES
Yosemite offers good public transportation within Yosemite Valley and minimal service along Tioga Rd to Tuolumne Meadows. For information, schedules and departure points, call **DNC Parks & Resorts at Yosemite, Inc** (DNC; ☎ 209-372-1240, 209-372-4386; www .yosemitepark.com) or stop by the **Yosemite Lodge Tour Desk** (☎ 209-372-1240) or the information desk at the Valley Visitor Center.

RED BEAR, DEAD BEAR

Every year in Yosemite, some 15 bears are killed by speeding motorists. As part of a rather ingenious campaign to stop speeding, the park service began placing signs along the road wherever bears have been killed by drivers. The signs depict a red bear and read 'Speeding Kills Bears.' In other words, slow it down – speeding endangers more than your fellow humans.

For information on public transit into and out of the park, see Getting There & Away (p260).

Yosemite Valley
The free Yosemite Valley Visitor Shuttle stops year-round at 21 numbered locations, from Happy Isles and Mirror Lake in the east (both inaccessible by car) to Yosemite Lodge in the west, with stops at all popular sites. This excellent easy-to-use, hybrid-fuel bus service operates 7am to 10pm daily at 10- to 20-minute intervals. Small, fold-up route maps are available free at most stores and lobby desks throughout the park.

Yosemite Valley–Glacier Point
In summer, the **Glacier Point Sightseeing Bus** (☎ 209-372-1240, 559-252-4848; adult/senior & child $33/26) loops from Yosemite Valley to Glacier Point and back, taking about four hours for the whole trip. It runs three times daily from about June to October. Hikers can pay for a one-way journey (adult/child/senior $20/12/18) and return to the Valley under their own steam. This is a very popular bus, so reservations must be made a day or two in advance.

Yosemite–Badger Pass
From approximately mid-December through March (when the Badger Pass ski resort is open), a free Badger Pass shuttle bus runs daily from Yosemite Valley in the morning, returning from the Badger Pass ski area in the afternoon.

Wawona–Yosemite Valley
A free shuttle bus between Wawona and Yosemite Valley departs every morning from Memorial Day until sometime in October. It leaves from the Wawona Hotel at 8:30am and departs from Yosemite Lodge for its return leg at 3:30pm.

Wawona–Mariposa Grove
Between about April and October, the free Wawona–Mariposa Grove Shuttle loops between the Wawona Store, the South Entrance and Mariposa Grove from 9am to 6pm daily. Taking the bus is not only a good idea, but sometimes it's your only option for visiting the grove. The small parking lot fills up quickly, and the shuttle guarantees that you can get in even when it's full.

Tuolumne Meadows

For free transportation in the Tuolumne Meadows area, use the free Tuolumne Meadows Shuttle Bus, which plies part of Tioga Rd daily from about mid-June to mid-September (the exact schedule varies annually). The shuttle travels between Tuolumne Meadows Lodge and Olmsted Point, starting at the lodge at 7am and operating at roughly 30-minute intervals until 7pm. The last eastbound shuttle usually departs Olmsted Point at 6:30pm. Another shuttle travels between Tuolumne Meadows Lodge and Tioga Pass, departing the lodge at 9am, noon, 3pm and 5pm; returns depart from Tioga pass at 9:30am, 12:30pm, 3:30pm and 5:30pm.

HIKERS' BUSES

From about mid-June to mid-September, buses run from Yosemite Valley to Glacier Point and Tuolumne Meadows, stopping at various points along the way. Hikers disembark at elevation and follow any number of trails back down to the Valley (or vice versa).

The Tuolumne Meadows Tour & Hikers' Bus travels between the Valley and Tuolumne. The bus departs daily from Curry Village at 8am, from Yosemite Village at 8:05am and from Yosemite Lodge at 8:20am, stopping at Crane Flat, White Wolf, May Lake Junction, Olmsted Point and Tenaya Lake. It arrives at the Tuolumne Meadows Store about 10:20am and Tuolumne Meadows Lodge at 10:30am.

On the return trip, the bus leaves Tuolumne Meadows Lodge at 2:05pm and arrives at Curry Village at 4pm, making all the same stops in between. You can also flag the bus for pickup from any trailhead or ask the driver to drop you at a trailhead along the way.

Reservations are strongly recommended; contact **DNC** (☎ 209-372-1240, 209-372-4386; www .yosemitepark.com) up to one week in advance or stop by the tour desk at Yosemite Lodge. Fares vary according to your trip. From Yosemite Valley, a one-way adult ticket to Tuolumne Meadows costs $14.50; children (aged five to 12) ride for half-price.

To get from the Valley to Tuolumne and other points along Tioga Rd, you can also ride the Yosemite Area Regional Transport System (YARTS) buses heading to Mammoth Lakes (see p174). The 5pm YARTS bus is the only eastbound evening service from the Valley to Tuolumne. Hikers can treat the DNC Glacier Point Tour bus (see p257) as a shuttle in either direction between Yosemite Valley and Glacier Point; many people take this bus up and walk down.

SIGHTS

YOSEMITE VALLEY

Yosemite Valley is the park's crown jewel. It's home to what most people think of when they imagine Yosemite: Half Dome, Yosemite Falls, El Capitan, the Royal Arches – all those mind-boggling sights that draw (believe it or not) over 3.3 million people to the park each year. But the numbers can be deceiving. Most visitors come in July and August, and many of them stay only for the day. Sure, the stores, the dining rooms and the food stands at Yosemite Village and Curry Village are a complete nightmare, and the traffic is maddening, but come sundown, when the day-trippers and tour buses disappear, you can stroll the loop trails along the Valley Floor and feel the tranquil magic that has always been here. Of course, visiting the Valley outside of summer makes finding solitude a cinch. If you don't mind nippy nights, then springtime, when the waterfalls are raging, is one of the very best times to visit. Winter is quiet, and the snow lends a serenity to the Valley that few people experience.

ORIENTATION

Meadow-carpeted Yosemite Valley is 7 miles long and 1 mile wide (at its widest point). The Merced River meanders down its middle, within sight of Half Dome on the east end, westward past El Capitan, and out of the park into the Merced River Canyon.

Northside and Southside Drives parallel the valley on either side of the river, each one way for most of its route (the former heads west, the latter heads east). Four bridges span the river, including Sentinel Bridge, which leads to Yosemite Village, the Valley's commercial center.

TWO CLASSIC ROADSIDE VIEWS

For two of the very best views over Yosemite Valley, you don't even have to stroll far from your car. The best all-around photo op of the Valley can be had from Tunnel View (Map pp90–1), a large, busy parking lot and viewpoint at the east end of Wawona Tunnel, on Hwy 41. It's just a short drive from the Valley floor. The vista encompasses most of the Valley's greatest hits: El Capitan on the left, Bridalveil Fall on the right, the green Valley floor below, and glorious Half Dome front and center. This viewpoint is often mistakenly called Inspiration Point. That point was on an old park road and is now reachable via a steep hike from the Tunnel View parking lot.

The second view, known as Valley View (Map pp90–1), is a good one to hit on your way out. It offers a bottom-up (rather than top-down) view of the Valley and is a lovely spot to dip your toes in the Merced River and bid farewell to sights like Bridalveil Fall, Cathedral Rocks and El Capitan. Look carefully to spot the tip-top of Half Dome in the distance. As you head west out of the Valley on Northside Dr, look for the Valley View turnout (roadside marker V11), just over a mile past El Capitan Meadow.

The Ahwahnee Hotel sits about a half-mile east of the village, while Yosemite Lodge is near the base of Yosemite Falls, less than a mile west of the village. Curry Village and the three Pines campgrounds lie south of the river, about a mile east of Sentinel Bridge.

Three highways diverge at the west end of the Valley. Big Oak Flat Rd leads north to Crane Flat (where it meets Hwy 120), Hetch Hetchy and Tuolumne Meadows; Hwy 140 heads west out of the park to El Portal and Mariposa; and Hwy 41 runs south to Glacier Point Rd, Wawona and Mariposa Grove.

INFORMATION

Yosemite Valley boasts the greatest concentration of visitor services. In addition to accommodations and dining options, you'll find stores, ATMs, a post office, internet access, a bookstore, laundry and shower facilities, medical and dental clinics, a wilderness center, a campground reservations office and the Yosemite Valley Visitor Center.

Yosemite Village

Regardless of your feelings toward commercial development in one of the world's natural wonders, you'll probably wind up here at one point or another, as the village offers just about every amenity – from pizzas and ice cream to fire wood and wilderness permits.

Commercial development began in the Valley almost as soon as the public became aware of the park. Quite a few hotels opened around the turn of the 20th century, and by the 1920s a collection of businesses – including hotels, photo studios, a dance pavilion and even a cinema – had risen just south of the river near Sentinel Bridge. This was the original Yosemite Village. By the 1950s, however, it was downgraded to the 'Old Village,' as businesses moved north of the river. The site of the Old Village has since reverted to meadow (look for road marker V20), though the chapel remains, albeit in a slightly different spot. A few buildings were moved to the Pioneer History Center in Wawona, and Best's Studio was moved to the present-day village and eventually renamed the Ansel Adams Gallery.

Though the smell of quick eats and a plethora of T-shirts and cheap souvenirs may get on your nerves, some businesses are quite useful, including the Village Store for groceries, and the **Sport Shop** (Map p93; 9am-6pm, reduced hours in winter) for last-minute camping supplies.

YOSEMITE VALLEY VISITOR CENTER

Rarely do visitors spend much time in the Valley without a stop at the park's **main visitor center** (Map p93; ☎ 209-372-0299; 8am-6pm, to 5pm off-season, to 7pm Jul & Aug). If you've never been to Yosemite, its an excellent place to load up on information. All places in this section share the same opening hours as the center.

At the main desk, rangers answer tourists' questions (remaining amazingly friendly amid the barrage) and can pretty much settle any query you might have. A rudimentary hiking map is available, and weather reports, trail conditions and road conditions

A STROLL INTO THE PAST

Dr Bonnie Gisel, one of Yosemite's premier historians, is the author of two books about John Muir: *An Inordinate Fondness for Plants: The Herbarium of John Muir* (Heyday, 2008) and *Kindred and Related Spirits: The Letters of John Muir and Jeanne C Carr* (University of Utah Press, 2001). Gisel is the director of the Sierra Club's LeConte Memorial Lodge (p104), where she and a group of volunteers keep aflame the environmental spirit that John Muir, Galen Clark and the lodge's namesake, Joseph LeConte, lit over a century ago.

We asked Dr Gisel to recommend some special spots in the Valley where one might absorb its unique past – places folks might otherwise miss. Here's what she suggested:

The research library above the Indian museum is open to the public and has lots of old photographs and books, and the librarian, Linda, is full of information. But it has peculiar hours.

On the south side of Sentinel Bridge, there's an old incense cedar out in a clearing. You have to look for it. A small house [known as the Big Tree House] was built around the tree and used as a reading room and gathering place for guests staying at Hutching's Hotel. The tree has since died, and the house is gone, but you can still see the nail holes in a slanted line where the roof was nailed to the tree. Look around and you'll see the remnants of the old hearth, as well as two stone markers which identify two corners of the old house.

The Four-Mile Trail to Glacier Point was the route most people used to take into the Valley. They traveled from Clark's Station [Wawona] up to Old Inspiration Point, then to Glacier Point and finally down the trail into the Valley.

Near Lower Yosemite Falls, an old wooden bridge parallels Northside Dr between the bus stop and the new restrooms. To me it has the spirit of [renowned landscape architect] Frederic Law Olmsted. He didn't design it, but I remember him when I'm on that bridge. It's one opportunity to say, 'Ah ha, the man was here.'

An old road leads northeast from the backpackers' campground [below the bicycle and foot paths]. Follow this road a short distance and you'll find a large tule marsh where the Ahwahneechee used to collect tule for their baskets. With its views of Half Dome and the Royal Arches, it was undoubtedly a special place for the Ahwahneechee. It still has that feeling. If you follow the footpath further east, you'll find a huge flat rock that was an important milling site with holes pounded into the rock.

As related to Danny Palmerlee

are posted behind the desk. There's also a park concessions courtesy phone.

To the left of the help desk is the **Yosemite Association Bookstore** (☎ 209-372-0731; www .yosemitestore.com), which stocks an outstanding assortment of Yosemite-related books and maps and a smattering of Yosemite paraphernalia. To the right of the help desk is the sparkling new **exhibit hall** (admission free), which opened in 2007 after a two-year, $1.3-million upgrade. The exhibit, which hadn't been updated in 40 years (and didn't even include a discussion of plate tectonics), offers an interactive walk through Yosemite's history from the dinosaurs to the present.

Behind the visitor center stands the **West Auditorium** (admission free), which screens the painfully dramatic, but beautifully photographed, 22-minute film *Spirit of Yosemite*. The movie starts every half-hour or so and offers an air-conditioned respite from the summer heat. On Sundays, the first screening is at noon.

YOSEMITE MUSEUM

Next to the visitor center, the **Yosemite Museum** (Map p93; ☎ 209-372-0200; admission free; 🕙 9am-4:30pm or 5pm, closed for lunch; 🕭) features a series of cultural and historical exhibits on the Valley's native Miwok-Ahwahneechee and Paiute people, covering the period from 1850 to today. It's worth a visit just to see the giant, intricately woven **Miwok-Paiute baskets** dating from the 1920s and, '30s. The baskets were woven (some over periods as long as three years) by famous weavers such as Lucy Telles, Carrie Bethel and Alice Wilson. A basket by Telles, the largest in the collection, took four years to make. She later declined an offer by Robert Ripley (of *Ripley's Believe It or Not!*) to purchase the basket.

The museum also features paintings and photographs from the museum's permanent collection, including some Ansel Adams prints, and has a small hands-on area where kids can play with Miwok games and ask Miwok interpreters questions.

Behind the museum, a free, self-guided interpretive trail winds through the **Indian Village of Ahwahnee**, where you can peek inside full-size, reconstructed Miwok buildings, including a traditional roundhouse. The building and the sweat lodge behind it are used for ceremonial purposes by the Miwok.

A couple items in front of the museum are worth a look: a cross section of a **giant sequoia** has been marked with rings to show its age. Its center is marked 'AD 923.' Nearby, a **time capsule** awaits the year 2090, when rangers will open it and use the materials inside to evaluate changes in the park since the capsule was created in 1990.

ANSEL ADAMS GALLERY

The **Ansel Adams Gallery** (Map p93; ☎ 209-372-4413; www.anseladams.com; ☾ 9am-6pm summer, to 5pm rest of year), east of the visitor center, is a privately run art gallery housed in a building that was originally Best's Studio, founded in 1902. Owner Harry Best was the father of Virginia Best, who married Adams in 1928. The gallery has since moved from its original site south of the river and been extensively remodeled. Today, instead of

---

YOSEMITE'S ARTISTS

From its very beginnings as a park, Yosemite has inspired a body of art nearly as impressive as the landscape itself. The artists who came to Yosemite with the first generation of tourists revealed a world of extraordinary beauty, even as miners, ranchers and lumbermen were tearing it apart in their lust for profit. From the illustrations of Thomas Ayres to the photographs of Carleton Watkins, art played a key role in the bid to establish Yosemite as a national park.

In the mid-19th century, the Hudson River School and related movements in American art strived to capture the face of God in the wild magnificence of nature. A parallel trend in literature expressed a distinctly American spiritualism tied to the wilderness; writers who explored such transcendental themes included Ralph Waldo Emerson, Walt Whitman, Emily Dickinson and Henry David Thoreau. Into this intellectual moment, which flourished on the East Coast, came the first paintings of Yosemite by a recognized artist, Albert Bierstadt, in 1863.

At that time, San Francisco was becoming the epicenter for a distinctly Californian school of art. Inspired by the vistas that Bierstadt and the photographers were capturing in Yosemite, many other artists embraced the Sierra as a subject matter. Mountain landscapes by Charles Nahl, Thomas Hill and William Keith soon adorned Victorian mansions in San Francisco and Sacramento, and painters became a regular fixture in the haunts of John Muir, who occasionally led groups of them on sketching expeditions into remote locations. Hill set up a studio at Wawona in 1884, beginning the tradition of resident artists and galleries in the park.

While the painters were often content to set up their easels in the meadows, photographers became known for seeking out more inaccessible regions. Sierra Club photographer-mountaineers such as Joseph LeConte and Norman Clyde captured extremely remote areas of the park. Yosemite's best-known photographer, of course, was Ansel Adams, who developed a level of craft not seen in the work of his predecessors. An early proponent of the idea that photography could adhere to the same aesthetic principles used by fine artists, he also became a strong advocate for the preservation of the wilderness, working on the frontlines of the growing conservation movement.

In 1929 Adams married Virginia Best, whose father's gallery in Yosemite Valley was the precursor to the Ansel Adams Gallery, found today in Yosemite Village. In 1940 Adams held a photography workshop at the gallery with fellow photographer Edward Weston, beginning a tradition of photography education that continues to this day.

Three of Adams' assistants – John Sexton, Alan Ross and Ted Orland – are lesser known but equally important to the greater body of Yosemite photography. Mountaineer-photographer Galen Rowell, who Adams himself highly regarded, took some of the most extreme photos of the park, continuing to expose those faraway places to the public eye.

NATIVE AMERICAN BASKET WEAVERS

Handwoven baskets were an integral part of indigenous Californian life. The exquisitely wrought baskets were so tightly woven that they could be used for drawing and carrying water. They also served as cooking vessels and dinner plates.

Ironically, the survival of the craft owes something to its commercial exploitation by mid-20th-century art collectors. Artists like Lucy Parker Telles, a descendant of Southern Miwok and Mono Lake Paiute, wove larger and more ornate baskets than those of their ancestors, fetching a higher price from collectors. Intricate geometric designs were painstakingly created along the sides of bulb-shaped baskets using natural dyes and special weaves. Larger baskets could span as wide as 3ft and often had narrow openings at their tops. The craft was also given a boost by that era's Yosemite Indian Field Days, when survivors of ancient tribes gathered to demonstrate their crafts.

Though Indian Field Days are no longer held, organizations like the **California Indian Basketweavers Association** (www.ciba.org) seek to preserve the craft and reaffirm its spiritual significance. One sacred part of that practice is the gathering of traditional materials – sedge, bracken fern, redbud, willow and waterproofing elements such as pine pitch and soap root. Thus, recent efforts have focused on environmental restoration of traditional gathering sites.

Lucy Parker Telles' daughter-in-law, Julia Parker, is a renowned basket weaver and teacher who makes traditional Kashaya Pomo baskets. Through marriage, she also learned the cultural traditions of her mother-in-law's Yosemite Miwok and Mono Lake Paiute ancestors, passing this knowledge to her daughter, Lucy Parker. Both Julia and Lucy continue to teach their craft and display their baskets and jewelry at Yosemite. The Yosemite Museum has a collection of extraordinary baskets, some of which took several years to weave.

Best's paintings, it specializes in Adams' photographs and the work of other contemporary artists; it also houses a great selection of art and ecology books and other gift items (candles, jewelry, ceramics, post cards etc).

Surprisingly, the gallery displays very few original Adams pieces, exhibiting works by other nature photographers instead. However, on Saturdays at 3pm, curator Glenn Crosby hosts a free **fine print viewing** in the private room for up to five people (reserve up to three days in advance). Sign up, and you'll get to see special edition Adams prints, and Crosby will explain their history.

On Tuesdays, Thursdays and Saturdays, the gallery hosts free **photography walks** at 9am, where you'll pick up tips on composition, technique and the best spots to shoot. Walks are for 15 people max, so sign up over the phone or in person.

ART ACTIVITY CENTER

In summer, the **Art Activity Center** (Map p93; ☎ 209-372-1442; ◷ 10am-2pm Apr-Oct) in Yosemite Village holds free art classes that feature a different artist and medium (watercolor, pastel, acrylic etc) nearly every day of the week. Classes usually take place outside, and students must bring their own supplies or purchase them at the center. No experience is necessary. Children older than age 10 can participate, but those under 12 must be accompanied by an adult. Sign up at the center at least a day ahead to ensure a spot.

Curry Village

Lying directly below Glacier Point, Curry Village is home to the Valley's second-biggest collection of restaurants, stores and overnight accommodations. Originally called Camp Curry, it was founded in 1899 by David and Jennie Curry as a place where everyday visitors could find 'a good bed and a clean napkin at every meal.' Starting with just a handful of tents, the camp quickly grew, thanks in large part to David Curry's entrepreneurial drive and booming personality. One of his biggest promotional schemes was the Firefall (p106), a nightly event and significant tourist draw. Curry Village is now owned and run by DNC.

More than 100 years later, the Camp Curry sign still hangs over the entrance, but this sprawling complex retains few traces of its turn-of-the-century roots. From the parking lot, a sea of tent cabins fans out toward the base of Glacier Point, radiating from a central cluster of stores and snack bars – not exactly a vision of rustic glory. Still, it's pleasant to settle in for pizza and beer on the patio that faces the amphitheater out back. There's even a small cocktail bar. Or you can head to the charming deck of the old Camp Curry Lounge for a catnap in one of the rocking chairs.

The **Curry Village Mountain Shop** (Map p93; ☎ 209-372-8396) offers the Valley's best selection of camping, mountaineering and backpacking supplies and is the year-round home of the Yosemite Mountaineering School (p155). The shop is world-renowned for its selection of big-wall climbing gear.

Half Dome

Rising 8842ft above sea level, and nearly a mile above the Valley floor, Half Dome (Map pp90–1) serves as the park's spiritual centerpiece and stands as one of the most glorious and monumental (not to mention best-known) domes on earth.

Its namesake shape is, in fact, an illusion. While from the Valley the dome appears to have been neatly sliced in half, from Glacier or Washburn Points you'll see that it's actually a thin ridge with a back slope nearly as steep as its fabled facade. As you travel through the park, witness Half Dome's many faces. For example, from Mirror Lake it presents a powerful form, while from the Panorama Trail it looks somewhat like a big toe poking out above the rocks and trees.

Half Dome towers above Tenaya Canyon, a classic, glacially carved gorge. Across this canyon rise North Dome and Basket Dome, examples of fully intact domes. In contrast, Half Dome's north face shattered along cracks as a small glacier undercut the dome's base. The resulting cliff boasts a 93% vertical grade (the sheerest in North America), attracting climbers from around the world. Hikers can reach its summit from the Valley via a long series of trails (p138). The final 45-degree stretch to the top was first made accessible by George Anderson, a local blacksmith who drilled holes in the granite in 1875 and installed a rope system (later replaced by the steel cables in use today).

Yosemite Falls

One of the world's most dramatic natural spectacles, Yosemite Falls (Map p93) is a marvel to behold. Naturalist John Muir devoted entire pages to its changing personality, its myriad sounds, its movement with the wind and its transformations between the seasons. No matter where you are when you see it (and it regularly pops into view from all over the Valley), the falls will stop you in your tracks.

In spring, when snowmelt gets Yosemite Creek really pumping, the sight is astounding. On those nights when the falls are full and the moon is bright, you might spot a 'moonbow.' In winter, as the spray freezes midair, an ice cone forms at the base of the falls.

Dropping 2425ft, Yosemite Falls is considered the tallest in North America. Some question that claim, however, as Yosemite Falls comprises three distinct tiers: towering 1430ft Upper Yosemite Fall, tumbling 675ft Middle Cascade and the final 320ft drop of Lower Yosemite Fall. If you want to make the grueling hike to the top, see p123.

The meandering walkways and natural areas around the falls underwent a two-year, $15-million makeover between 2003 and 2005. Under the direction of renowned landscape architect Lawrence Halprin, the project made the falls more accessible (wheelchairs should take the easternmost route), expanded the viewing platform, added interpretive plaques, enhanced indigenous sites and addressed environmental problems within the entire 56-acre biological area surrounding the falls.

CHAPEL IN A SANCTUARY

Built in 1879, the **Yosemite Valley Chapel** (Map p93; ☎ 209-372-4831; www.yosemitevalleychapel.org) is Yosemite's oldest structure that still remains in use. The church originally stood near the base of Four-Mile Trail, and in 1901 was moved about a mile to its present site. Sunday morning services are nondenominational. Should you desire to tie the proverbial knot in this 125-seat chapel, it will only set you back about $700 (a steal, considering what sites go for in much of California), and less if you use your own minister.

THE LEGEND OF HALF DOME

According to Native American legend, one of Yosemite's early inhabitants came down from the mountains to Mono Lake, where he married a Paiute named Tesaiyac. The journey back to the Valley was difficult, and by the time they reached what was to become Mirror Lake, Tesaiyac decided she wanted to return to her people at Mono Lake. Her husband refused to live on such barren, arid land with no oak trees where he could get acorns. With a heart full of despair, Tesaiyac fled toward Mono Lake, her husband in pursuit. When the spirits heard the couple quarreling, they grew angry and turned the two into stone: he became North Dome, and she became Half Dome. The tears she cried made marks as they ran down her face, forming Mirror Lake.

To get to the base of the Lower Yosemite Fall, get off at shuttle stop 6 (or park in the lot just north of Yosemite Lodge) and join the legions of visitors for the easy quarter-mile stroll. Note that in midsummer, when the snowmelt had dissipated, both the upper and lower falls usually dry up – sometimes to a trickle, other times stopping altogether.

Bridalveil Fall

On the southwest end of the Valley, Bridalveil Fall (Map pp90–1) tumbles 620ft. The Ahwahneechee people call it Pohono (Spirit of the Puffing Wind), as gusts often blow the fall from side to side, even lifting water back up into the air. This waterfall usually runs year-round, though it's often reduced to a whisper by midsummer. Expect to get soaked when the fall is heavy.

Park at the large lot where Wawona Rd (Hwy 41) meets Southside Dr. From the lot, it's a quarter-mile walk to the base of the fall. The path is paved, but probably too rough for wheelchairs, and there's a somewhat steep climb at the very end. Avoid climbing on the slippery rocks at its base – no one likes a broken bone.

If you'd rather walk from the Valley, a trail (part of the Loop Trails) follows Southside Dr, beginning near the LeConte Memorial Lodge and running about 3.8 miles west to the falls.

El Capitan

At nearly 3600ft from base to summit, El Capitan (Map pp90–1) ranks as one of the world's largest granite monoliths. Its sheer face makes it a world-class destination for experienced climbers, and one that wasn't 'conquered' until 1958. Since then, it's been inundated. Look closely and you'll probably spot climbers reckoning with El Cap's series of cracks and ledges, including the famous 'Nose.' At night, park along the road and dim your headlights; once your eyes adjust, you'll easily make out the pinpricks of headlamps dotting the rock face. Listen, too, for voices.

The road offers several good spots from which to ogle El Capitan. The Valley View turnout is one. For a wider view, try the pullout along Southside Dr just east of Bridalveil Fall. You can also park on Northside Dr, just below El Capitan, perhaps the best vantage point from which to see climbers.

Ahwahnee Hotel

Almost as iconic as Half Dome itself, the elegant Ahwahnee Hotel (Map p93) has drawn well-heeled tourists through its towering doors since 1927. Of course, you needn't be wealthy in the least to partake of its many charms. In fact, a visit to Yosemite Valley is hardly complete without a stroll through the **Great Lounge** (aka the lobby), which is handsomely decorated with leaded glass, sculpted tile, Native American rugs and Turkish kilims. You can relax on the plush but aging couches and stare out the 10 floor-to-ceiling windows, wander into the **Solarium**, or send the kids into the walk-in fireplace (no longer in use) for a photo. You can even sneak up the back stairs for a peek into the private **Tudor Room**, which has excellent views over the Great Lounge.

Take a wander around the outside, too. The hotel was built entirely from local granite, pine and cedar – against the backdrop the Royal Arches it's truly a sight to see. There's no mistaking the reasoning behind its National Historic Landmark designation. Dropping in for a meal at the restaurant or a drink and a snack at the bar (both covered on p169) are great ways to experience this historic hotel without coughing up three car payments' worth of cash in order to spend the night. For information on that, see p166.

The Ahwahnee was built on the site of a former Ahwahnee-Miwok village. In order to promote the relatively young national park, National Park Service director Stephen Mather dreamed up the idea of a majestic hotel to attract wealthy guests. The site was chosen for its exposure to the sun and its views of Half Dome, Yosemite Falls and Glacier Point. The hotel was designed by American architect Gilbert Stanley Underwood, who also designed Zion Lodge, Brice Canyon Lodge and Grand Canyon North Rim Lodge. If the Ahwahnee's lobby looks familiar despite you never having been there, perhaps it's because it inspired the lobby of the Overlook Hotel, the ill-fated inn from Stanley Kubrick's *The Shining*.

The Ahwahnee is located about a quarter-mile east of Yosemite Village.

Yosemite Lodge

Near the base of Yosemite Falls, the collection of buildings known as Yosemite Lodge includes modern, motel-like accommodations, restaurants, shops, bar, bicycle-rental stand, public pool, tour desk and other amenities. The amphitheater hosts regular evening programs, and the pool is open to the public. Unlike the Ahwahnee, it's not a very striking development.

Despite efforts to blend it into the natural surroundings, the place feels strangely like a suburban condo development. Though it doesn't appear very old, the lodge dates back to 1915. It underwent extensive redesign and remodeling in 1956 and 1998, retaining little to suggest its history.

The Yosemite Valley shuttle bus stops right out front, as do most YARTS and VIA

PHOTOGRAPHING YOSEMITE

Glenn Crosby came to Yosemite in 1986 with plans to stay for a year to photograph the park. He's now the curator of the Ansel Adams Gallery's fine print program – and he still shoots Yosemite year-round. We hit Crosby up for some photographic advice and got the following tips:

- Timing is everything. Having a tripod really makes a big difference because your ability to take advantage of the light increases your odds from *not getting it* to *maybe getting it.*
- Know your camera. Bring your manual. Scenes can change rapidly, and you have to be able to respond quickly.
- Be prepared. The biggest thing we get here at the gallery is people coming in and saying, 'I forgot my charger.'
- Some of the best photographs are made in really bad weather. In summer, when the air is bad and the sky is clear, it's hard to make a good image. Some of the most dramatic low-angle light occurs in winter.
- Time. If you're really into photography, it can be difficult to have nonphotographers with you. They want to go to dinner when you need to be out getting the light.
- Look at the photographic guide books and learn the 'best' time to go and avail yourself of the options you might have.
- Look at the work of other photographers who have been here: Bill Atkinson is one. Charles Cramer, Keith S Walklet and Michael Frye all lived here for some 15 years and, like Ansel Adams, were able to get to know the park and the light. Also John Sexton. Alan Ross, Ted Orland, Jeffrey Conley, Jerry Uelsmann. William Neill. *Yosemite In Time,* by Mark Klett, Rebecca Solnit and Byron Wolfe, puts famous photographs into visual context and is extremely interesting. Galen Rowell was more the adventure photographer whose physical ability put him in places others couldn't get to. And of course, there's Ansel.
- In spring, the Pohono Trail is excellent for taking pictures. From Tunnel View you can hike the rim to Stanford Point, Crocker Point and Dewey Point in a relatively short period of time and you see all the waterfalls, El Cap, the Valley and the high country. Or hike to the top of Yosemite Falls and continue to Eagle Peak or El Cap. The view from Eagle Peak is incredible, but it's 8 miles one way.

As related to Danny Palmerlee

buses. All guided tram tours, ski shuttles and hiker buses also leave from here; tickets are available from the tour desk in the lobby.

See p166 and p169 for details of its accommodations and eating options.

LeConte Memorial Lodge

Built by the Sierra Club in 1903, this small, rustic granite-and-wood **lodge** (Map p93; ☎ 209-372-4542; www.sierraclub.org/education/leconte; ☽ 10am-4pm Wed-Sun May-Sep) offers a glimpse into a relatively unknown chapter of California architecture. Designed by Berkeley architect John White, the building sits firmly within a style known as the First Bay Tradition, a movement that was intimately linked with the 20th-century Arts and Crafts Movement. The First Bay Tradition placed great importance on reflecting the natural world and insisted each work of architecture be specific to its surroundings.

The Sierra Club built the lodge in honor of Joseph LeConte (1823–1901), a University of California Berkeley geologist and a cofounder of the Sierra Club. The building was initially erected in Camp Curry, then moved here in 1919. LeConte Lodge is one of three National Historic Landmarks in Yosemite, along with the Ahwahnee Hotel and the Rangers' Club (a Valley building currently used as employee housing).

Sierra Club members staff the lodge, which houses exhibits and information on LeConte, Muir and Ansel Adams, along with an excellent library of park-related ecology, geology and other nature books free for the browsing. There's also a fun children's corner. Evening activities are posted out front and in *Yosemite Today*.

Nature Center at Happy Isles

Happy Isles lies at the Valley's southeast end, where the Merced River courses around two small islands. The area is a popular spot for picnics, swimming and short strolls in the woods. It also marks the start of the John Muir Trail and Mist Trail, where hikers begin treks to Vernal Fall, Nevada Fall, and Half Dome.

On the site of a former fish hatchery, the **nature center** (Map p93; admission free; ☽ 10am-noon & 1-4pm May-Sep; ⬛) features great hands-on exhibits that will enthrall kids and adults alike. Displays explain the differences between the park's various pinecones, rocks,

animal tracks and (everyone's favorite subject) scat. Out back, don't miss an exhibit on the 1996 rock fall, when an 80,000-ton rock slab plunged 2000ft to the nearby valley floor, killing a man, felling about 1000 trees and seriously damaging the nature center.

Happy Isles is about a mile from Curry Village. The road is closed to cars (except those with handicap placards); instead, reach it by either an easy walk or the free shuttle bus. There's a small snack bar at the shuttle stop and the islands themselves are wheelchair accessible.

GLACIER POINT & BADGER PASS

Constructed to replace an 1882 wagon road, the modern 16-mile stretch of Glacier Point Rd leads to what many people consider the finest viewpoint in Yosemite. A year-round destination, winter attracts skiers galore who whoosh down the Badger Pass slopes and traverse the unplowed road as a cross-country route. In warmer months, gawkers flock to the end of the road for its satiating Half Dome views and hikers file out from its many trailheads.

ORIENTATION & INFORMATION

From Yosemite Valley, it's 30 miles (about an hour's drive) to Glacier Point. Glacier Point Rd runs east from the Chinquapin junction on Hwy 41, dead-ending at Glacier Point itself. The road rises from about 6000ft at Chinquapin to 7700ft at the Sentinel Dome parking lot, then down again to 7214ft Glacier Point. Along the road are numerous trailheads for simple strolls or more ambitious backpacking trips. From the Chinquapin turnoff, Badger Pass Ski Area lies about 5 miles to the east; in winter, Glacier Point Rd is closed east of the ski area.

Glacier Point lies at the far eastern end of winding Glacier Point Rd. Along the road, hiking trails lead to more spectacular viewpoints such as Dewey Point and Sentinel Dome. The road also passes Bridalveil Creek Campground, adjacent to Bridalveil Creek, which runs north and drops into Yosemite Valley as Bridalveil Fall.

The only services in the area are at Glacier Point, where there's a small **snack bar** (Map p105; ☽ 11am-4pm) and an adjacent **gift shop** (Map p105; ☽ 9am-6pm). Rangers are stationed at viewpoint areas but the closest visitor center is in Yosemite Valley. No wil-

Glacier Point & Badger Pass

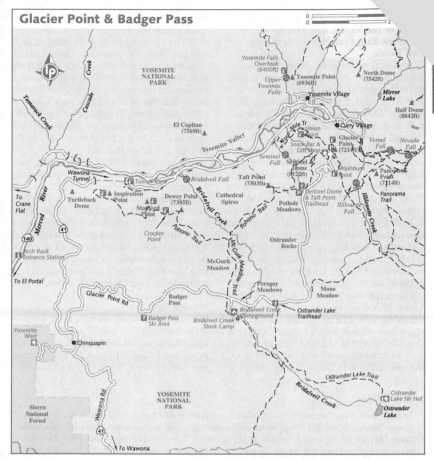

derness permits are available in the vicinity (except at Badger Pass in the winter); you must backtrack to either Yosemite Valley or Wawona if you develop warm weather backcountry urges.

A Valley–Glacier Point bus service operates in summer, and there's also a Valley–Badger Pass service in the winter; see Getting Around, p94.

Glacier Point

The views from 7214ft Glacier Point can make you feel like you cheated somehow – a huge array of superstar sights present themselves without any physical effort. A quick mosey up from the parking lot and you'll find the entire eastern Yosemite Val-

ley spread out before you, from Yosemite Falls to Half Dome, as well as the distant peaks that ring Tuolumne Meadows. Half Dome looms practically at eye level, and if you look closely you can spot ant-sized hikers on its summit. The cable approach is not visible, however.

To the left of Half Dome lies the glacially carved Tenaya Canyon, and to its right are the wavy white ribbons of Nevada and Vernal Falls. On the Valley floor, the Merced River snakes through green meadows and groves of trees. Sidle up to the railing, hold on tight and peer 3200ft straight down at Curry Village. The aqua rectangle of its swimming pool is clearly visible, as is the Ahwahnee Hotel just to the north. Basket ome also rise to the ...nd Liberty Cap and ...e seen to the right of

...k's inception, Glacier ...r destination. It used to be that getting up here was a major undertaking. That changed once the Four-Mile Trail (p124) opened in 1872. While not exactly an easy climb – neither then nor today – the trail did offer a more direct route to the point. James McCauley financed formation of the trail, for which he charged a toll; he later took over the reins of the Mountain House hotel, built in 1873 atop Glacier Point. In the 1870s he also conceived the famous Firefall (see the boxed text, below), though Curry Village later picked up and heavily promoted the event.

A wagon road to the point was completed in 1882, and the current Glacier Point Rd was built in 1936. As far back as 1929 (and again in the 1970s), there was talk of building an aerial tramway to ferry tourists from Yosemite Valley to Glacier Point. But since the cables would be an eyesore and the system would disturb fragile ecosystems, plans thankfully were abandoned. The spectacularly situated Glacier Point Hotel stood on the point from 1917 until 1969, when it burned down along with the adjacent McCauley Mountain House.

At the tip of the point is **Overhanging Rock**, a huge granite slab protruding from the cliff edge like an outstretched tongue, defying gravity and once providing a scenic stage for daredevil extroverts. Through the years, many famous photos have been taken of folks performing handstands, high kicks and other wacky stunts on the rock. You'll have to stick to the pictures though, as the precipice is now off-limits.

For information on the stargazing programs at the Glacier Point amphitheater, see p52.

To escape the crowds, consider a short hike down the first half-mile or so of the Four-Mile Trail, which drops gently into a quiet forest and – at this point at least – isn't too steep. After about 10 or 15 minutes, you'll round a corner to a view of El Capitan and Yosemite Valley's western half. Serious switchbacks begin below this point.

WASHBURN POINT

Named for the brothers who built the Wawona Hotel, this viewpoint along Glacier Point Rd is magnificent, though not quite as expansive as Glacier Point. The point faces east toward the Clark Range and lacks the

---

THE FIREFALL

Imagine the ruckus that would ensue today if someone built a bonfire and sent it toppling over Glacier Point. Rangers and fire crews would swarm the scene, and rangers would no doubt press arson charges. So it's hard to believe that this was a Yosemite evening tradition for 88 years, inciting public rapture and no official park condemnation. It sounds horrific to those schooled in the 'leave no trace' wilderness ethic, but countless Valley campers still testify to the beauty and excitement of the Firefall, regarded as a sublime summer moment in the enchantment of a summer's evening. Even the echoing signal call to Glacier Point from the Camp Curry campfire, 'Let the fire fall!' became a spine-tingling element of the tradition.

The Firefall originated around 1872, when a hotel was being built at the top of James McCauley's new 4-mile toll trail to Glacier Point. Perhaps as an advertisement for his enterprise, McCauley pushed his campfire off the cliff, creating a glowing waterfall of sparks that was so appealing that tourists in Yosemite Valley called on McCauley to repeat it. His sons transformed the Firefall into a family business, collecting $1.50 from each person who wanted to see it happen. When they found enough takers, a fire builder went up the trail to build a large fire of fir bark and pushed it off the cliff just after nightfall.

The McCauleys left Yosemite in 1897, but two years later David Curry reintroduced the Firefall as a way to draw business to his newly created Camp Curry. Apart from two brief hiatuses, one in 1913 and the other during WWII, the Firefall continued to hold a place in Yosemite evening activities until the National Park Service ended it in 1968, finally declaring the tradition to be incompatible with natural land management.

To read a compilation of Firefall memories, visit http://firefall.info.

sweeping view of Yosemite Valley. Still, a stop here serves as a great warm-up to Glacier Point, less than a mile down the road.

Badger Pass

The California ski industry essentially got its start in Yosemite Valley, and Badger Pass was California's first alpine ski resort. After Yosemite's All-Year Highway (now Hwy 140) was completed in 1926 and the Ahwahnee Hotel opened its doors the following year, the Valley quickly became a popular winter destination.

As the 1929 Winter Olympics approached, the newly formed Curry Company and the Yosemite Winter Club submitted an impassioned bid to host the games. They lost, and instead the events were held at Lake Placid, New York – where, in a freakish irony, no snow fell that winter. Bales of hay were used in lieu of snow, while the Sierra saw record snowfalls.

When Wawona Tunnel opened in 1933, skiers began congregating at Badger Pass. In 1935 a new lodge opened on Glacier Point Rd, and a newfangled device called 'the upski' was installed at the pass. The crude lift consisted of nothing more than two counterbalanced sleds, but it worked, and Badger Pass became California's first alpine ski resort.

In winter a free shuttle bus runs between the Valley and Badger Pass (see p94). So in winter, wilderness permits are available by self-registration at the **A-frame building** (☎ 209-372-0409), where the first-aid station and ski patrol are also situated. Rangers usually staff the office from 8am to 5pm, but coverage can be hit and miss.

WAWONA

Yosemite's historical center, Wawona was home to the park's first headquarters (supervised by Captain AE Wood on the site of the Wawona Campground) and its first tourist facilities. The latter was a simple wayside station run by Galen Clark, who homesteaded in Wawona in 1856. A decade later, Clark was appointed state guardian of the Yosemite Grant, which protected Yosemite Valley and the Mariposa Grove. In 1875 he sold his lodge to the Washburn brothers, who built what's known today as the Wawona Hotel. The Washburns also renamed the area Wawona – thought to be the local Native American word for 'big trees.'

Completed in 1875, the original Wawona Rd opened the floodgates for tourists curious to see the big trees – as well as wondrous Yosemite Valley to the north. The road was modernized in 1933, following construction of the Wawona Tunnel.

From 1891 to 1906, the current Wawona campground site was home base for the US cavalry, who were appointed as the first official protectors of the newly formed national park. The cavalry moved its headquarters to Yosemite Valley in 1906. Curiously, considering its significant role in the park's history, Wawona remained private property for decades and wasn't incorporated into the boundaries of Yosemite National Park until 1932. Some parts of the area are still in private hands, including the houses that line Chilnualna Falls Rd.

A blend of Victorian elegance and utilitarian New England charm, the Wawona Hotel is the commercial hub of the area. The unassuming white wooden building sits behind a large, manicured green lawn and a fountain inhabited by very vocal frogs. Across Hwy 41, there's the Wawona Golf Course (see p56) and the expansive Wawona Meadow, which doubled as the local airport in the early 20th century. To the north is the Pioneer Yosemite History Center, which includes some of the park's oldest buildings, relocated from various points including 'old Yosemite Village.' The center also features a nice collection of horse-drawn stagecoaches and buggies that brought early tourists to Yosemite.

Some 6 miles southeast of Wawona stands the Mariposa Grove of giant sequoias, the park's largest and deservedly popular sequoia grove. It's home to the 2700-year-old Grizzly Giant and, in the upper grove, the Wawona Tunnel Tree, which toppled over in 1969. Allow at least an hour to get to the grove from Yosemite Valley.

ORIENTATION & INFORMATION

Wawona lies on Hwy 41 (Wawona Rd), 4 miles north of the park's South Entrance, which is about 63 miles north of Fresno. Yosemite Valley is a 27-mile drive north. No public transportation serves Wawona; however, DNC's Grand Tour (see p257), which originates and ends in the Valley, is the only scheduled option for getting to Wawona without a car.

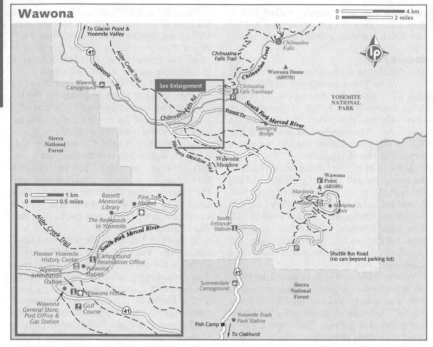

The South Fork of the Merced River passes through Wawona, running northwest out of the park. Most visitor services lie just to its south. North of the river is Chilnualna Falls Rd, which runs east into a development of private homes and rental properties.

The **Wawona Information Station** (Map p108; ☎ 209-375-9531; ⏲ 8:30am-5pm late May-early Oct) doubles as the area's visitor center and wilderness center. It issues wilderness permits and bear boxes, answers general park questions and sells some maps and books. The station is located inside Hill's Studio, a historic 1886 building (it was the studio of landscape painter Thomas Hill) adjacent to the Wawona Hotel. Small exhibits in the studio include a display of the park's various pinecones.

When the office is open for the season, it issues wilderness permits for all areas of the park. When it's closed (about October through May), backcountry-bound visitors can self-register for wilderness permits for trailheads in Wawona and Glacier Point Rd only.

At the corner of Hwy 41 and Forest Dr, just north of the hotel, are a general store, post office, ATM and gas station (24-hour with credit card).

The horse stables, the Pioneer Yosemite History Center and a small Campground Reservation Office are along Chilnualna Falls Rd; cross to the north side of the river and turn right. The Bassett Memorial Library (with free internet access), and the year-round Pine Tree Market are also on Chilnualna Falls Rd, about a mile northeast of Hwy 41.

Pioneer Yosemite History Center

In the 1960s, a large number of Yosemite's historic wooden buildings – including some from the original site of Yosemite Village – were transferred to the **Pioneer Yosemite History Center** (Map p108; admission free; ⏲ 24hr), forming a period village along the South Fork of the Merced River just north of the Wawona Hotel. Mostly furnished, the buildings include a Wells Fargo office, a jail and the Hodgdon homestead cabin. An evocative covered bridge (it dates from

1857 but was modified with walls and a ceiling by Vermont native Henry Washburn in 1875) crosses the river, and a barn south of the river holds a collection of vintage stagecoaches. In a reminder of daffy past land-management practices, there's also a 'mosquito wagon' that once sprayed oil on Tuolumne Meadows ponds to control bugs!

In summer, the buildings are staffed with folks dressed in period costume who explain their surroundings (though tours of the buildings are self-guided). In the spring, elementary school teachers and their students can spend the night and learn about pioneer life as part of the **Environmental Living Program** (www.nps.gov/yose /forteachers/elp.htm).

A nice spot to trip back in time, the center gives you a sense of what local life was like a century ago. For fun, hop aboard a 10-minute **stagecoach ride** (adult/child $3/2; ⊙ Wed-Sun Jun-Sep). For summer events like blacksmithing demonstrations or the occasional barn dance, check *Yosemite Today*.

Mariposa Grove

With their massive stature and multi-millennium maturity, the chunky high-rise sequoias of Mariposa Grove will make you feel rather insignificant. The largest grove of giant sequoias in the park, there are approximately 500 mature trees towering over 250 acres, with a number of mammoths right in the parking lot. A few walking trails wind through this very popular grove, and you can usually have a more solitary experience if you come during the early evening in summer or anytime outside of summer. The Mariposa Grove Rd closes to cars from about November to April, but you can always hike in (2 miles, 500ft of elevation gain) and experience it in its quiet hibernation.

Walk a half-mile up to the 2700-year-old **Grizzly Giant**, a bloated beast of a tree with branches that are bigger in circumference than most of the pines trees in this forest. The walk-through **California Tunnel Tree** is close by, and the favored spot for 'I visited the tall forest photos.' Incredibly, this tree continues to survive, even though its huge portal was hacked out back in 1895. The more famous **Wawona Tunnel Tree**, however, fell over in a heap in 1969 – its 10ft-high

hole gouged from a fire scar in 1881. Other notable specimens include the **Telescope Tree** and the **Clothespin Tree**. Three miles from the parking lot, the wide-open overlook at **Wawona Point** (6810ft) takes in the entire area. It's about a mile round-trip from the Wawona Tunnel Tree.

Depending on your energy level, you could spend half an hour or a few hours exploring the forest. Between the parking lot and the Wawona Tunnel Tree in the upper grove, the elevation gain is about 1000ft, but the trail is gentle. The upper grove is also home to the **Mariposa Grove Museum** (Map p108; ⊙ 10am-4pm May-Sep), a small building further dwarfed by the scale of the surrounding trees. The museum has exhibits on sequoia ecology.

You can also explore the grove on a one-hour guided tour aboard a noisy open-air **tram** (☎ 209-375-1621; adult/child/senior/ $16/11/14; ☎ Jun-Oct) that leaves from the parking lot.

BIG OAK FLAT ROAD & TIOGA ROAD

Those arriving on Hwy 120 first encounter this section of the park. While not the most spectacular part of Yosemite, it has a steady flow of visitors. Though many visitors just pass through, the campgrounds at Hodgdon Meadow and Crane Flat keep the area humming with people.

Big Oak Flat Rd was the second route into the park, completed in 1874, just a month after Coulterville Rd. Both were toll roads. Today, Big Oak Flat Rd follows a modified route into the Valley, though a portion of the old road remains open to cyclists and hikers headed for Tuolumne Grove. In winter the road is popular with cross-country skiers.

ORIENTATION & INFORMATION

Going east on Big Oak Flat Rd (Hwy 120) past the Big Oak Flat Entrance, you'll find the **Big Oak Flat Information Station** (Map p110; ☎ 209-379-1899; ⊙ 8am-4:30pm Apr-Oct, to 5pm midsummer). It serves as a mini-visitor center, with a good variety of books, maps and postcards for sale. The staff can answer questions and there is a courtesy phone inside to check available concessionaire-run lodging inside the park. In the same office is the **wilderness permit desk** (⊙ 8am-5pm Jun-Oct), which issues permits and doles out bear boxes ($5).

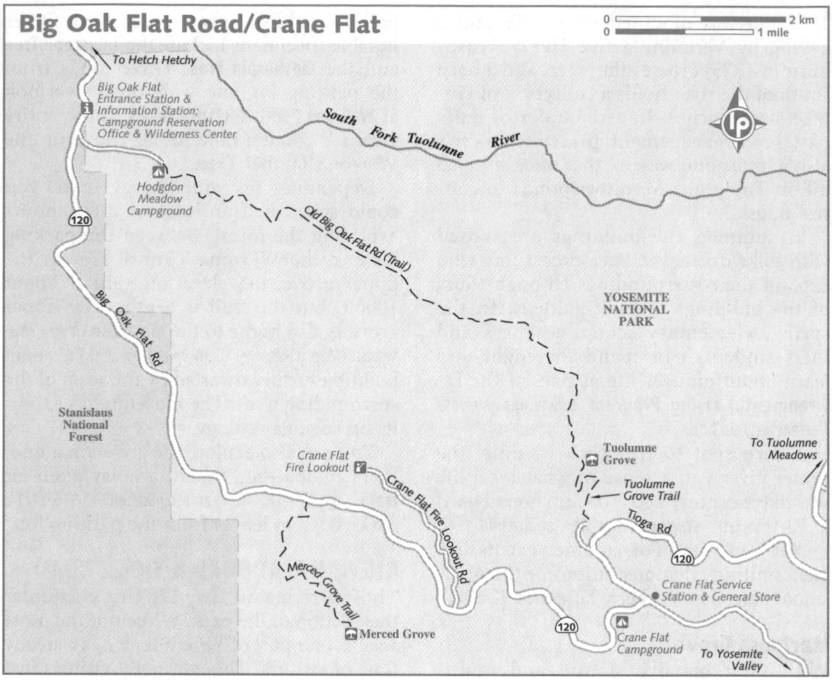

Next door to the information station, the staff at the small **Campground Reservation Office** (Map p110; ☎ 209-379-2123; ⏰ 8am-5pm summer, closed mid-Oct–Apr) offers advice on camping options and posts information on site availability at the first-come, first-served campgrounds at Tamarack, Yosemite Creek, Porcupine Flat and White Wolf, though they don't assign sites. They can also let you know if any reserved spaces at Hodgdon Meadow or Crane Flat campgrounds open up. Come in by 8am to put your name on the list for reserved sites that open up; the staff begin distributing them at 10:30am.

From the entrance station, Big Oak Flat Rd descends southeast into the Valley, passing through several tunnels that offer great overlooks of the Merced River Canyon.

At Crane Flat junction, the **Crane Flat Service Station & General Store** (Map p110; ⏰ 8am-8pm summer, 9am-5pm winter) sells firewood, ice, beer and a smattering of groceries and last-minute camping supplies. Perhaps most importantly, it also has decent fresh coffee. Hurrah! The gas station operates 24 hours year-round with a credit card, and there's a handy pay phone outside.

Going north, Tioga Rd (Hwy 120 East) rises from 6200ft at Crane Flat to 9945ft at Tioga Pass. Because of the high elevation, snow closes the road (and everything along it) in winter; the road's generally plowed and open from late May or mid-June to mid-November. Exact dates are impossible to predetermine, so always call ahead. From the Crane Flat junction until Tenaya Lake, there are few visitor services.

As Tioga Rd heads east toward Tuolumne Meadows, it passes four developed campgrounds. Some 15 miles northeast of Crane Flat is White Wolf, with a small lodge boasting a dining hall, tent cabins and a tiny store that sells mostly snacks and drinks. White Wolf sits on a short spur road a mile north of Tioga Rd.

During summer the Tuolumne Meadows Tour & Hikers' Bus (p96) is an excellent transportation option for one-way hikes that depart from Tioga Rd.

Crane Flat

Throngs of sandhill cranes once rested here as they crisscrossed the Sierra Nevada, and the birds gave the meadow (and surrounding area) its name. About 4 miles east of the entrance station is the road to the Merced Grove (see p121), a seldom-visited giant sequoia grove.

It's easy to miss the turnoff for the **Crane Flat Fire Lookout** (Map p110), so keep your eyes peeled to the north between Crane Flat campground and the Merced Grove parking area. At the top of a 1.5-mile spur road (RVs and trailers should not attempt the climb), a short walk from the parking area leads to the lookout, offering fantastic 360-degree views of the park, including the jagged peaks of the Clark Range to the south and (on cloudless days) the San Joaquin Valley to the west. The historic 1931 building is open to the public and contains an Osborne Firefinder, the circular map and plotting device used to pinpoint fires. The adjacent building houses the park's crack search and rescue and fire crews, and a working heliport sits a bit lower down.

Along Tioga Road

The only road that bisects the park is Tioga Rd (Map p112), a 56-mile scenic highway that runs between Crane Flat in the west (starting from Crane Flat junction) and Hwy 395 at Lee Vining, about 12 miles east of Tioga Pass, the park's easternmost gate. Along the way it traverses a superb High Sierra landscape. Be prepared to pull over regularly to gawk at sights such as glorious Tenaya Lake, mighty Clouds Rest and Half Dome from Olmsted Point.

Initially called the Great Sierra Wagon Rd, the road was built by the Great Sierra Consolidated Silver Company in 1882–83 to supply a mine at Bennettville near Tioga Pass. Ironically, no significant silver was ever found, and the mine closed soon after the road was completed. Tioga Rd was realigned and modernized in 1961. Only a few sections of the original roadbed remain, including the rough, 4.5-mile stretch that leads to Yosemite Creek Campground. Head down this narrow, tortuous road for a glimpse of how much more treacherous park roads used to be – and not even that long ago. You'll return to Tioga Rd

with newfound respect for this engineering marvel.

A half-mile from Crane Flat (going east on Tioga Rd toward Tuolumne Meadows) is the turnoff for Tuolumne Grove (see p121), a small grove containing two dozen mature giant sequoias.

The honey-hit-the-brakes viewpoint is **Olmsted Point** (Map p112). A lunar landscape of glaciated granite, it offers a stunning view down Tenaya Canyon to the backside of Half Dome. Midway between the May Lake turnoff and Tenaya Lake, the point was named for Frederick Law Olmsted (1822–1903), who was appointed chairman of the first Board of Commissioners to manage the newly established Yosemite Grant in 1864. Olmsted also helped to design Central Park in New York City and did some landscaping for the University of California and Stanford University. To experience an even better view, and without the company of your awestruck compatriots, stroll a quarter-mile down to the overlook, where you can get past the tree cover and see even deeper into the canyon.

Looming over the canyon's eastern side is 9926ft **Clouds Rest**, a massive mountain comprising the largest exposed chunk of granite in Yosemite. As its name implies, clouds often settle atop the peak. Rising 4500ft above Tenaya Creek, it makes a strenuous but rewarding day hike (see p129).

Just east of Olmsted Point, **Tenaya Lake** (8150ft; Map p112) takes its name from Chief Tenaya, the Ahwahneechee chief who aided white soldiers, only to be driven from the land by white militias in the early 1850s. Tenaya allegedly protested use of his name, pointing out that the lake already had a name – Pywiack, or 'Lake of Shining Rocks,' for the polished granite that surrounds it. The lake's shiny blue surface looks absolutely stunning framed by thick stands of pine and a series of smooth granite cliffs and domes. Dominating its north side is **Polly Dome** (9806ft). The face nearest the lake is known as **Stately Pleasure Dome**, a popular spot with climbers – you may see them working their way up from the lake. Sloping up from the lake's south shore are Tenaya Peak and Tresidder Peak.

For information on Tioga Pass and the eastern stretch of Tioga Rd, see p195.

Along Tioga Road

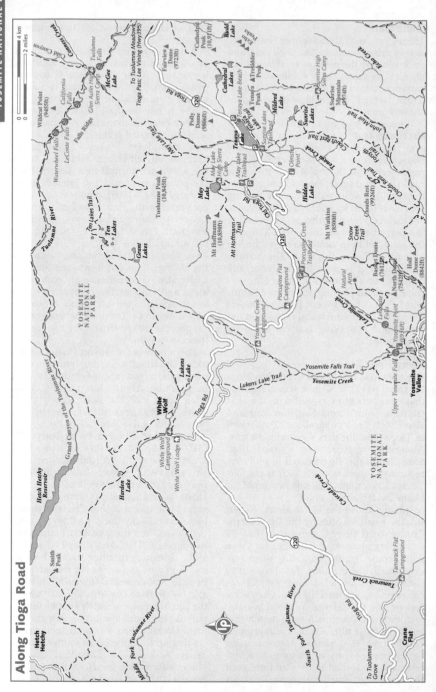

TUOLUMNE MEADOWS

Arriving at Tuolumne (*twol*-uh-me) Meadows after the drive up from the Valley is like stepping into another world, even though the two areas are only about 55 miles apart. Instead of being surrounded by waterfalls and sheer granite walls, you emerge in a subalpine wonderland marked by jagged peaks, smooth granite domes, brilliant blue lakes and the meadows' lush grasses and wildflowers. The flowers, which peak in July, are truly a highlight of any visit to Yosemite.

Flowing from the Sierra Crest, the Lyell and Dana Forks of the Tuolumne River – not to mention creeks such as Budd, Unicorn and Delaney – all converge at Tuolumne Meadows (8600ft elevation). At 2.5 miles long, the main flat cradles the Sierra's largest subalpine meadow. The surrounding peaks and domes make Tuolumne a paradise for climbers and hikers, with trails stretching in all directions.

Lying deep in the high country of the Sierra, the Tuolumne Meadows region enjoys a brief but glorious summer and, depending on weather conditions, is only accessible roughly between June and November. Despite the short season, Tuolumne is far quieter than the Valley, although the area around the store, campground and visitor center can get crowded, especially on midsummer weekends. Many hiking trails, such as Dog Lake, are also well traveled, but with a little effort you'll quickly find solitude.

ORIENTATION

Tuolumne Meadows sits along Tioga Rd (Hwy 120) west of the park's Tioga Pass Entrance. Limited parking is available for hikers and meadow meanderers in pullouts along Tioga Rd (or you can take the shuttle bus). You'll find larger parking lots near Lembert Dome, the visitor center and the wilderness center.

INFORMATION

Temperatures in Tuolumne Meadows and the surrounding high country are 15°F to 20°F cooler than in Yosemite Valley, a benefit for hikers and anyone else who struggles in the heat. At the same time, nights are much chillier up here, so pack warm clothes. And remember, snow can fall here in any month of the year, though typically no later than June and no earlier than September.

At the **Tuolumne Meadows Visitor Center** (Map p114; ☎ 209-372-0263; ☼ 9am-6pm Jul-Aug, to 5pm spring & fall), about a mile west of the campground, rangers answer questions, sell books and hiking maps, and have helpful handouts describing local trails. There are a few good displays that explain common glacial features. Especially handy is the wildflower display, which will help you identify what you see on your hikes. For further information about wildflowers, see p73.

The **Wilderness Center** (Map p114; ☼ 7:30am-6pm midsummer, 8am-5pm late spring & early fall) is the place to go for wilderness permits and trail information. Since Tuolumne's mountains, lakes and trails are such a draw for backpackers, it's often a busy spot. It stocks a small selection of books and maps, and offers current trail conditions. The center sits on the south side of Tioga Rd just east of Lembert Dome, on the spur road leading to Tuolumne Meadows Lodge.

The Tuolumne Meadows Store (see p170) stocks groceries and supplies and has a post office.

The **Tuolumne Meadows Sport Shop** (Map p114; ☼ 9am-5pm mid-Jun–mid-Jul, 8am-6pm mid-Jul–Sep), next door at the gas station, sells a variety of climbing gear, some backpacking supplies, maps, dehydrated food and bear-resistant food containers.

The Main Meadow

Stretching nearly 3 miles from Pothole Dome in the west to Lembert Dome in the east, Tuolumne's main meadow is a beautiful sight to behold, especially during sunset, when golden light ripples across the green grass and lashes up the sides of distant peaks into the still blue sky. Grab a fishing pole and dip into the gently rolling **Tuolumne River** as the sunlight drifts away, or just find a quiet spot to sit and stare at the landscape as the mood shifts and the colors shimmer.

The meadow is a perfect place for quiet contemplation, but there's actually a lot of activity going on here. Blanketed in snow for most of the year, the meadow explodes to life in summer, when the wildflowers, taking full advantage of the short growing season, fill the grassy expanse with color. For an explanation of what's happening beneath the meadow's deceptively still surface, check out the interpretive signs that line the dirt road between the stables and Soda Springs.

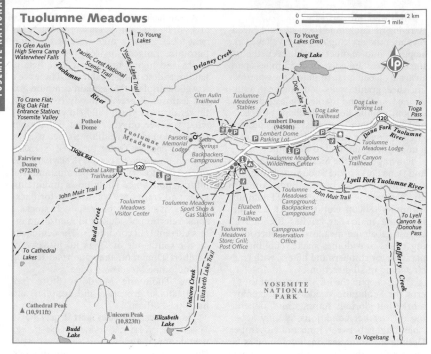

Pothole Dome

Pothole Dome marks the west end of Tuolumne Meadows. It's small by Yosemite standards, but the short, 200ft climb to the top offers great views of the meadows and surrounding peaks – especially, of course, at sunset. Park along Tioga Rd, then follow the trail around the dome's west side and up to its modest summit. It's a fairly quick trip and well worth the effort.

Lembert Dome

Prominently marking the eastern end of the main meadow, Lembert Dome (Map p114) towers about 800ft above the Tuolumne River. Its summit, which chalks in at 9450ft above sea level, is easily one of the finest places to watch the sunset in Yosemite. Its steep western face is a de facto granite playground for everyone from kids (who stick around the gently sloping bottom) to climbers (who rope up and head to the top). Nonclimbers can reach the summit by hiking up the backside (see p131). The dome was named for 19th-century shepherd Jean-Baptiste Lembert, who homesteaded in Tuolumne Meadows.

Soda Springs & Parsons Memorial Lodge

Above the northern shore of the Tuolumne River, carbonated mineral water burbles silently out of Soda Springs (Map p114), a small natural spring that turns its surroundings into a cluster of mineral-crusted, rust-red puddles. People (and animals) used to drink the stuff, though the park service now discourages the practice due to possible surface contamination – no big deal as it's not exactly an appealing method for quenching your thirst anyway.

Nearby stands Parsons Memorial Lodge (Map p114), a simple but beautifully rugged cabin built in 1915 from local granite. It initially served as a Sierra Club meeting room and was named for Edward Taylor Parsons (1861–1914), an adventurer and active Sierra Club member who helped found the club's outings program. Today, it opens as a shelter during thunderstorms (there's a huge fireplace inside), as well as for special events, ranger talks and other programs. See *Yosemite Today* for the current schedule. Above the lodge sits the old **McCauley Cabin**, now closed to the public.

The springs and lodge are a short, pleasant walk across the flat middle of the meadow. There are two approaches, both about 0.5 miles long. The first starts opposite the visitor center on Tioga Rd. The other begins in the Lembert Dome parking area.

Cathedral Range

Dominating the views to the south of Tuolumne Meadows, the jagged Cathedral Range runs roughly northwest from the Sierra Crest, marking the divide between the Tuolumne and Merced Rivers. Its granite pinnacles are immediately striking, in particular **Cathedral Peak** (10,911ft), visible from numerous spots in the region, including along Tioga Rd. At certain angles, its summit appears to be a near-perfect pinpoint, though in reality it's a craggy, double-pronged affair. Other mountains in the range include Tresidder Peak, Echo Peaks, the Matthes Crest and Unicorn Peak (10,823ft), another standout with a horn-shaped protuberance, just east of Cathedral Peak. Soda Springs offers a particularly good vantage point for viewing the range,

ROUND THE CAMPFIRE

Quite frankly, Soda Springs is a bit of a snoozer. But with a little imagination, you can conjure up the image of an historic campfire that, in 1889, crackled beneath a star-dusted sky beside this bubbling little mineral swamp. Around that fire sat two men, naturalist John Muir and writer Robert Underwood Johnson, discussing their visions of preserving the unique chunk of the Sierra Nevada that lay before them. Below them, Tuolumne Meadows bore the scars of sheep grazing, fueling their desires to keep the area as pristine as Muir had found it when he first traveled through here as a shepherd, years before. In 1890 Johnson published two articles in *Century Magazine* (he was the magazine's associate editor), in which Muir extolled the importance of preserving Yosemite for all time. The articles led to the creation of Yosemite National Park. Thank the stars for campfires!

For more on Muir, see the boxed text, p65.

as does the trail up to Young Lakes (p144). The Cathedral Lakes hike (p132) is the classic must-do hike into the range itself.

Tioga Pass

East of Tuolumne Meadows, Tioga Rd (Hwy 120) climbs steadily toward Tioga Pass (Map p196), which at 9945ft is the highest auto route over the Sierra. The short ride by car or free shuttle bus from Tuolumne Meadows takes you across dramatic, wide open spaces – a stretch of stark, windswept countryside near the timberline. You'll notice a temperature drop and, most likely, widespread patches of snow.

Tioga Rd parallels the Dana Fork of the Tuolumne River, then turns north, where it borders the beautiful Dana Meadows all the way to Tioga Pass. To the east you'll see great views of Mt Gibbs (12,764ft) and 13,053ft Mt Dana, the park's second-highest peak after Mt Lyell (13,114ft).

For descriptions of the spectacular area beyond Tioga Pass, see p195.

HETCH HETCHY

No developed part of the park feels as removed from the rest of the park as Hetch Hetchy. Despite the fact that 'Hetchy's' soaring waterfalls, granite domes and sheer cliffs rival its more glamorous counterparts in Yosemite Valley, Hetch Hetchy receives but a fraction of the visitors that the Valley does. This is mainly because Hetch Hetchy Valley is filled with water – the Hetch Hetchy Reservoir – and because, save for a couple of drinking fountains, a parking lot and a backpacker campground, there are practically no visitors services. Despite the former, and because of the latter, Hetch Hetchy is a magical place, and is definitely worth the detour north from the much busier Big Oak Flat Entrance.

Hetch Hetchy Valley was filled with water only after a long political and environmental battle that lasted a dozen years during the early 20th century. Despite the best efforts of John Muir, who led the fight against it, the US Congress approved the 1913 *Raker Act,* which allowed the city of San Francisco to construct O'Shaughnessy Dam in the Hetch Hetchy Valley. This blocked the Tuolumne River and created Hetch Hetchy Reservoir. Muir's spirit was crushed, and he died a year later, supposedly of a broken heart.

YOSEMITE NATIONAL PARK

Hetch Hetchy

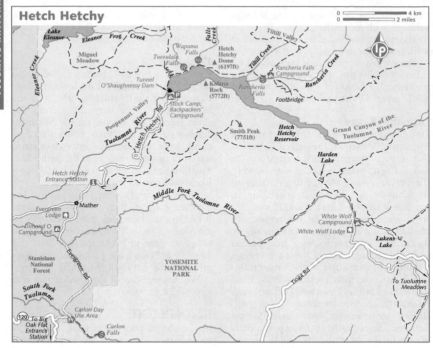

Today, the reservoir and dam supply water and hydroelectric power to much of the Bay Area, including Silicon Valley. When you turn on a tap in San Francisco, out pours Tuolumne River water from the Hetch Hetchy Reservoir. Some politicians and environmentalists (particularly the Sierra Club) still argue for pulling the cork and draining the valley. And who knows? Stranger things have happened in California.

There's one good thing you can say about the dam: by filling in the valley, it has prevented the overdevelopment that plagues Yosemite Valley. Hetch Hetchy remains a lovely, quiet spot – good for a quick day trip or as a jumping-off point for a serious backcountry experience.

Its low elevation makes Hetch Hetchy an especially suitable hiking destination in spring and fall, when much of the high country is still blanketed by ice and snow. In summer, however, it can be very hot and dry – bring a hat, sunscreen and plenty of water. Tueeulala and Wapama Falls (see p135) are best in spring. The former dries up by late summer.

ORIENTATION & INFORMATION
The 8-mile-long Hetch Hetchy Reservoir stretches behind O'Shaughnessy Dam, the site of the area's trailheads, parking area and backpackers' campground (available only to those with a valid wilderness permit).

Hetch Hetchy is a 40-mile drive from Yosemite Valley. From the park's Big Oak Flat Entrance, drive a mile or two west on Hwy 120 and look for the signed turnoff to Hetch Hetchy along Evergreen Rd; turn right (north), drive 8 miles to Camp Mather and turn right (east) on Hetch Hetchy Rd. The Hetch Hetchy Entrance Station is just a mile beyond the junction; here backpackers can register for a free wilderness permit.

From the entrance, it's about 9 miles to the parking lot beside O'Shaughnessy Dam. About 5.7 miles past the entrance, at roadside marker H3, you'll pass an overlook of the reservoir to the east and lovely Poopenaut Valley some 1200ft below.

The road to Hetch Hetchy is only open during daylight hours – approximately 7am to 9pm in summer, 7am to 7pm in spring and fall, and 8am to 5pm in winter. Hours vary year to year and season to season; they're posted on a sign at the Evergreen Rd turnoff. The gate is locked at night, and the road may close in winter due to heavy snows (carry chains). Vehicles over 25ft are not permitted on the narrow, winding road.

Don't expect any visitor services at Hetch Hetchy. The closest convenience supplies and lodging are at Evergreen Lodge, just south of Mather (p167).

HIKING

There's no better way – and often no other way – to see Yosemite than by hiking into it. It's impossible to say one area of the park is better for hiking than another. Really, it depends on the hiker's ability and interests and the time of year. For example, the vast wilderness surrounding Tuolumne Meadows is a hikers' mecca, but it's accessible only when Tioga Rd is open (usually late May through mid-November).

Hikes along Tioga Rd are likewise only accessible when the road is open, but when it is, the walking is phenomenal. There are easy hikes and day hikes to splendid lakes – including Harden, Lukens and May Lakes – all sans the heat and crowds of the Valley.

Offering what is likely the park's finest view, Glacier Point is also a good jumping-off point for hikes into the backcountry to the south. The area is also popular for the Valley rim walks along the Pohono Trail.

Yosemite Valley is accessible year-round, but in the height of summer the heat can be brutal, and the trails get crowded. Spring is a great time for hiking in the Valley as well as at Hetch Hetchy, another low-elevation area that experiences harsh summer heat. Temperatures in Wawona are similar.

If you're a hiker who hates return ascents, skip the sequoia groves in the Crane Flat area. Those in Mariposa and Wawona are more impressive anyway.

LEVELS OF DIFFICULTY

Yosemite Valley offers hikes for all levels. Those seeking gentle strolls can visit Mirror Lake and wander the Valley Loop trails as far as they wish. The rest of the Valley's trails involve significant elevation gains. At the far end of the spectrum is the

trek to the summit of Half Dome, perhaps the single most difficult (and popular) day hike in the entire park. Although no 'easy' hikes are included for Tuolumne Meadows, you can stroll around the meadow itself for hours without gaining 2ft in elevation. Just remember that the altitude can make you short of breath before you become acclimated (see p269). Wawona and the Tioga Rd have some good gentle strolls as well.

For more how we rate the hikes, see the boxed text, p39. For information on the John Muir and Pacific Crest Trails, see p41.

EASY HIKES

Although we've featured no easy hikes in Tuolumne Meadows or Hetch Hetchy (at least as we define the term), there's plenty of strolling to do. Meadow pathways in Tuolumne are great for easy walks, and the O'Shaughnessy Dam in Hetchy is well worth a stroll.

Yosemite Valley

Many of Yosemite's easiest hikes – some might call them strolls – are along the mostly flat floor of Yosemite Valley. It's a lovely place wander, especially in the evenings, when the day-trippers are gone and Half Dome glows against the sunset. See the Maps p93 and pp90–1.

GETTING AWAY FROM IT ALL

If you've come to Yosemite looking for peace and solitude, there are plenty of places to find it. Sure, the park gets packed every summer, but with a little effort you can find near-empty trails, quiet riverside hangouts and other hideaways tucked throughout the park. If solitude is a priority, avoid summer (especially August weekends). Winter and spring are both excellent times to visit. A good rule is to hit the trail just after sunrise or late in the day, when the crowds are either sleeping or running off to supper. Yosemite Valley is where most visitors throng, and roads, campgrounds and popular trails (such as that to Vernal Fall) are predictably packed. Even in summer, though, you may find peace and quiet along the Yosemite Valley Loop trails (see p118), a trail few Valley visitors seem to know about.

YOSEMITE NATIONAL PARK

YOSEMITE VALLEY LOOPS

Duration varies
Distance varies
Difficulty easy; elevation change +330ft
Start/Finish varies
Nearest Town/Facilities Yosemite Village
Transport YARTS buses
Summary Generally flat and paved, these easy-to-follow trails are a great way to acquaint yourself with Yosemite Valley and its many historic sites. Plaques along the way explain the valley's natural and human history, too.

Whether you want to plot a route from your campsite to the nearest hot shower, or take in the views from the meadows and bridges around the valley floor, the vaguely defined loop trails are an undeniably great way to get to know Yosemite Valley. Parts are even wheelchair- and stroller-friendly, and they connect the valley's most important historic and natural features. In some places the trail joins the road, in other places it peters out only to reappear later. Generally, it follows alongside Northside and Southside Drives, and it's nearly impossible to get lost.

For the ambitious, a well-marked path leads up and down the entire Valley, but it's easily broken into segments, making the journey manageable for just about any level of hiker.

You can walk a 2.6-mile loop around the eastern end of the Valley by starting at **Curry Village**. From here, head east along the edge of the day-use parking area, with the tent cabins on your right. When you hit the shuttle road, turn right and follow the road into and through the trailhead parking area. Southeast of the parking lot, two trails lead to **Happy Isles**: one skirts the shuttle road, and another leads into the trees and across a delicate meadow area known as The Fen. After visiting the Nature Center at Happy Isles (p104), cross the Merced River and follow the trail alongside the road, veering left when you can to stay along the banks of the river. Just before you reach the **stables**, head left (southwest) on the road across the river, past the entrances to Lower and Upper Pines Campgrounds. Then look for the sign pointing to Curry Village.

Further removed from the Valley's central commercial district, the 6.5-mile loop

on the west end of the Valley passes good swimming spots on the Merced and offers fabulous views of El Capitan and Bridalveil Fall. The trail basically follows Northside and Southside Drs between the base of El Capitan and **Pohono Bridge**, the westernmost bridge over the Merced River.

MIRROR LAKE & TENAYA CANYON LOOP

Duration 1–2 hours
Distance 4.8-mile round-trip
Difficulty easy; elevation change +100ft
Start/Finish Mirror Lake junction
Nearest Town/Facilities North Pines Campground
Transport YARTS shuttle stop 17
Summary Shallow Mirror Lake, reflecting Mt Watkins and Half Dome on its tranquil surface, is one of the valley's most photographed sites. Further northeast, Tenaya Canyon offers one of the quietest corners of Yosemite Valley.

Formed when a rockfall dammed a section of Tenaya Creek, Mirror Lake has been slowly reverting to 'Mirror Meadow' ever since the park service stopped dredging it in 1971. Only folks who visit in spring and early summer get the splendid sight that Mirror Lake is named for. By midsummer, it's just Tenaya Creek, and by fall, the creek is sometimes dried up altogether. Spring is also a marvelous time to visit for other reasons: the dogwoods are in full bloom and Tenaya Creek becomes a lively torrent as you venture further up the canyon. The Ahwahneechee called Mirror Lake Ahwiyah, meaning 'quiet water.'

From the Mirror Lake Trailhead, near shuttle stop 17, follow the Mirror Lake road to **Tenaya Bridge**. Cross Tenaya Creek and follow the partially paved trail 0.9 miles to **Mirror Lake**, where interpretive signs explain the area's natural history. From here you can return to the shuttle stop along the Mirror Lake road (for the sake of looping), or journey up Tenaya Canyon for a little solitude.

To head partway up **Tenaya Canyon**, continue along the trail that heads up the north (left) side of Tenaya Creek. After about 1.2 miles you'll reach a footbridge over the creek, which allows you to return to Mirror Lake on the opposite side of Tenaya Creek. The Tenaya Canyon loop adds about 3 miles to the shorter Mirror Lake loop, and there are plenty of good spots to picnic along Tenaya Creek.

When you cross the footbridge, you'll see an unmarked trail leading further up Tenaya Canyon. This potentially dangerous trail is officially off-limits due to loose talus and other hazards, and leads (after some technical scrambles) to wild Tenaya Falls. In spring, when Tenaya Creek is full, heading even partway up this trail gives you the impression that the trees themselves are bursting with water. It's a wild area, to say the least.

Glacier Point & Badger Pass

If you're looking for bird's-eye views of Yosemite Valley, then several Glacier Point Rd hikes will fit the bill perfectly. Dewey Point, Taft Point and the Sentinel Dome hikes all lead to spectacular overlooks of Yosemite Valley (see Map p105). The latter offers perhaps the widest, finest view of all, and the hike to its summit takes a mere half-hour. Some of the hikes link up with other top-notch trails, such as the Four-Mile Trail to Glacier Point (p124) and the trail from Wawona Tunnel to Inspiration Point (the westernmost leg of the Pohono Trail; p126).

MCGURK MEADOW

Duration 1 hour
Distance 1.6-mile round-trip
Difficulty easy; elevation change +150ft
Start/Finish McGurk Meadow Trailhead
Nearest Town/Facilities Bridalveil Creek campground, 1 mile
Transport private
Summary An effortless and relaxing walk through grassy wildflower meadows, this is a nice choice for families or those who want an easier, less-crowded hike.

For a short stroll with solitude and tranquility, lush, open McGurk Meadow fits the bill. Park at a pullout along Glacier Point Rd just west of the Bridalveil Creek campground entrance; the posted trailhead is about 100yd west of the parking area.

Shaded by lodgepole pines, a level and sun-dappled path meanders through quiet forest. After about a mile, a historic one-room **log cabin** appears on the left. Kids will love playing in and around this former seasonal shelter for cattle ranchers, and adults will need to double over to enter the low, half-scale doorway.

The meadow sits across a small footbridge just beyond the cabin, and its wildflowers peak in July, erupting in splashes of red, white and yellow. If you wish to continue on, another 3.2 miles takes you to **Dewey Point** and big, wide views down into the Valley.

TAFT POINT & THE FISSURES

Duration 1 hour
Distance 2.2-mile round-trip
Difficulty easy; elevation change +250ft
Start/Finish Sentinel Dome/Taft Point Trailhead
Nearest Town/Facilities water and restrooms, Glacier Point, 2.4 miles
Transport private
Summary A hike over easy terrain leads to a spectacular overlook and drop-off at the edge of a sheer 3000ft cliff. Sizeable boulders fill a series of enormous granite cracks.

Park in the Sentinel Dome/Taft Point lot on the north side of Glacier Point Rd, about 13 miles from Chinquapin. Note that the main parking area is not that large and often fills up by midmorning; it is less packed in the afternoons.

Taft Point (7503ft) is a fantastic, hair-raising viewpoint at the edge of a sheer 3000ft cliff, with impressive views of El Capitan and Yosemite Valley. On the same promontory are the Fissures, a series of deep, narrow cracks in the granite, many with large boulders wedged inside. Choose your steps carefully, especially when accompanying small children.

After a gentle descent through pleasant forest, you'll emerge on an open, rocky slope dotted with hardy wind-shaped trees. On your right are the **Fissures**, which drop hundreds of feet along the edge of **Profile Cliff**. Across Yosemite Valley, you'll see the Three Brothers, with similar yet longer cracks in the rock.

Ahead is Taft Point, guarded only by a short metal railing. Unless you have a profound fear of heights, approach and peer over the edge – the sheer drop is mind-boggling. Look west through binoculars to spot climbers on the southeast face and nose of El Capitan. After soaking up the views, which include a close-up look at Cathedral Spires, return on a gentle uphill climb to the parking lot.

SENTINEL DOME

Duration 1 hour
Distance 2.2-mile round-trip
Difficulty easy–moderate; change +370ft
Start/Finish Sentinel Dome/Taft Point Trailhead
Nearest Town/Facilities water and restrooms at Glacier Point, 2.4 miles
Transport private
Summary The easiest trail up one of the park's fabled granite domes will reward you with sprawling panoramic vistas of high peaks and falls. Ravaged and surreal trees strain to grow against the wind.

The hike to **Sentinel's summit** (8122ft) is the shortest and easiest trail up one of Yosemite's granite domes. For those unable to visit Half Dome's summit, Sentinel offers an equally outstanding 360-degree perspective of Yosemite's wonders. A visit at sunrise, sunset or during a full moon is spectacular. You can also combine a trip up Sentinel Dome with a walk to Taft Point and the Fissures, an equidistant hike from the same trailhead, or combine the two to form a loop via the solitary **Pohono Trail**.

Park in the same lot as the hike for Taft Point and the Fissures. From the roadside parking lot, take the trail's gently rising right fork. After 20 minutes, it heads northwest across open granite slabs to the dome's base. Skirt the base to an old service road, which leads to the dome's northeast shoulder. From here, head up the gentle granite slope to the top (wear good hiking shoes).

The gnarled, bleached bones of a windbeaten **Jeffrey pine** once crowned the top. The photogenic tree died in a drought in the late 1970s, but caused heartbreak to many when it finally fell in 2003.

From the top, the views take in almost the entire park. To the west are Cathedral Rocks and El Capitan, while to the north you'll spot Yosemite Falls and, in the distance, Mt Hoffmann. North Dome, Basket Dome and Mt Watkins line the valley's northeast side, and Clouds Rest and Half Dome rise dramatically above Tenaya Canyon. In the distance, above Nevada Fall, you'll see the notable peaks of the Cathedral and Ritter Ranges. To the east lie Mt Starr King and the peaks of the Clark Range.

Wawona

Mariposa Grove features quite a few lovely hiking trails, and you could easily spend a half-day or more crisscrossing its 250 acres. A trail connects the grove with Wawona, where an easy loop circles Wawona Meadow and a more difficult trail leads to Chilnualna Falls, one of the park's lesser-known waterfalls. From there, long-distance trails head to such remote areas the Buena Vista Crest and the Clark Range. See the Map p108.

WAWONA MEADOW LOOP

Duration 1–1½ hours
Distance 3.5-mile round-trip
Difficulty easy; elevation change +200ft
Start/Finish Wawona Hotel
Nearest Town/Facilities Wawona Hotel and store
Transport private
Summary A relaxed loop on a former stagecoach road, this level hike surveys a pretty meadow, with wildflowers raging in late spring and early summer.

Though you won't huff and puff too much on this gentle, shaded loop around pretty Wawona Meadow, you will have to dodge copious amounts of smelly horse manure plopped and squashed along the entire trail. Horseback riders and stagecoaches use the loop, throwing up lots of dust – another unpleasant element, especially on an already hot summer day.

On the other hand, this short, easy trail is a nice way to spend an hour or two beneath the trees beside the meadow. It's especially lovely in spring, when wildflowers are in bloom. If you're lucky, you might even be alone most of the way – aside from the horses.

From the Wawona Hotel, cross Hwy 41 on a small road through the golf course. The trail starts a short distance down on your left and follows an old dirt road around the meadow perimeter. On the return, you'll cross Hwy 41 again and wind up on the hotel's back lawn. Plunk down in an Adirondack chair and soak up the scene.

MARIPOSA GROVE TO WAWONA

Duration 2–3 hours
Distance 6.5 miles one way
Difficulty easy–moderate; elevation change -2000ft
Start Mariposa Grove
Finish Wawona Hotel
Nearest Town/Facilities Wawona Hotel and store
Transport shuttle
Summary Walk through a woodsy and winding downhill trail, sometimes in the company of horses, on this solitary alternative to the shuttle-bus route from Mariposa Grove.

Take the free shuttle bus up to the grove to enjoy this downhill one-way hike. You can actually do several miles' worth of hiking in Mariposa Grove alone, but this trail is a great way to escape the crushing crowds and recover some peace of mind on your way back to Wawona. The trail leaves from the outer loop on the west side of the grove; follow signs from either the museum (if you're in the upper grove) or the parking lot.

Crane Flat & Tioga Road

Two of the area's main hikes lead to groves of giant sequoias (see Map p110). Though neither grove is as magnificent as Wawona's Mariposa Grove, the crowds are mercifully thinner.

Day hikes and backcountry excursions are plentiful in Yosemite's subalpine wilderness, which stretches north and south from either side of Tioga Rd. Like Tuolumne Meadows further east, this truly is a hikers' paradise. Several trails from the south side of the road lead to Yosemite Valley, and if you take the hikers' bus up from the Valley, they're more or less downhill all the way – an exquisite and rare treat (see Map p112).

TUOLUMNE GROVE

Duration 1.5 hours
Distance 2-mile round-trip
Difficulty easy–moderate; elevation change +500ft
Start/Finish Tuolumne Grove Trailhead
Nearest Town/Facilities Crane Flat gas station and store, 0.5 miles
Transport private
Summary Descend into Yosemite's second-most-visited grove of giant sequoias, though the walk back up is a bit of a haul. There's even a tree you can walk through.

You can reach this moderately sized grove of sequoias via a short, steep hike down a section of the Old Big Oak Flat Rd (closed to cars). Follow the road and a few switchbacks to the first trees, then meander through the grove and along an interpretive nature trail. The most popular attraction is the **Tunnel Tree** (or 'Dead Giant'), already a stump when a tunnel was cut into it in 1878. Another interesting specimen is the **Leaning Towering Tree**. It fell over in 1983, and now looks like a huge set of cracked vertebrae. At one end, its roots shoot out like flares, and the hollowed-out core makes a fun tunnel for kids to explore.

The only bummer about this hike is the steady uphill climb back to the parking area. When it's hot, you'll be hurting – or panting at the very least. It's not awful though, and hikers of any age should be able to handle it given time and patience.

MERCED GROVE

Duration 1½–2 hours
Distance 3-mile round-trip
Difficulty easy–moderate; elevation change +600ft
Start/Finish Merced Grove Trailhead
Nearest Town/Facilities Crane Flat gas station, 4 miles
Transport private
Summary Another hike leading down to a beautiful sequoia grove, with crowds rarely present to break the solitude. The walk follows a dirt road to a dense cluster of giant trees.

The smallest sequoia grove in the park, Merced is also the quietest, thanks in part to its distance from major park sights. If you seek solitude amid the sequoias, this is for you. You'll start from a small parking lot along Big Oak Flat Rd midway between Crane Flat and the Big Oak Flat gate. The trail follows a dirt road (closed to cars), which remains flat for the first half-mile before dipping downhill into the grove. A handful of the trees surround a small log cabin. Reserve your energy for the hike out.

LUKENS LAKE

Duration 1 hour
Distance 1.6-mile round-trip
Difficulty easy; elevation change +200ft
Start/Finish Lukens Lake Trailhead
Nearest Town/Facilities food, water and restrooms at White Wolf, 3.2 miles
Transport private
Summary A gentle, quick jaunt to a wildflower meadow and a peaceful lake edged by shaded forest. Even small children can do this walk with ease.

Hike up here early in the morning or late in the afternoon, especially on a weekday, and you just might have the quiet blue lake, green meadow and surrounding sea of colorful wildflowers all to yourself. (Weekends are a different story.) Corn lilies trace the path leading up to the lake, and thousands of orange and black butterflies cluster on the ground in summer. If you hold still and listen, you can hear the low hum of omnipresent bees. Purple and white flowers erupt as you near the lakeshore, forming an exquisitely colored carpet. Revel in the idyllic setting and serenity in the 'golden hour' of early evening light. Even beginners can handle the short jaunt from Tioga Rd.

Start from the marked parking area a couple miles east of the White Wolf turnoff. Cross the road when the traffic's not coming and begin the trail in the soft woods. Climbing steadily, you'll reach a small ridge, then drop down to **Lukens Lake**. The trail follows the north shore to the far (west) end, where you'll find plenty of shady spots to rest, picnic or simply sit in quiet contemplation.

An alternative 2.3-mile trail leads to the lake's west side from White Wolf Lodge (p167).

TENAYA LAKE

Duration 1 hour
Distance 2-mile round-trip
Difficulty easy; elevation change +50ft
Start/Finish east Tenaya Lake parking lot
Nearest Town/Facilities water and restrooms at Tuolumne Meadows Visitor Center, 6 miles
Transport Tuolumne Meadows shuttle bus
Summary A back-and-forth stroll along one of Yosemite's prettiest lakes, with no need to head high into the backcountry to reach it. A long sandy beach tempts you into trying the chilly blue water.

A pleasant stroll, this loop trail skirts the south shore of one of the park's biggest natural lakes.

Begin from the parking lot on the lake's east end, adjacent to the popular sandy beach. Walk south along the beach, and look for the trail amid the trees just ahead. As the path traces the shore, small spurs lead down to the water. Though the shoreline is rocky, there are several nice spots for a picnic. When you reach the west end (and the Sunrise Trailhead), it's best to either wait for the free shuttle bus back to the parking lot or simply return the way you came.

DAY HIKES
Yosemite Valley
Nearly all day hikes from Yosemite Valley require some ascent. The popular Half Dome hike (see p138) is more relaxed as an overnighter. See Maps pp90–1 and p93 .

INSPIRATION POINT

Duration 1½–2½ hours
Distance 2.6-mile round-trip
Difficulty moderate–demanding; elevation change +1000ft
Start/Finish Tunnel View parking lot
Nearest Town/Facilities food, camping and lodging in Yosemite Valley
Transport private
Summary Some of the best vistas in all Yosemite are granted to those who hike this steep trail to this classic viewpoint.

Sure, Tunnel View offers an amazing look into the Valley. But the view is even more impressive along the steep trail to Inspiration Point. Best of all, you'll leave the crowds behind.

Inspiration Point used to be a viewpoint along an old road into Yosemite Valley. The roadbed still exists, but this hike (actually the western end of the Pohono Trail) is now the only way to reach the point. You'll start by climbing a series of switchbacks from the upper **Tunnel View parking lot** (which is on Hwy 41 immediately east of the Wawona Tunnel). Almost immediately the view improves, with fewer trees and no bus tourists to battle for camera positions. Short spur trails lead to open viewpoints.

The climb is steep and steady but, thankfully, fairly short. The view from Inspiration Point itself – a large open area – isn't as spectacular as what you get on the way up, but it's a worthy destination nonetheless, quiet and perfect for a picnic. If you've got the energy, continue up the trail 2.5 miles further to **Stanford Point** and even on to **Crocker Point**. Both offer epic views. The Inspiration Point trail is often doable in winter.

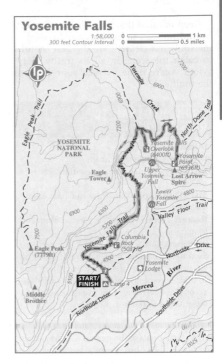

Yosemite Falls

1:58,000
300 feet Contour Interval

YOSEMITE FALLS

Duration 5–6 hours
Distance 6.8-mile round-trip
Difficulty demanding; elevation change +2400ft
Start/Finish Yosemite Falls Trailhead near Camp 4
Nearest Town/Facilities food, camping and lodging in Yosemite Valley
Transport YARTS shuttle stop 7
Summary This classic hike along one of the park's oldest trails leads from the Valley floor to the top of the falls. The stiff ascent (and equivalent descent) make it a real thigh-burning, knee-busting haul.

The heart-stopping views from atop Upper Yosemite Fall will make you quickly forget any pain endured on the hike up. If it seems a bit much, you can always hike just the first mile (and 1000 vertical feet) to **Columbia Rock** (5031ft), a justifiably classic viewpoint.

From the northeastern side of Camp 4, the Yosemite Falls Trail immediately starts in on the four dozen short switchbacks that zigzag up a talus slope through canyon live

oaks. After 0.8 miles, the grade eases as the trail follows more switchbacks east to Columbia Rock. Some people stop here.

In another 0.4 miles, the trail approaches the top of **Lower Yosemite Fall**, where breezes may shower you with a fine, cooling mist. After admiring the view of Upper Yosemite Fall, brace yourself for the numerous switchbacks that run steadily up a rocky cleft to the Valley rim. The falls once ran down this cleft.

The trail tops out 3.2 miles from the trailhead and bends east. At the junction, the trail going straight leads to **Eagle Peak** (7779ft). Turn right at this junction and follow the trail two-tenths of a mile to the brink of Upper Yosemite Fall at the **Yosemite Falls Overlook** (6400ft). The view of the falls is impressive, but views of El Capitan and Half Dome are obscured. For a wider perspective, go the extra 1.6 miles (and nearly 600ft more in elevation gain) to **Yosemite Point** (6936ft), where you'll get incredible views of Half Dome, North Dome, Clouds Rest, Glacier Point, Cathedral Rocks and Lost Arrow.

Keep in mind that the falls are often dry by midsummer, so late May and June (after the snow has cleared) are the best months to catch the scene in all its frothy glory. When you're done, retrace your steps to the trailhead.

FOUR-MILE TRAIL TO GLACIER POINT

Duration 4–8 hours
Distance 9.2-mile round-trip
Difficulty demanding; elevation change +3200ft
Start/Finish Four-Mile Trailhead near Leidig Meadow
Nearest Town/Facilities food, camping and lodging in Yosemite Valley
Transport YARTS shuttle stop 7
Summary Fulfilling day hike from Yosemite Valley that ascends the Valley's southern wall to Glacier Point, the park's most famous view-point. The reward for the grunt is one of the finest vistas in the entire country.

Sure, you can easily get to Glacier Point by car or bus, but there's something supremely rewarding about making the journey on foot. From shuttle stop 7, it's a short walk south along a paved footpath leading across Swinging Bridge to Southside Dr. From here walk parallel to the road a short distance west to the Four-Mile Trailhead.

Today the Four-Mile Trail actually spans closer to 4.6 miles, having been rerouted since it was first completed in 1872. It was originally intended as a toll pathway, at the time being the quickest way into the Valley.

The trail climbs steadily, passing 2000ft **Sentinel Fall** and **Sentinel Rock** (7038ft). At **Union Point**, 3 miles from the trailhead, you'll first catch a glimpse of Half Dome. Continue climbing until the trail levels out for the final leg to Glacier Point. Take in the views and check out that all-important snack stand.

When you're ready, return the way you came. Hardy hikers can turn this into an excellent loop trail (and avoid retracing their steps) by continuing on the Panorama Trail to Nevada Fall, then down to Happy Isles.

VERNAL & NEVADA FALLS

Duration 4–7 hours
Distance 6.5-mile round-trip
Difficulty moderate–demanding; elevation change +1900ft
Start/Finish Vernal & Nevada Falls/John Muir Trailhead near Happy Isles
Nearest Town/Facilities food, camping and lodging in Yosemite Valley
Transport YARTS shuttle stop 16
Summary Affording views that are unmatched anywhere else in the park, this well-trodden partial loop ascends the so-called Giant Staircase: the route of the Merced River as it plunges over Nevada and Vernal Falls.

If you can only do a single day hike in Yosemite – *and it's springtime* – make this the one. Not only are Vernal and Nevada Falls two of Yosemite's most spectacular waterfalls, but Yosemite Falls and Illilouette Fall both make appearances in the distance from select spots on the trail. If you prefer a shorter excursion, stop at the top of Vernal Fall.

There are two ways to hike this loop: up the **Mist Trail** and down the **John Muir Trail** (in a clockwise direction) or vice versa. It's easier on the knees to climb rather than descend the plethora of steep granite steps along the Mist Trail, so it's best to go for the clockwise route. Then you can lollygag along the John Muir Trail – which has astounding views of both falls – on the way down. The granite slabs atop Nevada Fall make for a superb lunch spot (as close to the edge as you want), with the granite dome of **Liberty Cap** towering above.

From the Happy Isles shuttle stop, cross the road bridge over the Merced River, turn right at the trailhead and follow the riverbank upstream. As the trail steepens, watch over your right shoulder for Illilouette Fall (often dry in summer) which peels over a 370ft cliff in the distance. From a lookout, you can gaze west and see Yosemite Falls. After 0.8 miles you arrive at the **Vernal Fall footbridge**, which offers the first view of 317ft Vernal Fall upstream.

Shortly beyond the Vernal Fall footbridge (just past the water fountain and restrooms), you'll reach the junction of the John Muir and Mist Trails. To do the trail clockwise, hang a left and shortly begin the steep 0.3-mile ascent to the top of **Vernal Fall** by way of the Mist Trail's granite steps. If it's springtime, prepare to get drenched in spray – wear some waterproof clothing! – and peer behind you as you near the top to see rainbows in the mist.

Above the falls, the Merced whizzes down a long ramp of granite known as the **Silver Apron** and into the deceptively serene Emerald Pool before plunging over the cliff. No matter how fun the apron looks on a hot day, don't slide down it: underwater currents in Emerald Pool have whipped swimmers over the falls.

From above the apron, it's another 1.3 miles via granite steps and steep switchbacks to the top of the Mist Trail, which meets the John Muir Trail, about 0.2 miles northeast of the falls. From this junction, it's 2.5 miles back to Happy Isles via the Mist Trail or 4 miles via the John Muir Trail.

Shortly after joining the John Muir Trail, you'll cross a **footbridge** (elevation 5907ft) over the Merced. Beneath it, the river whizzes through a chute before plummeting 594ft over the edge of **Nevada Fall**. Nevada Fall is the first of the series of steps in the Giant Staircase, a metaphor that becomes clear when viewed from afar at Glacier Point. Plant yourself on a slab of granite for lunch and views, and be prepared to fend off the ballsy Stellar jays and squirrels that will have your jerky in their jaws in no time, should you let down your guard.

Shortly after leaving Nevada Fall, the John Muir trail offers a fabulous glimpse of Yosemite Falls, passes the Panorama Trail junction and traverses a cliff, offering awesome views of Nevada Fall as it winds down the canyon. Soon you'll reach **Clark Point** and a junction that leads down to the Mist Trail. From here it's just over 2 miles downhill, through Douglas firs and canyon live oaks to Happy Isles.

If you choose to do this hike in summertime, be sure to hit the trail early to avoid the crowds and afternoon heat.

Glacier Point & Badger Pass

Bask in views as you descend from Glacier Point and ogle some of Yosemite's best waterfalls. See Map p105.

PANORAMA TRAIL

Duration 5 hours
Distance 8.5 miles one way
Difficulty moderate–demanding; elevation change -3200ft/+760ft
Start Glacier Point
Finish Happy Isles
Nearest Town/Facilities water and restrooms, Glacier Point
Transport bus
Summary Picture-postcard views accompany this trail and eye-popping sightlines of Half Dome are a highlight. Visit Nevada Fall as you descend down, down, down to the Valley floor.

Connecting Glacier Point and Nevada Fall, this trail is gorgeous, comprising several miles of Yosemite's most picture-perfect scenery. Hikers seeking a full loop from the Valley must first tackle the steep 3200ft ascent on the Four-Mile Trail (see opposite). Those starting from Glacier Point and heading down to the Valley must arrange a car shuttle or reserve a seat on the Glacier Point Hikers' Bus. Or you can simply hike to Nevada Fall and return to Glacier Point the way you came.

At Glacier Point, look for the Panorama Trail signpost near the snack bar. Descend a fire-scarred hillside south toward Illilouette Fall. The route down is largely easy, with magnificent views to your left – including Half Dome, which from here looks like the tip of a giant thumb. If you're lucky, you'll also find blue grouse on the trail, hooting and cooing in gentle, haunting tones. Make sure you bring sunscreen and a hat, as most of the tree cover has burned away.

After about 1.2 miles you'll meet the trail from Mono Meadow. Turn left and take a short series of switchbacks down to Illilouette Creek. The best place to admire 370ft Illilouette Fall is a well-worn viewpoint above the creek on the left.

At the 2-mile mark, a footbridge crosses Illilouette Creek, whose shaded banks invite a picnic. The trail leaves the creek and climbs east to **Panorama Point**, then **Panorama Cliff**. This 760ft climb is the only significant elevation gain on the hike. Vantage points high above the Merced River afford amazing views of the Glacier Point apron, Half

Dome, Mt Broderick (6706ft), Liberty Cap and Mt Starr King (9092ft).

The trail descends to a junction with the John Muir Trail. Turn right and follow the trail 0.2 miles to the top of **Nevada Fall**, 3.2 miles from Illilouette Creek.

To reach the Valley, descend the Mist Trail via Vernal Fall or take the slightly longer and gentler John Muir Trail. You'll emerge at Happy Isles on the Valley's east end (see the Vernal & Nevada Falls hike, p124).

POHONO TRAIL

Duration 7–9 hours
Distance 13.8 miles one way
Difficulty moderate–demanding; elevation change -2800ft
Start Glacier Point
Finish Wawona Tunnel parking lot
Nearest Town/Facilities water and restrooms at Glacier Point
Transport private or bus (one way)
Summary A panoramic traverse of the southern Valley rim between Glacier Point and the Wawona Tunnel overlook, this hike descends along a scenic ridge above three waterfalls.

Romantically named Bridalveil Fall was called Pohono by the Ahwahneechee, who thought the fall bewitched. According to Native American legend, an evil spirit who breathed out a fatal wind lived at its base; to sleep near it meant certain death. Some claimed to hear the voices of those who had drowned, warning others to stay away.

As the trailheads are many miles apart, you'll need either two vehicles or to arrange for pickup following your hike. The Glacier Point Hikers' Bus can take you to Glacier Point from the Valley, but it doesn't stop at the Wawona Tunnel parking area.

It's best to go from east to west, starting at **Glacier Point**. (The trail descends more than 2800ft, so hiking the opposite direction would involve a strenuous climb.) Though it's generally downhill, the trail does make some noticeable climbs here and there. Highlights include Glacier Point (7214ft), Taft Point, Dewey Point (7385ft), Crocker Point (7090ft), Stanford Point and Inspiration Point. The trail traverses an area high above three waterfalls – Sentinel, Bridalveil and Silver Strand.

Look for the well-marked trailhead near the snack bar at Glacier Point. After about a mile, you'll reach the trail junction for **Sentinel Dome**. You can either climb to the top or keep going, skirting just north of the dome along the Valley rim. After about 2 miles, you'll join the trail to **Taft Point** (see p119), which leads you across open rock, past the **Fissures** to the point itself. Peer over the railing before resuming your hike.

The trail continues west along the Valley rim, dipping to cross **Bridalveil Creek**. Past the creek, a trail veers left toward McGurk Meadow. Instead, bear right toward **Dewey Point** and another magnificent view (use extreme caution when peering over the edge). Across the Valley, you'll see 1612ft Ribbon Fall – when flowing, the highest single-tier waterfall in North America.

About a half-mile farther west is **Crocker Point**, again worth a short detour for the view, which takes in Bridalveil Fall. Another short walk brings you to **Stanford Point**, the last cliff-edge viewpoint on this trail. Once you cross Meadow Brook and Artist Creek, you'll begin the steep, 2.5-mile descent to **Inspiration Point**, an overgrown viewpoint along an old roadbed. The final 1.3-mile leg ends at the Wawona Tunnel parking lot.

Wawona

Take a break in spring or early summer and spy on these gushing cascades. See Map p108.

CHILNUALNA FALLS

Duration 4–5 hours
Distance 8.6-mile round-trip
Difficulty moderate–demanding; elevation change +2240ft
Start/Finish Chilnualna Falls Trailhead
Nearest Town/Facilities water, restrooms and food at Wawona Hotel and Store, 2 miles
Transport private
Summary Chilnualna Creek tumbles over the north shoulder of forested Wawona Dome in an almost continuous series of cascades. The largest and most impressive of these, Chilnualna Falls thunders into a deep, narrow chasm.

Unlike its Valley counterparts, this fall is not free-leaping, but its soothing, white-

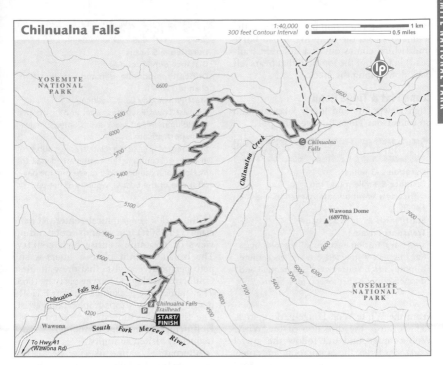

Chilnualna Falls

water rush makes it an attractive day hike. Carry lots of water, as the route can be hot. The top is a nice picnic spot. Like all Yosemite waterfalls, Chilnualna Falls is best between April and June when streams are at their fullest. July and August are often too hot for an afternoon hike, and by September the fall is limited by low water.

The trailhead is at the eastern end of Chilnualna Falls Rd. Follow Hwy 41 (Wawona Rd) a quarter-mile north of the Wawona Hotel and Store, and take a right just over the bridge on Chilnualna Falls Rd; follow it for 1.7 miles. The parking area is on the right, and the trailhead is marked.

The trail follows the northwest bank of **Chilnualna Creek** 0.1 miles to the first series of tumbling cascades, which in spring shower the trail with a cool mist. Ascend several brief sets of granite steps beside the falls. Above, the stock trail joins the footpath along the Yosemite Wilderness boundary, a short but steep 0.2 miles and 600ft above the trailhead.

The trail rises gently yet continually through open, mixed-conifer forest, leveling out as it passes the rushing creek. It then moves away from the creek, taking you on long, sweeping switchbacks. The sheer granite curve of Wawona Dome fills the sky to the east as you rise above forested Wawona Valley. About one to 1½ hours from the trailhead, you'll reach an unobstructed viewpoint from a granite **overlook** (5400ft); it offers the first good view of the fall. To the southwest are the forested Chowchilla Mountains.

The trail climbs several well-graded switchbacks, then a final dynamite-blasted switchback across a granite cliff to the top of **Chilnualna Falls** (6200ft). While you won't find any better view of the fall, it's worth continuing 15 minutes further to a nice picnic spot along Chilnualna Creek. If you're on an overnight trip, head for the campsites further up both Chilnualna and Deer Creeks.

Retrace your steps 4.3 miles to the trailhead in two hours or so, ignoring an inaccurate sign that reads '5.6 miles to

Wawona.' At a junction 0.2 miles from the trailhead, avoid the tempting, broad horse trail (which comes out at a different trailhead) in favor of the footpath that bears left back down along the creek.

Crane Flat & Tioga Road

High viewpoints and lovely lakes abound on trails from Tioga Rd. See Map p112.

HARDEN LAKE

Duration 2–3 hours
Distance 5.8-mile round-trip
Difficulty easy–moderate; elevation change +400ft
Start/Finish White Wolf Lodge
Transport private
Summary Tracing sections of the old Tioga Rd, this nicely forested out-and-back route is mostly level. Your reward is a tranquil and pretty lake basin that's good for a swim.

From the White Wolf Lodge parking area, start towards the direction of the White Wolf campground but follow the gravel road to the left of the campground entrance. The road is a section of the **old Tioga Road** and closed to public traffic. The roadway passes a mixed forest of lodgepole pine and Jeffrey pine, running parallel to the Middle Fork of the Tuolumne River. A few areas of fire damage are visible just before a discreet sewage-treatment facility appears off to the left. Continue through a stand of tall red firs, and at the 2-mile mark take a right off the road and onto a foot trail. Jittery leaves of quaking aspens flutter in the breeze, and the occasional pine drops plant can be spotted by its unusual red stalks.

Rejoin the road approximately 0.5 miles from the lake, and after a quarter-mile on the road, follow the junction sign and turn right off the road onto the lake trail. On the path towards the small boulder-littered shore, a meadow erupts with bulbous yellow Bigelow sneezeweed and white sprays of yampa.

Harden Lake is an unusually warm-water lake for these parts, primarily because it evaporates rapidly during the summer. So bring a towel and splash around without feeling like a polar bear. Retrace your steps to the parking lot.

MAY LAKE & MT HOFFMANN

Duration 4–5 hours
Distance 6-mile round-trip
Difficulty moderate–demanding; elevation change +2004ft
Start/Finish May Lake Trailhead
Nearest Town/Facilities water and restrooms at Tuolumne Meadows Visitor Center, 8 miles
Transport private
Summary May Lake is a relatively easy uphill to instant backcountry. The cairn-marked trail to Mt Hoffmann can be harder to see, and the payoff is one of the best viewpoints of the park.

At the park's geographical center, **Mt Hoffmann** (10,850ft) commands outstanding views of Yosemite's entire high country. The broad summit plateau offers a superb perspective, a vista that drew the first California Geological Survey party in 1863. They named the peak after Charles F Hoffmann, the party's topographer and artist. The first peak climbed in Yosemite, Mt Hoffmann remains one of the park's most frequently visited summits.

Alternatively, some hikers go no further than **May Lake** (9350ft), on the High Sierra Camps loop, a pristine mountain lake that cries out for a shoreline picnic. It alone is a satisfying destination, with great views of Half Dome, Cathedral Peak, and Mt Clark along the way. The hike takes only about 30 to 40 minutes in each direction.

To turn this into an overnight trip, you can stay at the nice backpackers campground next to the May Lake High Sierra Camp, or you can camp on Mt Hoffman's summit.

Start from the **May Lake Trailhead** (8846ft), 1.7 miles up a paved section of the old Tioga Rd. The turnoff from Tioga Rd is 2.2 miles west of Olmsted Point and 3.2 miles east of the Porcupine Flat Campground. Be sure to use the bear boxes in the parking lot.

The 1.2-mile stretch to May Lake is fairly easy, although it's a steady 500ft climb. At the lake the trail splits; the right fork leads to May Lake High Sierra Camp, the left traces the lake shore and then ascends to Mt Hoffmann. The Hoffmann trail winds through a talus field, where it often becomes indistinct. Follow a small stream, then cross a meadow where the trail turns sharply toward Mt Hoffmann's east summit. Don't be confused by the many paths marked with cairns along this rocky slope – all routes lead to the higher west summit.

The last bit up involves some basic scrambling. Don't be surprised if some curious marmots pop their heads out the rocks to check your progress. Be warned: the swarms of marmots living at the summit and in the rocks piles are not shy – they'll come right up to you. If you sit down, keep an eye on your day pack!

Camping is possible on the vast plateau near the east summit, although you must carry water from May Lake or use snowmelt. Retrace your steps to the May Lake Trailhead.

CLOUDS REST

Duration 6–7 hours
Distance 14.4-mile round-trip
Difficulty demanding; 2205ft ascent
Start/Finish Sunrise Lakes Trailhead
Nearest Town/Facilities water and restrooms at Tuolumne Meadows Visitor Center, 7.5 miles
Transport private
Summary A fair amount of effort and distance is required for this classic hike, but you'll be amply rewarded with phenomenal 360-degree views from one of the park's best vantage points.

Yosemite's largest granite peak, **Clouds Rest** (9926ft) rises 4500ft above Tenaya Creek, with spectacular views from the summit and along the trail. More than 1000ft higher than nearby Half Dome, Clouds Rest may well be the park's best panoramic viewpoint. The hike involves a strenuous ascent and equally significant descent (make sure you have a cold drink waiting for you!), but getting here is definitely worth the effort. This hike forms part of the Tenaya Lake to Yosemite Valley hike (see Map p142).

Start from the Sunrise Lakes Trailhead at the west end of Tenaya Lake. Trailhead parking is limited, and the lot fills early. If you're staying in Tuolumne Meadows, a great alternative to driving is the free Tuolumne

to Olmsted Point shuttle bus, which stops at the trailhead. The Tuolumne Meadows Tour & Hikers' Bus from Yosemite Valley also stops here, but only once a day in each direction.

Follow the trail along Tenaya Creek for your first glimpse of Clouds Rest and Tenaya Canyon's shining granite walls. As the trail climbs steadily up well-constructed switchbacks, the view expands to include prominent Mt Hoffmann (10,850ft) to the northwest and Tuolumne Peak (10,845ft) to the north. After a steady 30-minute ascent, the grade eases atop soft earth amid large red firs. Continue straight past the **Sunrise Lakes junction** and descend southwest. As Yosemite Valley and Sentinel Dome come into view, the trail reaches the level floor west of Sunrise Mountain (9974ft). Paintbrushes, lupines and wandering daisies bloom here, alongside mats of pink heather and bushes of poisonous white-flowered Labrador tea. Fifteen minutes past a shallow pond you'll reach a **creek** that's the last water source en route to the summit – so fill up here (and filter it).

Twenty minutes later you'll reach the **Forsyth Trail junction**, although it's not labeled as such on the sign. Bear southwest and ascend the ridgeline that culminates in Clouds Rest. To the southeast are fabulous views of wedge-shaped Mt Clark (11,522ft), the Cascade Cliffs and Bunnell Point in Merced Canyon. The granite swell of Mt Starr King (9092ft) rises to the southwest. The trail soon passes over a low rise and through a slight but obvious saddle. At a large white pine 20 minutes beyond the saddle, a small unmarked trail forks left; this is recommended for those not willing or able to hike the more exposed summit path.

A sign reading 'Clouds Rest Foot Trail' directs you along the granite ridge, which narrows rather thrillingly in one place. Never less than 5ft wide, the narrowest section might look intimidating but takes only five to 10 seconds to cross. The **summit** itself offers breathtaking views of Half Dome and the Valley. The view stretches from the Sawtooth Ridge and Matterhorn Peak along the park's north border to Mt Ritter and Banner Peak, standing dark and prominent to the southeast. Mts

Conness and Dana on the Sierra Crest and the closer Cathedral Range are all outstanding. This is one of the Sierra Nevada's most inspiring viewpoints – savor the sights before retracing your steps to the trailhead.

You can extend your hike by continuing down to Yosemite Valley (see the Tenaya Lake to Yosemite Valley hike, p141).

NORTH DOME

Duration 4½–5 hours
Distance 8.5-mile round-trip
Difficulty moderate; elevation change -1000/+422ft
Start/Finish Porcupine Creek Trailhead
Nearest Town/Facilities water, food and restrooms at White Wolf, 11 miles
Transport private
Summary Perhaps the best vantage point along the Valley rim, this trail sees relatively few hikers. A downhill trek outbound, so you'll be doing the ascent on the return.

The trail descends 1000ft and rises 422ft on the way there, so be ready for a climb on the return trip. A side trip to the natural arch on Indian Ridge adds another 240ft climb. Keep in mind that it's mostly downhill on the way out to North Dome (7542ft) and uphill on the way back, although the gradient is rarely steep.

From Tioga Rd, start at the **Porcupine Creek Trailhead** (8120ft), 1.3 miles east of Porcupine Flat Campground. To reach the trailhead from the campground, walk to the southern side of the highway from the camp entrance and follow the footpath that parallels the road.

An abandoned road leads beneath red firs until the pavement ends and the trail crosses **Porcupine Creek** via a log. After an easy 30-minute ascent into the forest, you'll reach a sign for the Snow Creek Trail to the Valley. Continue straight another 50ft to a second trail junction and take the left fork toward North Dome.

The trail climbs gently up Indian Ridge for 10 minutes to an inviting view across the Valley to Sentinel Dome and Taft Point. The trail soon turns sharply and ascends steadily for another 10 minutes, leading to the marked Indian Rock trail junction.

A worthwhile but optional 30-minute side trip leads to Yosemite's only visible **natural arch** (8360ft). Follow the short, steep spur trail to the arch. From the trail you can see the arch from all sorts of angles, and the arch affords good views of Clouds Rest, the Clark Range, Mt Starr King and Sentinel Dome. Clamber onto the rock for a view of Half Dome framed by the arch.

At the **Indian Rock trail junction**, the main trail continues south, leading to a spectacular viewpoint at the end of the ridge: front and center is Half Dome, and across the Valley is hard-to-see Illilouette Fall. North Dome lies directly below to the south, and Basket Dome's rounded peak (7612ft) lies to the southeast. This is a fantastic spot to camp; if you do decide to spend the night here (or on North Dome), you'll need to bring water, as none is available nearby.

The trail drops south off the ridgeline in the direction of Half Dome and descends on switchbacks across open granite. Cairns lead to the marked North Dome Trail junction. Turn east for the final half-mile stretch. The rough trail descends steeply before a short final ascent to the summit. West are the Sentinels, Cathedrals, El Capitan, the Three Brothers and Yosemite Point (Yosemite Falls lie hidden). To the northeast are Basket Dome, Mt Watkins, and the distant peaks of the Cathedral Range. Horse Ridge rims the horizon to the south, while dominating the scene is the sheer north face of Half Dome – surely one of Yosemite's most impressive sights. Clouds Rest rises on the far side of granite-walled Tenaya Canyon.

It will take about two hours to retrace your steps along Indian Ridge and return to the trailhead.

You can extend the hike by descending to the Valley on either the Snow Creek Trail (which heads down to Tenaya Canyon and Mirror Lake) or on the trail west to Yosemite Point and Yosemite Falls Overlook. From the latter, take the Yosemite Falls Trail down to Camp 4.

Use the hikers' bus from the Valley to reach the North Dome Trailhead in the morning. You can also start hiking from the Valley and visit North Dome on a very demanding round-trip of eight to 10 hours. For an especially vigorous day hike, traverse the Valley's north rim via North Dome by ascending the Snow Creek Trail's 100-plus switchbacks and returning via the Yosemite Falls Trail.

Tuolumne Meadows

The many day hikes out of Tuolumne Meadows are some of the finest in all of Yosemite, especially in July, when colorful wildflowers – poking up wherever they can – bring the high country to life. See the Maps p114 and p144.

LEMBERT DOME

Duration 2–3 hours
Distance 2.4-mile round-trip
Difficulty moderate; elevation change +850ft
Start/Finish Dog Lake parking lot
Nearest Town/Facilities gas, food, phones and camping at Tuolumne Meadows, 0.5 miles
Transport YARTS bus; Tuolumne Meadows Shuttle Bus stop 1; Tuolumne Hikers' Bus
Summary The short hike (and scramble) to the top of Tuolumne's most iconic dome offers fun on granite and fantastic views in all directions, especially at sunset.

Lembert Dome (9450ft) rises from the meadows' east end, opposite the campground. Scrambling around the base of the dome's steep southwest face is a favorite Tuolumne pastime, but the real pleasure is hiking up the backside and standing atop the summit, where the views are staggering. Mt Dana, the Cathedral Range, Tuolumne Meadows, Pothole Dome, Fairview Dome and the Lyell Fork Tuolumne are all visible from the top. To the east, the Sierra Crest stretches from Mt Conness to the Kuna Crest. It's magical just before sunset.

This hike is doable for most walkers, but reaching the summit requires scrambling up the granite at the end – not recommended for the slippery-footed or faint at heart. Once you're on top, however, you can picnic upon a ledge or walk the ridge, scramble down some rock and cross a tree-filled saddle to the section of Lembert Dome that's so prominent from the road below.

Two similarly named trails lead to Lembert Dome. The one from the Lembert Dome parking lot, at the very base of the

dome, is a steep, borderline unpleasant trail that's been damaged by storms. To reach the preferred Dog Lake Trail, drive east from the Tuolumne Meadows campground and turn right onto the road leading to Tuolumne Meadows Lodge. Park in the Dog Lake parking lot, about a half-mile up this road. From the north side of the lot, follow the signed Dog Lake/Young Lakes trail up and across Tioga Rd.

This trail, almost entirely shaded in pine forest, is the quickest way up the backside of the dome. From the top of the trail, you can scramble up the granite to the dome's summit.

DOG LAKE

Duration 2 hours
Distance 2.8-mile round-trip
Difficulty easy–moderate; elevation change +520ft
Start/Finish Dog Lake or Lembert Dome parking lots
Nearest Town/Facilities gas, food, phones and camping at Tuolumne Meadows, 0.8 miles
Transport YARTS bus; Tuolumne Meadows Shuttle Bus stop 2; Tuolumne Hikers' Bus
Summary This short hike skirts the base of Lembert Dome and climbs gently through lodgepole pine forest to scenic Dog Lake, a great spot for an afternoon picnic and, if you can take it, a chilly dip.

Pine tree-ringed **Dog Lake** (9170ft) is accessible via the same trails that head to Lembert Dome. The better one leaves from the appropriately named Dog Lake parking lot, near Tuolumne Meadows Lodge. Follow this trail to the base of **Lembert Dome**. When you reach the turnoff for the summit, continue straight. A half-mile or so up the fairly flat trail is another junction; turn right toward Dog Lake (left is a steep downhill to the Lembert Dome parking lot). It's about another half-mile to the lake. Although most topo maps don't show it, a trail circles the lake, allowing you to hike around it before heading home.

Be prepared to share this subalpine gem with fellow hikers – on weekends it may resemble your local reservoir, as people lug abundant picnic supplies and even inflatable rafts up to the lake's forested shores.

ELIZABETH LAKE

Duration 2½–4 hours
Distance 5.2-mile round-trip
Difficulty moderate; elevation change +800ft
Start/Finish Elizabeth Lake Trailhead, Tuolumne Meadows Campground
Nearest Town/Facilities gas, food, phones and camping in Tuolumne Meadows
Transport YARTS bus; Tuolumne Meadows Shuttle Bus stop 5; Tuolumne Hikers' Bus
Summary At the foot of jagged Unicorn Peak, this easily reached alpine lake offers spectacular views and plenty of opportunity for exploration beyond the lake itself.

Any time is a good time for a hike to this beautiful lake, but it's a particularly good choice if you've just rolled into the Tuolumne Meadows area and need a short acclimatization hike before sunset. Because it's fairly short, the trail gets busy, but heading up in the late afternoon means you'll encounter fewer people. That said, you could easily stretch a day out of this hike by exploring the saddles and ridges around the lake or, if you're experienced, by attempting the summit of **Unicorn Peak** (10,823ft), a class 3–4 climb.

The trailhead lies in the upper 'B' section of Tuolumne Meadows Campground. When you pull in, ask the ranger on duty for a campground map, or follow the sign to **Elizabeth Lake**. Once you're on the trail, the climbing kicks in immediately, and most of the elevation gain is out of the way within the first mile or so. Most of this section is shaded by lodgepole pines. The first real treat is the trail's encounter with **Unicorn Creek**, which drains into its namesake lake. After that, the trail widens and levels off, and finally meets a fork at the northeast end of the lake. Turn right, and you'll hit the water. Otherwise, you'll follow Unicorn Creek into a meadow (a reward in itself), where several side trails also lead to the lakeshore. Climbing the slopes on the south side of the lake affords views of Lembert Dome and, far beyond, 12,590ft **Mt Conness**. To return to the trailhead, retrace your steps.

If you choose to come earlier in the day, Elizabeth Lake makes a nice spot for a picnic lunch.

→ CATHEDRAL LAKES

Duration 4–7 hours
Distance 8-mile round-trip (upper lake)
Difficulty moderate; elevation change +1000ft
Start/Finish Cathedral Lakes Trailhead, 0.5 miles west of Tuolumne Visitor Center
Nearest Town/Facilities gas, food, phone and camping at Tuolumne Meadows, 1 mile
Transport YARTS bus; Tuolumne Meadows Shuttle Bus stop 7; Tuolumne Hikers' Bus
Summary Easily one of Yosemite's most spectacular hikes, this steady climb through mixed conifer forest ends with glorious views of Cathedral Peak from the shores of two shimmering alpine lakes.

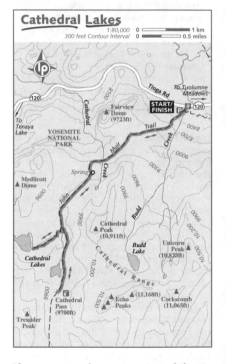

If you can only manage one hike in Tuolumne, this should probably be it. **Cathedral Lake** (9588ft), the lower of the two lakes, sits within a mind-blowing glacial cirque, a perfect amphitheater of granite capped by the iconic spire of nearby **Cathedral Peak** (10,911ft). From the lake's southwest side, the granite drops steeply away, affording views as far as Tenaya Lake, whose blue waters shimmer in the distance. Although it's only about two hours to the lower lake, you could easily spend an entire day exploring the granite slopes, meadows and peaks surrounding it. Continuing to the **upper lake** (9585ft) adds less than an hour to the hike and puts the round-trip walk at 8 miles, including the stop at Cathedral Lake. Admittedly, the upper lake is less spectacular when measured against the lower lake, but by all other standards it's utterly sublime.

Parking for the Cathedral Lake Trailhead is along the shoulder of Tioga Rd. Due to the popularity of this hike, parking spaces fills up fast, so arrive early or take the free shuttle. Camping is allowed at the lower lake (despite what some maps show), but be absolutely certain you're 100ft from the water *and* the trail, and that you choose an already impacted site to prevent further damage. Better yet, camp somewhere near the upper lake or off the pass.

From the Cathedral Lake Trailhead on Tioga Rd, the hike heads southwest along the John Muir Trail. Almost immediately, it begins to climb through forest of lodgepole pine, mountain hemlock and the occasional whitebark pine. After ascending over 400ft, the trail levels out and a massive slab of granite – the northern flank of Cathedral Peak – slopes up from the left side of the trail. Soon you'll see Fairview Dome (9731ft) through the trees to your right.

Before long, the trail begins its second ascent, climbing nearly 600ft before leveling off and affording outstanding views of Cathedral Peak. Three miles from the trailhead, you'll hit the junction that leads 0.5 miles southwest to Cathedral Lake. This trail crosses a stunning **meadow** (turn around as you cross it for the head-on view of Cathedral Peak) before arriving at the granite shores of the lake. Be sure to follow the trail around the lake and take in the views from the southwest side.

To visit the upper lake, backtrack to the main trail, turn right (southeast) and, after about 0.5 miles, you'll hit the lake. If you wish to stretch the hike out even further, you can continue past the upper lake to **Cathedral Pass** (9700ft), where you'll be rewarded with a stellar side-view of Cathedral

Peak and Eichorn Pinnacle (Cathedral's fin-like west peak). This side trip adds about 0.6 miles to trip.

GLEN AULIN

Duration 6–8 hours
Distance 11-mile round-trip
Difficulty moderate; elevation change -600ft
Start/Finish Glen Aulin Trailhead near Lembert Dome parking lot
Nearest Town/Facilities gas, food, phones and camping at Tuolumne Meadows, 0.5 miles
Transport YARTS bus; Tuolumne Meadows Shuttle Bus stop 1; Tuolumne Hikers' Bus
Summary The first leg of the multiday hike through the Grand Canyon of the Tuolumne makes for a great day hike, offering stunning views of the Cathedral Range before reaching Glen Aulin High Sierra Camp (see the boxed text, p165).

Except for the dip in the final stretch, most of the elevation change along this hike is gradual. It's an uphill return, so save energy for the climb home. The hike follows a section of the Pacific Crest Trail (PCT), the same stretch that horse packers use to supply the High Sierra Camp. It's a beautiful walk, but it's well worn and there's plenty of aromatic horse dung along the way.

The trailhead lies behind the Lembert Dome parking lot, which is immediately east of the Tuolumne Meadows campground and bridge. Follow the dirt road northwest toward the stables. When you reach the gate, swing west (left) toward Soda Springs, watching for the Glen Aulin Trail signs to the right of Parsons Lodge.

The trail leads through open lodgepole pine forest, crosses shallow **Delaney Creek**, then continues to a signed junction with the Young Lakes Trail, 1.3 miles from Soda Springs. Take the left fork, heading northwest through lodgepole pines. You'll emerge on riverside meadows with outstanding views of Fairview Dome (9731ft), Cathedral Peak (10,911ft) and Unicorn Peak (10,823ft).

Thirty minutes on, the level, cairn-dotted trail crosses a vast, glacially polished granite slab over which the **Tuolumne River** flows. The river's roar signals the end of Tuolumne Meadows and the start of a series of cascades that tumble toward the Grand Canyon of the Tuolumne.

The trail climbs briefly over a granite rib, affording distant views of Matterhorn Peak (12,264ft) and Virginia Peak (12,001ft) on Yosemite's north border and a first view of the huge, orange-tinged granite cliff above Glen Aulin. Descend through forest to a two-part wooden footbridge spanning the river, 2.3 miles from the Young Lakes Trail junction.

The trail descends steadily, alternating between forest and riverside before reaching **Tuolumne Falls**. Continue along the plunging river to a signed junction with the May Lake Trail and then a steel girder footbridge spanning the river. Cross it and you'll reach two trail junctions in close succession. To the right is the Glen Aulin High Sierra Camp. At the second junction, the PCT continues north (straight) to a backpackers' campground and on to Cold and Virginia Canyons.

You can hang out here, or turn west (toward Waterwheel Falls) and continue a short distance into Glen Aulin itself – a long, level forested valley where the river flows green and tranquil beneath a massive water-stained granite wall.

To extend this into an overnight excursion, see the Waterwheel Falls hike (p148).

GAYLOR LAKES

Duration 2–3 hours
Distance 3-mile round-trip
Difficulty moderate; elevation change +560ft
Start/Finish Gaylor Lakes Trailhead and parking lot, immediately west of Tioga Pass Entrance Station
Nearest Town/Facilities gas, food and camping at Tuolumne Meadows, 7 miles
Transport Mammoth Lakes–bound YARTS bus, summer only; Tuolumne Meadows–Tioga Pass shuttle bus
Summary This spectacular and popular trail climbs gently up to Gaylor Lakes, set in pristine alpine territory just inside the park boundary near Tioga Pass.

The hike to Gaylor Lakes is a high-altitude hike, so prior acclimatization (such as a day in Tuolumne) is a good idea. There can be snow any time of the year. Sound good? It is.

The trail begins from the parking lot and wastes no time in starting its steep ascent. At the crest, **Lower Gaylor Lake** (10,334ft) lies in a basin below you, with great views everywhere you turn. The trail skirts the lower lake and then climbs to **Upper Gaylor Lake** (10,510ft).

For an extra bonus, head past the lake and climb again to the site of the old **Great Sierra Mine**, where the views are even wider and more stunning. All told, the alpine countryside here is knockout beautiful, so budget some time for poking around.

MONO PASS

Duration 4 hours
Distance 7.4-mile round-trip
Difficulty moderate–demanding; elevation change +915ft
Start/Finish Mono Pass Trailhead at road marker T37, 1.4 miles south of Tioga Pass
Nearest Town/Facilities gas, food, camping at Tuolumne Meadows, 5.6 miles
Transport Mammoth Lakes–bound YARTS bus, summer only; Tuolumne Meadows–Tioga Pass shuttle bus
Summary This outrageously scenic, high-altitude hike from Dana Meadows starts at 9689ft and follows an ancient Native American trail past meadows and through open forest to the vast, lake-crowned Mono Pass.

A saddle on the Sierra Crest between the rounded summits of Mts Gibbs (12,764ft) and Lewis (12,296ft), Mono Pass was the highest point on an ancient Native American trade route that linked the Mono Lake area with Tuolumne and continued to Yosemite Valley via Cathedral Pass. Remnants of late-19th-century log buildings, relics of the mining years, remain along the trail among subalpine meadows and lakes. It's a fantastic walk through some of the highest of Tuolumne's readily accessible high country.

From the Mono Pass Trailhead and parking lot, the trail leads southeast through open forest within the shadow of 13,053ft **Mt Dana** to the northeast. After an easy half-mile hike alongside Dana Meadows, the trail crosses the Dana Fork of the Tuolumne River, then crosses two small ridges before passing beneath lodgepole pines beside several small, buttercup-filled meadows. Emerging from the pines, the trail makes a gentle ascent along **Parker Pass Creek**, with the reddish bulk of Mt Gibbs above and to the east.

When you reach the signed Spillway Lake trail junction, follow the left fork toward Mono and Parker Passes. The trail passes the remains of a log cabin and opens onto a large meadow beside a small creek, with impressive views of Kuna Crest and Mammoth Peak (12,117ft). Thirty minutes (1.4 miles) past the Spillway Lake junction, a small trail branches right toward Parker Pass. Keep going straight, however, past twisted whitebark pines and two small lakes to **Mono Pass** (10,604ft).

Tiny Summit Lake lies to the west, while east of the pass are Upper and Lower Sardine Lakes. Further down, Walker Lake lies in an area known as Bloody Canyon. Tree frogs chirp from the banks of Summit Lake in early summer. Flourishing in meadows along its north side are scrub willows, Sierra onions, and yellow potentillas. At the south end of the pass sit three historic log cabins.

Retrace your steps to the trailhead. To make this an overnight trip, camp at Upper Sardine Lake east of Mono Pass, just outside the park in the Ansel Adams Wilderness.

MT DANA

Duration 6–7 hours
Distance 5.8-mile round-trip
Difficulty demanding; elevation change +3108ft
Start/Finish unmarked trailhead immediately east of Tioga Pass Entrance
Nearest Town/Facilities gas, food and camping at Tuolumne Meadows, 7.2 miles
Transport Mammoth Lakes–bound YARTS bus, summer only; Tuolumne Meadows–Tioga Pass shuttle bus
Summary Starting at 9945ft, this strenuous hike is a leg-working, lung-busting climb to the top of Yosemite's second-highest peak, which, at 13,053ft, offers stunning views in every direction.

Mt Dana, which takes its name from American geologist James Dwight Dana, offers unrivaled views of Mono Lake, the Grand Canyon of the Tuolumne and the rest of the Yosemite high country from its summit. Remember, though, that this is a steep, high-altitude hike which *starts* at nearly 10,000ft. Prior acclimatization will ease your struggle.

The hiking season runs from July to mid-September, though snow may block the trail in early summer. Don't even start the hike if a storm threatens.

Parking for the trailhead is available on either side of the Tioga Pass Entrance. From Tioga Pass the trail heads east, passing between two broad, shallow pools before the ascent begins. The trail passes through flower-filled meadows on the 1700ft climb to a west-descending ridge, marked by a large, loose **cairn**, 1.8 miles from Tioga Pass.

From this cairn, several indistinct paths head up the rocky west slope to the summit. Shun the leftmost path through difficult talus in favor of paths to the right, which offer easier footing. The views from the summit of **Mt Dana** are so outstanding that some hikers spend the night on top in the shelter of two small rock windbreaks. From the summit, retrace your steps downhill to the trailhead.

Hetch Hetchy

Hetch Hetchy offers some outstanding hiking, but day hikers are essentially limited to the Wapama Falls Trail, which traces the reservoir's scenic north shore, a fairly easy hike for just about anyone.

TUEEULALA & WAPAMA FALLS

Duration 2½–3 hours
Distance 5.4-mile round-trip
Difficulty easy–moderate; elevation change +400ft
Start/Finish parking lot at O'Shaughnessy Dam
Nearest Town/Facilities food, store and lodging at Evergreen Lodge, 10 miles
Transport private
Summary This hike along the north shore of Hetch Hetchy Reservoir leads to the base of two neighboring falls: the free-leaping, seasonal Tueeulala Falls and the enormous triple cascades of year-round Wapama Falls.

Few – if any – trails in Yosemite bring you as close to the shower and roar of a giant waterfall as this one does to Wapama Falls.

In springtime, after a good snowmelt, the falls can rage so mightily that the Park Service occasionally has to close the trail itself as water rolls over the bridges. On your way, you'll pass the wispy Tueeulala Falls (*twee*-la-la), which spring spectacularly from the cliffs from more than 1000ft above the trail. All the while, **Hetch Hetchy Dome** (6197ft), on the north shore, and the mighty **Kolana Rock** (5772ft), on the south shore, loom over the entire scene. You can capture both falls and adjacent Hetch Hetchy Dome in a single striking photo. Kolana Rock's vertical north face provides nesting sites for peregrine falcons, once close to extinction but now present in healthier numbers.

The gentle north shore trail is fairly flat, but does have a few ups and downs that will challenge unfit hikers in the summer heat. Plan the hike for mid- to late spring, when temperatures are cooler, butterflies are abundant, wildflowers are in bloom and the falls are full.

From the parking lot (3813ft), cross **O'Shaughnessy Dam** and pass through the tunnel on its far side. The broad, oak-shaded trail then heads northeast, above and parallel to the north shore. In just over a mile, after rising gradually past several small seasonal streams, you'll reach a signed trail junction (4050ft).

Take the right (east) fork, following the sign reading '1.6 miles to Wapama Falls.' The trail descends gently, then bears left onto broad granite slabs before reaching **Tueeulala Falls**. Most of the falls end up flowing beneath the footbridge, but in spring a small section of the trail can fill with runoff. By June, the falls are usually dry.

The trail continues 10 minutes down a staircase that switchbacks gently to the base of thundering **Wapama Falls** (3900ft), where wooden footbridges span Falls Creek. In spring, water cascades over the trail beyond the first footbridge and almost covers the second. When the water is high, crossing is dangerous, but at other times the flow is ankle-deep. The frothy, gushing torrents create billowing clouds of mist that drench the entire area and make for a cool bath on a warm afternoon.

Return to the trailhead via the same route.

CARLON FALLS

Duration 2 hours
Distance 2.4-mile round-trip
Difficulty easy–moderate; elevation change +300ft
Start/Finish Carlon Day Use area
Nearest Town/Facilities food, store and lodging at Evergreen Lodge, 5 miles
Transport private
Summary This short but sweet hike follows the South Fork Tuolumne River up to Carlon Falls, which cascade down granite slabs into perfect swimming holes.

Most people blow right by Carlon Falls on their way to Hetch Hetchy, but a quick stop for this short venture is well worthwhile. The hike is especially satisfying on a hot day, when the swimming holes beneath the falls are paradisiacal. Folks who stay at Evergreen Lodge and Camp Mather frequent the falls, so arrive early to have the place to yourself. The only thing making this hike 'moderate' is a section of washed-out trail that requires surefootedness.

To get to the trailhead, drive northwest on Evergreen Rd, which departs Hwy 120 about 1 mile before the Big Oak Flat Entrance Station. About 1 mile after turning off, you'll see the **Carlon Day Use Area** at a bridge across the river. Park in the pullout on the far (north) side of the bridge and hike upstream from there. Although the trailhead is outside the Yosemite park boundary, you enter the park after about 0.1 miles.

Shaded by ponderosa pines, incense-cedars and the occasional dogwood, the trail winds along the north bank of the river, through patches of fragrant kitkitdizze (a exceptionally pungent shrub also known as Sierran Mountain Misery) and finally arrives at **Carlon Falls**. Better described as a cascade, the falls tumble nearly 40ft across moss- and fern-draped granite into two separate **swimming holes**. There's plenty of granite around for sunning, so be sure to bring lunch.

BACKCOUNTRY HIKES

Backcountry hiking and sleeping beneath the stars is one of the Yosemite's finest adventures. The vast majority of the 3.3 million people who visit Yosemite every year never leave the Valley floor, meaning the park's 1101 sq miles of wilderness is, for the most part, empty. There are a few painless bureaucratic hurdles to jump before heading out, however, but a little planning will make your trek a triumph.

For information on Wilderness Centers, see p92.

WILDERNESS PERMITS
Wilderness permits are required for all overnight backcountry trips (not for day hikes). To stem overuse of the backcountry, a quota system is in effect for each trailhead. You must spend your first night in the area noted on your permit – from there, you're free to roam.

Permits are available either in advance (between six months and two days ahead) or on a first-come, first-served basis from the nearest wilderness center. The park reserves 40% of its wilderness permits for walk-ups; these become available one day before the hike-in date. If you show up early the day before your hike, you should have no problem getting a permit. For popular hikes (such as Little Yosemite Valley, Cathedral Lakes or the High Sierra Camp routes), you should show up and get in line before the permit offices open the day before you hike. Always have a backup plan, as some spots fill very quickly. Hikers who turn up at the wilderness center nearest the trailhead get priority over someone at another wilderness center. For example, if there is one permit left for Lyell Canyon, the person at the Tuolumne Meadows Wilderness Center gets it, even if someone has been waiting at the Yosemite Valley Wilderness Center.

Reserving a **permit** (☎ 209-372-0740; www .nps.gov/yose/wilderness; Yosemite Association, PO Box 545, Yosemite, CA 95389) is the best way to ensure you get one. Between May and September you can do so by phone, online or through the mail, with a $5 processing fee per person, per reservation.

Study your maps, read your guidebooks and decide where you want to go before registering for a permit. Rangers can offer guidance about starting points and trail conditions, but they will not recommend one area over another because they don't know hikers' skills. For updated trail conditions, call the **park information number** (☎ 209-372-0200).

WILDERNESS REGULATIONS
For the sake of the bears more than your food, the use of bear-resistant food canisters is required at all backcountry campsites above 9600ft and *highly* recommended everywhere else. When you pick up your wilderness permit, you'll be required to rent a bear canister or show that you own one. They're also sold at stores throughout the park. These canisters weigh just under 3lb each and, when carefully packed, can store three to five days' worth of food for one or two people. As with the lockers, keep the canisters closed when cooking. As for the old string-up bear bag method of storing food, Yosemite's bears have figured out how to get them down.

Campfires are forbidden above 9600ft. Where available, use pre-existing campsites to reduce your impact, and camp at least 100ft from water sources and trails. Never put soap in the water, even 'biodegradable' types. Properly filter all drinking water or boil it for three to five minutes, and don't burn trash. Pack out everything you bring, including toilet paper.

Wilderness camping is prohibited within four trail-miles of Yosemite Valley, Tuolumne Meadows, Glacier Point, Hetch Hetchy and Wawona, and you must be at least one trail-mile from any road. No one is actually going bust out the measuring tape – the idea is to keep people from simply wandering into the trees and camping when they can't find open campsites in the park.

BACKPACKERS' CAMPGROUNDS
If you're like most backpackers heading into the Yosemite wilderness, you probably didn't reserve a campsite for the night before (or night after) your backcountry trip. Worry not, there's a place for us. To accommodate backpackers heading into or out of the wilderness, the park offers three walk-in backpackers' campgrounds: one in Yosemite Valley (Map p93), one in Tuolumne (Map p114) and one at Hetch Hetchy (Map p116). If you hold a valid wilderness permit, you may spend the night before and the night after your trip in one of these campgrounds. The cost is $5 per person per night, and reservations are unnecessary.

Yosemite Valley

Most hikes within and around Yosemite Valley proper are day hikes. Most overnight hikes from the Valley will take you out of its confines entirely. The hike to the top of Half Dome, Yosemite's most famous trek, is one major exception. See Map pp90–1.

HALF DOME

Duration 10–12 hours
Distance 17-mile round-trip
Difficulty demanding; elevation change +4800ft
Start/Finish Vernal & Nevada Falls/John Muir Trailhead near Happy Isles
Nearest Town/Facilities food, camping and lodging in Yosemite Valley
Transport YARTS shuttle stop 16
Summary Ideally done over two days, but do-able as a grueling day hike, the demanding trek to the top of Yosemite's signature peak offers views (and crowds and sore muscles) like you wouldn't believe.

For many visitors, this is the ultimate Yosemite hike, an achievement to boast about to the grandkids someday. The stand-alone summit of this glacier-carved chunk of granite offers awesome 360-degree views, and peering down its sheer 2000ft north face offers a thrill you'll remember the rest of your life. But, unless you get a crack-of-dawn start, you'll have people aplenty to deal with.

Ideally, Half Dome is best tackled in two days, allowing you more time to rest up and enjoy the gorgeous surroundings. But since it's so popular, you'll have a hard time getting a permit to sleep overnight at the limited legal camping areas on the route (the most popular being Little Yosemite Valley). If you do attempt this hike in a single day (and many people do), be ready for some serious exertion. Get an early start (6am), pack lots of water and bring a flashlight, because you may wind up hiking home in the dark.

Climbing gear is unnecessary. Instead, hikers haul themselves up the final 650ft to the summit between two steel cables. Climbing this stretch is only allowed when the **cable route** is open, usually late May to mid-

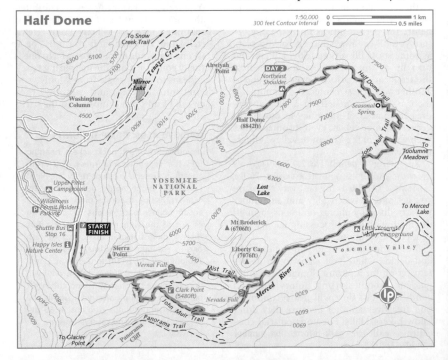

Half Dome

ALTERNATIVE HALF DOME ROUTES

As an alternative to the hugely popular route from Happy Isles (which can feel like rucksack rush hour on summer weekends), consider approaching Half Dome from other points in the park. Beginning from higher elevation also saves you the initial climb. Just about anywhere works, depending on how long you want to spend on the trail (overnighting requires a wilderness permit). Good starting points include Tenaya Lake and Glacier Point, the latter leading you along the gorgeous Panorama Trail. From Half Dome, you can descend via the Mist or John Muir Trails.

October, depending on snow conditions. If planning an early-season or late-season trip, confirm ahead that the cables are in place.

Start at **Happy Isles** and ascend to the top of **Nevada Fall** on either the John Muir Trail or the Mist Trail (see p124). Continue over a low rise to level **Little Yosemite Valley**, which boasts views of Half Dome's south side. You'll also find solar composting toilets, bear boxes and a seasonal ranger station, all welcome features at this well-used campground, which is one of the park's most heavily visited areas.

From the west end of Little Yosemite Valley, the Merced Lake Trail heads east along the river to the Merced Lake High Sierra Camp. Stay on the John Muir Trail, which turns north and climbs steeply through forest 1.3 miles to the **Half Dome Trail junction**, just 2 miles from the summit.

Take the left fork onto the Half Dome Trail. Ten minutes above the junction on the left is a hard-to-spot seasonal spring – the last source of water en route. (Filter or treat it.) Continue for 30 minutes, first through forest and then up switchbacks to the northeast shoulder (7600ft), an alternative camping spot with spectacular views. Visit the summit at sunset and sunrise for exquisite solitude.

From here, a rocky 20- to 30-minute trail snakes 650ft up two dozen **switchbacks** to a notch at the base of the cables. The twin steel cables are draped from posts bolted into the granite on the final 600ft ascent up an exposed 45-degree rock face. There are gloves available to protect your hands, and intermittent wooden cross-boards provide footholds. A trip in light crowds takes only 15 minutes,

but on crowded cables (or if you're jittery), expect it to take much longer. 'Sharing the road' will be your biggest challenge.

A word of caution: do *not* ascend the cables if there's any chance of a storm. The exposed summit is no place to be when lightning strikes (should you have any doubts, read Bob Madgic's *Shattered Air*, 2005), nor do you want to get stuck halfway up with your hands wrapped around virtual lighting rods.

The **summit** is fairly flat and about 5 acres in size. From here, enjoy amazing views of Yosemite Valley, Mt Starr King, Clouds Rest, the Cathedral Range and the Sierra Crest. As tempting as it is to linger, watch the time carefully to avoid a hazardous descent in darkness.

Camping on the summit is prohibited for three reasons: to reduce human waste, to protect the threatened Mt Lyell salamander and to save the last remaining tree – six of the seven trees previously growing here were illegally cut for campfires.

Glacier Point & Badger Pass

Trails from the south and east side of Glacier Point Rd wind into some of Yosemite's largest wilderness tracts (see Map p105). Serious backpackers interested in longer hauls can explore such rugged areas as the Merced headwaters or the Clark Range, along the park's southeast border.

OSTRANDER LAKE

Duration 2 days
Distance 12.4-mile round-trip
Difficulty moderate–demanding; elevation change +1550ft
Start/Finish Ostrander Lake Trailhead
Nearest Town/Facilities water and restrooms at Bridalveil Creek campground, 1.3 miles
Transport private
Summary A deservedly popular out-and-back trek to an atmospheric stone ski hut. A gorgeous granite bowl lake cuts into the forest, with water perfect for a brisk dip.

Sure this trail is doable as a day hike, but what's the rush? Doing the trek over two days gives you the chance to check out regenerating forest, enjoy wildflowers and spy some wild strawberries.

Park at the **Ostrander Lake Trailhead lot** (just over a mile east of Bridalveil campground road) and use the bear boxes to stockpile any food that you're not packing in. You soon cross over a footbridge and the level trail starts through a swathe of burned-through **lodgepole forest**. The rejuvenation is fascinating to see. The entire area is blanketed by trees of a uniform height, not more than 8ft tall. The trail, remaining level, fords through purple, yellow and white banks of waist-high wildflowers, ecstatic bees and ground-hugging wild strawberries.

The hiking path that you're following was once a jeep road, but it is now also a winter route to the Ostrander Ski Hut, and yellow and orange cross-country ski markings are posted on trees the whole way there.

At almost 2 miles, bear left at a signed junction. Another junction comes within a mile, and once again bear left, following the trail sign to Ostrander Lake. The right-hand side trail goes to Wawona, among other places. A climb gears up slowly, and Horizon Ridge appears to your left (east) through the skeletons of burned-out trees and the dainty little puffs of young fir trees. The climb becomes steeper, but a clearing just past the ridge offers energizing views, just when you need the extra encouragement. The jagged Clark Range perches to the northeast, and you can spy on Basket Dome, North Dome and Half Dome as well. In approximately a half-mile, the pitched roof of the handcrafted stone Ostrander Ski Hut (see the boxed text, p158) comes into view, framed by Ostrander Lake with a slope of rock boulders tumbling down its far shore from **Horse Ridge**.

You can trace the lake's western bank to find established campsites, and then cool off with a refreshing dip in the lake. When you're ready, you can return following the same trail.

Crane Flat & Tioga Road

Sometimes the best way to appreciate the beauty of Yosemite Valley is to sneak up on it from above. The Old Big Oak Flat Rd to Yosemite Falls hike skirts the Valley's northern perimeter (see Map p110), while the Tenaya Lake to Yosemite Valley hike drops down from Tioga Rd (see Map p112).

OLD BIG OAK FLAT ROAD TO YOSEMITE FALLS

Duration 2 days
Distance 18.8 miles one way
Difficulty demanding; elevation change +3080ft
Start Old Big Oak Flat Trailhead
Finish Yosemite Fall Trailhead
Nearest Town/Facilities Crane Flat gas station, 6 miles
Transport Tuolumne Meadows Hikers' Bus
Summary Climb up to bird's-eye views of Yosemite Valley, Half Dome and the Clark Range on a trail that never gets crowded. Spent the night on top of El Capitan before descending Yosemite Falls.

When planning for this hike, note that the creeks along the way run dry in summer. So unless you don't mind carrying in *all* your water, this is best done as a late-spring trip. Ask at the Yosemite Valley wilderness office about the status of water sources en route.

DAY 1: BIG OAK FLAT ROAD TRAILHEAD TO EL CAPITAN
7–8 hours, 10.1 miles
From Yosemite Valley, get the Tuolumne Meadows Tour & Hikers' bus (reserve a spot; see p96) to drop you a quarter-mile west of Foresta turnoff on Big Oak Flat Rd, in the 'Old Big Oak Flat Rd ' parking lot. The trailhead (across the street) begins with switchbacks, climbing through an area charred by the 1990 Foresta fires.

Over 4 miles, cross **Wildcat Creek** and then **Tamarack Creek** before coming to a junction at a footbridge. To the left, it's just over 2 miles to Tamarack Flat campground via the Old Big Oak Flat Rd. Instead continue right (southeast), crossing the footbridge over Cascade Creek. The path is forested with red fir, Jeffrey pine and canyon live oak. Pass through Ribbon Meadow, with corn lilies and, in wet years, many mosquitoes. Cross Ribbon Creek and veer a quarter-mile south off the trail to camp on the top of **El Capitan** (at just over 10 miles). You can camp anywhere here; just don't wander off the edge during the night. At eye level, the surrounding peaks look like frothy waves, with the iconic Half Dome to the east. It's a stunning viewpoint to see the evening alpenglow.

Old Big Oak Flat Road to Yosemite Falls

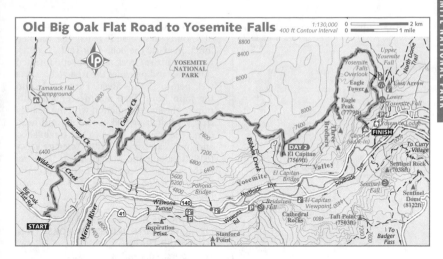

1:130,000 / 400 ft Contour Interval   0 — 2 km / 0 — 1 mile

DAY 2: EL CAPITAN TO YOSEMITE FALLS
6–7 hours, 8.7 miles

Rejoin the trail and continue east for 1.7 miles to the **Three Brothers**. A half-mile jut takes you to **Eagle Peak** (7779ft), the upper of the trio, with more awesome views of the Valley and the Clark Range. Continue northeast, and at the junction of the Yosemite Creek Trail, turn south to reach the top of **Yosemite Falls** in about a half-mile. It's 3.6 miles down more than a hundred switchbacks and 2700ft of knee-knocking descent to the Valley floor.

TENAYA LAKE TO YOSEMITE VALLEY

Duration 2 days
Distance 17.2 miles one way
Difficulty demanding; elevation change +2205ft
Start Sunrise Lakes Trailhead
Finish Happy Isles
Nearest Town/Facilities water and restrooms at Tuolumne Meadows Visitor Center, 6 miles
Transport bus
Summary Instead of driving between Tioga Rd and Yosemite Valley, why not consider hiking? The Tenaya Lake to Yosemite Valley hike is one of the classics, allowing you an up-close look at the major landscape changes.

The most spectacular trail from Tioga Rd to Yosemite Valley traverses the summit of Clouds Rest (9926ft), arguably Yosemite's finest panoramic viewpoint. An easier variation bypasses Clouds Rest completely and follows Sunrise Creek. Both hikes descend through Little Yosemite Valley and pass world-renowned Nevada and Vernal Falls to Happy Isles. Hearty hikers can also include a side trip to the top of Half Dome. On stormy days, steer clear of both Half Dome and Clouds Rest.

The trailheads are almost 50 miles apart by road. Unless you plan to shuttle two vehicles, instead use YARTS or the Tuolumne Meadows Tour & Hikers' Bus (make sure to reserve a spot in advance) for the uphill leg.

DAY 1: TENAYA LAKE TO LITTLE YOSEMITE VALLEY
8–10 hours; 12.3 miles

Start from the well-marked Sunrise Lakes Trailhead, at the west end of Tenaya Lake off Tioga Rd. Trailhead parking is limited, and the lot fills early. Those leaving from Tuolumne Meadows can instead use the free Tuolumne to Olmsted Point shuttle bus, which stops at the trailhead.

See the Clouds Rest hike (p129) for the trail to the summit. From there, head down steps off the south side to the ridge below. In 0.6 miles there's a **signed junction** with a bypass trail for horses. Continue straight, down through pines, chinquapins and manzanitas, for 20 minutes. Pass beneath granite domes and continue the descent on switchbacks for another hour. Near the bottom of the 2726ft descent, the trail enters shady forest.

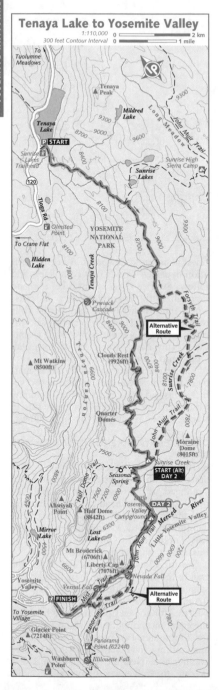

Tenaya Lake to Yosemite Valley

Two hours (3.8 miles) from the summit of Clouds Rest, you'll reach the marked junction with the **John Muir Trail** (7200ft). Nearby Sunrise Creek offers several forested campsites and provides the first water since well before Clouds Rest. Turn west onto the John Muir Trail and descend a half-mile to the signed junction with the heavily traveled **Half Dome Trail**. Go south and head down the trail 1.3 miles to the established and busy campsites in **Little Yosemite Valley** (6100ft) along the Merced River. Beware: both Sunrise Creek and Little Yosemite Valley experience chronic problems with bears.

ALTERNATIVE ROUTE: TENAYA LAKE TO LITTLE YOSEMITE VALLEY VIA FORSYTH & JOHN MUIR TRAILS
7–9 hours, 10.9 miles
Those not inclined to visit the Clouds Rest summit can follow an easier, forested alternative trail along Sunrise Creek, which eventually meets the trail from Clouds Rest and descends to Little Yosemite Valley.

To begin, follow the Day 1 description above for 2.5 hours (4.7 miles) to the signed junction (9100ft) with the Clouds Rest and Forsyth Trails. Bear southeast and follow the **Forsyth Trail** across a meadow into the pine and granite landscape. The trail leads down a slope of red firs, offering good views of the Clark Range, Merced Canyon and Mt Starr King. Follow Sunrise Creek until a slight ascent takes you to the marked junction (8000ft) with the John Muir Trail, also known here as the **Sunrise Trail**. Go southwest on the John Muir Trail 0.1 miles to another junction, where a trail to Merced Lake heads east. Stay on the John Muir Trail, heading west along Sunrise Creek, then descend switchbacks to the junction (7200ft) with the Clouds Rest Trail. Continue a half-mile to the busy Half Dome Trail, then turn south and descend the John Muir Trail to Little Yosemite Valley.

DAY 2: LITTLE YOSEMITE VALLEY TO HAPPY ISLES VIA THE JOHN MUIR TRAIL
2–3 hours, 4.8 miles
Today you can follow either the Mist Trail or the **John Muir Trail** (JMT) some 1065ft down to Happy Isles in Yosemite Valley. We recommend the JMT because the granite steps on the Mist Trail tend to pound your

knees on the descent. If you do take the Mist Trail, it's 3.9 miles to Happy Isles.

From Little Yosemite Valley, follow the JMT for 0.5 miles, where it traces the Merced River and then contours to the south of **Liberty Cap**. At 1.1 miles, meet the Mist Trail (and follow it to the right, if you wish). Continue southwest along the JMT, fording the footbridge over the rushing Merced at **Nevada Fall**. Pass the junction with the Panorama Trail and, at approximately 4 miles, cross the river again. From here it's less than a mile to the trailhead, walking along the eastern riverbank.

Tuolumne Meadows

In addition to the following multiday hikes, several of the day hikes can be extended into overnight excursions, including Cathedral Lakes, Mt Dana, and Glen Aulin. Also see the Map p114.

LYELL CANYON

Duration 2 days
Distance 17.6-mile round-trip
Difficulty easy–moderate; elevation change +200ft
Start/Finish Lyell Canyon Trailhead at Dog Lake parking lot
Nearest Town/Facilities gas, food and camping at Tuolumne Meadows, 0.5 miles
Transport YARTS bus; Tuolumne Meadows Shuttle Bus stop 3 or 1; Tuolumne Hikers' Bus
Summary This flat section of the John Muir Trail meanders deep into Lyell Canyon to the base of Mt Lyell, the park's highest peak. Fishing, relaxing, views and side trips are all excellent.

If destinations like Cathedral Lake and Nevada Fall slap you in the face with their shockingly good looks, Lyell Canyon gently rolls its beauty over you like a blanket on a cool day. The Lyell Canyon trail takes you through a special place, along a section of the John Muir Trial as it follows the Lyell Fork of the Tuolumne River through a gorgeous subalpine meadow hemmed in by tree-covered granite peaks. The final reward is the view of 13,114ft Lyell Peak and its eponymous glacier, towering over the meadow beyond Donohue Pass. This is also a great choice for those who loathe uphill climbs.

The best place to park is the **Dog Lake parking lot**, off the road to Tuolumne Lodge. If that's full, park in the wilderness center parking lot, further west on the same road. From the latter, look for a hidden trail sign reading 'John Muir Trail' and walk southeast, paralleling the road. After about 0.2 miles, you'll pass the trail that comes down from the Dog Lake lot. Soon, you'll cross the **Dana Fork** (Tuolumne River) by bearing right at a junction (continuing straight would take you to the lodge) and crossing the footbridge over the river. Soon you'll hit another junction; veer right toward Donohue Pass (hint: always head toward Donohue Pass). About 0.5 miles further, you'll cross the **Lyell Fork** over two footbridges and come to yet another junction. This time, bear left.

Another 0.5 miles on, the trail passes the Vogelsang/Yosemite Valley junction and crosses **Rafferty Creek**. Finally it turns southeast into **Lyell Canyon**, and you can start paying attention to the scenery rather than the trail junctions. After 4.2 miles you'll pass the turnoff to Ireland and Evelyn Lakes, cross **Ireland Creek** and pass beneath the inverted cone of Potter Point (10,728ft).

If you wish to camp in Lyell Canyon – a highlight of any Yosemite trip – you'll find several sites alongside the river; just make sure you're at least 4 miles from the trailhead. Basically, anything south of Ireland Creek is fine. Some of the best sites are about 0.5 miles before the head of the canyon, where you can see **Mt Lyell** (13,114ft) looming over the southeast end of the meadow. There are sites on both sides of the river and above the trail. Once you start heading up the 'staircase' at the head of the canyon, campsites are few until you reach Lyell Base Camp, a busy climbers' camp below Donohue Pass.

You can take a day-long side trip to the **summit** of Mt Lyell, but only experienced climbers should attempt it. The ascent alone gains over 4000ft, and the difficult route traverses a glacier, involves steep and complex climbs, and requires safety ropes. Another option is setting up your own base camp in the canyon and continuing another few miles up the John Muir Trial to **Donohue Pass** (a 2000ft climb), admiring the impressive peaks and glaciers along the way.

On your second day, the task is simple: follow the John Muir Trail along the Lyell Fork back to the trailhead.

YOSEMITE NATIONAL PARK

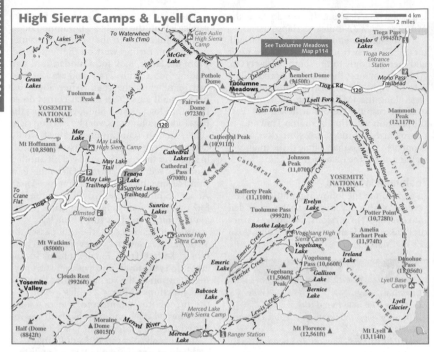

High Sierra Camps & Lyell Canyon

YOUNG LAKES

Duration 2 days
Distance 13-mile round-trip
Difficulty moderate; elevation change +1300ft
Start/Finish Dog Lake Trailhead near Lembert Dome parking lot
Nearest Town/Facilities gas, food and camping at Tuolumne Meadows, 1 mile
Transport YARTS bus; Tuolumne Meadows Shuttle Bus stop 4; Tuolumne Hikers' Bus
Summary After climbing through forests of lodgepole pines, this trail opens up to offer sweeping views of the Cathedral Range before reaching shimmering Young Lakes, at the base of gnarly Ragged Peak

DAY 1: TRAILHEAD TO YOUNG LAKES
3–4 hours, 6.2 miles

Set at elevations between 9950ft and 10,050ft, the three **Young Lakes** make for a vigorous day hike but offer much more – particularly at sunrise and sunset – to those who make an overnight journey out of it.

If the permit quota for Cathedral Lakes is full, this is a good alternative. Some walkers knock this off their favorite-hikes list because much of it is through pine forest, meaning fewer vistas. But the rewards at the lakes above make up for this tenfold.

Day hikers can park at the Lembert Dome parking lot; overnighters must park along the dirt road leading from the lot to the stables. From the parking lot, follow the Dog Lake trail into the trees, with Lembert Dome on your right. After 1.3 miles you'll pass the trail to Lembert Dome. After another 0.3 miles, you'll hit the junction to 9240ft **Dog Lake**, good for a quick detour and snack stop.

Back on the Young Lakes trail, you'll ascend gradually to about 9400ft before descending to **Delaney Creek**, which burbles along the edge of a lovely meadow. Cross Delaney Creek and follow the trail across the meadow and around the western side of a granite peak. Shortly thereafter, the trail meanders into a clearing and you'll see snarled Ragged Peak to the north. After entering a gently sloping meadow spotted with wildflowers and stunted whitebark pines, you're presented with a magnificent view to the south: the entire Cathedral Range and all its major peaks, including Cathedral Peak, Unicorn Peak and Echo Peaks (with Cockscomb just behind Unicorn). To the far left stands Mt Lyell (13,114ft), Yosemite's highest peak.

Cross **Dingley Creek** (a good spot to fill up the water bottles), and follow the trail over a small crest, with Ragged Peak on your right. The trail winds down through the pines and boulders to meet a junction (the return route). Keep to your right and continue around the northwest shoulder of Ragged Peak until, after 1.5 miles from the junction, you arrive at the lowest of the **Young Lakes**.

There are numerous places to camp along the northwest shore, and trees offer shade and shelter from any wind that might pick up. The lake itself sits within a sort of granite amphitheater formed by the northern flanks of Ragged Peak, which takes on a fiery golden glow at sunset, lighting up the lake with its reflection in the water.

From the northeast side of the lake, a trail leads up to **middle Young Lake**. From the middle lake's eastern shore, a vaguely defined, steep trail climbs alongside a pretty waterfall before reaching a meadow and gently sloping down to the third lake. It's a truly stunning alpine setting boasting marvelous views in every direction. There are a couple of campsites eked out above the northwestern shore.

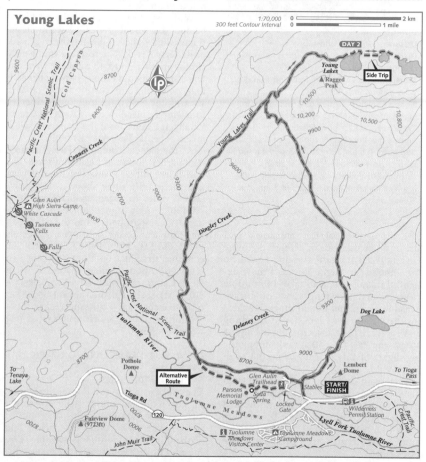

Young Lakes

DAY 2: YOUNG LAKES TO TRAILHEAD
3–4 hours, 6.8 miles

To return from the lower lake, follow the same trail out until, 1.5 miles from Young Lake, you reach the junction you passed on the way up. Stay to your right. The views are less impressive along the return trail, but it makes for variation. After 3.7 miles of mostly downhill walking you'll join the **Pacific Crest Trail**. After crossing Delaney Creek, the trail becomes extremely worn, sandy and mule-trodden. At a junction you can either stay to your left to reach the stables and the road where you parked, or head to your right to visit Soda Springs (p114).

VOGELSANG

Duration 3 days
Distance 27-mile round-trip
Difficulty moderate–demanding; elevation change +3852ft
Start/Finish Lyell Canyon Trailhead from Dog Lake parking lot
Nearest Town/Facilities gas, food and camping at Tuolumne Meadows, 0.5 miles
Transport YARTS bus; Tuolumne Meadows Shuttle Bus stop 3 or 1; Tuolumne Hikers' Bus
Summary This exquisite but very popular semi-loop crosses Tuolumne and Vogelsang Passes through Yosemite's Cathedral Range, offering a remarkable circuit through John Muir's 'Range of Light.'

The sloping subalpine meadows and streams on either side of gentle Tuolumne Pass (9992ft) provide a scenic backdrop for some of the Sierra Nevada's most delightful hiking. The trail takes in multiple cascades and sweeping views of distant peaks in several mountain ranges, including the hard-to-see Clark Range. Camping at Vogelsang Lake and crossing the alpine Vogelsang Pass (10,660ft) rank among the highlights of this journey around Vogelsang Peak.

Vogelsang Peak, Lake and Pass, and High Sierra Camp (HSC), all take their name from the Vogelsang brothers, who headed the California Fish and Game Board from 1896 to 1910. The name itself translates aptly from German as 'a meadow where birds sing.'

DAY 1: LYELL CANYON TRAILHEAD TO VOGELSANG LAKE
4–6 hours, 7.2 miles

On Day 1, follow the Lyell Canyon hike (p143) to the Pacific Crest/John Muir Trail. After 0.8 miles, at Rafferty Creek, turn south, leaving the John Muir Trail. The 2½-hour, 4.9-mile ascent along **Rafferty Creek** begins with a rugged uphill climb. Gouged out by the steel-shod hooves of packhorses and mules that supply the Vogelsang HSC, the trail clambers over granite steps and cobblestones through forest for some 20 to 30 minutes before it eases and nears Rafferty Creek's left bank. To the north you'll see Mt Conness and White Mountain, while the **Lyell Fork Meadows** spread out some 500ft below to the east.

With the steepest part of the trail now behind you, you'll gradually ascend an attractive little valley, following the west bank of Rafferty Creek. The forested trail gently climbs another 30 to 40 minutes, then enters a small open meadow. Passing beneath lodgepole pines and crossing several smaller streams, the well-worn trail finally emerges into a lovely meadow along Rafferty Creek. Finally, 6.1 miles from the trailhead, you'll arrive at gentle **Tuolumne Pass** (9992ft).

At the signed Tuolumne Pass junction, take the left fork and head southeast. The trail offers enticing views of Boothe Lake and the granite ridge above it as it travels 0.8 miles to **Vogelsang High Sierra Camp** (10,130ft). At a signed junction, a backpackers' campground lies to the left (east), while the trail to the right (west) descends to Merced Lake High Sierra Camp. Instead, continue straight (south) to **Vogelsang Pass** (10,660ft). About 0.5 miles beyond the High Sierra Camp you'll reach large **Vogelsang Lake** (10,341ft), set in a picture-perfect cirque beneath Fletcher and Vogelsang Peaks. Above the northeast shore are campsites set among whitebark pines.

DAY 2: VOGELSANG LAKE TO EMERIC LAKE
5–7 hours, 10.2 miles

The trail ascends above the southwest end of Vogelsang Lake, eventually crossing a large, cold stream just below its spring-fed source. The view of the lake below and Cathedral Range beyond is sublime. Five minutes further you'll reach the pass, in the

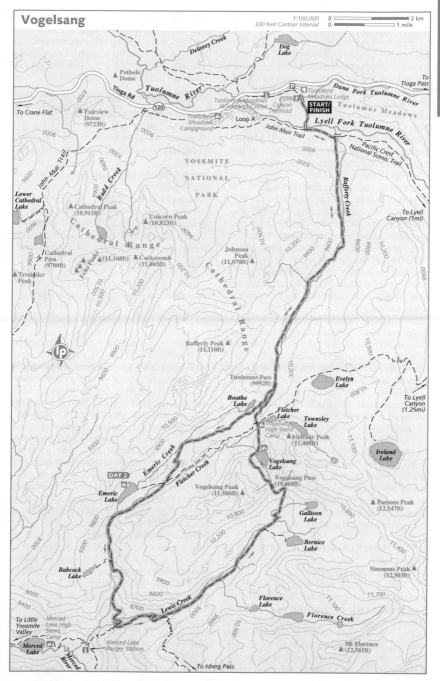

Vogelsang

1:100,000
300 feet Contour Interval

0 — 2 km
0 — 1 mile

serrated granite **ridge** that descends from Vogelsang Peak (11,506ft).

From here the trail rises a bit and provides a long view of the upper Lewis Creek Basin. Lovely **Gallison Lake**, surrounded by meadow, issues forth a cascading stream. Large **Bernice Lake** spreads out at the base of a massive granite ridge beneath Mt Florence (12,561ft). Half a dozen more lakes lie hidden in a chain above Gallison Lake, fed by permanent snow from the slopes of Simmons Peak (12,503ft) at the valley's head. To the southwest is the more distant Clark Range, sweeping from the west to the southeast.

Descend the **switchbacks** that follow the course of a small stream. At the base, enter a forest along the level valley floor. Streams course across the meadow, involving a few crossings. Continue straight past the Bernice Lake junction, heading downstream along **Lewis Creek** as the descent grows steeper.

Three miles from Bernice Lake trail junction, you'll pass the Isberg Pass trail junction. Continue 1 mile down the trail through a dramatic canyon for a view of distant Half Dome before passing the signed Merced Lake trail junction (8160ft). Turn north at the junction and follow the trail up **Fletcher Creek**. After crossing a footbridge, the trail climbs beside the creek, crosses several side streams and climbs high above the left bank of Fletcher Creek. The trail levels out about one hour past the footbridge, offering a fabulous vista over Merced Canyon and the Clark Range.

Leaving the views behind, head beneath lodgepole pines past the signed Babcock Lake trail junction. After 25 minutes, the trail emerges in a lovely meadow and finally hits a four-way trail junction. Turn northwest and head 0.4 miles to the large **Emeric Lake** (9338ft). Cross its inlet to reach good campsites above the northwest shore.

DAY 3: EMERIC LAKE TO LYELL CANYON TRAILHEAD
4½–5 hours, 9.1 miles
On Day 3, retrace your steps to the four-way junction. Turn north on the route to **Boothe Lake** (rather than the heavily used trail to Vogelsang HSC). This lovely lake, which lies 2.7 miles from the junction, was the original site of the High Sierra Camp before the camp was moved and renamed Vogelsang. The trail stays well above the lake, where camping is prohibited. Arrive once again at **Tuolumne Pass**, 0.4 miles beyond Boothe Lake. From here, retrace your steps: 4.9 miles down Rafferty Creek to the John Muir Trail and 1.1 miles to the Lyell Canyon Trailhead.

WATERWHEEL FALLS

Duration 2 days
Distance 18-mile round-trip
Difficulty demanding; elevation change +2260ft
Start/Finish Glen Aulin Trailhead near Lembert Dome parking lot
Nearest Town/Facilities gas, food, phones and camping at Tuolumne Meadows, 0.5 miles
Transport YARTS bus; Tuolumne Meadows Shuttle Bus stop 1; Tuolumne Hikers' Bus
Summary Follow this hike along the Grand Canyon of the Tuolumne River to Waterwheel Falls. It's the last and most impressive of six cascades along the river, before it plunges into the canyon on its descent toward Hetch Hetchy Reservoir.

For the first several miles of the hike, follow the Pacific Crest Trail (PCT) to Glen Aulin (p133). About 0.2 miles after **Tuolumne Falls**, head northwest along the trail to Waterwheel Falls, which is 3.3 miles downstream from where you leave the PCT. The trail meanders between through ghost forest to the river's edge, inviting a dip in the placid waters, then crosses an area made marshy by a stream that descends from Cold Mountain to the north.

After a 40-minute stroll, you'll reach the far end of the peaceful glen, where the river flows briskly to the brink of the first in a series of near continual cascades. The trail, too, plunges along the river, dropping over gorgeous orange-tinted granite. Ahead, the **Grand Canyon of the Tuolumne** stretches as far as the eye can see. The trail continues between the sheer, polished granite walls of **Wildcat Point** (9455ft) to the north and the 8000ft granite wall of Falls Ridge on the opposite bank. **California Falls** and **LeConte Falls** are the most prominent cascades in this section; most are unnamed. If you have to ask yourself, 'Is this Waterwheel Falls?' keep going – you'll know it when you see it.

An hour after leaving the glen, you'll reach a small unsigned junction where a hard-to-see spur trail branches southwest (left) to a viewpoint of **Waterwheel Falls**. The obvious roar tells you this is the spot, although the falls remain hidden from view. From the main trail, walk two minutes to the edge of the massive falls, named for the distinctive 15ft- to 20ft-high plumes of water that curl into the air like a wheel midway down the more than 600ft-long falls.

After admiring the cascade, return to the main trail, turn west (left), and descend another 10 minutes. As you approach the scattered junipers beside an obvious dark granite rib perpendicular to the trail, turn south (left) and head down a sandy slope through manzanita, following a trail that parallels the rocky rib. It leads to a large, forested **campsite** (6440ft) that's partly visible from the main trail above. Camp beneath big ponderosa pines and incense cedars, about 0.3 miles below Waterwheel Falls, with the green and tranquil Tuolumne River about 200ft away.

On day two, retrace your steps 9 miles to the trailhead.

Hetch Hetchy

Hetch Hetchy offers some excellent backpacking opportunities, as well as access to some of the park's most remote areas, north of the reservoir. Summers can be brutally hot, which is why the trails out here are busiest in spring and fall. See Map p116.

RANCHERIA FALLS

Duration 7 hours–2 days
Distance 13-mile round-trip
Difficulty moderate–demanding; elevation change +786ft
Start/Finish Rancheria Falls Trailhead, O'Shaughnessy Dam
Nearest Town/Facilities food, store and lodging at Evergreen Lodge, 10 miles
Transport private
Summary This classic Hetch Hetchy hike passes the spectacular Tueeulala and Wapama Falls, then takes you to the gentler Rancheria Falls, where swimming holes abound and the scenery is outrageous.

Rancheria Falls is doable as a day hike, but it's best enjoyed as an overnighter, allowing you to experience sunset over Rancheria

Creek and Hetch Hetchy Reservoir. This part of Yosemite can be brutally hot in summer and, like the Tueeulala and Wapama Falls hike, is best in the spring. Still, it can be rewarding in July and even August, despite the heat, thanks to fewer people and the excellent swimming holes near the falls. Watch out for poison oak along the trail.

Follow the hike to **Wapama Falls** (p135). After the falls, the trail climbs into the shade of black oaks and laurels, offering relief from the sun. It then ascends a series of switchbacks and skirts around the base of **Hetch Hetchy Dome** (6197ft), passing two epic viewpoints over the reservoir on the way. Alternately climbing and falling through shaded oak forest and hot, exposed stretches, the trail finally arrives at two footbridges over **Tiltill Creek**, which mark the end of the no-camping zone.

After climbing up from Tiltill Creek, you'll begin to notice the charred manzanita and fire-scarred trees from the 2003 Tiltill Valley Fire, started by an arsonist who shot himself after setting the forest ablaze. Soon, you'll get your first glimpse of **Rancheria Falls** as they shoot down a granite apron into the reservoir below. Camping below the falls looks inviting, but, because the area has become so impacted, it's best to continue 0.25 miles further to the established **Rancheria Falls campground**.

After chucking your sack and pitching your tent, walk further up the trail, past the Tiltill Valley junction (stay to your right) to the footbridge over **Rancheria Creek**. During summer, when the water levels are low, there are two superb emerald green swimming holes set in a chasm of granite, both with rock- and bridge-jumping opportunities for the adventurous. The views of Rancheria Creek and the reservoir from here are sublime.

To return on day two, retrace your steps.

CYCLING

Bikes are prohibited from all trails within Yosemite, so break out that road bike or beach cruiser if you want to do any pedaling in the park. Moderate-level bike rides within Yosemite, which is dominated by steep grades except in Yosemite Valley, are few and far between. Generally it's either easy (ie the Valley) or demanding (everywhere else).

BICYCLE RENTALS

If you can't bring your own bike, single-speed beach cruisers can be rented at the **Yosemite Lodge Bike Stand** (Map p93; ☎ 209-372-1208; Yosemite Lodge; ☉ 8:30am-7pm) and the **Curry Village Rental Stand** (Map p93; ☎ 209-372-8319; Curry Village; ☉ 8:30am-7pm). Both places charge about $7.50 per hour or $25 per day. Also available are bike trailers so you can drag the young ones along. You're required to leave either a driver's license or credit card for collateral. Neither location accepts reservations, but you should be fine if you arrive before 11am or so. Also see Bicycle, p265.

CYCLING ROUTES

The following routes are all doable in less than a day. All but the Yosemite Valley Loops route require a good road bike and physical fitness. Many people bicycle along formidable Tioga Rd, though it's not a route for the casual cyclist. If you succumb to the temptation, keep in mind that this winding, climbing route has many blind spots and often fields a lot of traffic. It's a tough, relentless grind, so start riding early in the morning and keep well hydrated. From Crane Flat, it's just under 100 miles to Tioga Pass and back. Also see Cycling p47.

YOSEMITE VALLEY LOOPS

Duration 1–3 hours
Distance up to 12 miles round-trip
Difficulty easy
Start/Finish Curry Village
Nearest Town/Facilities Curry Village
Transport YARTS shuttle stop 13
Summary Whether done in segments or in its entirety, this easy pedal around the floor of Yosemite Valley is as relaxing as it gets – and the views are amazing.

Twelve miles of paved, mostly flat bicycle paths run up and down the length of Yosemite Valley (see Map p93), making for some very relaxed and superbly enjoyable peddling, whether you're solo or a family of five. The free hiking map provided at the visitor center shows the bike route in detail, and it's easy to whip out while riding.

You can pick up the bike path near just about anywhere you're staying in the Valley. Most people start where they rent bikes at either Curry Village or Yosemite Lodge. From the latter, follow the path down to the riverside, past the lodge buildings, across a meadow and west to **Swinging Bridge** (which actually doesn't swing at all). Cross over the Merced River, veer east along Southside Dr, take in the magnificent view of Yosemite Falls, then Half Dome. Soon you'll pass Curry Village, the Royal Arches will appear on your left and you'll finally hit the road to **Happy Isles**. Pass the Nature Center at Happy Isles and continue along the road to loop around to North Pines Campground. Cross the Merced again, then cut north to Northside Drive, which you can follow back to Yosemite Lodge.

GLACIER POINT ROAD

Duration 3 hours
Distance 32-mile round-trip
Difficulty moderate–demanding; elevation change +1770ft
Start/Finish Chinquapin junction
Nearest Town/Facilities water and restrooms, Chinquapin junction
Summary Along a peaceful pine-fringed road, this is one of Yosemite's prettiest rides. The pavement's smooth, the traffic is usually not too heavy and the vistas at Glacier Point are worth the climbs.

To ride the full 16 miles each way, begin at the pullout near Chinquapin junction (see Map p105). There's ample parking near the phone and restrooms.

In the first 5 miles to the **Badger Pass Ski Area**, the road ascends approximately 1000ft. Your first big sight is to the west, where the **Merced Canyon** drops 4500ft below into El Portal. In another half-mile, a saddle marks the high point in this area, and you begin a descent to **Peregoy Meadows** near the Bridalveil Creek campground, where you can refill your water bottle if necessary. There are views of the Clark Range to the east and 9500ft Horse Ridge to the south, which borders Ostrander Lake.

The ride continues on rolling terrain until about a half-mile before Mono Meadow, where the road turns abruptly north and climbs 550ft over 2 miles to **Pothole Meadows**. After some level terrain, the road descends about 500ft in switchbacks to the runner-up views at **Washburn Point**. As you pass the point and wind around the last curve, Half Dome rises into view in all its magnificent glory. Return along the same route.

For a shorter but equally gorgeous ride, start from the parking area near the Sentinel Dome Trailhead. From here, it's just under 3 miles to the Glacier Point overlook.

CARLON TO HETCH HETCHY

Duration 3–4 hours
Distance 34-mile round-trip
Difficulty moderate; elevation change +550ft/-1205ft
Start/Finish Carlon Falls Day Use Area
Nearest Town/Facilities food and lodging at Evergreen Lodge, 6 miles
Transport private
Summary With a gentle ascent to the Hetch Hetchy Entrance Station and an adrenaline-spiking descent to the reservoir, this ride offers fabulous views and a spectacular destination.

With relatively little traffic, this ride to Hetch Hetchy Reservoir (see Map p116) offers a splendid way to take in the scenery along the northwest boundary of the park. Fuel up with a good picnic lunch at the reservoir: the return climb is much more strenuous than the exciting drop on the way there. In summer, it can get extremely hot out here, so get an early start. In spring, it's divine.

To get to the starting point, drive northwest on Evergreen Rd, which departs Hwy 120 about 1 mile west of the Big Oak Flat Entrance Station. About 1 mile after turning off, you'll see the **Carlon Day Use Area** at a bridge across the South Fork Tuolumne River. Park in the parking lot and ride out to Evergreen Rd, cross the bridge and you're off. The first 9.5 miles rise and fall fairly gently with a modest overall elevation gain of about 550ft. About 1.5 miles after the park entrance station (which lies about 7 miles from Carlon), you'll hit the crest of the ride (topping out around 5000ft) and begin the 1205ft descent to the reservoir. The views over the Poopenaut Valley are outstanding – be sure to stop for a breather at one of the viewpoints.

After you reach the reservoir and peddle out onto the dam (a must), gobble down your energy bars, take a deep breath and slog your way back to the car.

DRIVING

Driving is hardly the proper way to see Yosemite Valley (unless you enjoy craning your neck in traffic to see the sights otherwise blocked by your roof), but it's an undeniably superb way to experience the high country – and beyond – via the spectacular Tioga Rd. This is the only road that bisects the park between its eastern and western borders. All park roads, however, are lined with beautiful scenery, so basically you can't go wrong. And if you have limited time, driving through Yosemite Valley is better than nothing – just try to avoid doing it on weekends.

YOSEMITE VALLEY

Duration varies depending on traffic
Distance 12.5-mile round-trip
Start/Finish Yosemite Village
Nearest Town/Facilities Yosemite Village
Transport private
Summary The only driving route in Yosemite Valley takes you past the Valley's classic sights and viewpoints, including Bridalveil Fall and Yosemite Falls.

This loop follows the only two roads in and out of Yosemite Valley (see Map pp90–1): **Northside Drive** and **Southside Drive**. Each is (mostly) one way and, as their names suggest, they sit on either side of the Merced River. You can easily drive this loop in less than an hour, but budget more time as you'll want to stop frequently. Despite the fact that the park service has tried to limit the number of cars in the Valley, it remains a popular driving tour. The free YARTS shuttle covers most of this route, so consider parking the car and doing this by public transport.

Starting in **Yosemite Village**, head west on Northside Dr, which leads past Yosemite Falls, the Three Brothers and El Capitan to **Valley View** (roadside marker V11), a great viewpoint along the Merced River. To complete the loop, turn left (south) at the **Pohono**

Bridge, just past Valley View, and cross the Merced River. Then head east on Southside Dr back toward Yosemite Village. From that road you get wider views of Yosemite Falls and El Capitan on the north rim and a closer look at south rim features such as Cathedral Rocks, Sentinel Rock, and Bridalveil Fall. You also drive by the old site of **Yosemite Village**, near where the chapel now sits. The road dead-ends just past Curry Village, or you can turn at **Sentinel Bridge** back toward Yosemite Village.

TIOGA ROAD TO MONO LAKE

Duration 2–4 hours
Distance 60-mile round-trip
Start Crane Flat
Finish Mono Lake
Nearest Town/Facilities Crane Flat
Transport private
Summary Get ready to ascend over 3500ft as you drive over dizzying Tioga Pass (elevation 9945ft) before zigzagging down the steep eastern side to surreal Mono Lake.

Without a doubt, this is one of California's ultimate drives. From Crane Flat, the tour follows Tioga Rd (see Map p112) up through the trees to **Olmsted Point**, **Tenaya Lake** and **Tuolumne Meadows**. It then flanks beautiful **Dana Meadows** before crossing the dizzying **Tioga Pass**. You can either turn around here or, if you have enough time, continue down the precipitous eastern side of the Sierra Crest to the town of Lee Vining and beautiful Mono Lake. The scenery along this route – the spiky peaks of the Cathedral Range, the granite domes around Tuolumne Meadows, the stunted subalpine forests, the meandering creeks and shimmering lakes – will give you whiplash harder than driving into a giant sequoia.

Tioga Rd is only open during summer and fall, usually from mid-June to late October. From Yosemite Valley, it's only about 1½ hours to Tuolumne Meadows, but that's not including stops for views (Olmsted Point is a must), hikes or lunch at the Tuolumne Meadows Grill. From Tioga Pass, it's another half-hour east to Hwy 395 and Mono Lake. While you could easily make the drive in about two hours, it's best to take all day.

WAWONA ROAD & GLACIER POINT ROAD

Duration 2 hours
Distance 52 miles one way
Start Tunnel View
Finish Glacier Point
Nearest Town/Facilities water and food at Yosemite Village, 8 miles; Wawona Store, 20 miles
Transport private
Summary Some of the best park views are along this route south of Yosemite Valley. The Tunnel View and Glacier Point overlooks give excellent Valley views from different angles.

Start your expedition from the east side of the Wawona Tunnel (see Map p105) in the spectacular pull-off point of **Tunnel View**. No, you will not be staring slack-jawed at a dark traffic structure, but at the magnificent landscape to the east. Best in the spring when snowmelt has it gushing, 620ft **Bridalveil Fall** leaps off a plateau. When it thins out in summer, it sways like a string in the wind. The sheer wall of El Capitan rises to the north side of the Valley, and Half Dome pops out in the background past deep green forest.

Buckle up and proceed west through Wawona Tunnel, the longest one in the park at almost a mile. Two miles after your return to daylight, you approach **Turtleback Dome**, a slab of exfoliating granite that looks like it's been sliced horizontally into pieces of crumbling bread.

ROADSIDE KNOWLEDGE

Ever wonder what those little wooden roadside markers are? You know, the ones with the Half Dome symbol and a code like H15 or T32. Well, wonder no longer. They demarcate sights along roadways throughout Yosemite. But in order to decipher the code, you have to carry a copy of the handy little *Yosemite Road Guide* ($3.50), a booklet published by the Yosemite Association featuring descriptions that correspond to the codes on the signs. Also packed with some great park history, the booklet is a must-have for any drive through the park. Pick one up at a visitor center or Yosemite Association bookstores anywhere in the park.

In six more miles you'll come to the **Chinquapin** junction; turn left onto Glacier Point Rd to begin the forested 16-mile stretch to Glacier Point. In 2 miles is the wide western view of **Merced Canyon**, which descends 4500ft below you. The **Badger Pass Ski Area** appears in three more miles, though the lifts and lodge will be deserted in warm weather. In winter, the road is closed beyond here. Pass Bridalveil Creek campground, with nearby views of the Clark Range to the east.

The road turns abruptly north near **Mono Meadow**, reaching **Pothole Meadows**, where strangely small bowls of water collect during wet months. A quarter-mile more lands you at **Sentinel Dome** (8122ft), one of the park's easiest-to-hike granite domes (see p120). Switchbacks descend through red fir forest to **Washburn Point**, which has views *almost* as good as those from Glacier Point. Winding through into Glacier Point, the peak of **Half Dome** parades before you.

Retrace your route back to the Chinquapin junction, and turn left to continue south on the Wawona Rd (Hwy 41). The final 12-mile stretch passes Yosemite West, a private community that's accessible only through the park, and crosses the South Fork of the Merced River before reaching the **Wawona Hotel**, a landmark lodging dating from 1879.

OTHER ACTIVITIES

ROCK CLIMBING & BOULDERING

When it comes to rock climbing, Yosemite reigns supreme. While covering Yosemite's climbing routes is beyond the scope of this book (try something by Don Reid), at least we can point the first-time climber or visitor in the right direction (also see boxed text, p154). If you're new to climbing, consider taking a class at the Yosemite Mountaineering School (see boxed texts, p155).

Yosemite Valley

First, know this: all ropes lead to Camp 4 (p162). Most of the Valley's climbing activity revolves around this walk-in campground and historic hangout for climbing's most legendary figures. Camp 4 is where you go when you want to stop reading and start asking real people questions about where to climb, what to carry and what to expect. It's also where

you find climbing partners, pick up used gear (among other things) and find the car keys you left sitting at the base of the climb.

As for bouldering, the possibilities are limitless. Popular areas include the west end of Camp 4, Sentinel Rock, the Four-Mile Trail Trailhead, and the rocks near Housekeeping Camp and around Mirror Lake, to name only a few.

Crane Flat & Tioga Road

The big draw in these parts is Polly Dome, right next to Tenaya Lake. Stately Pleasure Dome, on the side of Polly adjacent to the lake, is the most popular spot, offering a good mix of easy and moderate routes. The granite rocks in this part of the park are well suited for slab and friction climbing, and both are well represented here.

For more difficult climbing, try the backside of Pywiack and Medlicott Domes, both just northeast of the lake toward Tuolumne Meadows. The beach at the east end of Tenaya Lake is an ideal spot for watching climbers.

For good bouldering, head to The Knobs, just over a mile north of Tenaya Lake on the west side of the road. Beginners will find excellent climbing on nearby Low-Profile Dome, particularly along the Golfer's Route.

Tuolumne Meadows

Come summertime, when temperatures in the Valley regularly top 90°F, climbers head to Tuolumne Meadows where the cool, high-country air is much more conducive to climbing. Thanks to the altitude, the air is also thinner, so climbing here requires at least a day's acclimatization for most people.

Cathedral Peak and its fin-shaped west peak, the frightening Eichorn Pinnacle, are both epic and extremely popular climbs. It's fun watching climbers tackle these peaks from the Cathedral Lakes trail (p132). The Northwest Books route on Lembert Dome is one of the most popular climbs on that iconic dome. Mt Conness, on the park's eastern border, is a challenging all-day climb.

HORSEBACK RIDING
Guided Trail Rides

There's ample opportunity to ride in Yosemite, but unless you bring your own horse you'll be on the back of a mule. For kids, it's a great way to take in the scenery, breath some dust and have a little fun.

ROCK SOLID ADVICE

Dave Bengston, director of the Yosemite Mountaineering School (YMS), has been climbing in Yosemite since 1974. He began guiding in 1985 and has served as YMS director since 1999. Dave agreed to chat with us one afternoon outside the Curry Mountain Shop, where we picked his brain on climbing in Yosemite.

Climbers new to Yosemite – where should they start?

The internet is a great source of information. Come into the [Curry Village] Mountain Shop (p101), pick up a guide book and ask the guys at the counter any questions. There are bulletin boards at Camp 4 in the Valley and in front of the Tuolumne Store in Tuolumne Meadows. The Tuolumne Store is really the central meeting area up there. Everyone gets their coffee at the Grill and hooks up with their partner. People from Camp 4 often go over to Yosemite Lodge and grab coffee and pancakes, that sort of thing.

What separates Yosemite from other climbing areas?

First it's the quality, amount and size of the rock. The granite is extremely hard (it doesn't break off easily) and the climbs here are huge. Then there's Yosemite's accessibility; you don't have to take a bush plane into the middle of nowhere to get to a climb. Finally there's the weather; in the middle of summer it's sunny all day, and it'll probably be like that tomorrow. And, of course, the crack climbing – or traditional climbing – here is *super* high quality.

Where can nonclimbers go to watch climbers climb?

Avoid El Capitan Meadow, where meadow damage has been a serious problem. Instead watch from the El Capitan Bridge, where you get a great view of the right side of El Cap. Of course, you have to have binoculars. To the left of Yosemite Falls, across from the lodge, is a spot known as Swan Slab, and there are almost always climbers there. Church Bowl is good. It's to the right of the health clinic and sort of up and to the left.

Do you have any favorite spots in Yosemite?

That's hard. I love the variety of Yosemite – that's where it's at for me. I have a new favorite place every weekend. Someone asked John Muir once what he would do if he had one day in Yosemite. He said he'd sit by the river. And that's not a bad place. I'd say get up high. Whether that's a trail or a climb.

Do you have any other advice for successful climbing or hiking?

The best way to practice Leave No Trace principles is to plan ahead and prepare. Know the park regulations. For example, certain cliffs are nesting grounds for peregrine falcons, so you need to know which routes are closed. Know where to camp to minimize your impact. Educate yourself about a route so you don't have to spend the night below the climb or build a fire. Get information about the descent trail. You can greatly minimize your impact by planning.

Guided mule rides are offered at three stables within the park from roughly spring through fall.

For guided rides throughout the park, no experience is necessary, but riders must be at least seven years old and 44in tall and weigh less than 225lb. Don't sign on for a full-day trip unless you're in good physical shape – you'll regret it. During the summer months, reservations are advised, particularly for the longer rides from the Valley. Prices at all three park-operated stables are the same: $55 for two hours, $70 for a half-day trip and $100 for a full-day trip. During the popular summer months, you should make a reservation, particularly for the longer rides, by calling the stable directly.

In Yosemite Valley, rides depart from **Yosemite Valley Stables** (Map p93; ☎ 209-372-8348), near North Pines Campground. Some of the park's most scenic riding trips leave from the **Tuolumne Meadows Stables** (Map p114; ☎ 209-372-8427).

From early April to mid-October, the **Wawona Stables** (Map p108; ☎ 209-375-6502) offer guided horseback riding behind the Pioneer Center ($55 for two hours) and to Chilnualna Falls ($70 for a half-day). If you reserve at least a month in advance, you can book a full-day trip; rates vary depending on the number of people.

Just outside the park's South Entrance, the **Yosemite Trails Pack Station** (☎ 559-683-7611) offers rides to the Mariposa big trees. Or you can rent pack and saddle animals, and the services of a packer, if you want to go it alone.

High Sierra Camps

The **Yosemite High Sierra Camps Saddle Trips** (☎ 559-253-5674, freight 209-372-8427; tent cabin per person $$$$) are far and away the most popular (though definitely not the cheapest) way to see the park from a saddle, with mules schlepping you and all the supplies. These four- to six-day trips include all meals and depart from the Tuolumne Stables for the spectacular High Sierra Camps circuit (see p165). They fill up months in advance; for availability, navigate to the High Sierra Camps section of the **DNC website** (www.yosemitepark.com). If you just want to carry your own weight and have mules carry your gear, it'll cost you $4 per pound.

Stock Camps

If you're bringing your own pack animals, you can use the stock camps at Tuolumne Meadows (Map p114), Wawona, Bridalveil Creek (Map p105) and Hetch Hetchy (one-night stay only). Each site ($20) accommodates six people and six animals. You can reserve sites up to five months in advance through **Recreation.gov** (☎ 877-444-6777; www.recreation.gov). The camp in Hetch Hetchy is available by reservation during the summer and on a first-come, first-served basis the rest of the year. Stock are allowed on all Yosemite trails except those posted on the Stock Closure list on the **NPS website** (www.nps.org/yose). For more information on traveling with your own animals, see p62.

Custom Trips

You can also hire mules to carry you and/or your gear to a destination of your choosing. Pack and saddle mules both cost $94 per animal per day, and you're required to hire a guide to go with you (an additional $185 per day). One guide is required for every five animals you hire.

RAFTING & KAYAKING

Bad news first: there are no rapids to ride within the park – you'll have to head outside Yosemite for that (see p50). The good news is that the Merced River flows lazily through Yosemite Valley, offering rafters and kayakers a marvelous way to take in the scenery on a hot summer day. That said, you do have to share the water with a plethora of other boats, but with the right sense of humor and a little Merced River water running down your face, it's undeniably fun.

Rafts, kayaks, air mattresses and inner tubes (or whatever strange, nonmotorized flotation device you're using) are allowed only along the 3-mile stretch between Stoneman Bridge (near Curry Village) and Sentinel Beach. The waters are gentle enough for children, and **raft rentals** (Map p93;

YOSEMITE MOUNTAINEERING SCHOOL

Since 1969 **Yosemite Mountaineering School** (YMS; Map p93; ☎ 209-372-8344; www.yosemitemountaineering.com) has been teaching and guiding rock climbers, mountaineers and back-country skiers of all levels. While you can learn everything from basic backpacking skills to building a snow cave, the school's specialty is teaching folks how to move their bodies up slabs of granite. Whether you're a 12 year old who wants to learn the basics of climbing, belaying and rappelling or a sport climber who wants to learn the art of big walls, you'll find this school a gold mine of opportunity. Beginners over the age of 10 can sign up for the Go Climb a Rock seminar, which is pretty much guaranteed to inspire participants to go on for more. For parents, it's a great and constructive way to turn the kids loose for a day.

Other YMS class offerings include anchoring, leading/multipitch climbing, self-rescue/aid and crack climbing, for which Yosemite, of course, is famous. You can even create your own custom climbing trip or hire guides to take you climbing.

The school is based out of the Curry Village Mountain Shop (p101) year-round. From late June through early September (when Tioga Rd is open) YMS also maintains a branch at the Tuolumne Meadows Sport Shop (p113). At both places, the friendly and knowledgeable staff will offer suggestions based on your skill level and objectives.

For more on climbing, see the boxed text, p50.

☎ 209-372-8319; ☷ 10am-4pm) for the 3-mile trip are available at Curry Village. Rates include all equipment and a return shuttle to the rental kiosk. No permit is required to use your own raft, canoe or kayak on the Merced. Shuttles depart every 30 minutes and cost $2 for those bringing their own flotation devices.

Whenever you disembark, be sure to do so only on sand or gravel bars – *not* vegetated riparian areas which cannot handle the human impact.

Rafting is also fun in Wawona on the South Fork of the Merced, between the campground and Swinging Bridge. On Tioga Rd, near Tuolumne Meadows, Tenaya Lake is a great place for a float and especially good for kayaking.

SWIMMING

River swimming throughout Yosemite is best mid- to late summer, when the water levels are low and the current gentler. The Merced River is Yosemite's biggest killer, so never swim where you're not certain the current is safe.

Yosemite Valley

On a hot summer day in Yosemite Valley (Map pp90–1), nothing beats the heat like lounging in the gentle Merced River. Provided you don't trample the riparian life on your way, you can jump in just about anywhere, but there are several locations proving particularly good: at the beach just behind Housekeeping Camp; on the stretch behind Yosemite Lodge; and at the Cathedral Beach and Devil's Elbow areas opposite the El Capitan Picnic Area. The beach immediately below Swinging Bridge is hugely popular and, thanks to calm waters, great for families. Tenaya Creek offers good swimming as well, especially near the bridge leading toward Mirror Lake.

Skin too thin? Curry Village and Yosemite Lodge provide public outdoor **swimming pools** (Map p93; adult/child $5/4; ☷ mid-May–mid-Sep). The price includes towels and showers.

Wawona

You'll find nice swimming holes both near the campground and by Swinging Bridge (Map p108). The latter is reached via a 2-mile drive east along Forest Dr, which parallels the south bank of the Merced River.

Park in a lot beyond private Camp Wawona and walk the short distance to the river.

Crane Flat & Tioga Road

If you can handle cold water, Tenaya Lake (Map p112) offers some of the most enjoyable swimming in the park. It's hard to resist this glistening lake that beckons with sapphire waters. A sandy half-moon beach wraps around the east end. Sunbathers and picnickers are also drawn to the rocks that rim its north and west sides.

Want to work a little for that dip? May Lake is an easy hike (p128) and gorgeous, if a bit chilly. You can swim anywhere except a signed section of the western side where the May Lake High Camp draws its drinking water. Further west, Harden Lake (p128) is unusually warm compared with other nearby lakes because much of its volume evaporates in summer. A late- or even mid-season swim is practically balmy.

Tuolumne Meadows

The Tuolumne River (Map p114) is an excellent choice for high-country swimming, with many easy-to-reach sandy-bottomed pools and slightly warmer temperatures than other High Sierra rivers. From the pullout at the west end of Tuolumne Meadows, follow the trail along Pothole Dome and the river for about a mile to a gorgeous waterfall and hidden swimming spot.

You'll also find a couple of small but good swimming holes at the twin bridges crossing the chipper Lyell Fork Tuolumne; to get there, head out the trail to Lyell Canyon (see p143). If you don't mind hiking a bit further, the Lyell Fork also has some great (albeit shallow) swimming areas. Elizabeth Lake (p132) can be a bit bone-chilling, but on a hot summer day, plenty of people take the plunge and love it.

FISHING

Yosemite may not be the sort of place you go to catch whopping trophy trout, but the setting is fabulous, and wettin' a line, so to say, in the Merced or Tuolumne River is pretty darn satisfying. In Wawona (Map p108), the South Fork of the Merced offers some of the best stream fishing in the park. In and around the Valley (Map pp90–1), you can fish the Merced River between Vernal and Nevada Falls and above Washburn

Lake, although if you catch a rainbow trout, you'll have to throw it back. In Yosemite Valley, you're only allowed five brown trout per day, and bait is prohibited (artificial lures or barbless flies only).

The park's most satisfying fishing, especially for fly casters, is undoubtedly in Tuolumne Meadows (Map p114). Although the fish aren't big, they're fun, and the setting is unbeatable. The Dana Fork Tuolumne and especially the Lyell Fork Tuolumne are good, with easy access from shore and no wading required. As for lakes, Elizabeth Lake (p132) is the most easily accessible. If you're heading up to Young Lakes (p144), bring a pole. Some of the best lake fishing is on Saddlebag Lake, just outside the park, east of the Tioga Pass entrance, off Hwy 120.

Hetch Hetchy Reservoir (Map p116) is said to house a trove of very large trout; casting is permitted from the shore only, though no live bait is allowed. Above the reservoir, the Tuolumne River is supposedly very good.

You can pick up tackle and supplies at the Yosemite Village Sport Shop, the stores in Tuolumne Meadows, Wawona and Crane Flat. For more information on fishing regulations and suggestions on where to fish outside the park, see p53.

WINTER ACTIVITIES
Yosemite Valley
It wouldn't be difficult to argue that Yosemite Valley is at its very best just after a fresh snowfall. **Snowshoeing** around the Valley, past icy monoliths, frozen waterfalls and meadows blanketed in snow, is a truly magical activity. The John Muir Trail, which begins at Happy Isles, is a popular destination.

Another delightful way to spend a winter's afternoon is twirling about on the large outdoor **Curry Village Ice Rink** (Map pp90-1; ☎ 209-372-8319/41; 2½hr session adult/child $8/6, skate rental $3). The rink is open from November through March, with daily sessions at 3:30pm and 7pm and additional sessions at 8:30am and noon on weekends.

Wawona
Mariposa Grove (Map p108) contains a series of well-marked **cross-country skiing** trails, including an 8-mile loop trail from the South Entrance. Trail maps can be purchased at the park or printed from the park website. The trails also connect to marked Sierra National Forest trails just south of the park in Goat Meadow and along Beasore Rd. Trail map are available at the United States Forest Service (USFS) office in Oakhurst (p183).

Off-limits in summer, the peaceful and protected Mariposa Grove is open for **snow camping** from December to mid-April. You'll need a wilderness permit, and you must set up your tent uphill from Clothespin Tree. The Wawona campground also stays open for winter camping on a first-come, first-served basis.

Glacier Point & Badger Pass
DOWNHILL SKIING & SNOWBOARDING
California's oldest ski slope, **Badger Pass Ski Area** (Map p105; ☎ 209-372-8430; www.yosemitepark .com/badgerpass.aspx; adult/child/youth lift tickets $40/15/35; ☻ mid-Dec–early Apr) sits at 7300ft on Glacier Point Rd, about 22 miles from the Valley. Known as a family-friendly mountain geared toward beginners and intermediates, it features an 800ft vertical drop, nine runs, two terrain parks, five lifts, a full-service lodge and equipment rental ($25 for a full set of gear). For great money-saving deals, check out the stay-and-ski packages at the Wawona Hotel, Yosemite Lodge and Ahwahnee Hotel, and note that lift-ticket prices drop considerably during midweek. They also rent tubes for snow tubing.

The excellent on-site Yosemite Ski School is highly regarded for its top-notch instruction, particularly for beginners. Group lessons are $30, private lessons start at $65 per hour and the 'Guaranteed Learn to Ski/Snowboard' package costs $60 to $100. Badger's gentle slopes are well suited for first-time snowboarders.

In winter, a free daily shuttle runs from the Valley to Badger Pass in the morning, returning to the Valley in the afternoon.

CROSS-COUNTRY SKIING
Twenty miles of groomed track, 90 miles of marked trails and 23 skating lanes fan out from Badger Pass. From here, you can schuss out to the Clark Range Vista and Glacier Point, an invigorating 21-mile round-trip. Pick up a trail map or download one from the Yosemite website.

The **Yosemite Cross-Country Ski Center** (☎ 209-372-8444) offers learn-to-ski packages

---

WINTER SKI HUTS

When the park is hushed and white, three classic ski huts are open for overnight guests who make the trek on snowshoes or cross-country skis. The journeys aren't easy, but certainly worth the work. Make sure to self-register for a wilderness permit before you head out.

The **Glacier Point Ski Hut** (Map pp90-1; ☎ 209-372-8444; www.yosemitepark.com) is operated by the park concessionaire, and reached by way of a guided 10.5-mile trip on an intermediate trail. Led by the Cross-Country Ski Center, one-night trips cost $160 to $200 per person; two nights run $240 to $300. All tariffs include meals, wine, accommodations and guides.

The handcrafted stone **Ostrander Lake Ski Hut** (Map p105; ☎ 209-372-0740; www.ostranderhut .com; bunk $), operated by the Yosemite Association, can accommodate up to 25 skiers in a gorgeous lakeside spot beneath Horse Ridge. Cooking facilities are provided, but you must ski in with all of your supplies. The 10-mile trip requires experience and a high fitness level. Staffed throughout the winter, the hut is open to backcountry skiers and snowshoers, and a drawing is held for reservations in early November.

Are you up to this challenge? The **Tuolumne Meadows Ski Hut** is a 16-mile trek from the eastern side of the park, crossing Tioga Pass. The Ski Hut is the stone building facing Tioga Rd just west of the bridge across the Tuolumne River, right at the entrance to the Tuolumne Meadows Campground. It has a wood-burning stove, sleeps 10, and is first-come, first served. If you're hesitant to try this on your own, the Yosemite Cross-Country Ski Center runs tours there for $800 per person.

($20), guided tours (from $45 for a half-day, three people minimum), telemark instruction ($35), private lessons (starting at $30), and equipment rental ($25 for skis, boots and poles). The school also hosts very popular overnight trips to the Glacier Point Ski Hut (see the boxed text, above).

SNOWSHOEING
You can rent snowshoes ($19.50/16.50 per half-/full day) at Badger Pass, where rangers lead two-hour naturalist treks that are informative, fun and almost free ($5). Check *Yosemite Today* for schedules. From February to April, rangers offer two-hour 'Full Moon Snowshoe Walks' ($14.75 with equipment rental; $5 without) on nights of, and leading up to, a full moon. Sign up at the Yosemite Lodge Tour Desk or by calling ☎ 372-1240.

SNOW CAMPING
The Yosemite Cross-Country Ski Center offers an overnight trip at Badger Pass ($250 per person, including meals), with instruction in snow-camping fundamentals and survival skills.

Crane Flat & Tioga Road
You'll find good marked cross-country skiing and snowshoeing trails in the Crane Flat area, including Old Big Oak Flat Rd, which leads to Tuolumne Grove and Hodgdon Meadow. Trail maps are available at the park and on the park website. When Tioga Rd is closed in winter, it becomes a popular, though ungroomed ski route.

If tubing down a hill is more your fancy, there's a snow-play area located in Crane Flat.

HANG GLIDING
Glacier Point & Badger Pass
You can actually hang glide from Glacier Point for a mere $5, provided you're an active member of the **USHGA** (☎ 719-632-8300; www.ushga.org), have an advanced standing or level 4 certification, and you preregister online with the **Yosemite Hang Gliding Association** (YHGA; www.yhga.org). On Saturdays and Sundays from late May to early September, weather permitting, qualified hang gliders can launch from the overlook between 7am and 9am, well before any thermal activity rolls in, and float down by 10am to Leidig Meadow, just west of Yosemite Lodge. Arrive at the launch pad before 7am (by as early as 6am) and avoid a late landing, or you may face stiff consequences (like a night in jail or hefty fine). The YHGA monitors all jumps, but you must bring your own equipment; no paragliding or tandem flying is allowed. One of the best free shows in the park is watching the colorful gliders sprint off the edge and soar over the Valley like tiny paper airplanes.

BOATING
Crane Flat & Tioga Road
Motorless boats of any kind can use beautiful and easy-to-access Tenaya Lake – hands down the best place to boat in the park. Lounging at the foot of John Muir's beloved Mt Hoffmann is tranquil May Lake, a lovely place to paddle an inflatable; that is, unless you want to hoof anything heavier for the 1.2 miles from the trailhead along Tioga Rd.

CAMPFIRE & PUBLIC PROGRAMS
There's something almost universally enjoyable about group campfire programs. Pull a bench around a roaring bonfire, with stars above, big trees behind you and lots of friendly folks all around, and it's as if you've left the world's troubles behind.

During the summer, free campfire programs are held at the following Yosemite campgrounds: Tuolumne Meadows, Wawona, Bridalveil Creek, Crane Flat, White Wolf and Lower Pines. Check *Yosemite Today* for that week's programs and times. Rangers, naturalists and other park staff lead the programs, and topics include the history, ecology and geology of the local region, a few tips on dealing with bears, and maybe some stories and songs. They're geared toward families and people of all ages.

Similar evening programs are also held at amphitheaters behind Yosemite Lodge and Curry Village – even in the absence of an actual campfire, the mood remains the same. These programs include general talks about the area, with occasional slide shows and films.

The Sierra Club's LeConte Memorial Lodge (p104) hosts programs each week. A little more in-depth than the average campfire talk, these cover such topics as the founding of the John Muir Trail and the history of Hetch Hetchy.

Glacier Point rangers lead weekly programs at a lovely stone amphitheater near the snack bar, and sometimes offer sunset talks along the railing overlooking the Valley. Over at Tuolumne Meadows, talks take place during rainy afternoons at Parsons Memorial Lodge (p114), reachable via an easy half-mile hike.

The busiest time is, of course, during the summer, usually June to September. Limited programs are, however, offered in the off-season, and they're held during cold weather at indoor locations such as Yosemite Lodge and the Ahwahnee Hotel.

GROUP HIKES
If you haven't done much hiking before – or even if you have – taking a ranger-guided hike with a group of fellow travelers is a great way to get to know this massive park better. Rangers lead hikes year-round, most often in the summer. Check *Yosemite Today*. Like most ranger programs, the hikes are generally free and require no reservations.

Hikes take place in all major areas of the park and range from mild (walks to Mirror Lake or through the Mariposa Grove) to moderately strenuous (out to Mono Pass or up Mt Hoffmann). Short hikes may be just an hour or two, while longer excursions can last all day.

CLASSIC KEEPSAKES
Alright, you didn't come to Yosemite to shop. But c'mon, you know when you stroll over to the Village Store for that tube of toothpaste that you forgot to pack, you're going to glance over at the souvenirs. Of course, you'd never *buy* that dumb key chain or silly beer cozy. But that box of Chiura Obata greeting cards is pretty cool…

Here are our top five goodies to take home from Yosemite:

- 'Restore Hetch Hetchy' bumper sticker
- 'Go Climb a Rock' T-shirt, sold at the Curry Village Mountain Shop (p101)
- A small, special edition print from the Ansel Adams Gallery (p99)
- Box of Chiura Obata's Yosemite greeting cards
- John Muir's *The Yosemite*, featuring Galen Rowell's photography

SLEEPING

One of the biggest questions facing Yosemite visitors is where to spend the night. Nearly four million people visit Yosemite each year, some as day visitors but many vying for one of the 1505 campsites or 1517 rooms and tent cabins available in the park. During the height of summer, visitors fill open reservations faster than blue jays descend on a picnic. Newcomers with visions of sleeping soundly under the stars often find that campsites and rooms are full, having been reserved months in advance.

Most lodges and campgrounds both inside and outside the park open and close at slightly different times each year, depending on weather. Always check before you go. If you're stuck without a place to sleep inside the park, look outside its borders.

CAMPING

During the height of summer, when all facilities are open, more than 9000 people may be packed into Yosemite's campgrounds on any given night. Those hoping to get in touch with nature may find they're more in touch with their neighbors, who are often clanging pans, slurping beer by the fire or snoring in their tents just 10ft or 20ft away. It gets especially crowded in Yosemite Valley. Overnighters looking for a quieter, more rugged experience are better off in spots like Bridalveil Creek, Yosemite

---

HEY STINKY, WANNA SHOWER?

Yosemite campers have one thing in common: they all need a wash. No campgrounds in the park have showers. Should you feel the need to remove that four-day layer of grime or wash your hair, head to the public showers at Curry Village (p100), Housekeeping Camp (p165) or, during summer, the Tuolumne Meadows Lodge (p167; noon to 3:30pm only). All three places have hot public showers and charge about $5 for nonguests. If you didn't bring enough underwear and socks, Housekeeping Camp also offers public laundry facilities.

Creek and Porcupine Flat. For general camping information, see p250.

Campgrounds in Yosemite range from primitive backpacker camps to developed sites that can accommodate large RVs. Most have flush toilets and potable water. The exceptions are the park's three primitive sites (Tamarack Flat, Yosemite Creek and Porcupine Flat), which have vault (pit) toilets and require you to bring your own water or a means of purifying water from nearby streams. All park campsites include a picnic table, a fire pit with a barbecue grill, and a bear-proof locker for food storage. None of the campgrounds have showers.

Campground elevations are important to consider. For instance, the campgrounds along Tioga Rd and in Tuolumne Meadows, some of which sit above 8000ft, may boast warm weather during the day, but come nightfall you'll be wishing you'd packed that wool sweater.

Yosemite has four campgrounds open all year: Upper Pines, Camp 4, Wawona and Hodgdon Meadow. The rest are open seasonally.

Yosemite Valley

While Yosemite Valley campgrounds (Map p93) are convenient to many of the park's major sights and activities, they're also very crowded, often noisy and definitely lacking in privacy. Don't camp here expecting to get away from it all – for solitude, you're better off in less-visited areas of the park.

Yosemite Valley's three Pines campgrounds (North Pines, Upper Pines and Lower Pines) are all located east of Yosemite Village at the far end of the Valley and are open to both RVs and tent campers. For tips on securing one, read the boxed text (opposite).

Upper Pines (sites $; year-round) With 238 sites spread under a forest of pine, Yosemite's second-largest campground is close-quarters camping at its finest. It sits along the bus and pedestrian road to the Nature Center at Happy Isles and trailhead, only a short walk away from Curry Village.

Lower Pines (sites $; Mar-Oct;) Directly west of North Pines, Lower Pines is smaller but almost identical to Upper Pines, set amid the trees on the south shore of the

HOW TO SCORE A CAMPSITE IN YOSEMITE

If you're one of those folks who can't bear the thought of driving four hours or more without knowing whether there's a campsite waiting for you, then you'd better make a reservation if you want to camp in Yosemite. It's the only way to ensure you'll have a place to lay your head. However, if you'd rather chance it – or if you couldn't get (or never got around to making) a reservation before you came – there are options.

Reservations

Reservations for all campgrounds within the park are handled by **Recreation.gov** (☎ 877-444-6777, 518-885-3639; www.recreation.gov; ☺ 7am-7pm Nov-Feb, to 9pm Mar-Sep), formerly the National Park Reservation Service. Campsites can be reserved up to six months in advance. Reservations become available on the 15th of every month in one-month blocks. Be sure to act quickly, as most dates in summer fill up the first day reservations become available – sometimes within minutes!

Campgrounds *requiring* reservations include: North Pines, Upper Pines and Lower Pines in Yosemite Valley (only Camp 4 is first-come, first-served); Wawona and Hodgdon Meadow (between May and September only); Crane Flat; and half of the sites in Tuolumne Meadows. The rest of the park's campgrounds (and Hodgdon Meadow and Wawona during the off-season) are available on a first-come, first-served basis. If you're rolling into Yosemite without reservations and would like to stay in a reservation-only campground, swing by one of the Campground Reservation Offices (see next section).

If you still have questions regarding the whole process or simply wish to speak with a human being in Yosemite, call the **Yosemite Valley Campground Office** (☎ information only 209-372-8502). Also, check the **Yosemite National Park website** (www.nps.gov/yose). Unaffiliated with the park, **Yosemitesites.com** (www.yosemitesites.com) is a good place to conduct initial research; you can see exactly what's available before reserving a site through Recreation.gov.

If you already have a reservation, proceed directly to the campground gate to check in. If you're going to be more than 24 hours late, call the campground office; otherwise you may lose your reservation.

Trying Your Luck

If you arrive at Yosemite without reservations, there are several options. If you want to stay in Yosemite Valley, you can either try the first-come, first-served, walk-in campground at Camp 4 or head straight to the **Yosemite Valley Campground Reservation Office** (Map p93; ☎ information only 209-372-8502; ☺ 8am-5pm) in the day-use parking lot near Camp Curry. Practically every day, reservation-only campsites become available due to cancellations or early departures, and these are sold on a first-come, first-served basis from the reservation offices.

If nothing's available, you can put your name on a waiting list and return at the prescribed time (usually 3pm) to find out if you've gotten one. At this point, it's usually better to simply try Camp 4 or one of the other first-come, first-served campgrounds outside the Valley. These are Bridalveil Creek, Tamarack Flat, White Wolf, Yosemite Creek, Porcupine Flat and half the sites at Tuolumne Meadows.

There are also reservation offices in **Wawona** (Map p108; ☎ 209-375-9531; ☺ 8:30am-5pm late May–early Oct); **Big Oak Flat** (Map p110; ☎ 209-379-2123; ☺ 8am-5pm May–mid-Oct), just inside its namesake entry; and **Tuolumne Meadows** (Map p114; ☎ 209-372-4025; ☺ 8am-5pm mid-Jun–mid-Sep), near the campground entrance.

Also see p251.

Merced River. Damaged during the 1997 flood, this campground has been reduced to only 60 sites.

North Pines (sites $; ☺ Apr-Sep) Across the Merced River from Lower Pines, the 81-site North Pines campground is probably the quietest of the valley's campgrounds. Although most of its sites are similar to those at the other Pines, it boasts a handful of riverside sites that are comparatively outstanding.

YOSEMITE NATIONAL PARK CAMPGROUNDS

Campground	Location	No of sites	Elevation	Open (approx)	Reservations required?
Bridalveil Creek	Glacier Point Rd	110	7200ft	Jun-early Sep	no
Camp 4	Yosemite Valley	35	4000ft	year-round	no
Crane Flat	Crane Flat	166	6191ft	Jun-Sep	yes
Hodgdon Meadow	Big Oak Flat Rd	105	4872ft	year-round	May-Sep
Lower Pines	Yosemite Valley	60	4000ft	Mar-Oct	yes
North Pines	Yosemite Valley	81	4000ft	Apr-Sep	yes
Porcupine Flat	Tioga Rd	52	8100ft	Jul-Sep	no
Tamarack Flat	Tioga Rd	52	6315ft	Jun-early Sep	no
Tuolumne Meadows	Tuolumne Meadows	304	8600ft	Jul-Sep	half reserved
Upper Pines	Yosemite Valley	238	4000ft	year-round	yes
Wawona	Wawona	93	4000ft	year-round	May-Sep
White Wolf	Tioga Rd	74	8000ft	Jul-early Sep	no
Yosemite Creek	Tioga Rd	40	7659ft	Jul-early Sep	no

All campgrounds have: bear boxes, parking, picnic tables, fire pits and trash receptacles.

 Drinking Water   Flush Toilets   Ranger Station   Wheelchair Accessible   Dogs Allowed (On Leash)   Grocery Store Nearby

Camp 4 (tent sites $; year-round) Formerly known as Sunnyside, legendary Camp 4 is Yosemite's only first-come, first-served campground and, for over half a century, has been hub and home for Valley climbers. Outside climbing season, however, you'll find as many families (who couldn't get into the Pines campgrounds) as you will rock jocks. Each of the 35 sites holds six tents, so be ready to share your table, your campfire and the night's conversation with others. It's a fun, low-key place. It's also a walk-in campground; cars must be left in an adjacent parking lot, and sites are for tent campers only.

Backpackers' Campground (tent sites per person $5; summer) The 20 quiet, wooded sites at Yosemite Valley's backpackers' campground are open only to backpackers holding valid wilderness permits. It's a walk-in self-registration campground, reached via a bridge over Tenaya Creek from the west end of North Pines campground.

Glacier Point & Badger Pass

Bridalveil Creek Campground (Map p105; Glacier Point Rd; sites $; Jul-early Sep) If the Valley's stewing through a summer heat wave, remember that the altitude here (7200ft) keeps things much cooler. Tucked 25 miles (a mere 40 minutes) away from the Valley buzz, this 110-site campground is the only developed place to stay in the Glacier Point Rd area. Sites are well spaced beneath pretty pine forest, and the ones near the amphitheater front a long granite outcropping that's perfect for watching the sunset in solitude. Located 8 miles up from Hwy 41, it's first-come, first-served, has drinking water and flush toilets, and there's a horse camp at the back.

Facilities	Description	Page
	Near Glacier Point; some attractive sites; removed from Valley crowds	opposite
	Walk-in campground, popular with climbers; fee is per person; campers share sites; tent-only	opposite
	Large family campground spread across five loops, varied sites; easy drive to Yosemite Valley	below
	Close to park entrance, utilitarian, can be crowded and noisy; easy drive to Yosemite Valley	below
	Smaller Valley campground, minimum privacy	160
	Smaller Valley campground with pleasant sites, slightly removed from development; adjacent to stables	161
	Primitive, close to road but relatively quiet; RV access front half only	164
	Quiet, secluded, primitive; accessed via a rough 3-mile road; tent only	164
	Park's biggest campground, many sites well dispersed over large, forested area	164
	Largest Valley campground, expect little privacy, especially in summer; close to Happy Isles	160
	Located along river; nicer sites in back section (open summer only); short drive to store	below
	Only nonprimitive campground in area; walking distance to store and restaurant	164
	Park's most secluded, quiet primitive campground; accessed via rough 4.5-mile road; tent only	164

 Payphone   RV Dump Station

Wawona

Wawona Campground (Map p108; sites $; year-round;) The south fork of the Merced River cuts through this southernmost section of Yosemite, and this campground includes some sites situated right alongside its banks. It's a pleasant place to set up your tent or RV, though some of the nicer 93 spots are in the back section and are only open during summer (approximately May to September), when the whole campground goes on the reservation system. The rest of the year it's first-come, first-served. Horse sites are available.

Crane Flat

Hodgdon Meadow (Map p110; sites $; year-round) Just east of the Big Oak Flat Entrance, this popular campground has 105 decent sites; a few of the nicer ones are walk-ins, though you won't have to go more than 20yd. All campsites here must be reserved during summer (May through September) but are first-come, first-served the rest of the year.

Crane Flat (Map p110; sites $; Jun-Sep) Around 8 miles east is this even bigger campground, which sits near the Crane Flat store and the junction with Tioga Rd. Sites lie along five different loops, most in the trees and some very nicely dispersed (there's 166 in total). The central location is great for those wanting to split their time between Tuolumne Meadows and Yosemite Valley. Reservations are required year-round.

Tioga Road

If you're in the mood for some solitude and crisper evening air, you'll find a number of options along Tioga Rd (Hwy 120) as it

---

PSST! IGNORE THE SIGNS

Both the Tamarack Flat and Yosemite Creek campgrounds are first-come, first-served and located at the end of bruising dirt roads. 'Full' signs are posted on the Big Oak Flat Rd respective turnoffs when all of their spots have been claimed. However, park staff don't check availability on a daily basis, so you won't know for sure until you get there. Especially in the mornings, there's a good chance that you can snag one of these remote sites, even when the signs say otherwise.

---

heads east from Crane Flat to Tuolumne Meadows. When it's been a light snow season, early birds may get the place all to themselves.

All four campgrounds along Tioga Rd operate on a first-come, first-served basis, and two of them are the most rugged, quiet and beautiful in the park. White Wolf offers flush toilets, while the other three are primitive, with only vault toilets and no water tap, so be sure to bring your own water or be prepared to purify it from adjacent streams.

Tamarack Flat (Map p112; sites $; ⟨☽⟩ Jun-early Sep) One of the most serene and spacious places in the park to set up your tent is 3 miles down a rough, barely paved road that's as steep and narrow as it is woodsy and beautiful. Expect about a 15-minute drive off Tioga Rd each way, and don't attempt the journey with an RV or big trailer. The 52 tent-only sites are well dispersed among trees, with some near a creek – which lends the campground a very open feel, with lots of sun and sky. The parts of the park accessible by road are rarely this quiet.

White Wolf (Map p112; sites $; ⟨☽⟩ Jul-early Sep) Don't feel like cooking over the ol' Coleman every night but don't want to deal with Valley throngs? Located north of Tioga Rd on a mile-long spur road, this 74-site campground, adjacent to the White Wolf Lodge and store, enjoys a relaxed setting among pine trees and granite boulders beside a lazy stream. It's an attractive and convenient alternative to the food options available to Valley campers

without forsaking *all* the creature comforts of civilization.

our pick Yosemite Creek (Map p112; sites $; ⟨☽⟩ Jul-early Sep) Halfway down this rutted road, you may ask yourself if it's really worth it. Don't fret, it is. Drive 4.5 miles (about 20 minutes) down a stretch of the old Tioga Rd – a narrow, winding and very chopped-up piece of roadway that's no good for RVs or trailers – and you find yourself in the most secluded, spacious and serene car-accessible campground in the park. The 40 sites are surprisingly well dispersed: some in the trees, others in the open. A trail from here leads to the top of Yosemite Falls.

Porcupine Flat (Map p112; sites $; ⟨☽⟩ Jul-Sep) If you want easy access to Tioga Rd and don't mind treating or bringing your own water, try this 52-site campground, which sits about halfway between Crane Flat and Tuolumne Meadows, the latter only a 20-minute drive away. The sites up front can handle RVs and campers, but the quieter and more rustic back half is for tents only. There's some road noise in the daytime, but it dissipates after dark. At 8100ft, it's the second-highest developed campground in the park, and a good place to spend the night acclimatizing before hitting the high country.

Tuolumne Meadows

our pick Tuolumne Meadows Campground (sites $; ⟨☽⟩ Jul-Sep) This is the largest campground in the park, with 304 sites for tents or RVs (35ft limit). Despite its size, many of the sites are tucked into the trees, making the place feel far less crowded than other park campgrounds. Some of the sites in the 'E' and 'F' sections are delightfully peaceful. The premises also include a horse camp, group camp and walk-in backpackers' campground for those with wilderness permits. Half the sites here are on the reservation system, while the other half are kept first-come, first-served.

Hetch Hetchy

The only place to stay in this area is the **backpackers' campground** (Map p116; sites $), which is one of the park's nicest. But it's brutally hot in summer and available only to holders of valid wilderness permits for Hetch Hetchy.

Once you leave the park, you can drive down any of the dirt Forest Service roads and camp for free wherever you wish. The nearest official campground is the pleasant **Dimond O Campground** (Map p116; ☎ 877-444-6777; www.recreation.gov; Evergreen Rd; sites $; ⊗ Apr-Oct), which lies 6 miles north of Hwy 120 on Evergreen Rd, in the Stanislaus National Forest. Some can be reserved; others are first-come, first-served.

LODGING

Of the Yosemite lodging options, tent cabins are the most basic. Curry Village, White Wolf Lodge and Yosemite Lodge feature motel-like standard rooms with showers and bathrooms. Top of the heap are rooms at the park's two historic hotels, the lovely Wawona and the uber-deluxe Ahwahnee.

Yosemite Valley

Yosemite Valley (Map pp90–1) offers a fair range of accommodations, from simple tent cabins to standard motel units to luxurious accommodations at the historic Ahwahnee. Tent cabins at Curry Village and Housekeeping Camp are great for families who wish to avoid both exorbitant hotel costs and the labor of setting up camp.

Housekeeping Camp (4-person tent cabins $$; ⊗ Apr-Oct; ♿ ⚹) A 10-minute walk from Yosemite Village, Housekeeping Camp is a conglomeration of 266 tent cabins grouped tightly together on the southern shore of the Merced River. Each cabin has concrete walls, a canvas roof, an electrical outlet, cots, an enclosed outdoor table and a fire pit. The complex can feel pretty cramped, especially with all the cars parked around the cabins, but they're pleasant nonetheless. One guest offered a friendly tip: bring a space heater if it's cold. Our tip – expect noise and bring your sense of humor! The cabins along the riverbank are excellent. Housekeeping Camp offers the only lodging facilities that allow cooking. There's a small store (where you can get newspapers), hot showers ($5 for nonguests) and laundry facilities (from 8am to 10pm). Bring your own linens and pillows or rent bedding from the front desk (about $2.50 per item per person).

Curry Village (tent cabins, cabins & r $$; ⊗ year-round; ♿ ⚹) Resembling a cross between

---

HIGH SIERRA CAMPS

In the backcountry near Tuolumne Meadows, the enormously popular High Sierra Camps (HSCs; Map p144) provide accommodations and meals for hikers who would rather not carry a tent. The camps are at Glen Aulin, May Lake, Sunrise, Merced Lake and Vogelsang, each within a leisurely day's hike of one another (less than 10 miles). The Tuolumne Meadows Lodge completes the circuit, although the lodge is also open to the public. Some hikers do the whole circuit, a weeklong loop on established trails. Others visit just one or two camps.

The camps consist of dormitory-style canvas tent cabins with beds and wool blankets or comforters, plus showers and a central dining tent. Breakfast and dinner are included in the fee (for current rates, see www.yosemitepark.com). Guests bring their own sheets and towels. The accommodations are hardly luxurious, but the knockout settings – not to mention the convenience of not having to carry a tent and food – make the High Sierra Camps appealing.

The seasons are so short (roughly June to September) and the camps so popular that reservations are doled out by lottery. Applications for the lottery are accepted no later than January 15 each year, and requests for an application must be made before December 31. To obtain an application, contact **DNC** (☎ 559-253-5674; www.yosemitepark.com). Folks with flexible schedules can sometimes get in at the last minute to at least one camp due to cancellations. Call DNC or check the availability list on the website.

While the High Sierra Camps are only for reserved guests, each has an adjacent backpackers' campsite available to anyone with a wilderness permit. The backpackers' campsites come complete with bear boxes, toilets and potable water taps. It's also possible to reserve meals only at a High Sierra Camp, which can ease the burden of carrying your own food; call a day or two in advance.

LODGING RESERVATIONS IN YOSEMITE

Nearly all the lodging in Yosemite National Park, from tent cabins and High Sierra Camps to the Ahwahnee Hotel, is managed by **DNC Parks & Resorts at Yosemite, Inc** (DNC; ☎ 559-253-2003, 559-253-5635; www.yosemitepark.com; ☸ reservations 7am-9pm Mon-Fri, to 7pm Sat & Sun, reduced hours winter). The only accommodations DNC doesn't manage are the Ostrander Ski Hut (p158) and the homes and cabins in Foresta (a private vacation settlement south of Big Oak Flat Rd), Yosemite West (below) and the Redwoods in Yosemite (opposite).

Reservations are available through DNC 366 days in advance of your arrival date. Places get snapped up early for summer months, especially on weekends and holidays, but if you're flexible, there's often some space available on short notice, especially midweek. You can go on the website and easily view everything that's available.

If you roll into the park without a reservation, the Yosemite Valley Visitor Center (p92) and all the lodging front desks have courtesy phones so you can inquire about room availability throughout the park. That said, it's important to remember that rooms *rarely* become available midsummer.

---

a summer camp and a labor camp, the vast, crowded and historic Curry Village offers several types of accommodations. The 427 canvas tent cabins sleep up to five people each and include linens but lack heating, electrical outlets and fire pits. Cars must park outside the cabin area, however, which cuts down on the noise. Some tents have propane heaters and are open during winter. The wooden cabins are a bit nicer: 80 share central bathroom units and have propane heaters but are still crowded together; another 102 boast private bathrooms, electric heat and outlets, plus more spacious and cozy quarters. Curry Village also contains 19 straightforward motel-style rooms without televisions or phones.

Yosemite Lodge (☎ 209-372-1274; standard/lodge r $$/$$$, children under 12yr free; ☸ year-round; ✸ ▢ ▣ ⚷ ♿) Located a short walk from the base of Yosemite Falls, the modest and meandering Yosemite Lodge makes for great family accommodations, thanks to its giant swimming pool, an array of hosted activities, tours, bike rentals, a small amphitheater, a store and 229 spacious 'lodge family rooms.' Its 19 'standard' rooms are comfy for couples but about as exciting as a Motel 6 in Barstow, California. There are also restaurants and a bar on the premises (see p169 for details). Despite the number of rooms, the place fills up a year in advance (so plan ahead).

Ahwahnee Hotel (☎ 209-372-1407; r, ste & cottages $$$$; ✸ ▢ ▣ ⚷) A National Historic Landmark, the Ahwahnee has been offering its guests the royal treatment since 1927. A stunning work of architecture, the hotel is by far the most luxurious place in the park. The 99 rooms, all tastefully decorated with Native American touches, boast great views and supremely comfortable beds. Other options include 24 cottages out back and a handful of suites. Tucked away in its own quiet, secluded corner of the Valley, the Ahwahnee is worth a visit even if you're not staying overnight. The hotel features an upscale restaurant and friendly bar (both covered on p169, swimming pool, tennis courts, wireless internet access, occasional evening programs and an amazing series of public common rooms.

Glacier Point & Badger Pass

The **Yosemite West** (Map p105; www.yosemitewest .com; accommodations $$$-$$$$) private development rents contemporary homes, cabins, rooms and apartments in a community just west of Hwy 41. Although it is outside the park proper, Yosemite West is only accessible from inside the park. Look for the turnoff about half a mile south of the intersection with Glacier Point Rd. Drive about a mile and you'll reach a sign, where there are maps and phone numbers of the local establishments. Rates are for double occupancy, but larger units are available; prices rise with the size of the group.

Inside the Yosemite West development are also a few B&Bs, including the **Yosemite**

Peregrine (☎ 209-372-8517, 800-396-3639; www .yosemiteperegrine.com; 7509 Henness Circle; r $$$) and the **Yosemite West High Sierra** (☎ 209- 372-4808; www.yosemitehighsierra.com; 7460 Henness Ridge Rd; r $$$).

Wawona

Wawona Hotel (Map p108; ☎ 209-375-6556, reser- vations 559-253-5635; www.yosemitepark.com; r with/ without bathroom incl breakfast $$$/$$; ⊙ Easter–Oct, weekends Nov–Mar; 🖃 👶 👣) This National Historic Landmark, dating from 1879, is a collection of six graceful, New England– style buildings, each painted white and lined with wide porches. The 104 rooms come with Victorian furniture and other period items, and most open up onto a veranda. About half the rooms share bath- rooms, and nice robes are provided for the walk there. Rooms with private facili- ties are a bit larger, and most rooms can be configured to connect to others, which is handy for families. None has a TV or phone. The grounds are lovely, and the spacious lawn is dotted with Adirondack chairs. There's an excellent restaurant (see p169) in the main building, as well as bar service nightly in the lobby lounge or out on the porch.

Redwoods in Yosemite (Map p108; ☎ 209-375- 6666; www.redwoodsinyosemite.com; 8038 Chilnualna Falls Rd; homes per night $$$-$$$$) This private enterprise rents some 127 fully furnished accommodations of various sizes and levels of comfort, from rustic log cabins to spacious vacation homes. (Hot tub, anyone?) There's a three-night minimum stay in summer; two nights otherwise. The main office (where there is free coffee and tantalizing fresh popcorn) is 2 miles east of Hwy 41 on Chilnualna Falls Rd; look for the junction just north of the Wawona Store.

Tioga Road

White Wolf Lodge (Map p112; tent cabins $$, cabins with bathroom $$; ⊙ summer only) This complex enjoys its own little world a mile up a spur road, away from the hubbub and traffic of Hwy 120 and the Valley. It also features nice hiking trails to Lukens and Harden Lakes. There are 24 spartan tent cabins and four very in-demand hard-walled cabins housed in two duplex buildings. There's also a dining room and a tiny counter-service store (see p170 for details of both). The four-bedded tent cabins include linens, candles and wood stoves with wood, but have no electricity; they share central bathrooms. A step up are the hard-walled cabins, which have the feel of a rustic motel room. Each unit contains a private bathroom, two double beds, a porch and propane heat. The generator cuts out at 11pm, so you'll need a flashlight until early morning. When there's enough water in its well, the lodge sells showers to the public.

Tuolumne Meadows

If you don't want to camp in Tuolumne Meadows (Map p114), you have one option – a minor but definite step up.

Tuolumne Meadows Lodge (☎ information 209- 372-8413; tent cabins $$; ⊙ Jun–mid-Sep; 👣) Don't let the name confuse you. This 'lodge' con- sists of 69 wood-framed, canvas-covered tent cabins, each set on a cement floor and boasting a prehistoric wood-burning stove, card table, roll-up canvas window and candles (no electricity). The lodge complex – which is part of the original High Sierra Camp loop – also includes a dining hall serving great breakfasts, box lunches and dinner. Bathrooms and show- ers are shared, and each cabin has four twin beds or two twins and a double. Lin- ens are included, but bring your sleeping bag if you want to be extra warm. Cook- ing is prohibited. To guarantee you get a room, make a reservation 366 days in advance.

Hetch Hetchy

There is no lodging in Hetch Hetchy (Map p116). The nearest accommodations are at the lovely **Evergreen Lodge** (☎ 209-379-2606; www.evergreenlodge.com; 33160 Evergreen Rd; cabins $$- $$$; 🍴 🖥 👣), about 1.5 miles outside the park border, just south of Camp Mather (a summer camp open to San Francisco residents by lottery). The lodge consists of a series of lovingly decorated and comfy cabins spread out among the trees just off the side of the road. The place has just about everything you could ask for, in- cluding a bar (complete with pool table), general store, restaurant, live music, horse shoes and all sorts of guided hikes and activities.

EATING & DRINKING

With the exception of dining at the Wawona and Ahwahnee Hotels, Yosemite is hardly defined by its culinary wonders – except, of course, when setting comes into play. As for the food, content yourself with reliably prepared, fill-the-stomach-type meals that are slightly overpriced but certainly do the trick after a good hike. Some places, such as the Tuolumne Meadows Grill (where the French fries are undoubtedly phenomenal) or the Wawona Hotel (for brunch), do have a sort of cult following among visitors in the know. Whether you're looking for a sit-down meal or a sandwich for the road, the following listings will guide you to just about every option available in Yosemite.

All Yosemite restaurants in the park are run by **DNC** (☎ 209-372-1000, 559-252-4848; www.yosemitepark.com), and everything (except dinner at the Ahwahnee) is child-friendly.

YOSEMITE VALLEY

Yosemite Village and Curry Village (Map p93) are the best options for relatively cheap eats and to-go items.

Yosemite Village

Frankly, the restaurant choices in Yosemite Village won't set the gourmands among you salivating. But, like they say, hunger's the best sauce.

Village Store (🕙 8am-10pm summer, to 8pm rest of year) The biggest and best grocery store in the park is located smack in the center of Yosemite Village. Whether you're after last-minute items or full-fledged dinners, there's no denying the place comes in handy. The store carries decent produce, fresh meat and fish, and even some surprising items like tofu dogs, hummus, udon noodles and polenta. You'll also find a small section of camping supplies along with plenty of souvenirs.

Degnan's Deli (lunch $; 🕙 7am-6pm; 🕭) Likely the best of the bunch in the Yosemite Village complex, this store-cum-deli whips up fresh sandwiches, soups and lots of snacks and beverages. Good for sandwiches to go.

Degnan's Cafe (snacks & drinks $; 🕙 7am-5pm; 🕭) Beside the deli, Degnan's Cafe serves espresso drinks, smoothies and pastries, which you can guzzle down over a newspaper purchased at one of the stands outside.

Degnan's Loft (pizzas & mains $-$$; 🕙 5-9pm Apr-Oct) Upstairs from the café, this no-frills pizza parlor has a totally unadorned, ski-lodge feel. Despite the lack of atmosphere, it's a great spot for pizza (or lasagna, calzones or salad) and cold beer. It opens at noon on rainy days.

Village Grill (burgers $; 🕙 11am-5pm Apr-Oct; 🕭) A few buildings south of the Degnan's empire, the Village Grill is a standard fast-food counter with patio seating and subpar burgers, chicken sandwiches and the like. At least the fries are good.

Curry Village

Curry Village's dining choices are hardly exciting, but they're convenient if you're staying in one of the Curry tent cabins or returning hungry from a grueling hike via the nearby Happy Isles Trailhead.

Curry Village Store (🕙 year-round; 🕭) The Curry Village store is undoubtedly handy if you're in the neighborhood and need snacks, sodas, gifts or beer.

Curry Village Taqueria (Taco Stand; mains $; 🕙 11am-5pm mid-Apr–Oct; 🕭 🕭) Although it's a far cry from a proper California taqueria, this walk-up taco stand does the trick if you're craving something even vaguely Mexican. Think fast-food Mexican food. Portions are substantial.

Pizza Patio (mains $; 🕙 mid-Apr–mid-Oct; 🕭 🕭) Also called the Pizza Deck, this popular joint serves mediocre pizzas (which, after a long hike, taste amazing with a pint of beer from the bar next door), chili dogs and 'veggie bowls.' The sunny outdoor patio gets packed on summer evenings. On rainy days, take your pizza (and beer) inside the next-door dining hall and devour it over a game of cards and sports TV.

Curry Village Dining Pavilion (breakfast $, dinner $$; 🕙 7-10am & 5:30-8pm Apr-Oct; 🕭 🕭) All-you-can-eat breakfasts and dinners draw ravenous families to Curry Village's giant cafeteria. The breakfast is a great way to fill up before a hike, but to enjoy dinner you'll have to toss your sense of taste and summon your sense of humor. But, hey, carrying vast quantities of warm chicken and pasta, decent salads, standard soup and –

if you're a kid – platefuls of jiggling green Jell-O back to the table is an experience everyone should share at least once.

Coffee Corner (☙ year-round; ☕) Fill up on pastries, ice cream and espresso drinks at this small café inside the Curry Village Dining Pavilion.

Terrace Bar (☙ noon-11pm) Directly beside the Pizza Patio window, this tiny bar pulls a couple of decent microbrews and pours a full range of cocktails.

Yosemite Lodge

Near the base of Yosemite Falls, this 'lodge' is not a single rustic building but rather a cluster of contemporary condo-type hotel units, gift shops and restaurants.

Yosemite Lodge Food Court (mains $; ☙ year-round; ☕ ☕) The lodge's cheapest option is this self-service cafeteria, just behind the hotel's main lobby. Sauntering over from Camp 4 for breakfast and coffee before the climb is a Valley tradition. Dinner choices range from basic burgers to hot pasta plates.

Mountain Room Restaurant (mains $$-$$$; ☙ 5:30-9pm; ☕) Dig into a plate of Southwestern chicken, seafood pasta, halibut, mahi-mahi or one of several cuts of deliciously grilled beef at the lodge's classy restaurant. Views of Yosemite Falls compete with the food for diners' attention. Great cocktails, no reservations.

Mountain Room Lounge (☙ 4:30-11pm Mon-Fri, noon-11pm Sat & Sun; ☕) Across the courtyard from the restaurant, the Mountain Room Lounge is an undeniably fine place to knock back a couple of cocktails, thanks to the spacious interior and big windows.

Ahwahnee Hotel

Ahwahnee Dining Room (☎ 209-372-1489; breakfast & lunch $$, Sunday brunch adult/child $$$$/$$, dinner $$-$$$$; ☙ 7-10:30am, 11:30am-3pm & 5:30-9pm; ☕) Sit by candlelight beneath the 34ft-high beamed ceiling and lose yourself in the incredible scenery, viewed through massive picture windows – it's nothing less than spectacular. The food is excellent, though compared with the surroundings it may come in second. There's a dress code at dinner, but you can wear shorts and sneakers at breakfast and lunch. The outrageously decadent Sunday brunch is a classic Yosemite experience. Reserva-

tions highly recommended for brunch and dinner.

Ahwahnee Bar (☙ 11am-11pm; ☕) Pinching pennies? Worry not – you can still experience the Ahwahnee's charms at the casual Ahwahnee bar. Drinks aren't exactly cheap, but the atmosphere on the patio is splendid. The food (salads, chicken-Waldorf sandwiches, cheese-and-fruit plates and the like) is affordable and quite good, making it an excellent choice for a light dinner.

GLACIER POINT & BADGER PASS

The Glacier Point Rd area (Map p105) is not the place to end up if you want a good sit-down meal, at least not in the warmer months. When the road is open, the unexciting **snack stand** (☙ 11am-4pm; ☕) at Glacier Point is your only food option.

In the wintertime, Badger Pass runs the **Slider's Grab-N-Go** (dishes $; ☕), which as the name suggests, serves food that is not slow. Pick up some pizza, burgers or nachos and go go go! On weekends and holidays, the **Snowflake Room** (dishes $; ☙ 11am-4pm) has a cozy wood-beamed room with a view of the lifts, a grill food menu, and beer and wine available. Its walls are covered with cool old ski photos and pieces of vintage ski equipment.

WAWONA

You'll find two small stores in this enclave (Map p108) near the South Entrance to the park, and both are open all year. The Wawona General Store, a short walk from the Wawona Hotel, offers a few picnic and camping items but focuses more on snacks and gifts.

Pine Tree Market (☎ 209-375-6343; 7995 Chilnualna Falls Rd; ☙ 8am-8pm summer, 8:30am-6:30pm Mon-Thu & Sun, 8:30am-7pm Fri & Sat rest of year) This tiny and superfriendly market sells groceries and bags of divine locally roasted coffee (take a deep breath in the aisles), and in summer it sells flats of seasonal fruit grown by regional farmers. It's located a mile east of Hwy 41 amid the Redwoods in Yosemite; turn east off Chilnualna Falls Rd, which is just north of the Pioneer History Center.

Wawona Hotel Dining Room (☎ 209-375-1425; breakfast $, lunch $-$$, dinner $$$; ☙ breakfast, lunch & dinner, daily Easter-Oct, weekends Nov-Mar) Inside the

---

TOP TAPROOMS & TAVERNS

When you're thirsty but sick of sucking on your hydration pack, it can only mean one thing: its drink time! These spirited joints are the best places for martinis, highballs and brews in and near the park.

- **Ahwahnee Hotel** (p169) Sip a martini out on the patio while squirrels run around your feet. The setting? One of the best in the West.
- **Wawona Hotel** (p169) Knock 'em back at the piano-lounge lobby or the tables outside.
- **Yosemite Bug Rustic Mountain Resort** (p177) The yarns spin faster as the draft gets drunk at this Midpines hostel bar.
- **Iron Door Grill & Saloon** (p182) Groveland's honky-tonking saloon claims to be the oldest in California.
- **H-B Saloon** (p180) Can't make it to San Francisco without a drink? Shame on you. Guess you'll have to stop at this classic Western bar in Oakdale.
- **Pines Bar** (p186) There's nothing quite like a rowdy weekend night at Bass Lake.
- **Inn at Mono Lake** (p199) What'll it be: the deck with astounding views or the huge stone fireplace with comfy chairs?

---

historic 1879 Wawona Hotel, this old-fashioned white-tablecloth dining room is lit by beautiful painted lamps, and the Victorian detail makes it an enchanting place to have an upscale (though somewhat overpriced) meal. 'Tasteful, casual attire' is the rule for dinner dress. Seating is first-come, first-served, though reservations are required for parties of six or more. The restaurant is also open during the Thanksgiving and Christmas seasons, and it puts on barbecue on the lawn every Saturday during summer. The Wawona's wide, white porch makes a snazzy destination for evening cocktails, served from 5pm to 9:30pm. In the hotel's lobby – which doubles as its lounge – listen for pianist Tom Bopp, who's been running through his repertoire of Yosemite-themed chestnuts since 1983.

TIOGA ROAD

A mile north of Tioga Rd, the White Wolf Lodge area (Map p108) has a miniscule store that sells snacks, ice-cream bars and coffee. At lunchtime, it has prepared sandwiches available, and there's always a vegetarian option available. The small, rustic **dining room** (☎ 209-372-8416; buffet $, dinner $$$$; ⊗ lunch & dinner) is open for a buffet breakfast and in the evening for family-style dinners inside or on the front porch. Reservations are highly advised for dinner, with four seating times available.

TUOLUMNE MEADOWS

As with everything else along the Tioga Rd (Map p114), eating establishments are open roughly June to mid-September only. Exact dates depend on snowfall.

Tuolumne Meadows Store (⊗ 8am-8pm) Browse the busy aisles of the Tuolumne Meadows Store, which stocks just about every necessity item you could have possibly forgotten: wine, beer, chips, dehydrated food, a smattering of produce, tofu dogs, dorky hats, camp cups, firewood, candy bars, fishing tackle and camping supplies, all at marked-up prices.

our pick Tuolumne Meadows Grill (breakfast & lunch $; ⊗ 8am-5pm; ⅏ ⅏) You can hardly say you've visited Tuolumne without smacking down a burger and a basket of fries in the parking lot in front of the Tuolumne Grill. The soft-serve ice-cream cones and hearty breakfasts – not to mention the people-watching – are equally mandatory.

Tuolumne Meadows Lodge (☎ 209-372-8413; breakfast $, dinner $$-$$$; ⊗ 7-9am & 5:50-8pm) For yet another classic Yosemite experience, make a dinner reservation (for breakfast, just show up) at the Tuolumne Meadows Lodge. The place is as basic-looking as they come, but the breakfasts are hearty and the dinners are good. Best of all, good company is pretty much guaranteed (or at least required): tables are shared. Breakfasts are predictable, and dinners run the gamut from 'cowboy style' steak to linguini, shrimp kebabs, trout and burgers. Snacks and cold drinks are sold all day at the lodge lobby.

HETCH HETCHY

There are no eating establishments or stores in Hetch Hetchy (Map p116), but you can eat yourself silly at the excellent **Evergreen Lodge** (☎ 209-379-2606; www.evergreenlodge.com; 33160 Evergreen Rd; breakfast & lunch $, dinner $$; & &), just a mile outside the park border. The restaurant serves four types of burgers (Black Angus beef, turkey, buffalo and veggie) as well as sandwiches and salads. Breakfasts are big and delicious, and dinner choices include everything from barbequed spareribs to broiled elk tenderloin. The lodge also has a general store with basic supplies, books, snacks and souvenirs.

Around Yosemite

Think of Yosemite as the filet mignon of the Sierras. It's the finest cut (by most standards), but there's so much more to experience. Sure, life just isn't complete without a taste of Yosemite Valley, but you may just find you prefer the flavor of other regions around it. You'll find many a happy camper who'd argue the unbeatable merits of the Eastern Sierra, which is home to sights such as Mono Lake, Mammoth Lakes, hidden hot springs, shimmering alpine lakes and some of the most dramatic mountain scenery in the Sierras. Northwest of Yosemite, you'll find some of the state's best white-water rafting, a network of seemingly rules-free forest roads in the Stanislaus National Forest and superb mountain biking, lake paddling and fishing.

West of Yosemite, Hwy 120 and Hwy 140 provide the main access routes into the park. For those who take the time to stop the car, the highways hold some wonderful little gold rush–era towns with restaurants, boutiques and groovy old-time saloons. South of Yosemite, Hwy 41 passes all sorts of wonderful distractions, including the Nelder Grove of giant sequoias and the beautiful Sierra Vista National Scenic Byway. It finally rolls into Wawona in southern Yosemite.

HIGHLIGHTS

- Marveling at the tufa formations at **Mono Lake** (p199) against the backdrop of the Eastern Sierra
- Shredding a path through fresh powder from the dizzying peak of **Mammoth Mountain** (p205)
- Paddling, bouldering, hiking and mountain biking along Hwy 4 near **Ebbetts Pass** (p194)
- Soaking in a superheated Eastern Sierra **hot spring** (p207) under a glittering night sky
- Hiking to the high-alpine **East Lake** (p201), the largest lake in the Hoover Wilderness

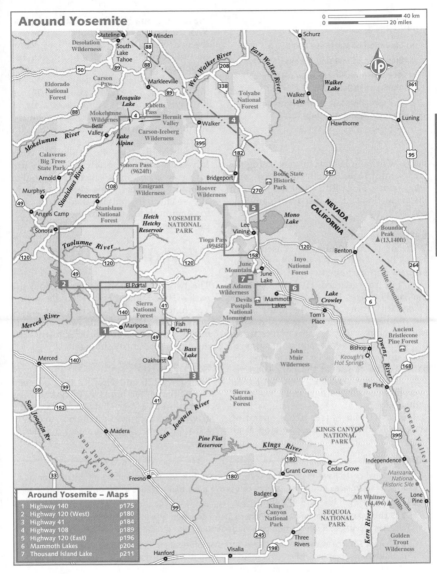

Around Yosemite

0		40 km
0		20 miles

AROUND YOSEMITE

Around Yosemite – Maps

1 Highway 140   p175
2 Highway 120 (West)   p180
3 Highway 41   p184
4 Highway 108   p189
5 Highway 120 (East)   p196
6 Mammoth Lakes   p204
7 Thousand Island Lake   p211

Information

You'll find more camping options here than within the park itself – both United States Forest Service (USFS) campgrounds and dispersed camping, which is allowed in most national forests. Dispersed camping is a great way to go if you crave solitude (no nearby campers) and affordability (it's free) – but remember, you're entirely on your own, which means no toilets or potable water (bring your own or come with a means to filter or purify stream water). If you're going to build a fire, you'll also need a free fire permit, which you can pick up at one of the local USFS ranger stations. Ranger stations also sell detailed USFS

FAST FACTS

- **Elevation of Mariposa** 2000ft
- **Elevation of Mammoth Lakes** 8000ft
- **Average high/low temperature in Mariposa in July** 95/60°F (35/16°C)
- **Average high/low temperature in Mammoth Lakes in July** 75/45°F (24/7°C)

maps, which are helpful for navigating the maze of dirt roads. Finally, note that some areas (along Tioga Rd east of the park, for instance) don't allow dispersed camping; watch for signs.

Getting Around

Whether you're heading to Yosemite by car or bus, you'll travel along one of four primary approaches: Hwy 41 from Fresno, Hwy 140 from Merced, Hwy 120 W from the San Francisco Bay Area or Hwy 120 E (Tioga Rd) from Lee Vining. Many of the old mining towns along these routes are worth a stop – they're great places to refuel your car and refill your stomach or to stock up on groceries before entering the park. Towns closest to the park (particularly along Hwy 120 and Hwy 140) offer overflow accommodations and a variety of eating options.

The YARTS buses (see p262) operating between Merced and Yosemite stop at all the towns along Hwy 140, west of the park. YARTS also runs buses from Yosemite Valley over Tioga Pass (Hwy 120) to Mammoth Lakes. The bus will stop on demand so you can get off at any trailhead or campground along Tioga Rd (Hwy 120). The bus does the June Lake Loop (p202) on its way, making this region accessible by bus as well. This service is offered during summer only, with Saturday and Sunday service starting when Tioga Pass opens (usually mid-May). Beginning in early July, daily buses are offered, with a return to the weekend-only schedule beginning around September. This changes seasonally, so check the online schedule. The bus to Mammoth leaves from the Valley Visitor Center.

WEST OF YOSEMITE

The two most important arteries into the park – Hwy 140 and Hwy 120 – lie west of Yosemite. Aside from offering easy access to the national park, the highways are home to some marvelous little historic towns resting along their dusty shoulders.

HIGHWAY 140

Both Hwy 120 and Hwy 41 may be open during the winter, but Hwy 140 is known as Yosemite's 'All-Year Highway,' a nickname given when the road first opened to cars in 1926. Its lower elevation makes it easier to

---

THE INFORMATION HIGHWAY

The national parks have their official websites (p27), but sometimes finding information on all those glorious places outside the parks can prove a bit tricky. Here's a few online resources to get you heading in the right direction:

- **395.com** (www.395.com) Interesting Eastern Sierra community website featuring local news, weather reports, and information on skiing, climbing and other activities in the region.
- **US Forest Service** (www.fs.fed.us/r5/forests.html) For information on everything from campgrounds to river rafting, fishing and more, log onto the indispensable USFS website. It covers all the national forests surrounding Yosemite in outstanding detail.
- **Yosemite Gold** (www.yosemitegold.com) Paid-advertising listings make this snappy website slightly less than comprehensive or objective, but it's definitely worth a look if you're planning to explore the foothills region. It also covers parts of the Eastern Sierra.
- **Yosemite-Sierra Visitors Bureau** (www.yosemite-sierra.org) Based in Oakhurst, the Yosemite-Sierra Visitor's Bureau offers this site with lots of general information about Yosemite, Sierra National Forest, Bass Lake and other areas south of the park.

Highway 140

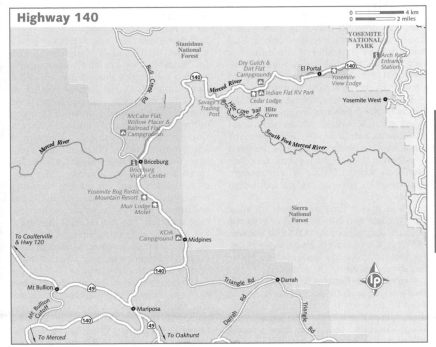

keep the road clear in bad weather, and it has traditionally been the chief year-round route into the park. However, in 2006 a rockslide buried a section of the road about 8 miles west of El Portal, and a temporary bridge was put in place as a bypass. One-way traffic controls may still be in place, and while they do not cause significant delay, because the turns on and off the bridge are very tight absolutely no vehicles over 28ft are permitted. The magnitude of the slide has transportation officials pondering lots of long-term options, though it's expected that these restrictions will be in place for a minimum of a few years. For updated road conditions, go to www.dot.ca.gov or call ☎ 800-427-7623.

Between Merced and Yosemite, the highway meanders past rolling foothills of gold and green, rich in the warm light of summer sunsets. It climbs to meet Mariposa, the last 'real' town on the route, and then tiny Midpines before dropping into the magnificent Merced River Canyon. From here, the highway follows the Merced River through El Portal to the park's Arch Rock Entrance. The route also parallels the bed of the long-defunct Yosemite Valley Railroad, which operated from 1907 to 1945.

Merced

☎ 209 / pop 69,500 / elev 170ft

At the junction of Hwys 140 and 99 in the central San Joaquin Valley, Merced is about two hours' drive from Yosemite – too far to qualify as a home base while visiting the park. That aside, it is a convenient stopover for those passing through by bus, train or car, with plenty of cheap accommodations, including a good hostel. Hwy 140 heads east toward Yosemite from an exit off Hwy 99 about a mile south of downtown.

Downtown Merced lies east of Hwy 99 along Main St, between R St and Martin Luther King Jr Way. The **California Welcome Center** (☎ 384-2791, 800-446-5353; www.visitmerced.travel; 710 W 16th St), adjacent to the bus depot, has local maps, information on Yosemite and coupon books offering local motel discounts.

AROUND YOSEMITE

While a little rundown on the edges, Merced's downtown can be quite pretty during the day, with tree-lined streets, Victorian homes, a handful of movie theaters and several antique shops. A popular **farmers market** (19th & N St) operates year-round in downtown every Saturday morning.

The main attraction, though, is the 1875 **Merced County Courthouse**. Surrounded by a lovely parklike square, it's the town's architectural patriarch, the only survivor among eight county courthouses designed by Albert A Bennett. Inside is the excellent **Courthouse Museum** (☎ 723-2401; mercedmuseum .org; admission free; ❧ 1-4pm Wed-Sun), well worth a quick peek.

If you have a little more time on your hands, check out the field full of restored military aircraft at the **Castle Air Museum** (☎ 723-2178; 5050 Santa Fe Dr, Atwater; adult/child $8/6; ❧ 10am-4pm Oct-Mar, 9am-5pm Apr-Sep) in Atwater, about 6 miles north of Merced.

Merced Home Hostel (☎ 725-0407; mercedhostel@juno.com; dm & d $; ❧ closed 8am-5:30pm) is a family-style hostel in the home of longtime Merced residents who know tons about Yosemite; they even offer a travel talk nightly at 9pm. The hosts will pick up and drop off travelers at points in town, including the bus and train stations. They also rent sleeping bags and tents ($5) for travelers on the way to the park. Discounts are given to HI members.

GETTING THERE & AWAY

A major transportation hub, Merced is the end of the line for Amtrak train and Greyhound bus passengers. From here, passengers can take the YARTS (Yosemite Area Regional Transportation System) bus along Hwy 140 into the park, making this route the easiest option for travelers without cars. **YARTS** (☎ 388-9589, 877-989-2787; www .yarts.com) buses run between Merced and Yosemite Valley, stopping in most towns and key spots along the way. They depart daily from several Merced locations, including the **Merced Transpo Center** (16th St at N St) and the **Amtrak station** (24th St at K St). See p262 for details.

Greyhound (☎ 722-2121; 800-229-9424) also operates from the Transpo Center, while **Amtrak** (☎ 722-6862, 800-872-7245) passengers transfer to buses in Merced to reach the park. For complete details, see p262.

Mariposa
☎ 209 / pop 1400 / elev 2000ft

Before you enter the park, stop in the former gold-rush settlement of Mariposa (Spanish for 'butterfly') for any last-minute groceries or a full night's sleep in a comfortable, clean motel that's not terribly overpriced. This cute town is just under an hour's drive from the park (around 34 miles). The largest of the state's original 27 counties, Mariposa County was founded in 1850. The town of Mariposa was named the county seat a year later. Today the town feels like a cross between a mountain community and a wannabe tourist haven. On the one hand, it's filled with antique shops, cute boutiques and upscale restaurants; yet it's also home to ragged muscle cars and colorful characters. But it's a safe and, for the most part, charming place – the down-to-earth element helps to counterbalance a touristy vibe that might otherwise get too cute too fast.

Hwy 49 joins Hwy 140 at the south end of town, then splits off again at the north end, heading toward Coulterville and Sonora. At the intersection, the **Mariposa County Visitor Center** (☎ 966-7081, 866-425-3366; www.homeofyosemite.com; 5158 N Hwy 140; ❧ 7am-8pm Mon-Sat, 8am-5pm Sun summer, 8am-5pm Mon-Sat winter) can supply a good county map ($1) and loads of brochures on both Yosemite and Mariposa.

The town straddles Hwy 140, though some historic buildings lie one block east on Bullion St, including the **Mariposa County Courthouse** (Bullion St at 8th St), a cute wooden building worth a quick look. Built in 1854, it's the state's oldest active courthouse.

Rock hounds should drive to the Mariposa County Fairgrounds, 2 miles south of town on Hwy 49, to see the 13lb 'Fricot Nugget' and other gems and machinery at the **California State Mining & Mineral Museum** (☎ 742-7625; www.parks.ca.gov; admission $3; ❧ 10am-6pm May-Sep, to 4pm Wed-Mon Oct-Apr; ♿). An exhibit on glow-in-the-dark minerals is very cool.

If you're still looking for something to pass a few hours, the **Sixth Street Cinema** (☎ 742-6666; www.sixthstreetcinema.org; upstairs, Old Masonic Lodge, 6th St at Bullion St) shows an eclectic offering of indie films, and a quarter-mile up County Park Rd is an outdoor **swimming pool** (☎ 966-2498; admission $1; ❧ 1-5pm summer) that's great for a summer dip.

SLEEPING

Mother Lode Lodge (☎ 966-2521, 800-398-9770; www.mariposamotel.com; 5051 Hwy 140; r $$; 🖳 🕿) Close to downtown and with the cheapest rates around, this small lodge offers simple rooms set back from the road. Some rooms are rented out for longer stays.

ourpick River Rock Inn (☎ 966-5793, 800-627-8439; www.riverrockncafe.com; 4993 7th St; r incl breakfast $$; 🔀) A bold splash of psychedelic purple and dusty orange paint spruces up what claims to be the oldest motel in town. Rooms done up in artsy earth tones have TVs but no phones, and calming ceiling fans resemble lily pads. A block removed from Hwy 140 on a quiet side street, it features a small courtyard deck and deli café, with live acoustic music on weekend evenings in summer.

Mariposa Lodge (☎ 966-3607, 800-966-8819; www.mariposalodge.com; 5052 Hwy 140; r $$; 🔀 🖳 🕿 👌) More of a generic motel, the simple, well-kept Mariposa sports clean, quiet rooms (with TVs and phones) and friendly staff. It earns pluses for the good-sized rooms and for the blooming flowers that border the grounds.

EATING

Pioneer Market (☎ 742-6100; 5034 Coakley Circle; 🕥 7am-9pm Mon-Sat, 8am-9pm Sun summer, 8am-8pm daily winter) A medium-sized supermarket with a decent selection, it's a good place to stock up on groceries. You'll find it about a mile east of downtown on Hwy 140; turn left (north) on Coakley Circle, just past the Burger King.

Pony Espresso (☎ 966-5053; 5053 Hwy 140; snacks $; 🕥 6:30am-7pm Mon-Fri, 7am-5pm Sat, 8am-4pm Sun, extended hours summer; 🖳) For coffee and snacks, the best bet in town is this small café, with yummy espresso drinks, smoothies, bagels and muffins.

Happy Burger (☎ 966-2719; Hwy 140 at 12th St; meals $; 🕥 5:30am-8pm Sun-Thu, to 9pm Fri & Sat; 🖳) Boasting the largest menu in the Sierra, this buzzing roadside joint decorated with old LP album covers serves the cheapest meals in Mariposa. Its all-American cuisine means burgers, sandwiches, Mexican food and a ton of sinful ice-cream desserts. Breakfast's available till 11am.

High Country Café (☎ 966-5111; Hwy 140 at Hwy 49; sandwiches $; 🕥 9am-3pm Mon-Sat) If you want some healthy fare, this café serves

salads, soups, and both vegan and meat-filled sandwiches, including falafels and burritos. The adjacent health-food store stays open later, if you want to stock up for your trip.

ourpick Savoury's (☎ 966-7677; 5027 Hwy 140; mains $$-$$$; 🕥 5-8:30pm Tue-Sat, until 9:30pm summer) Owner Miriam Wackerman describes it as 'fine dining without all the frou-frou,' and this classy contemporary restaurant is pretty damn fine. With only 10 tables and cozy Victorian wooden booths, the gorgeous moss-green and pale-yellow room sets an intimate stage for classic dishes like a flat-iron steak or creative mains like chipotle chicken and rice. It double its tables with patio dining in summer, but reservations are always recommended.

GETTING THERE & AWAY

YARTS (☎ 209-388-9589, 877-989-2787; www.yarts.com) runs buses along Hwy 140 into Yosemite Valley, stopping at the Mariposa visitor center. For details, see p262.

Midpines

☎ 209 / pop 980 / elev 2400ft

There's not much to see or do in Midpines, a rural community about 25 miles west of Yosemite's Arch Rock Entrance. The small **Midpines Country Store** (☎ 966-2600; 6428 Hwy 140; 🕥 8am-6pm winter, until 7pm summer) marks the center of 'town,' which is actually spread thin over several miles along Hwy 140. Run by the current owners for almost 30 years, the store has an ATM and a gas station (which isn't 24-hour). From Midpines, Hwy 140 drops down into the beautiful Merced River Canyon.

The highlight of this almost nonexistent town is **Yosemite Bug Rustic Mountain Resort** (☎ 966-6666, 866-826-7108; www.yosemitebug.com; 6979 Hwy 140; dm/tent cabin/r $/$/$$; 🖳 👌), tucked away on a forested hillside about 25 miles from the park. Removed from the busy highway, it's more of a convivial mountain retreat than a typical hostel. There's a range of sleeping options, from inexpensive dorm beds to uniquely decorated cabins with private bath, and they now have a spa just down the road with a hot tub, yoga lessons and massages available. It rents mountain bikes ($17 per day) and snowshoes ($8 per day), and the property has laundry facilities, free wi-fi and free computer access. If you don't have a car, you can often catch a ride into Yosemite with another visitor or buy a discounted round-trip ticket for the YARTS bus, which stops on the highway just a quarter-mile up the driveway. Its Bug Bus tours (see p257) offer a range of hiking trips (including overnights) to Yosemite and does shuttles for area mountain biking.

If you don't want to whip up something in the well-stocked community kitchen, the resort's **café** (mains $; ☻ 7am-9pm, drinks until 11pm) is the best grazing spot this side of Yosemite. At night, friendly folks of all ages from around the globe gather in the rustic wood-beam lodge to share stories, music and inexpensive, delicious meals. There's a cozy fireplace, lots of board games, hot chocolate, wine by the glass and even Guinness on tap. Tasty meals always include one awesome vegan option, and filling dinners include smoked pork, trout or pasta. And, no, you don't have to be an overnight guest to partake of the Bug's bounty.

The **KOA Campground** (☎ 966-2201, 800-562-9391; tents & RVs $, cabins $$; ☻ Mar-early Nov; ▢ ▣ ▧ ▨) has pseudo-log cabins that sleep can four to six people, plus a playground and a small on-site store.

If you're looking for a motel room, the aging rooms at **Muir Lodge Motel** (☎ 966-2468; www.yosemitemuirlodge.com; 6833 Hwy 140; dm $, r $-$$; ▢) are clean and affordable though very basic. The 'dorm' space is more like a shared single-sex room.

YARTS (☎ 209-388-9589, 877-989-2787; www .yarts.com) runs buses along Hwy 140 into Yosemite Valley, stopping at the Midpines post office. For details, see p262.

Briceburg

☎ 209 / pop 2 / elev 1200ft
Some 20 miles from Yosemite's Arch Rock Entrance, where Hwy 140 meets the Merced River, is the **Briceburg Visitor Center** (☎ 379-9414, 916-985-4474; ☻ 1-6pm Fri, 9am-6pm Sat & Sun mid-Apr–Aug). The interesting granite building, originally a tavern and restaurant, dates from 1927 and now belongs to the Bureau of Land Management (BLM). Here you can get local camping, hiking and recreation information.

Turn north on the small dirt road adjacent to the center, travel a few miles, and

you'll find three primitive **BLM campgrounds** (sites $) – McCabe Flat, Willow Placer and Railroad Flat – with 31 sites along the river between Briceburg and Bagby. You must cross a beautiful 1920s wooden suspension bridge to ford the river, so long trailers and large RVs are not recommended.

El Portal

☎ 209 / pop 1000 / elev 2100ft
Once the terminus of the Yosemite Valley Railroad, El Portal is now home to a collection of gateway services (motels, restaurants, a pricey gas station and a small store), housing for park staff and park administrative offices. Just west of the Arch Rock Entrance and about 14 miles west of Yosemite Village, the town is curiously narrow and long, stretching 7 miles alongside the Merced River.

Adjacent to the store, El Portal Rd leads one block north to a **post office** (☻ 8:30am-12:30pm & 1-5pm Mon-Fri) and a small outdoor **Yosemite Valley Railroad exhibit** that includes a restored locomotive and caboose next to a people-powered turnaround.

SLEEPING

Indian Flat RV Park (☎ 379-2339; www.indianflat rvpark.com; 9988 Hwy 140; tent & RV sites $, tent cabins/ cabins/r $/$$/$$$; ▨) Primarily an inexpensive private campground, it also has a number of interesting housing options, including two pretty stone cabin cottages with air-conditioning. It's conveniently located right on the way to the park, and the prices can't be beat. Nonguests can pay to use the showers.

Cedar Lodge (☎ 379-2612, 800-321-5261; www
.yosemiteresorts.us; 9966 Hwy 140; r $$ with kitchen $$$,
ste $$$$; ⊠ ⬜ ⬜ 🐾) Approximately 9 miles
west of the Arch Rock Entrance, the Cedar
is a sprawling establishment with more
than 200 adequate rooms, an indoor and a
seasonal outdoor pool, and a couple of restaurants. It's owned by the same company
as the Yosemite View Lodge, but it's not
nearly as nice.

Yosemite View Lodge (☎ 379-2681, 800-321-5261;
www.yosemiteresorts.us; 11136 Hwy 140; r $$$, ste $$$-
$$$$; ⊠ ⬜ ⬜ 🐾) Less than 2 miles from
the park entrance is this big, modern complex with hot tubs, restaurants and four
pools. Among the 336 rooms, the nicest
feature kitchenettes, gas fireplaces and views
of the Merced River, and the ground-floor
rooms have big patios. The souped-up 'majestic suites' are massive, with crazy-opulent
bathrooms featuring waterfall showers and
plasma TV entertainment centers.

Dry Gulch and Dirt Flat are small but
reservable **USFS campgrounds** (☎ 877-444-6777;
www.recreation.gov; Incline Rd; sites $) on the north
shore of the Merced River; tents only.

EATING

El Portal Market (☎ 379-2632; 🕑 8am-8pm summer, 9am-7pm winter) This tiny market marks
the center of town, with groceries, booze,
produce and some microwaveable burritos
on hand. It also stocks fishing tackle and
rents out movies.

¡QUE VIVA SAL!

When the infamous flood of 1997 washed
out Hwy 140 on both sides of town and cut
off traffic here for a few years, El Portal was a
sad and lonely place. Park employees, a majority of the town's residents, had to drive
two to three hours around to get to work,
and town morale was at an all-time low.
That's when Sal's taco truck began coming
every other week, spreading culinary sunshine and sparking a festive tradition that
continues today. Starting at about 5pm
every other Thursday – which conveniently
coincides with payday for government employees – look for a line of hungry locals
between the Community Hall and the post
office, listening to live bands and happily
munching on Mexican food.

Otherwise, head for the lodges. At
Cedar Lodge the **Hound Dog Bar & Grill** (mains
$; 🕑 11am-9:30pm, shorter hours winter) offers grill
food and cocktails in a room that looks like
an overeager cross between a sports bar and
a 1950s diner. Steaks, pasta and chicken are
on hand in the adjacent **Cedar Lodge Restau-
rant** (☎ 379-2316; breakfast $, dinner mains $$-$$$;
🕑 breakfast & dinner).

Yosemite View Lodge houses the casual
Little Bear's Pizza (pizzas & sandwiches $; 🕑 5-9pm
Sun-Thu, 5-10pm Fri & Sat, closed winter) and the
Yosemite View Restaurant (breakfast $, dinner mains
$$-$$$; 🕑 7-11am daily, 5-9pm Sun-Thu, 5-10pm Fri
& Sat, shorter hours winter), offering pasta and
stir-fry dishes along with a range of meaty
mains.

GETTING THERE & AWAY

YARTS (☎ 209-388-9589, 877-989-2787; www.yarts.com)
runs buses along Hwy 140 into Yosemite Val-
ley, stopping at Cedar Lodge and Yosemite
View Lodge. For details, see p262.

HIGHWAY 120 (WEST)

Most folks visiting from the San Francisco
Bay Area take Hwy 120 into the park, enter-
ing Yosemite at the Big Oak Flat Entrance
(p87). This is also the main route to Hetch
Hetchy, but instead of entering at Big Oak
Flat, you head north on Evergreen Rd, just
before entering the park.

From the Bay Area, it's a straightfor-
ward drive, taking about 3½ to four hours
to reach Yosemite Valley or Hetch Hetchy.
After crossing the flat San Joaquin Valley,
Hwy 120 slowly enters the foothills and
finally faces the precipitous Priest Grade,
which climbs some 1500ft over 2 miles. At
Priest Grade, you can choose the modern,
circuitous Hwy 120 or opt for Old Priest
Grade Rd (not recommended for RVs or
trailers), a much steeper and narrower –
though somewhat shorter – drive to the
top, where it rejoins Hwy 120. The highway
then passes the historic towns of Big Oak
Flat (not to be confused with the entrance
station) and Groveland, passes Evergreen
Rd and finally enters the park.

Your best bet for finding last-minute
camping supplies and groceries is Oakdale.
Groveland, which is much cuter and closer
to the park, is a nice place to spend the
night in an old hotel and have a good sit-
down dinner.

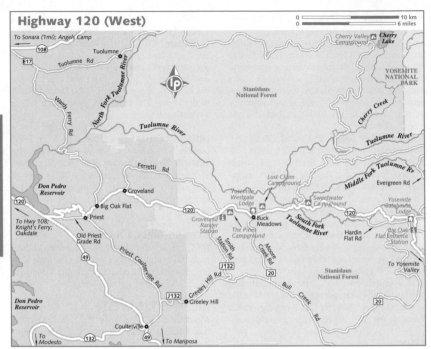

Oakdale

☎ 209 / pop 18,628 / elev 155ft

Unless they're stopping to fill up the tank (Oakdale is the last place for cheap gas west of the park), most folks whiz on through the town that deems itself the Cowboy Capital of the World.

There are, however, a few reasons to stop. Oakdale holds a highly regarded rodeo in April (check out www.oakdalerodeo.com, pardner), which might nicely complement a springtime trip to Yosemite. Then there's the **H-B Saloon** (Bachi's Family Style Dinners; ☎ 847-2985; 401 E F St; lunch $, dinners $$-$$$; ☀ lunch Mon-Fri, dinner Wed-Sat), an old Western-style restaurant that serves massive, family-style meals that include soup, salad, beans, stew, French fries and wine. The saloon itself is perfect for knocking back a brew with the local hee-haws.

Another reason to stop is the **Oak Ridge Market** (☎ 845-9800; Hwy 120/108 at Maag Ave; ☀ 6am-10pm), one of the best places to stock up on food supplies in the San Joaquin Valley; it even has a 'British foods' aisle. Then, of course, there's the kitschy **Oakdale Cowboy Museum** (☎ 847-5163;

www.oakdalecowboymuseum.org; 355 East F St; admission $1; ☀ 10am-2pm Mon-Sat; ♿), conveniently located next door to the H-B Saloon (drink up *before* hitting the museum).

Knights Ferry

☎ 209 / pop 98 / elev 193ft

Roasting in the sun on the banks of the Stanislaus River, this lazy, historic town gets passed up by just about everyone on their rush to Yosemite. Because it lies about a mile north of the highway, it feels almost hidden from the outside world. Most people who do visit stick to the river (boating, fishing and swimming are hugely popular), which offers welcome respite from the heat. Aside from the Stanislaus itself, Knights Ferry lays claim to a 330ft-long **covered bridge**, built in 1863 and said to be the longest covered bridge west of the Mississippi. Upstream, the town itself is a handful of old wooden buildings transporting you back in time.

If you don't bore easily, spend the night at one of the town's two historic hotels: the replica **Washington Hotel** (☎ 881-3381; www.washingtonhotelandgardens.com; 17712 Sonora Rd; r $$-$$$;

[X] [□]) or the quaint old **Knights Ferry Hotel** (☎ 881-3111; r $$), directly across the street.

For food and drink, sidle on over to the **Knights Ferry General Store, Café & Saloon** (☎ 881-3340; 17701 Sonora Rd; mains $; ✆ closed Tue & Wed), where you can drink with the Harley crowd or feast on hamburgers. Nearby, the **Knights Ferry Creamery** (snacks & lunch $) serves excellent milkshakes, sandwiches and espresso drinks.

To get to Knights Ferry, watch for the sign pointing you north of Hwy 120 via Sonora Rd.

Big Oak Flat

Home to some of the most impressive brick buildings left in Gold Country, Big Oak Flat is a wee town at the top of Old Priest Grade Rd, about 2 miles west of Groveland. Its worth stopping the car and taking a peak at the old **IOOF Hall**, which was built in 1852 from slabs of schist (a stone that was plentiful in the area). The upper half of the building was added in the 1920s. The other important building in town is the **Gamble Block**, built in the early 1850s to house three separate stores. The town also has a gas station.

Groveland

☎ 209 / pop 1500 / elev 2800

There's no missing Groveland – it's as if Hwy 120 rolls right into a Spaghetti Western, taking you with it. As the road slows to a crawl, it becomes Main St, passing two blocks of exceptionally well-preserved gold rush–era buildings, the most famous of which is the Iron Door Saloon, *said* to be the oldest watering hole in California.

About 25 miles west of Yosemite's Big Oak Flat Entrance, Groveland is a picture-perfect old mining town that, together with nearby Big Oak Flat, was originally called Savage's Diggings, after James Savage, who found gold here in 1848. In 1875, long after the gold rush was over, the town name changed to Groveland. Groveland boomed again with the damming of nearby Hetch Hetchy Valley, drawing loads of workers into town to work on the dam and water project. Today the town is a major draw – and rightfully so – for tourists on their way to Yosemite.

About 8 miles east of Groveland, the USFS **Groveland Ranger Station** (☎ 962-7825; 24545 Hwy 120; ✆ 8am-4:30pm Mon-Fri, 8:30am-3:30pm Sat & Sun Jun-Jul, reduced hours Sep-May) offers information on camping, rafting, fishing and other activities in the surrounding Stanislaus National Forest and nearby Tuolumne Wild and Scenic River Area. If you arrive after hours, check the big national forest map posted outside for the location of local campgrounds.

SLEEPING

Groveland's two hotels are on Main St (Hwy 120), plus there are B&Bs and rental properties further east along the highway.

TOP 10 EATS AROUND YOSEMITE

Whether you've been cooking one-pot meals on a Coleman camp stove all week, or you're tired of paying for overpriced slop in Yosemite Valley, an honestly priced and properly prepared sit-down meal becomes imperative at least once on every trip. And no visit to the Sierras is complete without feeding at one or more of the following. They're classics, after all.

- Whoa Nellie Deli (p199), junction Hwy 120 E and Hwy 395
- Grounds (p191), Murphys
- Happy Burger (p177), Mariposa
- Knights Ferry Creamery (above), Knights Ferry
- Groveland Hotel (p182), Groveland
- Giant Burger (p192), Arnold
- Tioga Pass Resort (p195), Tioga Pass
- Narrow Gauge Inn (p188), Fish Camp
- Erna's Elderberry House Oakhurst (p185), Oakhurst
- Mono Inn at Mono Lake (p199), Mono Lake

THE 'BIG OAK'

About a mile east of the top of Old Priest Grade, the run-down former mining town of Big Oak Flat looks like a ramshackle old town, but it holds an interesting place in history. This the source of the 'big oak' that gave the town – and the historic road into Yosemite – its name. The tree itself is long gone, however, having suffered many trials and tribulations, including fire, storms and, finally, damage from overeager miners. Supposedly, in their search for gold, the men removed so much soil from around its roots that the tree finally bit the dust.

Hotel Charlotte (☎ 962-6455; www.hotelcharlotte .com; 18736 Main St; r $$-$$$; 🍴 🖳) Since Italian immigrant Charlotte DeFerrari opened this historic hotel in 1918 a few things have changed: now it has flowery wallpaper and bedspreads, carpet on the floor, private bathrooms, new owners and, thankfully, air-conditioning. It's a splendid little place, with friendly owners.

our pick **Groveland Hotel** (☎ 962-4000, 800-273-3314; www.groveland.com; 18767 Main St; r/ste $$$/$$$; 🍴 🖳 ♿) Built in 1850, this stately historic property now houses an upscale restaurant, a wee wine bar and 17 quaint, lovingly decorated rooms. With teddy bears adorning the beds, it definitely qualifies as cute. A couple of downstairs rooms are wheelchair accessible, but bathrooms are unmodified.

EATING & DRINKING

Main St is home to everything from an old-time soda fountain to a coffee shop, pizzeria and even a Mexican restaurant.

Main Street Market (Hwy 120 at Ferretti Rd; 🕑 8am-9pm) With a good stock of produce and groceries, this is the best place (make that *only* place) to stock up in Groveland. It's on the east end of town just north of the highway and directly behind PJ's Cafe and the pizzeria.

Cocina Michoacana (☎ 962-6651; 18730 Main St; mains $-$$; 🕑 7am-9pm) Sometimes you just can't beat a big Mexican dinner, and this friendly joint definitely does the trick.

Café Charlotte (☎ 962-6455; 18736 Main St; mains $$$; 🕑 5:30-9pm Thu-Sun) The owners here do plenty of recipe research in order to keep the menu changing regularly. The dishes are imaginative and run the gamut from Asian chicken to rack of lamb.

Groveland Hotel (☎ 962-4000; www.groveland .com; 18767 Main St; mains $$$-$$$$; 🕑 7-10am daily, 5:30-9pm Tue-Sun; ♿) The most elegant meal option in town is the Victorian dining room at the historic Groveland Hotel. The menu, which changes regularly, includes items like baby-back ribs and salmon, and the wine list (all 38 pages of it) is renowned. Reservations recommended.

Iron Door Grill & Saloon (☎ 962-8904; www .iron-door-saloon.com; 18761 Main St; 🕑 11am-late) Several bars in California claim to be the oldest bar in the state, but the Iron Door does a great job of convincing you. It's a dusty, atmospheric old place, with big swinging doors, a giant bar, high ceilings, mounted animal heads and hundreds of dollar bills tacked to the ceiling (a requisite for any bar worth its salt in Gold Country). The adjacent dining room serves good burgers, steaks and pasta dishes, and there's live music every weekend night.

our pick **Mountain Sage** (☎ 962-4686; www.mtn sage.com; 18653 Main St; 🕑 7am-6pm Sun-Thu, to 7pm Fri & Sat) Likely one of the best reasons to stop in Groveland, Mountain Sage is café, store, nursery and live-music venue all rolled into one. Owned by two biologists who converted it from grandma's historic house, the place stocks Fair Trade and organic products (including clothes and coffee), maps, books and artistic souvenirs. It also holds an excellent summer concert series.

Buck Meadows & Around

☎ 209 / pop 150 / elev 3200ft

A former stagecoach stop en route to Yosemite, the blink-and-you'll-miss-it settlement of Buck Meadows was called Hamilton Station until its name was changed in 1916. Only 20 minutes' drive from the park entrance, Buck Meadows today is a good alternative to staying inside the park.

A half-mile east of Buck Meadows, **Lost Claim** (☎ 209-962-7825; sites $; 🕑 May-Sep) is arguably the most attractive Forest Service campground along this stretch, but watch out for the poison oak. About 3.2 miles further east, **Sweetwater** (☎ 209-962-7825; sites $; 🕑 Apr-Oct) is unexciting but will do fine in a pinch. Spot the turnoffs for the campgrounds by the little brown tent signs.

Though barely worthy of the title camp-ground, the **Pines** (☎ 962-7825; sites $; ◯ year-round) has a handful of unexceptional sites in a small clearing surrounded by oak, pines and manzanita. It's about 3 miles west of Buck Meadows.

Just 1 mile west of the Big Oak Flat Entrance, the aptly named **Yosemite Gatehouse Lodge** (☎ 379-2260; www.yosemitecabins.com/gatehouse; 34001 Hwy 120; r & cabins $$) Gatehouse Lodge offers four handsome, rustic cabins and a couple of modest motel rooms all set among the trees. It also has a small general store.

In Buck Meadows proper, **Yosemite Westgate Lodge** (☎ 962-5281, 888-315-2378; fax 962-5285; 7633 Hwy 120; r weekdays/weekends $$/$$$; ⬚ ▣ ▣ ▣) is a generic but totally toler-able motel featuring standard rooms with modern amenities overlooking a large parking lot and a wee pool.

Also in town, **Blackberry Inn Bed & Break-fast** (☎ 962-4663, 888-867-5001; www.blackberry-inn .com; 7567 Hamilton Station Loop; r $$$; ▣) is owned by a local Yosemite expert (need info, she's got it). In a stunningly converted house, it offers three rooms, *big* breakfasts, daily home-baked chocolate-chip cookies and plenty of visiting hummingbirds.

For whopping portions of reliable road-side food in Buck Meadows, pop into **49'er Restaurant** (☎ 962-6877; 7589 Hwy 120, ◯ 7am-9pm May-Oct).

SOUTH OF YOSEMITE (HIGHWAY 41)

If you're heading up from Los Angeles (six hours away) or other Southern California points, this is the highway you'll likely wind up driving. From Fresno, it's about a 60-mile drive north through busy Oa-khurst to the park's South Entrance Sta-tion near Wawona. Hwy 41 is generally open year-round. Along the way you pass through the small town of Fish Camp, and 10 miles east of Oakhurst is the popular resort of Bass Lake. The Sierra National Forest stretches south from Yosemite some 100 miles to King's Canyon National Park. Public transportation is limited to infre-quent intercounty buses that don't go to the park.

OAKHURST

☎ 559 / pop 13,500 / elev 2400ft

Oakhurst isn't a picturesque beauty, but value and convenience, not charm, are its strong points. If you're on your way to Yosemite, or other scenic points in the area, it makes great sense to spend the night here as you can stay in a (relatively) affordable motel and grab a halfway (but only halfway) decent dinner just down the street.

The town was first settled in 1912, when the area was known as Fresno Flats, now the name of a local historic park. It didn't grow into much until recently, though modern Oakhurst is still not much to look at. The town is basically a sprawl of tourist-oriented businesses along either side of Hwy 41, near the point where the road meets the southern terminus of Hwy 49, which heads north to Mariposa, Sonora and the rest of the Gold Country.

A great place to gather information on Yosemite National Park, as well as the local area, is the **Yosemite Sierra Visitors Bureau** (☎ 683-4636; www.yosemitethisyear.com; 40637 Hwy 41; ◯ 8:30am-5pm Mon-Sat, 9am-1pm Sun), about a half-mile north of the Hwy 41/Hwy 49 intersection. Loaded with brochures, it also sells maps of the area and patiently doles out helpful advice to the seemingly endless stream of Yosemite tourists. If you roll in after hours, a phone outside lets you make free calls to 30 local accommodations. In the same office is a seasonal **Forest Service office** (☎ 658-7588; ◯ variable hours & days Apr-Sep) that issues wilderness permits.

If you're in town for the night, there are a few diversions. You can catch a movie at the five-screen **Met Cinema** (☎ 683-1234; 40015 Hwy 49; ▣), in Raley's shopping plaza at the corner of Hwys 41 and 49. If you've got kids ages two to 12, then the **Children's Museum of the Sierra** (☎ 658-5656; www.childrens museumofthesierra.org; 49269 Golden Oak Dr; admission $3; ◯ 10am-5pm Tue-Sat Jun-early Sep, 10am-4pm Tue-Sat & 1-4pm Sun mid-Sep—May) can entertain them with its hands-on exhibits, including a Castle Room, a theater and a teddy bear hospital (the road's off Rd 426). Further afield are drives to Bass Lake (p185) or along parts of the Sierra Vista National Scenic Byway (p187), which are definitely worthwhile if you have the time. You can also take a steam-train ride at Fish Camp (see p187).

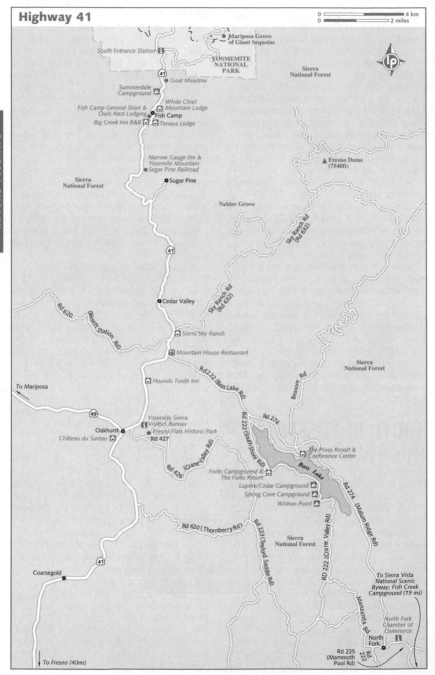

Fresno Flats Historic Park is a collection of old wooden buildings that were brought to this suburban setting beginning in 1975. It's a nice distraction if you like cute, pieced-together villages of restored historic buildings. Some interpretive plaques touch on the history of logging and local Native Americans. Folks dress up in costume once in a while, parading about and giving the place some life. To reach the park from Hwy 41, head east on Rd 426, then turn left on Rd 427 (School Rd).

Sleeping

Oakhurst Lodge (☎ 683-4417, 800-655-6343; www .oklodge.com; 40302 Hwy 41; r $$; ❂ 🖳 🕱 ⚘) Right in the center of town, this 60-unit motel presents a fine no-frills budget option, with quiet, clean kitchenette rooms.

our pick **Sierra Sky Ranch** (☎ 683-8040; www.sierra skyranch.com; 50552 Rd 632; r $$; ❂ 🖳 🕱) This former ranch dates back to 1875 and has numerous outdoor activities available on 14 attractive acres. The homespun rooms are phone-free and pet-friendly, with double doors that open onto shady verandas. The rambling and beautiful old lodge features a restaurant (dinner only) and a rustic saloon.

Hounds Tooth Inn (☎ 642-6600; www.hounds toothinn.com; 42071 Hwy 41; r incl breakfast $$-$$$; ❂ 🖳 ⚘) A few miles north of Oakhurst, this gorgeous garden B&B is swimming in rosebushes and Victorianesque charm. Its 13 airy rooms, some with spas and fireplaces, feel a bit like an English manor house. Complimentary wine and hot drinks are available in the afternoon.

Château du Sureau (☎ 683-6860; www.chateaudu sureau.com; r & ste $$$$; ❂ 🖳 🕱 ⚘) Never in a billion years would you expect to find this in Oakhurst. A luxe and discreet full-service European-style hotel and world-class spa, this destination property is prepared to pamper you.

Eating

Raley's (☎ 683-8300; ❂ 6am-11pm) For groceries, you have a few good supermarket choices, including the massive and modern Raley's, in a shopping complex at the traffic-clogged intersection of Hwys 41 and 49. The deli and sandwich counter makes good stuff to go.

Yosemite Coffee Roasting Company (☎ 683-8815; www.yosemitecoffee.com; 40879 Hwy 41; pastries & sandwiches $; 🖳) About a mile north of town, this on-site roastery and café sells coffee, espresso drinks, pastries and sandwiches. Weekends in summer bring in live music, with a mix of teen-oriented (ie, rockin') and mellower dinner shows; check the website for schedules.

Jade Gazebo (☎ 683-8600; 40487 Hwy 41; mains $; ❂ lunch & dinner Tue-Sun) A popular Chinese restaurant done up in green and white with red paper lanterns, it's a cheerful stop for big and inexpensive helpings. It has a fair number of vegetarian options available, as well as lunchtime specials.

Ol' Kettle Restaurant (☎ 683-7505; 40650 Hwy 41; mains $; ❂ 7am-7pm Mon-Sat, to 2pm Sun Oct-Mar, 7am-9pm Mon-Sat, to 2pm Sun Apr-Sep) Every town needs a homey family diner where the brood can kick back in a booth and order something that comes with a pile of fries. The Ol' Kettle fills this noble niche, tossing in a sunny dining room, long-time employees and kitschy salt and pepper shakers fashioned from mini-wine bottles. There's even a forest view!

Three Sisters Café (☎ 642-2253; 40291 Junction Dr; mains $$$; ❂ 9am-9pm Wed-Sat, to 7pm Sun) A romantic red and yellow dining room features German specialties, fresh fish and organic veggies from a local co-op. On warm evenings, enjoy your schnitzel and Black Forest ham at one of its outdoor café tables. From the intersection of Hwys 41 and 49, go north on Hwy 49 and right at the first light.

Erna's Elderberry House (☎ 683-6800; prix-fixe dinner $$$$; ❂ lunch Sun, dinner daily) Got a stack of extra cash or an expense account to burn up? Then definitely make a reservation at Erna's. It offers a renowned California-French dining experience in humble Oakhurst, at the super-swank Château du Sureau hotel. Look for it about a mile south of town on the west side of Hwy 41.

BASS LAKE

☎ 559 / pop 600 / elev 3300ft

In commercialized contrast to the serenity of Nelder Grove (p187), this hugely popular resort area is just a short drive from Oakhurst and Hwy 41. Surrounded by thick forest, Bass Lake is a great place to play, but don't expect to have it to yourself. Boaters, anglers, swimmers and car campers pack the place all summer long.

Most development lies on the northeast shore, where you'll find the Pines Village, a massive modern hotel and restaurant complex that includes galleries, gift shops, a grocery store and a post office. To get there, follow Bass Lake Rd (Rd 222) for a few miles until it forks; bear left onto Malum Ridge Rd (Rd 274). A couple miles further, turn right on Beasore Rd (Rd 434).

Sleeping

The closest **campgrounds** (☎ 877-444-6777; www .recreation.gov; sites $; ☺ May-Sep) lie along the lake's south shore, accessed via Rd 222, including (from west to east) Forks, Lupine/ Cedar, Spring Cove and Wishon Point.

Forks Resort (☎ 642-3737; www.theforksresort.com; 39150 Rd 222; cabins $$-$$$; ☒ ☖) Pine and plaid adorn these camp-style rooms and cabins near the lake, some sleeping up to eight people. Only some have air-conditioning, and none have phones. Weekly rates are available, as are canoe rentals. A friendly place, it's been family-owned and -operated for three generations.

Pines Resort & Conference Center (☎ 642-3121, 800-350-7463; www.basslake.com; chalets $$$, ste incl breakfast $$$; ☐ ☖) This 100-plus unit resort sprawls near the north edge of the lake, offering a mix of modern B&B Jacuzzi suites and fully equipped chalets. Take your pick from tennis, a spa, a hot tub and boating from the marina.

Eating & Drinking

Mountain House Restaurant (☎ 683-5191; 42525 Hwy 41; mains $-$$; ☺ 6am-9pm daily summer, 7am-9pm Mon-Fri, 6am-9pm Sat & Sun winter; ☐) About 13 miles south of Yosemite at the corner of Rd 222, the Mountain House serves standard pastas, sandwiches, salads, and steak and chicken dinners. It rotates 14 beers on tap throughout the year.

Ducey's on the Lake (39255 Marina Dr; breakfast $, mains $$$-$$$$; ☺ breakfast & dinner) Located behind the Pines Resort, here you can sup on crabmeat-stuffed rainbow trout or nibble on duck confit as you gaze out at the water. An extensive wine list features bottles from California and local wine makers.

Pines Bar (☎ 642-3750) Near the lobby of the resort, this is a loud, party-friendly place with pool tables and great mountain and lakeside views. (John Candy and Dan Aykroyd were filmed drinking at the bar in the 1988 comedy *The Great Outdoors*.) The jukebox has decent tunes, and classic rock bands take over on summer weekends.

SIERRA NATIONAL FOREST

The Sierra National Forest blankets the area between the Merced and Kings Rivers and brushes Yosemite from the south. You'll find lots of camping, much of it rather rustic, as well as excellent fishing, hiking and swimming.

More than 60 developed campgrounds dot the forest; to reserve a site call ☎ 877-444-6777 or check the internet at www. recreation.gov. Dispersed camping is also allowed. Available at area USFS offices is a Sierra National Forest map, which is a big help in navigation, and developed campgrounds are clearly marked.

The Sierra National Forest's **Summerdale Campground** (☎ 877-444-6777; www.recreation .gov; sites $; ☺ May-Sep) is the closest campground to the park and where most folks head to when the Wawona campground in Yosemite is full. It's a pleasant spot down along Big Creek (which is stocked with trout) with 28 well-dispersed sites in an area of grassy meadow and trees.

North Fork, a small community about 18 miles southeast of Oakhurst, is the main service and information center for points in the Sierra National Forest. You'll find a supermarket, an ATM and a post office at the intersection of Rds 225 and 222 (pick up a local map, as it's easy to get turned around). From the intersection, a driveway leads to the USFS **Bass Lake Ranger Station** (☎ 559-877-2218; www.fs.fed.us/r5/sierra; ☺ 8am-4:30pm Mon-Fri), which offers information on campgrounds, hikes and sights in the forest. The office is-

---

SCRAMBLING FOR A CAMPSITE?

If you get to the park and everything's full, try one of these nearby campgrounds in the Sierra National Forest:

- Summerdale (above) on Hwy 41 just outside the park
- Forks, Lupine/Cedar, Spring Cove, and Wishon Point (left) in Bass Lake
- McCabe Flat, Willow Placer and Railroad Flat (p178) in Briceburg
- Dry Gulch and Dirt Flat (p178) in El Portal

sues free fire permits, which are necessary if you want to build a campfire (you may be fined without one). You can also obtain wilderness permits here for overnight trips in the nearby Ansel Adams Wilderness.

Sierra Vista National Scenic Byway

Not every beautiful California mountain highway runs through Yosemite or even makes it across the Sierra Nevada. Set entirely within Sierra National Forest, this scenic byway follows USFS roads in a loop that takes you from 3000ft near Oakhurst and North Fork up to nearly 7000ft. Along the way are dramatic vistas, excellent fishing, and camping almost anywhere you like (dispersed camping is allowed in most areas). It's a great way for car campers – and curious day-trippers – to lose themselves within the mountains.

Begin your drive in North Fork, where you can pick up a map from the **Chamber of Commerce** (☎ 559-877-2332; www.north-fork-chamber.com; 33023 Rd 222/Main St; ☙ 9am-5pm Mon-Sat). The route takes a half-day to complete, emerging on Hwy 41 a few miles north of Oakhurst. Open from June to November, the road is paved most of the way, but is narrow and laced with curves. For camping information, stop by the ranger station at Bass Lake (opposite).

The byway accesses trails into the Ansel Adams Wilderness, most notably Clover Meadow, where a small ranger station opens each summer. It also passes Mile-High Vista, with views as sweeping as the name promises; Mammoth Pool Reservoir, a popular fishing, camping and swimming spot; Fresno Dome, well worth a hike to the top; and the Nelder Grove of giant sequoias. To follow the byway from North Fork, go southeast on Rd 225, northeast on Forest Rd 81, west onto Beasore Rd and northwest onto Sky Ranch Rd.

Numerous campgrounds line the byway, including **Fish Creek** (sites $; ☙ May-Sep), a small, woodsy, creekside campground that's the first you encounter after driving the 19 miles from North Fork. You'll find other popular campgrounds near Mammoth Pool Reservoir and Clover Meadow.

Nelder Grove

It's for good reason that crowds pack Yosemite's Mariposa Grove most days of the year. But if all you want is to walk in sol-

itude among majestic giant sequoias – with nary a chattering tourist in sight – head to this small but lovely grove in the Sierra National Forest instead. The trees aren't as plentiful as in Mariposa, but the scenery is moody and mystifying and the atmosphere impressively quiet (you just might be the only visitor, even in summer).

To reach the grove from Yosemite's South Entrance, follow Hwy 41 south 10 miles to Rd 632 (Sky Ranch Rd). Turn left, then follow the winding road (part of the Sierra Vista National Scenic Byway) about 7 miles to a turnoff for the grove. Signs mark the way. After another mile, head left toward the Shadow of the Giants Trail, with pit toilets at the trailhead. The easy 1-mile stroll beneath the trees takes just 30 minutes.

FISH CAMP

☎ 559 / pop 600 / elev 4300ft

Fish Camp is practically just a bend in the road, but a very pretty one. It's a tiny place with a small general store, a post office, and a handful of lodges and worthwhile B&Bs. The town is only 2 miles from Yosemite's southernmost entrance, so it makes a good base for visiting the park.

By far the biggest and boldest attraction in town is the **Yosemite Mountain Sugar Pine Railroad** (☎ 683-7273; www.ymsprr.com; 56001 Hwy 41; tours adult $13-17, child $6.50-8.50), at the south end of Fish Camp next to the Narrow Gauge Inn. Tours on either the old 'Logger' steam train (wheelchair accessible) or the Jenny railcar take place several times daily between March and October. Call for reservations or just show up. The Moonlight Special ($45/$22.50 per adult/child), on selected Saturday and Wednesday nights, includes a steak dinner, live music and a reenacted train robbery; reservations are essential.

Sleeping

White Chief Mountain Lodge (☎ 683-5444; www .sierratel.com/whitechiefmtnlodge; 7776 White Chief Mountain Rd; r $$) The cheapest option in town is this year-round 1950s-era motel with simple, standard kitchenette rooms and a restaurant on the grounds. It's located a few hundred yards east of Hwy 41; watch for the sign and go up the little wooded country road.

Owls Nest Lodging (☎ 683-3484; www.owlsnest lodging.com; 1237 Hwy 41; ste/cabins $$/$$$; ☻ Apr-Nov) If you're staying for a few days, the Owls Nest offers two spacious camp-style rentals that are a great value. There's a private cabin with full kitchen that sleeps six or seven, and a smaller kitchenette suite that's perfect for two. There's a two-night minimum stay.

our pick **Narrow Gauge Inn** (☎ 683-7720, 888-644-9050; www.narrowgaugeinn.com; 48571 Hwy 41; r incl breakfast $$-$$$; ☻ 🖳 ☻) Adjacent to the popular Sugar Pine Railroad, this beautiful, friendly and supremely comfortable 26-room inn has a hot tub, small bar and one of the finest restaurants around. Each tastefully appointed room features unique decor and a pleasant deck facing the trees and mountains, and some top-floor rooms were recently remodeled with air-con and flat-screen TVs.

Big Creek Inn B&B (☎ 641-2828; www.bigcreekinn .com; 1221 Hwy 41; r incl full breakfast $$$; 🖳) Each of the three white-palette rooms has peaceful creek views and a private balcony, and two have gas fireplaces. From the comfortable rooms or the bubbling hot tub, you can often spot deer and beavers, or hummingbirds lining up at the patio feeder. Amenities include in-room DVD players and a large movie library and kitchenette use.

Tenaya Lodge (☎ 683-6555, 888-514-2167; www .tenayalodge.com; 1122 Hwy 41; r $$$-$$$$, ste $$$$; ☻ 🖳 ☻ 🔥) A hulking, modern hotel and conference center just 2 miles from Yosemite's South Entrance, this 244-room resort and spa was formerly a Marriott, which explains why it looks and feels like a convention hotel. Despite the location outside the park, it's actually owned by the Yosemite concessionaire.

Eating

Fish Camp General Store (☎ 683-7962; 1191 Hwy 41; sandwiches $; ☻ 7am-8pm summer, to 6pm rest of year) This small place pretty much defines the 'center of town,' and it's been open since the 1920s. Open 365 days a year, it sells sandwiches and boxed lunches, a limited amount of groceries, snow chains and (not surprisingly) fishing supplies. There's also an ATM.

our pick **Narrow Gauge Inn** (☎ 683-6446; dinner mains $$$-$$$$; ☻ 5:30-9pm Wed-Sun Apr-Oct) Excellent food coupled with knockout views

make the dining experience at the Narrow Gauge Inn one of the finest in the Yosemite region. It's on the expensive side, but the dinners are creatively prepared, the lodge-like atmosphere is casual but elegant, and windows look out on lush mountain vistas. Reservations are recommended. Cozy up to the fireplace on colder evenings or warm yourself up at the small Buffalo Bar, perfect for a cocktail or glass of chardonnay.

NORTHWEST OF YOSEMITE

The vast **Stanislaus National Forest** (www.r5.fs .fed.us/stanislaus) dominates the area northwest of Yosemite, covering more than 250,000 acres of open terrain and 800 miles of rivers and streams. The result? Some of the best river rafting, lake canoeing, mountain biking, fishing and swimming in the entire Yosemite area. To the north, the forest wreathes all of Emigrant Wilderness and portions of the Carson-Iceberg and Mokelumne Wilderness areas, which you can access via Hwys 108, 4 and 120.

If you plan to explore any part of the national forest, be sure to stop by the **Groveland Ranger Station** (☎ 209-962-7825; 24545 Hwy 120), near the town of Groveland (p181), for friendly advice, maps and detailed trail descriptions. For more information on activities in this area, see p38.

CHERRY LAKE

Cherry Lake, the largest lake within Stanislaus National Forest, lies along Yosemite's border just west of Hetch Hetchy. Getting there, however, involves some meandering, so study your road map carefully. If motorboats don't bother you, Cherry Lake is a fine place to swim, paddle and fish, thanks in no small part to the spectacular vistas of the Tuolumne River Canyon.

You'll find several hikes off Cherry Lake Rd, including the 4½-mile **Preston Flat Trail**, an easy, scenic option. Stop on the right just past the bridge and follow the trail along the north side of the Tuolumne River. You'll pass several swimming holes and big rocks that are ideal for lounging about or having a picnic.

The **Cherry Valley Campground** (sites $; ☻ Apr-Oct) features 46 first-come, first-served sites.

HIGHWAY 108
Sonora
☎ 209 / pop 4625 / elev 1825

Settled in 1848 by miners from Sonora, Mexico, the historic town of Sonora once thrived as a cosmopolitan center, complete with Spanish plazas, elaborate saloons and the Southern Mines' largest concentration of gamblers, drunkards and gold. The Big Bonanza Mine, at the north end of Washington St, where Sonora High School now stands, yielded 12 tons of gold in two years (including a 28lb nugget). Today the Tuolumne County seat, it's no longer the quaintest of the Gold Country towns, but the bustling downtown is well preserved, and it's a good base for white-water rafting on the Stanislaus and Tuolumne Rivers (see p50). Sonora is about two hours from Yosemite's West Entrance, at the southwest end of Hwy 108.

The **Tuolumne County Visitors Center** (☎ 533-4420; www.thegreatunfenced.com; 542 Stockton St; ☯ daily) provides loads of information. For guided rafting trips, contact **Sierra Mac River Trips** (☎ 532-1327, 800-457-2580; www.sierramac.com)

and for canoe and kayak rentals, hit **Sierra Nevada Adventure Company** (SNAC; ☎ 532-5621; www.snacattack.com; 173 S Washington St).

For a good night's rest try the **Sonora Days Inn** (☎ 532-2400, 866-732-4010; www.sonoradaysinn .com; 160 S Washington St; motel r $$; ✖ ☐ ☝ ☝) or the less expensive but more historic **Gunn House Hotel** (☎ 532-3421; www.gunnhousehotel.com; 286 S Washington St; r $$; ✖ ☐ ☝).

Outlaws BarBQ (☎ 532-1227; 275 S Washington St; www.outlawsbarbq.com; mains $-$$; ☯ Tue-Sun) serves up gob-smackin' good barbeque.

Scenic Sonora Pass
Northeast of Sonora, Hwy 108 winds through dense forest and aspen-filled meadows before cresting out at Sonora Pass (9624ft). From here, the road corkscrews down the Eastern Sierra at a frightening 26% grade (in stretches), before leveling out and joining Hwy 395. Not for the road-weary, the absolutely stunning drive sometimes feels more like a roller coaster than a highway. It zigzags past pristine roadside Sierra scenery, including several good places to hike or simply take in the sights.

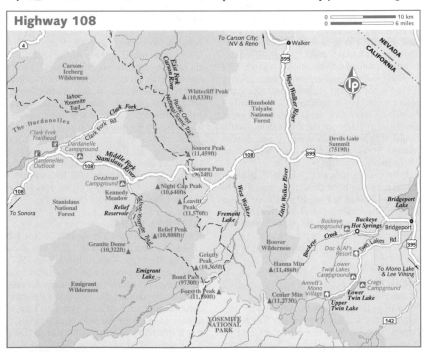

From the Vista Trail at the **Dardenelles Outlook** on Hwy 108, about 1¼ hours east of Sonora, you can enjoy an unobstructed view of the Dardanelles volcanic cones and the sprawling Carson-Iceberg Wilderness. The nearby **Clark Fork Trailhead**, accessed via Forest Rd 6N06, is a good starting point for hikes into both the Carson-Iceberg and Emigrant Wilderness areas. The 4-mile hike to Boulder Lake is a popular choice, as is the 7-mile Dardanelles Loop, a challenging day hike. Some of the best wilderness access is from **Kennedy Meadow**, along the Stanislaus River on Hwy 108, about 6 miles east of Dardanelle.

There are literally a dozen or so pleasant **campgrounds** along the stretch of road from Dardanelle to Sonora, and even in the thick of summer you stand a good chance of finding a sweet spot. Read up on the different campgrounds online at www.r5.fs.fed.us/stanislaus/visitor/camping.htm.

HIGHWAY 4

Stretching along an illustrious gold-rush mining route, scenic Hwy 4 jogs through a handful of quaint Gold Country towns, bisects the Stanislaus National Forest, skirts three wilderness areas, crosses Ebbetts Pass and finally plunges into the Humbolt-Toiyabe National Forest. For outdoor fanatics it's a road trip through paradise. The highway offers easy access to outstanding hiking among giant sequoias and along the Sierra Crest. It passes some of California's best lake canoeing and kayaking, great swimming holes on the Stanislaus River, bouldering sites, cross-country and downhill ski areas, and an endless network of 4WD roads. Yep, this is funville.

From Yosemite's Big Oak Flat Entrance, it's an easy two-hour drive to Angels Camp, via Hwy 120 west to Hwy 49 north. Although Ebbetts Pass closes after the first major snowfall, Hwy 4 is usually plowed from the west as far as Bear Valley ski resort.

There is no public transportation along Hwy 4.

Angels Camp

☎ 209 / pop 3150 / elev 1379ft

Famous as the place where Mark Twain collected notes for his short story 'The Celebrated Jumping Frog of Calaveras County,' Angels Camp is a classic Gold Country town at the junction of Hwy 49 and Hwy 4. Although residential development has dramatically transformed this once tiny town, the main drag is still as nostalgic as ever, and frog jumping still reigns supreme: the **International Frog Jump Competition** takes place the third weekend in May, and bronze frogs, embedded along the sidewalk of Main St, commemorate the International Frog Jump champions of the past 50 years. **Mark Twain Days** happen over the Fourth of July weekend.

There are several lodging options in town, including the friendly **Gold Country Inn** (☎ 736-4611, 800-851-4944; r $$; 🍴 🖥 👍 🐕) and the comfy **Angels Inn Motel** (☎ 736-4242, 888-753-0226; 600 North Main St/Hwy 49; r/ste $$/$$$; 🍴 🖥 🐾 👍 🐕).

Sue's Angels Creek Café (☎ 736-2941; 1246 S Main St; breakfast & lunch $) is where locals go for pancakes, eggs, hamburgers and hot sandwiches.

Murphys

☎ 209 / pop 2060 / elev 2300ft

With a main street that looks like a cross between a Norman Rockwell painting and a Randolph Scott Western, Murphys is, without a doubt, one of the finest historic towns in the Mother Lode. Although boutique shops and restaurants dominate its main drag, the town hasn't succumbed entirely to the kitsch and cliché that dominate so many Gold Country towns. With great restaurants, an excellent bakery, loads of wine-tasting rooms, several art galleries, bookstores and a theater company, Murphys has definitely gone upscale, but at least it has done so in style.

The best way to tap Murphys historical roots is to join the free one-hour walking tour that leaves every Saturday at 10am from outside the **Murphy's Old Timers Museum** (☎ 209-728-1160; Main St; ☺ 11am-4pm Fri-Sun, 10:30am-4:30pm Mon Memorial Day to Labor Day).

SLEEPING & EATING

Murphys Historic Hotel & Lodge (☎ 728-3444, 800-532-7684; 457 Main St; r $$; 🍴 🐕) If it was good enough for Mark Twain, Black Bart, William Randolph Hearst and Ulysses S Grant then, hey, it's gotta be good enough for you. Provided, of course, that you don't need air-conditioning or heat and you don't mind ghosts (ask about Elenor). Built in 1856, this is one historic hotel with a fun staff and old-fashioned rooms – so old-fashioned, in fact, that they all have shared bathrooms. Guests desiring more modern amenities (like air-con) can sleep in the modern sector out back.

Dunbar House (☎ 728-2897; 800-692-6006; www .dunbarhouse.com; rooms $$$-$$$$; ✷ 🖵) Relive the gold-rush days in style at this swanky but totally unpretentious B&B located downtown.

ourpick Grounds (☎ 728-8663; 402 Main St; ☺ 7am-8pm Wed-Sat, 8am-8pm Sun, 8am-3pm Mon & Tue; breakfast & lunch $, dinner $$$; 🅑) Stylish and sophisticated, yet totally casual and always welcoming, this excellent eatery chefs up California cuisine with the freshest ingredients.

Aria (☎ 728-9250; 458 Main St; coffee, baked goods & sandwiches $; ☺ 6am-4pm Mon-Sun, to 6pm Fri; 🅑) The town's best bakery also serves Murphys' best cup of coffee.

Murphys Historic Hotel & Lodge's **restaurant** (breakfast $, lunch $-$$, dinner $$-$$$; ☺ 7am-2pm & 5-8pm Mon-Thu, 7am-3pm & 5-9pm Sat & Sun; 🅑) serves salads, burgers, fried chicken, rack of lamb, pasta and a damn-good prime rib.

DRINKING & ENTERTAINMENT

Murphys Creek Theatre (☎ 728-8422; www.murphys creektheater.org; tickets $18-22, child $13; ☺ performances Thu-Sun) Every weekend at the Stevenot Winery's outdoor amphitheater, this small troupe presents its excellent and enthusiastic Theatre Under the Stars. Purchase tickets online, over the phone or by stopping into the box office (323 Main St at Church St), located inside Moon Alley candle shop on the main drag. Stevenot Winery is about 2.5 miles out of town via Sheep Ranch Rd.

Ironstone Vineyards (☎ 728-1251; www.iron stonevineyards.com; 1894 Six Mile Rd) Dance yourself silly to bands that fall into that past-their-prime-but-still-kickin' category (think Bryan Adams or Earth, Wind & Fire) before they head on to Las Vegas. The vineyard is located about 1 mile southwest of Murphys.

The old-time **saloon** (☺ 11am-close) at Murphys Historic Hotel & Lodge is arguably the joint's finest feature, with deer heads mounted to the walls, a giant bar and a friendly crowd.

Arnold

☎ 209 / pop 4300 / elev 4000

Arnold is the last sizable town before Hwy 4 winds its way up and over Ebbetts Pass. Surrounded by fragrant pine forest, the town

---

WINE TASTING IN CALAVERAS COUNTY

Wine making has long been associated with Gold Country. During the 1870s, Calaveras County alone boasted more than 100 wineries. But as the gold rush ended, so did the call for wine, and the makers who did hang on were later hit hard by Prohibition. After that, grape growing and wine producing virtually disappeared, except for a few families who continued to bottle their own. But the 1960s ushered in a newfound passion for California wines. Blessed with dry mountain air, warm temperatures and lots of golden sunshine, the Sierra foothills drew a fresh generation of wine makers to restore old vineyards, plant new varietals and produce quality handcrafted wines.

These days, Calaveras County houses a trove of small-production vineyards, with old-time Murphys the unofficial hub of wine tasting. Specialty varietals seem to thrive in the rolling hills and nutrient-rich soils. And a perfect collection of microclimates and varied elevations also help produce niche styles of grapes that ordinarily hail from sun-splashed regions of Europe, like nebbiola, viognier, roussanne, barbera, sangiovese, tempranillo, and cabernet frank, plus a handful of Portuguese varietals used for making port in Sonora.

Wine touring through the foothills can be an enjoyable and intimate experience, with crowd-free tasting rooms, complimentary tasting flights and some exceptional wines. The best way to hit the maximum number of tasting rooms in a day – and not have to drive home – is by strolling downtown Murphys, where nearly a dozen wineries have tasting rooms. They include **Stevenot** (www.stevenotwinery.com), **Zucca Mountain** (www.zuccawines.com), **Milliaire Winery** (www.milliairewinery .com), **Solomon Wine Company** (www.solomonwine.com), **Twisted Oak** (www.twistedoak.com), **Newsome-Harlow** (www.newsomeharlow.com), **Domaine Becquet** (www.becquetwinery.com), **Lavender Ridge** (www.lavenderridgevineyard.com) and **Ironstone Vineyards** (www.ironstonevineyards.com).

If you really want to check out the goods up close, head to the **Calaveras Grape Stomp**, held the first weekend of October in Murphys. Check out www.calaveraswines.org for information.

is as thick with cabin rentals as it is with trees, meaning it's a great base for families and groups who want adventure by day and comfort by night.

On the right, just as you roll into town from the west, is the **Sierra Nevada Adventure Company** (SNAC; ☎ 795-9310; www.snacattack.com; 2293 Hwy 4), which rents canoes and kayaks and stocks a wide variety of outdoor gear, paddling supplies and topo maps. It's also a great source of information.

If you're pinching pennies, go for the down-home **Meadowmont Lodge** (☎ 795-1394; 2011 Hwy 4; r $$). For a real treat, book a room at the beautifully rustic **Black Bear Inn** (☎ 795-8999, 866-795-8999; www.arnoldblackbearinn.com; 1343 Oak Circle; r $$$; ⊗ 🖥 �ⓖ), a B&B just off Hwy 4, east of the golf course. For cabin rentals, check out **Don Fry Realty** (☎ 795-4094, 800-641-4441; www.donfryrealty.com; Hwy 4); the Blue Lake Springs area is especially attractive.

There are several eating options along Hwy 4, but nothing beats milkshakes, burgers and onion rings at the outdoor tables at **Giant Burger** (☎ 795-1594; 846 Hwy 4; mains $; 🕙 10am-8pm). It's on the east end of town.

Calaveras Big Trees State Park
☎ 209 / elev 5000ft
'Big Trees' is a bit of an understatement. The behemoths which give this **state park** (www.parks.ca.gov; day pass per vehicle $6) its name are no less than *giant*, which, of course, brings us to their other name: giant sequoias. About 4 miles northeast of Arnold on Hwy 4, the park encompasses two easily accessible giant sequoia groves, 6000 acres of mixed-conifer forest, beautiful Beaver Creek and the mighty Stanislaus River. The trout fishing, river swimming and boulder-hopping are all outstanding, while the hikes among the big trees are humbling lessons in size. During winter, part of the park stays open for snow camping and cross-country skiing.

At the park entrance, you'll find the **visitor center** (☎ 795-2334; 🕙 11am-3pm), the **ranger station** (☎ 795-2334; 🕙 11am-3pm) and the main parking lots.

The best **swimming** is along the Stanislaus, near the bridge, where the river has sculpted the granite into perfection, with outstanding rock-jumping, slides, rapids, and peaceful pools in which to immerse yourself after sunning atop the wide rock slabs. From the park entrance, follow the main road 6 miles to the bridge; the fun stuff is just upstream.

HIKING
The **North Grove Big Trees Trail**, a 1-mile self-guided loop, begins next to the visitor center and winds along the forest floor past the Big Stump and a tree named Mother of the Forest. A 4-mile trail that branches off from the self-guided loop climbs out of the North Grove, crosses a ridge, and descends 1500ft to the Stanislaus River.

SOUTH GROVE NATURAL PRESERVE

Duration 2–4 hours
Distance 3.5–5 miles round trip
Difficulty moderate; elevation change +560ft
Start/Finish South Grove trailhead and parking lot
Nearest Town/Facilities gas, food and lodging in Arnold, 12 miles; visitor center, 9 miles
Transport private
Summary Ditch the crowds and hike this gentle trail that wanders among the biggest giant sequoias in Calaveras Big Trees State Park.

Inaccessible by car and devoid of any picnic areas or campgrounds, the South Grove is accessible from a trailhead about 9 miles from the park's entrance, and makes for an excellent alternative to the well-known trails through the giant sequoia groves of Yosemite. Even on busy weekends, this path rarely feels crowded. Even so, be sure to hit it early enough to beat the heat and to have the trees to yourself. The trail is particularly beautiful in springtime, when the dogwoods light up the trail with their myriad flowers.

The well-signed trail leaves the South Grove parking lot, crosses a small meadow and arrives at delightful **Beaver Creek** (take a good look, as this water will reward you upon your return). Cross Beaver Creek and begin your walk into the fragrant mixed-conifer forest. Pass the trail that detours left into the **Bradley Grove** (a group of sequoias planted in the 1950s) and you'll soon begin to climb out of the Beaver Creek drainage. A mile or so from the trailhead you'll come to a dirt road. Cross it and continue for approxi-

---

TERRIBLE TREE-TMENT

Even before tourists discovered Yosemite Valley in 1855, they were flocking to the Calaveras Grove of giant sequoias along the Stanislaus River, northwest of Yosemite. A series of businessmen had the idea that the trees should go on tour, and in 1853 a tree was cut down and shipped to New York City and London. The following year, another giant tree was stripped of its bark, and the bark was sent off with the same itinerary.

Back at the grove, one stump was polished up to serve as a dance floor for the wealthy city folk who were looking for novel entertainment. The revelers could dance into the wee hours and then tumble off to bed in a hotel built on the stump of another downed giant.

Entrepreneurs also bored through living trunks so tourists could tell the folks back home that they had driven their carriage through one of the colossal trees. And just because it was possible to do so, the carriages rumbled along the length of downed trees or through decaying tunnels that occur naturally inside of them. Today, of course, these practices no longer occur, but at Calaveras Big Trees State Park, you can still hike among the giants that survived the abuse.

---

mately 0.5 miles to the loop trail junction; veer right and you'll shortly see the first of the South Grove's astounding trees. The trail passes several giant sequoias – including a fallen, hollow sequoia that will make you feel you like a hobbit – before finally arriving another junction.

If you turn left at this junction, you'll return to the parking lot, having hiked a total of 3.5 miles. Turn right to see the two biggest trees in the park: the **Palace Hotel Tree** and the **Agassiz Tree**. With a diameter of 25ft (measured 6ft above the ground), the Agassiz Tree is the largest in the park and ranks among the world's 10 largest trees.

To return to the trailhead, retrace your steps, but pass the junction which put you on the final leg of the trail. You'll return instead via the loop trail.

SLEEPING

At the park entrance, you'll find **North Grove Campground** (sites $). Less crowded is the **Oak Hollow Campground** (sites $), about 5 miles further on the park's main road. Tent sites at both can be reserved through **Reserve America** (☎ 800-444-7275; www.reserveamerica.com).

Bear Valley

☎ 209 / pop 150 / elev 7073ft

Most people who've heard of Bear Valley know it for the ski resort. But over the years, Bear Valley Village (the resortlike population center) has become an enclave of outdoor fun, with everything from rock climbing to mountain biking within a short distance from the village. The nearby ski area of **Bear Valley Mountain Resort** (☎ 753-2301; www.bearvalley.com; lift tickets $48-54;), which boasts 2000ft of vertical rise and 12 lifts, is still the primary draw. The resort's somewhat off-the-beaten-track location gives it a friendly, local feel.

During summer, the village makes an excellent base for the network of mountain-biking trails that wind their way anywhere from 3 to 10 miles down to the Village. You'll find good rock climbing with 70ft to 100ft crack and face climbs in Box Canyon, less than a mile east of Bear Valley. West of Bear Valley, there's excellent bouldering at Hells Kitchen and Tamarack Boulders. For maps and directions to these sites, stop in at the **Alpine Ranger Station** (☎ 753-2811; Apr-Oct), west of town.

All sorts of backcountry skills courses, from wilderness medicine to avalanche education, are offered by **Mountain Adventure Seminars** (☎ 753-6556; www.mtadventure.com). Register in advance.

Bear Valley Adventure Company (☎ 753-2834; www.bearvalleyxc.com), on the left as you pull into the Village from Hwy 4, is the one-stop shop for outdoor supplies, kayak and mountain-bike rentals, and information on just about everything there is to do in the area. It can arrange mountain-bike shuttles (if you don't feel like pedaling) and has excellent maps. In winter, the shop stows the kayaks, pulls out the skis and becomes the de facto cross-country ski center.

Food supplies are available at the Bear Valley General Store, towards the back of the village complex. Both the **Headwaters Coffee**

House (☎ 753-2708; 3 Bear Valley Rd; ☺ 7am-2:30pm Nov-Sep) and **Bear Valley Pizza Company** (☎ 753-2872; ☺ 5-9pm Thu-Mon) serve good food.

Lake Alpine

☎ 209 / elev 7350ft

Lake Alpine is a large, stunningly beautiful alpine lake skirted by slabs of granite, several great beaches and a handful of campgrounds. Kayaking, canoeing, swimming and fishing are all excellent, which is why it's jammed with people on summer weekends. No matter how many people descend upon the place, however (and there are far fewer midweek), it's a hard setting to beat. It's particularly fun for families.

There are several nearby trailheads, and the **hiking** is excellent. The short climb to Inspiration Point (1.4 miles) is outstanding and accessible from the Lakeshore Trail near Lake Alpine's Pine-Martin Campground. The uphill scramble rewards you with spectacular views of Spicer Reservoir and the Dardanelles. Down at the boat ramp, on the lake's northern shore (right off Hwy 4) a **boat rental** kiosk rents rowboats, paddle boats, kayaks and canoes for $25 to $50, depending on the time; motorboats cost $40 to $80.

Across Hwy 4 from the boat ramp, **Lake Alpine Lodge** (☎ 753-6358; Hwy 4; tent cabins $, cabins $$; ☺ May 1-Oct 15) offers a handful of fully equipped and cozy one- and two-bedroom cabins, as well as tent cabins. Its **restaurant** (mains $-$$; ☺ 11am-3pm Mon-Sat, 10am-3pm Sun mid-Jun–Sep, weekends only fall & spring) serves pasta, meats and seafood, and features a long deck with views of the lake. The lodge also has a general store and a bar, and the outdoor tables make a great spot for a posthike pint.

Several first-come, first-served **campgrounds** (sites $) ring the lake and offer easy access to the water. The best are on the lake's eastern shore (it's signed). All have faucets and pit toilets and most sites have a picnic table and fire pit.

Ebbetts Pass

elev 8730ft

Although Ebbetts Pass, designated a National Scenic Byway in 2005, officially runs from Arnold to Hwy 89, it's the dramatic stretch east of Lake Alpine that really gets the heart pumping. After Lake Alpine, the narrow highway continues past picturesque **Mosquito Lake** and the **Pacific Grade Summit** (el-evation 8060ft) before slaloming through historic **Hermit Valley** (7060ft), entering the Toiyabe National Forest, and finally winding up and over the actual summit of **Ebbetts Pass**. Near the pass, there's an easy access point to the Pacific Crest Trail (p41). There are simple self-registration **campgrounds** (sites $) all along this stretch, including at Mosquito Lake, Pacific Valley and Hermit Valley. Most have fire rings, picnic tables and pit toilets only.

NOBEL LAKE

Duration 3.5–5 hours
Distance 8 miles round-trip
Difficulty moderate
Start/Finish Ebbetts Pass Trailhead, 0.4 miles east of Ebbetts Pass
Nearest Town/Facilities Hermit Valley Campground, 7 miles; food and supplies at Lake Alpine Lodge, 4 miles
Transport private
Summary This outstanding, well-marked stretch of the Pacific Crest Trail offers nonstop views along the Sierra Crest, strange volcanic cliff formations, conversations with PCT hikers and some of the best wildflowers anywhere.

The Ebbetts Pass Trailhead lies at a parking lot reached by a short dirt road 0.4 miles east of the Ebbetts Pass sign. From the southwest side of the parking lot, follow the trail into the trees and connect with the Pacific Crest Trail (PCT) after 0.2 miles. Turn left (northeast) onto the PCT, and within minutes the wildflower show begins. Head over a rocky bluff, dotted with Mariposa lilies and California corn lilies, and you'll enter a forest of fir and pines with volcanic cliffs towering behind them to the right. As you skirt these cliffs, which form the western wall of **Noble Canyon**, you'll pass several snow-fed creeks and patches of dazzling wildflowers.

About 30 minutes from the trailhead, the trail passes to the left of a seasonal pond. It then bends northeast and begins to drop and passes an outcropping of boulders at the edge of a ridge, offering beautiful views over Noble Canyon. The trail then skirts along a steep sector of upper Nobel Canyon with granite boulders scattered above the trail to your right and splendid views of the canyon on your left. You'll cross several cheerful creeks, brimming with lupine, before the trail turns north around the head of the canyon to flank the other side. It crosses the main creek (a great spot for a head-dunk) and soon passes the Nobel Canyon trail junction.

On the dryer, rockier southwest side of the canyon, the trail affords incredible views as it gently switchbacks up the mountain. The wildflowers differ here, with flowering sage, yarrow and even some patches of thistle. The trail tops out and shortly arrives the northeast shore of **Noble Lake**. The small lake seems almost an afterthought to the outstanding features of the rest of the hike.

To return, retrace your footsteps.

THE EASTERN SIERRA

Compared with the western side, the Eastern Sierra is another world. While rolling oak-covered foothills grace the Western Sierra and impede views of the mountains from a distance, a sweeping, nearly treeless desert basin abuts the steep eastern slopes. The result? Views – whether from the basin floor or from high in the mountains – like you wouldn't believe. Within this dramatic setting, National Forest roads lead to marvelously uncrowded campgrounds, hiking areas and undeveloped hot springs. There's superb mountain biking and world-class skiing at Mammoth Lakes. The fishing, cycling and hiking around the June Lake Loop is superb. Hiking into the high country from Twin, Lundy and Virginia Lakes will astound you. And capping it all off is ancient Mono Lake, the mineral tufa formations of which are one of the most surreal sights anywhere.

GETTING AROUND

Hwys 120 and 108 both lead over the Sierras to Hwy 395, the main north–south artery through the Eastern Sierra. Due to heavy snowfall, both are only open roughly May or June through September. For public transportation between Yosemite, Mammoth Lakes and points between, see p174.

TIOGA PASS TO MONO LAKE

The stretch of Hwy 120 between Tioga Pass and Lee Vining is the most epic route into or out of Yosemite National Park –

TAKE THE HIGH ROAD

Tioga Rd (Hwy 120 between Crane Flat and Lee Vining) is the highest road across the Sierra Nevada, topping out at Tioga Pass, the dizzying 9945ft elevation of which makes it the highest auto pass in California. The road was initially built in 1883 in order to supply a silver mine at Bennettville (p197), near Tioga Pass. But the mine failed shortly after the road's completion, and both fell into disrepair. Decades later, with Yosemite becoming an increasingly popular tourist destination, Tioga Rd was rehabilitated for the sake of tourism. It was finally rebuilt, rerouted and widened in the 1960s.

---

and one of the most stunning anywhere in California. The roadbed is scratched into the side of steep, dramatic Lee Vining Canyon, with sheer drop-offs, rugged rock walls and sweeping views. It's incredible to witness how quickly and significantly the scenery changes from one side of Tioga Pass to the other. Once you cross the pass heading east and start downhill, you'll leave behind the lush grasses and tall pines of Tuolumne and Dana Meadows for the dry, sagebrush-coated landscape of the Great Basin Desert. At the end of Hwy 120 lies Mono Lake, a massive expanse of saltwater at the edge of the Great Basin Desert.

Several excellent first-come, first-served campgrounds are found along Tioga Rd, most run by **Inyo National Forest** (☎ 760-647-3041; www.fs.fed.us/r5/inyo).

Tioga Pass

The campground closest to Tioga Pass is at **Tioga Lake** (Hwy 120; sites $), which has a handful of sunny, exposed sites right on the lake but visible from the road.

Founded in 1914, **Tioga Pass Resort** (www .tiogapassresort.com; r $$-$$$) justifiably attracts a loyal clientele with its 10 rustic cabins tucked into the rocks and trees beside Lee Vining Creek, just 2 miles east of Tioga Pass. The cabins are basic but cozy, and each includes a kitchen, porch, bathroom and linens. Book via email. Although the attached **diner** (breakfast & lunch $, dinner $-$$; ☙ 7am-9pm) has only a small counter and

AROUND YOSEMITE

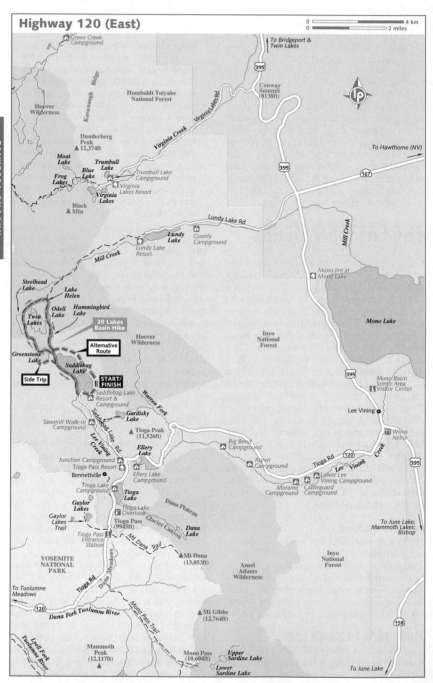

Highway 120 (East)

AROUND YOSEMITE

two tables, the intimate, old-time character makes for a superb setting. The lodge is open roughly from late May to mid-October, depending on snow. During the winter the lodge serves as a base camp for backcountry skiing forays into the surrounding wilderness. Winter visitors approach from Lee Vining and park their cars along Hwy 120. From there, they ski more than 6 miles to the resort.

Saddlebag Lake & Around

Reflecting its bleak, high-alpine surroundings at an elevation of 10,087ft, Saddlebag Lake lies at the end of a 2.5-mile dirt road that branches north from Hwy 120, about 2 miles east of Yosemite's Tioga Pass Entrance. The dam here was built in 1919 to help power Lee Vining before the water was diverted to LA. A favorite haunt for anglers, Saddlebag itself pales in comparison to the scenery surrounding it. With countless lakes, and stunning views of North Peak (12,242ft) and Mt Conness (12,590ft) on the Yosemite border and pointy Tioga Peak (11,513ft) to the southeast, the area is utterly spectacular. Saddlebag Lake (which is actually a reservoir) is California's highest car-accessible lake.

The Saddlebag Lake Resort operates a **water taxi** (adult/child/senior round-trip $10/6/9, one way $7/5/6) to the other side of the lake, rents **fishing boats** (2/5/10hr $30/60/90) and sells fishing licenses.

HIKING

Overnight camping is prohibited within the Monroe Hall Research Area, west of Saddlebag Lake. If you backpack (overnight) into the 20 Lakes Basin, you must obtain a wilderness permit from either the Tuolumne Meadows Wilderness Center (p93) or the Mono Basin Scenic Area Visitor Center (p199) near Lee Vining.

From Junction Campground (at the turnoff to Saddlebag Lake from Hwy 120), a mile-long trail leads to the former site of **Bennettville**, a one-time mining town. About a mile north on Saddlebag Lake Rd you'll find a trailhead for **Gardisky Lake**, an oft-overlooked gem tucked beneath 11,526ft Tioga Peak. The hike is short but steep, with an elevation gain of almost 800ft in about a mile.

20 LAKES BASIN

Duration 3–5 hours
Distance 5.2–8.8 miles
Difficulty Moderate; elevation change +250ft
Start/Finish Saddlebag Lake
Nearest Town/Facilities food and camping at Saddlebag Lake
Transport private
Summary Never dropping below 10,000ft, this mostly level trail meanders past some of the most breathtaking scenery in the entire Yosemite region.

AROUND YOSEMITE

Because it involves little elevation gain, this popular loop offers an outstanding opportunity to experience a real high-alpine setting – complete with glacial lakes, elf-land-like meadows, delightful cascades and dramatic peaks – without *too* much effort. For the more adventurous, it also offers plenty of opportunity to scramble up surrounding peaks and saddles for fantastic views, especially above Greenstone and Steelhead Lakes, both dominated by North Peak.

The trail begins at the south shore of Saddlebag Lake, heads up the western shore and continues past **Wasco Lake** to **Steelhead Lake**. It then cuts northwest along a signed unmaintained trail. At the sign, you have to cross the creek that drains Steelhead Lake and make your way over a rock outcropping.

The trail then disappears and reappears (watch for cairns) among the rocks and talus, passes **Twin Lakes** and makes its way around the north shore of **Lake Helen** before hitting the Lundy Canyon junction. Hang a right, head up a talus-filled ravine and return to Saddlebag via **Odell Lake**, **Lundy Pass** and **Hummingbird Lake**.

Note that many maps do not show the use-trail connecting Steelhead and Helen Lakes. You can chop 3.6 miles off of the hike by taking the water taxi from Saddlebag Lake Resort to the opposite side of the reservoir. The trail along the western shore of Saddlebag is almost a mile shorter than the more scenic trail on the eastern shore.

If you're not camped at Saddlebag Lake, park at the Saddlebag Lake Trailhead Parking lot, immediately above the trailhead.

SLEEPING & EATING

Inyo National Forest (☎ 760-647-3041; www.fs.fed .us/r5/inyo) runs the following three small primitive campgrounds in this area. Due to their size, large RVs and trailers are effectively prohibited, making for extremely pleasant tent camping:

Junction (cnr Hwy 120 & Saddlebag Lake Rd; sites $) Named for its location at the intersection of Hwy 120 and the Saddlebag Lake road, this 13-site campground offers sunny sites near Lee Vining Creek. They're fairly close to the highway, but when the sun hits in the morning they're sublime.

Sawmill Walk-in (Saddlebag Lake Rd; sites $) One of the most scenic established campgrounds in the entire Sierra Nevada, Sawmill offers 12 sites on the edge of the beautiful Monroe Hall Research Area. From the parking area (midway up the Saddlebag Lake road), it's an approximately 0.25 mile walk to the campground.

Saddlebag Lake (Saddlebag Lake; sites $) Perched atop a hill overlooking the reservoir, this is a favorite with anglers. All sites are small and well kept and some have splendid views over the lake.

Saddlebag Lake Resort (www.saddlebaglakeresort .com; Saddlebag Lake; breakfast & lunch $; ☺ 7am-7pm Mon-Sat, to 5pm Sun Jul-Oct) On the southeast shore of Saddlebag Lake, this diner-cum-general store (no lodging) serves up egg and pancake breakfasts, burgers, sandwiches and homemade pie.

Ellery Lake

elev 9538ft

Nestled into the rocks between the base of some seriously spectacular cliffs and Hwy 120, Ellery Lake makes for a splendid roadside stop and good fishing (unlike lakes within the park, it's stocked). It also boasts the small but pretty **Ellery Lake Campground** (sites $; Hwy 120), with tiny sites tucked into the bushes and pines out of sight of both the road and the lake. It's close-quarters camping, but it's a beautiful spot.

Along Lee Vining Creek

Once you drop out of Lee Vining Canyon and get closer to Lee Vining, you'll find several quiet campgrounds to the south of the highway. They're all first-come, first-served and set among pine, aspen and desert sage alongside Lee Vining Creek. About 10 miles

east of Tioga Pass is the turnoff for Poole Power Plant Rd; after turning off here, follow the signs left to **Moraine** (sites $) or right to **Aspen** (sites $) and **Big Bend** (sites $), all on Poole Power Plant Rd. Less than a mile further east along Hwy 120 are two more campgrounds: **Cattleguard** (sites $; Hwy 120) is the first you come to and the nicer of the pair; **Lower Lee Vining Campground** (sites $; Hwy 120) is next.

LEE VINING

☎ 760 / pop 490 / elev 6781ft

Never mind that this tiny town is flooded with tourists all summer long. Its old-time buildings, roadside motels, flickering neon signs and unbeatable setting above the western shore of Mono Lake make it a mandatory stop on any trip through the Eastern Sierra. A superb base for exploring the lake, Lee Vining is only 12 miles (about a 30-minute drive) from Yosemite's East Entrance.

Before you leave town, take a quick look at the **Upside-Down House**, a kooky tourist attraction created by silent film actress Nellie Bly O'Bryan. Originally situated along Tioga Rd, it now resides in a park in front of the tiny **Mono Basin Historical Society Museum** (admission $1; ☺ 10am-5pm Thu-Mon, noon-5pm Sun, summer only). To find it, turn east on 1st St and drive one block to Mattley Ave.

Information

Gas is outrageously expensive. There are ATMs at the Mono Market and inside the Mobil gas station at the corner of Hwys 395 and 120. You can do laundry at **Nicely's Laundromat** (☎ 647-6477; Hwy 120; ☺ 7-9pm).

For info head to the excellent Mono Basin Scenic Area Visitor Center (opposite) or the Mono Lake Committee Information Center & Bookstore (opposite). The latter provides public **internet access** (per 15min $2).

Sleeping

All of Lee Vining's modest, family-run motels are along Hwy 395.

Murphey's Motel (☎ 647-6316, 800-334-6316; www.murpheyosemite.com; Hwy 395; r $; ☐ ☒) At the north end of town, this large and friendly motel offers comfy rooms with all mod cons.

El Mono Motel (☎ 647-6310; www.elmonomotel.com; Hwy 395; r $$; ☺ Apr-late Oct; ☐) Lee Vining's oldest continually operating building went up in 1927, and has served as the town's tiniest motel ever since. Some rooms have shared bathrooms, all are little and all are lovingly painted in soothing colors and decorated with local art. They have TVs but no phones.

Yosemite Gateway Motel (☎ 647-6467, 800-282-3929; www.yosemitegatewaymotel.com; Hwy 395; r $$; 💻) Think vistas. This is the only motel on the east side of the highway, and the views from some of the rooms are phenomenal.

Lee Vining Motel (☎ 647-6440; Hwy 395; r $$) If you didn't make a reservation and everything else is booked, try this first-come, first-served motel. Reception opens at 4pm.

Eating & Drinking

Lee Vining has plenty of eating options, a couple of which are downright excellent.

Mono Market (🕑 7am-10pm summer, 7:30am-8pm winter) Stock up on quality groceries at the local market. The deli in back serves delicious breakfast burritos, pastries and coffee, all to go.

our pick **Whoa Nellie Deli** (☎ 647-1088; mains $-$$; 🕑 7am-9pm; ♿) If you're going to eat out just once in the Eastern Sierra, do it at the Whoa Nellie Deli. Ironically (or brilliantly) located inside the Mobil gas station at the junction of Hwys 120 and 395, this famed deli serves everything from buffalo meatloaf and grilled pork tenderloin to fish tacos and chicken jambalaya. Portions are huge, the prices are fair and the views from the outdoor patio are as great as the food.

Mono Inn at Mono Lake (☎ 647-6581; www.monoinn.com; 55620 Hwy 395; mains $$-$$$; 🕑 Wed-Mon mid-May–Oct 31; ♿) Run by Sarah Adams, granddaughter of photographer Ansel Adams, this restored 1922 lodge is now an elegant restaurant with outstanding food, fabulous wine and views to match it all. It's located about 5 miles north of Lee Vining. Reservations recommended.

Latte Da Coffee Cafe (☎ 647-6310; Hwy 395 at Third St; 🕑 7am-9pm Easter-Halloween) Part of El Mono Motel, this tiny café serves up organic coffee, espresso drinks and muffins from a shop inside the hotel lobby.

MONO LAKE

☎ 760 / elev 6379ft

Sunrise on Mono Lake, when the strange mineral tufa glow fiery orange above the water's mirrored surface, is unforgettable. Heck, it's pretty darn spectacular the rest of the day, too, which is why this is one of California's most impressive sights. The lake is North America's second oldest, spread lazily across a chalky white desert basin beneath the dramatic backdrop of the jagged Eastern Sierra.

Although the basin and the lake are both Ice Age remnants, formed more than 700,000 years ago, the area's most interesting features spring from more recent volcanic activity. Rising like weathered sand castles on or near the lakeshore, Mono's tufa (*too*-fah) towers are composed of calcium carbonate that bubbles up from freshwater springs beneath the surface. From the shore, you can see **Paoha**, the white island, and **Negit**, the black island, formed when magma pushed sediment above the surface between 300 and 1700 years ago. It's possible to boat to both, though the islands are closed from early April through August to protect nesting gulls.

Information

The **Mono Basin Scenic Area Visitor Center** (☎ 647-3044; 🕑 8am-5pm Mon-Thu, 8am-7pm Fri & Sat summer, 9am-4:30pm winter), about 2 miles north of Lee Vining, features a stunning view of the lake, good interpretive displays, a well-stocked bookstore and bear canister rentals. It also provides wilderness permits for Inyo National Forest and for overnight hikes from Lundy and Virginia Lakes.

Another great source of information is the **Mono Lake Committee Information Center & Bookstore** (☎ 647-6595; www.monolake.org; 🕑 9am-5pm late Jun–mid-Sep), located in Lee Vining on the west side of Hwy 395. Here you'll find maps, a great selection of books and a free 30-minute video about the history and geology of the Mono Lake area – as well as people who are passionate about preserving the lake.

Sights & Activities

The most impressive grouping of tufa lie at the **South Tufa Reserve** (adult/child $3/free; 🕑 24hr), on the lake's south rim, where a mile-long interpretive trail winds along the lakeshore. They're easily explored on your own, but from roughly June to Labor Day the visitor centers offer free, highly informative **interpretive walks** three times a day. They depart at 10am, 1pm and 6pm from the reserve's parking area, and no reservation is required. Simply turn up.

LONG LIVE MONO LAKE

In 1941 the City of Los Angeles Department of Water and Power (DWP) bought vast tracts of land throughout the Mono Basin and diverted four of the five streams that feed Mono Lake to the California Aqueduct to provide water to Los Angeles. Over time, the lake dropped 40ft and doubled in salinity.

Aside from its beauty, Mono Lake is of major importance to California gulls, which use the lake for breeding and nesting. Roughly 85% of California's 'seagulls' are born at Mono Lake. Historically, the lake's islands, which had no natural predators for the gulls, were the primary nesting grounds. But as lake levels dropped, land bridges emerged, giving coyotes and other predators access to the islands and the nests. For the gull population, the result was disastrous.

In 1976 environmental activist David Gaines began to study the effects of the diversion and projected that the lake would dry up within about 20 years. Because of Mono Lake's importance for gulls, along with eared grebes and red-necked phalaropes, its potential demise posed a major ecological threat. Gaines formed the Mono Lake Committee in 1979 and, through numerous campaigns and court battles, managed to win water back from Los Angeles.

A fluke of nature aided the struggle. In 1989 heavy snows caused dams to overflow into previously dry spillways, rejuvenating streams that had not seen water for 10 years. When fish were found in the streams, the courts ruled that although the DWP technically owned the water rights, the department could not allow the fish to die and, thus, was obliged to maintain the streams at life-sustaining levels. In 1994 the courts required that the lake level return to 6377ft above sea level (estimated to take 15 years) before the DWP can take water from the lake or its tributaries. Bumper stickers and T-shirts bearing the 'Save Mono Lake' slogan changed to 'Restore Mono Lake.' Mono is indeed rebounding, and faster than expected. Although still far below its highest historic levels, the lake is only about 7ft from the target level. Today, the lake is widely considered healthy, and bumper stickers now read 'Long Live Mono Lake.'

The best spot for swimming and launching a kayak or canoe is **Navy Beach**, just east of the South Tufa Reserve. Saltier than the ocean, the lake will make you (or your boat) noticeably more buoyant. Be warned, however, that there are no showers and the lake water can leave a thick, salty residue (yum!). The Mono Lake Committee also offers one-hour **canoe tours** (adult/child $24/12), which begin at 8am, 9:30am and 11am every Saturday and Sunday from roughly mid-June to early September. Reservations are required.

Away from the lakeshore, on a dirt road between the South Tufa Reserve and Hwy 120, you'll find **Panum Crater**, the youngest (about 640 years old), smallest and most accessible of the craters that run south from the lake. A panoramic trail circles the crater rim (about 40 minutes), and a short but steep 'plug trail' puts you at the crater's core.

On the north shore are the **Black Point Fissures**, narrow crags that formed when Black Point's lava mass cooled and contracted about 13,000 years ago. To reach the fissures requires an often hot and dry 5-mile round-trip hike. Check in at one of the visitor centers for directions before heading

out; it can be tricky getting out there and following the trail.

Also on the north shore, free guided **bird walks** depart from Mono Lake County Park at 8am on Friday and Saturday from roughly mid-June to early September.

BODIE STATE HISTORIC PARK

☎ 760 / pop 5 / elev 8375ft

The combination of its remote location and unrestored buildings makes **Bodie** (www.parks.ca.gov/bodie; adult/child $2/free; ☼ 8am-7pm late May-Sep, to 4pm Oct-Apr; ♿) one of California's most authentic and well-preserved ghost towns. Gold was discovered along Bodie Creek in 1859, and within 20 years the place grew from a rough mining camp to an even rougher mining town, with a population of 10,000 and a reputation for lawlessness sustained by gambling halls, cigar stores, brothels and no fewer than 65 saloons. Robberies, street fights and stagecoach holdups occurred almost daily, and the 'bad men from Bodie' were known far and wide.

All told, more than $100 million worth of ore came from the 30 mines in the surrounding hills, but when the supply petered out people moved on (mostly to the Comstock Lode in Nevada) and left Bodie's buildings to the elements and a devastating fire in 1932. About 5% of them still remain, maintained by the State Park Service – five resident employees live there year-round – but untainted by restoration. An excellent **museum and visitor center** (☎ 647-6445; ☒ 10am-5pm late May-Sep; ☒) offers historical maps, exhibits and free daily guided tours.

Easily accessible from Yosemite's Tioga Pass Entrance Station, Bodie is about a 45-minute drive from the junction of Hwys 120 and 395. Take the latter road north, then turn east onto Hwy 270 and follow it for 13 miles. Note that Hwy 270 is unpaved for the last 3 miles and often closed in winter.

LUNDY LAKE
elev 7083ft

About 7 miles north of Lee Vining, Lundy Lake Rd leads 5 miles west to its shimmering namesake. A gorgeous spot, especially when wildflowers are abloom or fall foliage lights up the canyon, it's nonetheless often overlooked and, thus, uncrowded.

On a flat dirt road a few miles past Lundy Lake Resort is trailhead parking for the Hoover Wilderness, with self-service wilderness permits. From here it's a lovely but strenuous **day hike** over Lundy Pass to the 20 Lakes Basin and Saddlebag Lake.

Anglers and hikers are the main patrons of the low-key **Lundy Lake Resort** (☎ 626-309-0415; Lundy Lake Rd; tent & RV sites $; cabins $$; ☒ late Apr–mid-Oct), which also has a small first-come, first-served campground with flush toilets and hot showers. The facilities include a laundry, boat rentals, and a small store. Before you reach the lake, the road passes a decent **county campground** (Lundy Lake Rd; sites $) with pit toilets and running water.

VIRGINIA LAKES
☎ 760 / **elev 9840ft**

North of Lundy Lake, Virginia Lakes are a series of gorgeously set high-country lakes flanked by Dunderberg Peak (12,374ft) and Black Mountain (11,797ft). The area, reached from Hwy 395 via the 6-mile Virginia Lakes Rd, offers superb hiking and excellent fishing.

From a trailhead at the end of the lakes, it's an easy hike into Hoover Wilderness

and onto the Pacific Crest Trail, which follows Cold Canyon down into Yosemite. On Yosemite's border, **Summit Lake** (5 miles each way) is an outstanding day hike.

You can sleep and rent fishing tackle at **Virginia Lakes Resort** (☎ 647-6484; www.virginia lakesresort.com; Virginia Lakes Rd; cabins $$-$$$; ☒ mid-May–mid-Oct), where snug, rustic cabins sleep up to six. The small and extremely scenic **Trumbull Lake Campground** (Virginia Lakes Rd; sites $) makes for excellent camping.

GREEN CREEK

Those who desire that feeling of getting away from it all should follow the bumpy 8.5-mile dirt road from Hwy 395 out to **Green Creek Campground** (Green Creek Rd; sites $; ☒ May-Oct), at the base of a glorious, aspen-filled canyon. Green Creek Rd, as it's called, is totally manageable for normal passenger vehicles, but you'll have to take it slowly. The campground and Green Creek Trailhead are the starting point for excellent hikes into the Hoover Wilderness and the northeastern regions of Yosemite.

GREEN CREEK TO EAST LAKE

Duration 3–4 hours
Distance 7 miles round-trip
Difficulty moderate
Start/Finish Green Creek Trailhead
Nearest Town/Facilities Bridgeport, 13 miles
Transport private
Summary The hike up the Green Creek drainage, first to Green Lake and then to East Lake (the largest lake in the Hoover Wilderness), is replete with fantastic views of jagged peaks and aspens aplenty.

The hike up to East Lake (9458ft) makes for a great day out, though you could easily turn it into an overnighter. You can camp at both Green and East Lakes, or continue past the latter to **Gilman Lake** (9486ft), **Hoover Lakes** and, with enough time, spectacular **Summit Lake** (10,175ft) on Yosemite's eastern border.

If you're not staying at the Green Creek Campground, park at the well-signed trailhead and head southwest along the trail into the trees. You'll rejoin the dirt road after about 15 minutes or so, which passes two paradisiacal homes before petering out into a proper trail. It soon begins its moderate ascent, passing beautiful groves of aspen before climbing a series of switchbacks away from Green Creek. The trail soon opens up to fantastic views and passes some marvelously twisted specimens of western juniper.

After 2.3 miles it hits a junction: the right (northwest) path leads 1.4 miles to **West Lake** (9875ft), a worthy detour. Veer south (left) to reach the eastern shore of **Green Lake** (8945ft). From here, the trail ascends gentle switchbacks that are almost continually shaded by mountain hemlock and pines. About 1.2 miles from Green Lake, you'll hit **East Lake** (9458ft), a marvelous spot to have lunch before continuing on or returning to the trailhead the way you came.

TWIN LAKES & AROUND
☎ 760

Just north of Bridgeport, these lakes are shadowed by the jagged Sawtooth Ridge, which includes 12,279ft Matterhorn Peak. Primarily a fishing resort revered for its trout and Kokanee salmon, Twin Lakes (elevation 7081ft to 7092ft) is another good access point into Hoover and Yosemite's lake-riddled eastern reaches. Several trails fan out from the west end of Barney Lake.

The road to Twin Lakes intersects Hwy 395 at the town of Bridgeport and crosses rolling pastures and foothills, passing five good first-come, first-served forest service campgrounds on Robinson Creek. The route has little traffic, a smooth surface, and few serious hills, making it an excellent 12-mile scenic **biking** excursion.

Just before reaching the lower lake, S Twin Rd heads south to two USFS campgrounds: **Lower Twin Lakes Campground** (☎ 877-444-6777; www.recreation.gov; S Twin Rd; sites $; May–mid-Oct) sits on the lake's east shore, but the adjacent **Crags Campground** (☎ 877-444-6777; www .recreation.gov; S Twin Rd; sites $; May–mid-Oct) is sunnier and more spread out. Neither is very attractive, but will do in a pinch. Reservations can be made for both.

At the far end of the upper lake, the road ends at the sprawling **Annett's Mono Village** (☎ 932-7071; www.monovillage.com; tent/RV sites $, r & cabins $$; late Apr-Oct), which offers cheap but cramped motel-type lodging, cabins, boat rentals and – likely its finest feature – a delightfully nostalgic diner-style **restaurant** (mains

$; 6am-7:30pm). The campground offers 300 first-come, first-served spaces. Certain locals refer to it as 'the zoo.'

For a step up, try **Doc & Al's Resort** (☎ 932-7051; cnr Twin Lakes Rd & Buckeye Rd; tent & RV sites $, cabins & trailers $$), set beside burbling Robinson Creek. Homey cabins sleep four to 10 people and have showers and kitchenettes; cheaper units share showers and toilets. You can also rent a trailer.

Buckeye Hotsprings
Fancy a dip in some hot, murky mineral water? Shallow as they are, these little hot springs set beside Buckeye Creek are just what those sore hiking muscles need. The springs surface atop a steep embankment above Buckeye Creek and trickle down into two rock-ringed pools. The largest pool, right beside the creek, is cold when the creek is high, while the higher one can get deliciously hot. Clothing is optional.

If you're heading southwest on Twin Lakes Rd from Hwy 395, turn right on Buckeye Rd, at Doc & Al's Resort. Drive the dirt road nearly 3 miles and cross Buckeye Creek. Right after crossing the bridge, veer right on the road signed 'to Hwy 395' and pull off at the large dirt parking area on the right. It's a short hike down to the springs.

JUNE LAKE LOOP
☎ 760

Just 15 miles from Yosemite's Tioga Pass Entrance Station, Hwy 158 makes a 16-mile loop west off of Hwy 395. This scenic route passes Grant, Silver, Gull and June Lakes, flanked by massive Carson Peak to the west and Reversed Peak to the east. The mountains to the near west are part of the Ansel Adams Wilderness, which runs smack into Yosemite.

All four lakes have excellent trout fishing, and Grant and Silver Lakes both offer free public boat launches. You'll find a colorful commercial hub in June Lake Village and a sandy beach at the south end of the lake. The route also makes for a very enjoyable bike ride. You can park your car near the information kiosk at the loop's southern entrance and do an out-and-back if you don't want to brave Hwy 395 on the return.

Much smaller and less crowded than nearby Mammoth (though owned by the same company), **June Mountain Ski Area** (☎ 648-7733, 888-586-3686; www.junemountain.com; lift tickets adult/senior & child/teen $60/30/45) is a friendly kind of place. And at 10,090ft it's no molehill either. There's nary a line at the seven lifts, including two high-speed quads, which serve 500 acres of trails along 2600 vertical feet. The area also includes two terrain parks and a superpipe. Season passes for Mammoth Mountain are good here as well.

At Silver Lake, the **Frontier Pack Train** (☎ summer 648-7701, winter 873-7971) offers guided horseback rides ($25/60/90 for one hour/half-day/full day) and multiday trips into the Sierra backcountry (from $550), including a five-day trip over Donohue Pass into Yosemite and Tuolumne Meadows ($950).

In summer, fishing is hugely popular, and numerous boat- and tackle-rental places operate along the loop. Most also sell fishing licenses. Get some friendly advice at **Ernie's Tackle & Ski Shop** (☎ 648-7756) in downtown June Lake. **Gull Lake Marina** (☎ 648-7539) rents paddleboats and canoes for $15 to $20 per hour.

Between the resort and pack station, the Rush Creek Trailhead is a departure point for wilderness trips; here you'll find a day-use parking lot, posted maps and self-registration permits. Gem and Agnew Lakes make spectacular day hikes, while Thousand Island and Emerald Lake (both on the Pacific Crest/John Muir Trail) are good overnight destinations in the Ansel Adams Wilderness (see p210). For information on day hikes, visit the Mono Lake or Mammoth Lakes ranger stations.

Sleeping & Eating

There are six **USFS campgrounds** (☎ 877-444-6777; www.recreation.gov; sites $) with sites along the full loop, including June Lake Campground, small and shady but crowded; Silver Lake, with gorgeous high mountain views; and Oh! Ridge Campground, on an arid ridge above the lake's south end, with nice views and beach access but not much shade. All have running water and are open from mid-April through October.

Haven (☎ 648-7524, 800-648-7524; www.junelake haven.com; studios & cottages $$) A block off June Lake's main drag on Knoll Ave, this is a homey and comfortable abode, with a long

wooden deck, whirlpool, tasteful furnishings and two-story cottages and studios, some with fireplaces or woodstoves. Winter is its high season, and it has massage services to sooth those cranky après ski muscles.

Silver Lake Resort (☎ 648-7525; www.silverlake resort.net; cabins $$-$$$; ☺ summer) Across the street from Silver Lake and tucked in at the base of Carson Peak, this family-friendly camp was originally opened as a trout fishing retreat in 1916. The 16 comfortable yet simple housekeeping cabins sleep between two and eight people, and are all nonsmoking. Its cozy country café (open 7am to 2pm) serves hearty breakfasts, burgers and sandwiches.

Double Eagle Resort & Spa (☎ 648-7004; www .doubleeagle.com; r incl breakfast $$$; cabins $$$$; ▣ ▨) A mighty swanky spot for these parts, this resort specializes in fishing and pampering. Sleek cedar cabins come complete with VCRs and outside decks, and the standard rooms have whirlpool tubs. The posh spa boasts a full menu of indulgences, including 11 types of massage, and a fancy fitness center. Spa-weary folk can sign up for a guided fishing outing with the on-site fly shop ($100 and up), or hook a trout right on the grounds.

Tiger (☎ 648-7551; 2620 Hwy 158; dishes $-$$; ☺ breakfast, lunch & dinner) A town hallmark since 1932, this is the place to visit in the evening for burgers, burritos, fish and beer. It also has good breakfasts and lunches.

Double Eagle Resort restaurant (☎ 648-7897; breakfast & lunch $, dinner $$-$$$$) This woodsy and elegant place features a high ceiling, cozy booths, a huge fireplace, and a warm saloon with timber bar stools and a flagstone floor.

MAMMOTH LAKES

☎ 760 / pop 7400 / elev 8000ft

This small resort town just won't let it rest. From winter until very late spring, you can tear through the powder on dizzying 11,053ft Mammoth Mountain. When the snow finally fades, it's an outdoor wonderland of mountain-bike trails, excellent fishing, endless alpine hiking and blissful spots for hot-spring soaking. The Eastern Sierra's commercial hub and a four-season resort, outdoorsy Mammoth is backed by a ridgeline of jutting peaks, ringed by clusters of crystalline alpine lakes and enshrouded

AROUND YOSEMITE

Mammoth Lakes

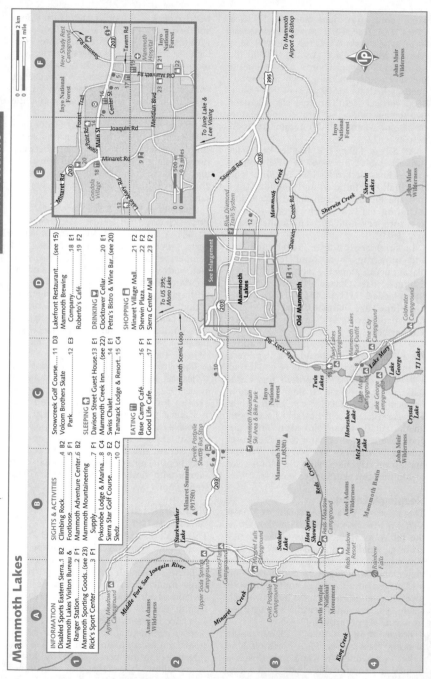

INFORMATION

Disabled Sports Eastern Sierra.1 B2
Mammoth Lakes Visitors Bureau &
Ranger Station..................2 F1
Mammoth Sporting Goods..(see 23)
Rick's Sport Center............3 F1

SIGHTS & ACTIVITIES

Climbing Rock...................4 B2
Footloose.......................5 F1
Mammoth Adventure Center..6 B2
Mammoth Mountaineering
Supply..........................7 F1
Pokonobe Lodge & Marina....8 C4
Sierra Star Golf Course..........9 E2
Sledz...........................10 C2

Snowcreek Golf Course......11 D3
Volcom Brothers Skate
Park............................12 E3

SLEEPING

Davison Street Guest House.13 E1
Mammoth Creek Inn.......(see 22)
Swiss Chalet...................14 E1
Tamarack Lodge & Resort..15 C4

EATING

Base Camp Café................16 F1
Good Life Cafe.................17 F1

Lakefront Restaurant.......(see 15)
Mammoth Brewing
Company.....................18 E1
Roberto's Café................19 F2

DRINKING

Clocktower Cellar.............20 E1
Petra's Bistro & Wine Bar..(see 20)

SHOPPING

Minaret Village Mall.........21 F2
Sherwin Plaza.................22 F1
Sierra Center Mall.............23 F2

by the dense Inyo National Forest. And if you venture out, you'll find stunning and surprisingly crowd-free wilderness areas.

Mammoth's humble origin as a ski resort began in the 1930s, when just a few adventurous souls made use of a few simple rope tows; the first chairlift went up in 1955. Long before that, Mammoth was a mining and lumber town with stamp mills, sawmills, flumes, waterwheels and a rough-and-tumble main street of tent cabins and saloons. Most of the original town, on the west end of Old Mammoth Rd, burned to cinders in 1880, but a 14ft flywheel and some other old structures remain.

Mammoth, as most people refer to it, is laid-back, friendly and decidedly unpretentious. People come more to see and play in the stellar surroundings than to be seen in Prada. But outdoor frolicking rules the place to such an extent that the locals have perhaps paid too little attention to the aesthetic consequences of burgeoning commercial growth. Shopping centers and clusters of lackluster condominiums crowd downtown Mammoth, though the A-frame aesthetic still persists on the periphery.

Orientation & Information

At the Mammoth Lakes turnoff from Hwy 395, Rte 203 heads west for 3 miles to town. After the first traffic light, Rte 203 becomes Main St, which continues as Lake Mary Rd past the second traffic light. (In winter Lake Mary Rd is closed past Twin Lakes.) North from the same intersection, Minaret Rd leads past the Village at Mammoth to the Mammoth Mountain Ski Area; in summer the road continues south to the Reds Meadow/Devils Postpile area.

The **Mammoth Lakes Visitors Bureau** (☎ 934-2712, 800-367-6572; www.visitmammoth.com; ☺ 8am-5pm) and the **Mammoth Lakes Ranger Station** (☎ 924-5500; www.fs.fed.us/r5/inyo; ☺ 8am-5pm) share a building on the north side of Hwy 203, just before the first traffic light. This one-stop information center issues wilderness permits and offers accommodations and campground listings, road- and trail-condition updates, bike route maps and details on local attractions. From May through October, trail quotas are in effect and walk-in wilderness permits are released at 11am the day before; permits are self-issue the rest of the year.

Activities
SKIING & SNOWBOARDING

The pride and joy of the southern Sierra, the **Mammoth Mountain Ski Area** (☎ 934-0745, 800-626-6684; www.mammothmountain.com) is a true skiers' and snowboarders' resort, where playing hard and having fun are more important than what kind of car you drove to the mountain. An inactive volcanic peak, Mammoth offers a fantastic combination of tree-line and open-bowl skiing, and the 3100 vertical promise some long runs; at the top are some nearly vertical chutes. The resort includes 28 chairlifts, two gondolas and enough terrain to keep any type of snow hound busy for a week – about 25% of the runs are beginner, 40% intermediate, and 35% advanced and expert.

Lift tickets for adults cost $60/80 per afternoon/full day, $45/60 for ages 13 to 18 and $30/40 for seniors over 65 and children aged seven to 12, and prices tend to go up a few dollars every year. Multiday tickets are cheaper. Slopes are open 8:30am to 4pm daily; night skiing until 9pm is offered weekends and holidays. Mammoth season passes can also be used at the June Mountain Ski Area (p202).

Five hubs line the base of the mountain: Main Lodge, Canyon Lodge, the Mountain Centre (in the Village), Eagle Lodge and the Mill Cafe – each with parking and ticket sales. At Main Lodge and Canyon Lodge,

---

ACCESSIBLE OUTDOOR SIERRA

Everyone has the right to be active, and **Disabled Sports Eastern Sierra** (☎ 934-0791; www.disabledsportseasternsierra.org; Mammoth Mountain Adventure Center) does its damnedest to make it happen. A nonprofit formed in 2003, the membership- and volunteer-based organization is housed at Mammoth Mountain and leads activities throughout the year for both adults and children with physical and cognitive disabilities. Summer sports include kayaking, hand cycling, horseback riding and rock climbing, and wintertime features private ski instruction on a range of ski types. Reservations are required, scholarships are available and it has comprehensive training for volunteers that wish to teach adaptive sports.

AROUND YOSEMITE

AROUND YOSEMITE

ski schools and state-of-the-art rentals are available. You'll usually find slightly better prices at outfitters in town, including **Footloose** (☎ 934-2400; 3043 Main St) and **Mammoth Sporting Goods** (☎ 934-3239; Sierra Center Mall).

A gondola from the Village at Mammoth connects the ski mountain with the town, so it's often unnecessary to drive up to the slopes. If you're staying downtown, you can just walk to the gondola.

CROSS-COUNTRY SKIING

You can do free cross-country skiing along the Blue Diamond Trails System behind New Shady Rest Campground, along Sawmill Rd about a half-mile north of Hwy 203. Maintained by the USFS, trails are mostly ungroomed.

A better, if more costly, option is the **Tamarack Cross Country Ski Center** (☎ 934-2442, 800-626-6684; Lake Mary Rd; per adult twilight/afternoon/full day $14/20/25, 7-12yr $7/10/13, senior & 13-18yr $11/15/19; ☉ first snowfall–mid-Apr). Right at Twin Lakes on Lake Mary Rd, Tamarack features 45km of groomed track, skating lanes, marked backcountry trails, guided nature tours, rentals and lessons. It's also a good spot for snowshoeing. Rentals for skis and snowshoes cost $22/18 per full day/afternoon, and lessons start at $30.

For backcountry skiing, try the popular network of beautiful trails from Agnew Meadows; the route to Reds Meadow is a favorite.

OTHER WINTER ACTIVITIES

Mammoth has all sorts of snow-play areas where you can tumble around in the fluffy white stuff. If you have your own equipment, you can go anywhere in the Inyo National Forest. On Minaret Rd between Earthquake Fault and Mammoth Mountain's Main Lodge, **Sledz** (☎ 934-7533) has a groomed run and a rope tow that deposits you at a good altitude for tubing with a smidgeon of speed. Look out below!

A new ice-skating rink was in the works at the time of research and should be open by the time you read this. Contact the Visitors Bureau for details.

MOUNTAIN BIKING

No, it's not a movie set for an apocalyptic *Mad Max* sequel. Over the years, Mammoth has morphed into a hotbed for mountain bikers, and the dudes and dudettes decked out in body armor are just trying to keep themselves intact. Come summer, Mammoth Mountain becomes a massive **Mammoth Mountain Bike Park** (☎ 934-0706; day pass adult/child $37/19), with more than 80 miles of well-tended single-track trails and a crazy terrain park. Several other trails traverse the surrounding forest. In general, Mammoth-style riding is characterized by plenty of hills and soft, sandy shoulders, which are best conquered with big knobby tires. But you don't need wheels (or a medic) to ride the vertiginous **gondola** (adult/senior $18/9) to the apex of the mountain, where there's an interpretive center and a snack bar.

When the park's open, it runs a free **bike shuttle** (☉ 9am-5:30pm late Jun-Sep) from the Village area to the Main Lodge. Shuttles depart every 30 minutes, and bikers with paid mountain passes get priority over pedestrians.

Footloose (☎ 934-2400; 3043 Main St) rents a nice range of spiffy bikes ($10 per hour or $40 to $60 per day) just right to float through Mammoth's volcanic terrain; the shop also rents a good selection of kid-sized bikes ($7/28) and offers excellent trail tips, maps, and other biking information.

MOUNTAIN VIEW TRAIL

Duration 0.5 hours
Distance 5.6 miles one way
Difficulty moderate; elevation change -900ft
Start Minarets Vista parking area
Finish Earthquake Fault parking area
Nearest Town/Facilities water, food and restrooms at Mammoth Mountain
Transport private
Summary A nice rolling ride, this cross-country single-track and jeep-road trail runs parallel to scenic Mammoth Mountain, winding down through evergreen forest from the exceptional overlook at Minaret Vista.

From the Minaret Vista parking lot, descend a jeep road into a shallow gulley. Ride through two switchbacks before the road turns to rolling single-track. At almost 1.5 miles from the start, descend another jeep road. Turn left at another jeep road, then hit the next right and in quick succession, a left onto more single-track. The trail crosses two bridges before coming to a jeep road again at 3.6 miles from your starting point. Go right down a well-graded dirt road to another single-track that continues to the left. The track changes to narrow road; turn right at the following junction and left at the next one. The jeep road you're now on descends through red fir forest and finally winds into the Earthquake Fault parking area. In stretches, you can see the Inyo Craters, the small volcanoes that speckle the region.

HIKING & ROCK CLIMBING

Hikers have a choice of three main trailheads, all with parking lots and access to good day hikes and longer trails over the Sierra Crest. **Horseshoe Lake**, in Mammoth Basin, is at a high elevation, so you needn't hike far to reach the gorgeous alpine scenery of the Inyo National Forest; its good trails venture down into Reds Meadow and up to McLeod Lake and Mammoth Pass.

Also in Mammoth Basin, **Lake Mary**, on Lake Mary Rd, offers easy access to several small alpine lakes backed by the impressive Mammoth Crest; the **TJ Lake** and **Crystal Lake Trails** make good choices from here.

Trails from **Agnew Meadows** (past the ski resort, on the road to Devils Postpile) go north along the Pacific Crest/John Muir Trail into the Ansel Adams Wilderness, surrounded by the **Minarets**, some of the Sierra's most stunning sawtooth peaks, and cirque lakes. **Shadow Lake**, about 7 miles round-trip from Agnew Meadows, is a spectacular day hike. Also from here, the High Trail traverses a high shoulder along the San Joaquin River leading to lakes at the base of the Ritter Range (see Thousand Island Lake hike, p210).

Mammoth Mountaineering Supply (☎ 934-4191; www.mammothgear.com; 3198 Main St) offers friendly advice, topo maps, equipment rentals and guided wilderness excursions.

Southern Yosemite Mountain Guides (☎ 800-231-4575; www.symg.com) leads year-round guided rock-climbing trips for all skill levels in the

AROUND YOSEMITE

HOT SPRINGS HEAVEN

If you live to soak, the Eastern Sierra will fulfill your every hot-spring fantasy. Thanks to its volcanic past and wealth of underground mountain-fed springs, the stretch of Hwy 395 from just north of Bridgeport south to Lone Pine is sprinkled with secluded spots for simmering. Over the years, first shepherds, then locals, have crafted actual drainable tubs, with rubber hosing used to divert the springs. Many are well known and thus can get crowded on weekends, so if you're after seclusion, it's best to spring-hop in midweek or off-season.

Nestled between the White Mountains and the Sierra Range near Mammoth is a tantalizing slew of natural pools with snowcapped panoramic views. When the high-altitude summer nights turn chilly and you can hear the coyotes cry, you'll never want to dry off. About 9 miles south of town, **Benton Crossing Rd** juts east off of Hwy 395, accessing a trove of hot springs. Locals call this 'Green Church Rd,' because of the road's unmistakable marker. About 1 mile down Benton, Forest Rd 2507 cuts north, eventually connecting with Hot Creek Rd, and more springs. All told, there are no fewer then 10 different hot springs along this loop. The **Hot Tub** is easy to find, well maintained and one of the best. Head east on Benton Crossing Rd for 1.2 miles (passing the Whitmore Public Pool on the right) and turn left on Forest Rd 2507. After 1.1 miles, turn right onto a faint but distinct dirt road; the tub is ahead about 100yd. Here you'll find a nice patio area and sweeping vistas of the Sierra Nevada. The tub, which has a well-designed drain for emptying after use, can fit four comfortably.

In case you take thermal springs for granted, think again. **Hot Creek**, one of the more public places near Mammoth, used to be a popular, if somewhat scary, place to bathe where springs bubbled up into a chilly creek. But in 2006, a significant increase in geothermal activity was detected at the site, and violent geysers began to send boiling water shooting into the air. The site was still closed to swimmers at the time of research, and will stay off-limits until activity has stabilized.

For a soaking to-do list with detailed directions and maps, pick up the bible – Matt Bischoff's excellent *Touring California and Nevada Hot Springs*. And keep in mind these three golden rules: no glass, no additives to the water and, if you can, no bathing suit.

Mammoth area. A full-day private guide for one to six people costs $365; add $70 for each additional participant (up to 10). They also lead Half Dome hikes.

Kids in particular like the **Climbing Rock**, on the lawn between the Yodler and Panorama Stations (the lifts used by mountain bikers). Single, staff-belayed climbs cost $10; additional climbs are $5. There's also a ropes course.

OTHER ACTIVITIES

Mammoth is a terrific place for horseback riding, thanks in part to the area's easy wilderness access. **Mammoth Lakes Pack Outfit** (☎ 934-2434, 888-475-8747; Lake Mary Rd) offers a wide selection of one-hour to half-day trips to many of the surrounding lakes ($35 to $80) and a full-day outing to Barney Lake ($110).

Starting on the last Saturday in April, the dozens of lakes that give the town its name lure in fly and trout fishers from near and far. California fishing licenses are available at sporting goods stores throughout town. For equipment and advice, head to **Rick's Sport Center** (☎ 934-3416; Main St at Center St).

The **Pokonobe Store and Marina** (☎ 934-2437), on the north end of Lake Mary, rents motor boats ($16 per hour), rowboats ($8), canoes ($14) and kayaks ($12 to $16). **Caldera Kayaks** (☎ 935-1691) has single ($40 for a half-day) and double kayaks ($60) for use on Crowley Lake.

High-altitude golfing anyone? Mammoth also boasts the two highest golf courses in California, the 18-hole **Sierra Star Golf Course** (☎ 924-4653; www.mammothmountain.com) and the nine-hole **Snowcreek Golf Course** (☎ 934-6633; www.snowcreekresort.com/golf.htm). Supposedly the balls fly higher, but you'll have to test that one out yourself.

Sleeping

Most of the 20 or so USFS campgrounds in and around Mammoth Lakes are open from about mid-June to mid-September. You'll find some of the nicest campsites on the shores of Twin Lakes, Lake Mary, and Lake George. Sites are available on a first-come, first-served basis. Head to the Visitors Bureau for a full campground list, specific opening dates and information about space availability.

Mammoth overflows with holiday condominiums, which can be an excellent and affordable option, especially for groups of four or more. Contact **Mammoth Reservation Bureau** (☎ 934-2528, 800-462-5571; www.mammothvacations.com) or **Central Reservations of Mammoth** (☎ 934-8816, 800-321-3261; www.mammothlakes.com).

Davison Street Guest House (☎ 924-2188, reservations 619-544-9093, 858-755-8648; www.mammoth-guest.com; 19 Davison St; dm/r $/$$) A cute A-frame chalet hostel on a quiet residential street, this is the best bargain in Mammoth. You can whip up elaborate meals in the stocked kitchen and enjoy sweeping views from the living room with fireplace or sun deck. However, it's quite a laissez-faire establishment, as the place is often left open for self-registration. It's possible to stay here in the slower summer season without ever seeing an employee.

Swiss Chalet (☎ 934-2403, 800-937-9477; www.mammoth-swisschalet.com; 3776 View Point Rd; r $$) An older motel perched just off the main road, this charming two-story lodge has friendly owners and simply decorated rooms with painted furniture, comfy beds, fridges, TVs and telephones. The rooms also have screen doors in front and back to catch summer breezes. After a day on the trails or slopes, you can wind down in the hot tub or sauna, both with superb mountain views.

Tamarack Lodge & Resort (☎ 934-2442, 800-626-6684; www.tamaracklodge.com; lodge r $$-$$$, cabins $$-$$$$; 🖥 ⚐) Kind people run this charming year-round resort on the shore of Lower Twin Lake. In business since 1924, the cozy lodge includes a fireplace, bar, excellent restaurant, 11 rustic rooms and 34 cabins. The cabins range from very simple to simply deluxe, and come with full kitchen, telephone, private bathroom, porch and wood-burning stove. Some can sleep up to nine people.

our pick **Mammoth Creek Inn** (☎ 934-6162, 866-466-7000; www.mammothcreekinn.com; 663 Old Mammoth Rd; r $$$, loft r & studios $$$$; 🖥) With a fabulous location at the end of a commercial strip, the Mammoth Creek Inn is within walking distance of shops and restaurants but has unobstructed mountain views. Contemporary rooms are decorated in warm colors, and have little luxuries like toiletries and robes. The standard rooms are medium-sized, but the upstairs loft rooms are superspacious and good for groups, and kitchen suites are available as well. Two comfortable lounges make good reading nooks, and a hot tub and sauna downstairs feel perfect after a day on the slopes.

Eating

Base Camp Café (☎ 934-3900; 3325 Main St; mains $; ☻ 7:30am-9pm Thu-Sun, to 3pm Mon-Wed; ▣) An excellent start to your day, this place serves organic coffee and tea and lots of filling choices for breakfast, and comfort food like Tex-Mex onion straws and pesto chicken fajitas throughout the day. Boxed lunches are available if you're jonesing to hit the trail. The restaurant's decorated with various backpacking and mountaineering gear, and the bathroom has a hysterical photo display of backcountry outhouses.

Good Life Café (☎ 934-1734; Mammoth Mall, Old Mammoth Rd; mains $; ☻ 6:30am-3:30pm) Healthy food, generously filled veggie wraps and big bowls of salad make this a perennially popular place. The front patio area is blissful for a long brunch on a warm day.

Roberto's Café (☎ 934-3667; 271 Old Mammoth Rd; dishes $; ☻ 11am-9pm, to 10pm summer) Serving Mammoth's hands-down best Mexican food and a selection of more than 30 tequilas, this fun restaurant is usually bustling. Locals pack the outdoor deck to look out on a beautiful wildflower garden, or quaff margaritas in the tropical-themed upstairs cantina.

our pick **Lakefront Restaurant** (☎ 934-3534; lunch $-$$, dinner $$$-$$$$; ☻ lunch & dinner) For a splurge, the Tamarack Lodge has an intimate and romantic dining room overlooking Twin Lakes. The chef crafts French-California specialties like elk medallions au poivre and heirloom tomatoes with Basque cheese, and the staff are superbly friendly. Reservations recommended.

Drinking

Clocktower Cellar (☎ 934-2725; Minaret Rd; ☻ 5-11pm) In the winter especially, locals throng this half-hidden basement of the Alpenhof Lodge. The ceiling is tiled with a swirl of bottle caps, and it stocks 31 beers on tap – especially German brews – and about 50 bottled varieties.

Petra's Bistro & Wine Bar (☎ 934-3500; 6080 Minaret Rd; ☻ 5:30-late Tue-Sun) Just next door, Petra's is the Clocktower Cellar's upscale grapey equivalent, with 28 California and international wines available by the glass using its cruvinet system, and 250 vintages by the bottle.

Mammoth Brewing Company (☎ 934-2555; Lake Mary Rd; ☻ 5-9pm summer, 4-9pm winter) Upstairs at Whiskey Creek Mountain Bistro, it's a popular and noisy hangout with a pool table and large-screen TVs, with the decibels rising during the early-evening happy hour. It serves beers brewed on-site as well as fancy pub grub.

Getting There & Away

Mammoth Mountain operates a free winter shuttle that runs through town to the Tamarack Lodge, Main Lodge, Canyon Lodge and the Juniper Springs/Little Eagle areas. The free Town Trolley runs between the Gondola Village and Old Mammoth Rd via Main St from mid-June through October.

Inyo Mono Transit (☎ 872-1901, 800-922-1930; www.inyocounty.us/transit/transit.htm) CREST buses

---

MAMMOTH LOVES THE LITTLE ONES

Kids are well catered for in Mammoth. In addition to skiing and biking on Mammoth Mountain, here are a few more ideas for fun things to do:

■ Hay rides at **Sierra Meadows Ranch** (☎ 934-6161; Sherwin Creek Rd; ☻ Jun-Sep; adult/child $30/15; ☻ summer) head out three times a week.

■ The zip line at **Mammoth Mountain** (1 zip $10, additional $5, ☻ summer) behind the Adventure Center is just for kids 12 and under.

■ Dog sled rides with **Mammoth Dog Teams** (☎ 934-6270; www.mammothdogteams.com; 30min ride adult/child $55/30; ☻ winter) are thrilling, and the dogs love to be petted.

■ Skateboarding at the very rad **Volcom Brothers Skate Park** (☎ 934-2712; Meridian Blvd; admission free; ☻ dawn-dusk) will eliminate teenage ennui.

service Bishop ($3.50) and Reno ($23), and
reservations are recommended. And in the
summertime, **YARTS** (☎ 877-989-2787; www.yarts
.com) runs buses to and from Yosemite Valley
(see Getting Around, p174).

ANSEL ADAMS WILDERNESS

The former Minarets Wilderness was renamed in 1984 to honor California's most
famous photographer, who spent lots of
time in this part of the Sierra. The wilderness hugs Yosemite's southeast border,
and is located in both the Sierra and Inyo
National Forests. Access is from the west,
as well as from the east via Mammoth
Lakes and the June Lake Loop. Visitors
enjoy backpacking amid the region's rugged scenery.

For those entering from the west, the
Bass Lake Ranger Station in North Fork
(see p186) issues permits for overnight excursions; those entering from the east can
visit the Mammoth Lakes Visitors Bureau
(p205). Permits are $5; you can also make
a reservation in advance.

A handful of nice first-come, first-served
campgrounds sit on the road to Reds
Meadow just west of Mammoth Mountain. Some, like Minaret Falls, are right
on the Middle Fork of the San Joaquin
River, and are very popular with anglers.
The kiosk at the road entrance lists which
campgrounds are full. Even if you don't
stay overnight there, you can use the free
hot-springs showers at the Reds Meadow
campground (not the resort), which is
a decadent treat after a long hike. From
mid-June through to mid-September, a
mandatory shuttle (see p212) is in place.
Campers may drive in, but still must pay
the transportation fee ($7 per adult or $20
per car).

Even if you take the shuttle through another time, it's worth driving up to check
out the spectacular view from Minaret
Vista, about 1 mile from the ski area and
just off to the right at the ranger kiosk.
Here you'll find one of the best views
around, looking over the San Joaquin
River valley and out toward Banner Peak,
Mt Ritter and the picturesque Minarets,
named for their resemblance to the spires
of mosques. At sunset, these lacy granite spires seem to come alive in the rosy
alpenglow.

THOUSAND ISLAND LAKE

Duration 3 days
Distance 24 miles round-trip
Difficulty moderate–demanding; elevation
change +1820ft
Start/Finish Agnew Meadows campground
Transport shuttle
Summary A glorious high-country loop via
sections of both the John Muir Trail and the
Pacific Crest Trail, this hike visits a bevy of al-
pine lakes and brings you up close to dramatic
snow-dipped Sierra peaks.

DAY 1: AGNEW MEADOWS TO EDIZA LAKE
3–4 hours, 6.9 miles

From the second trailhead parking area at
Agnew Meadows (8340ft), cross a creek and
walk 1 mile northeast, descending briefly
via the joint River/Shadow Trail. Continue for 0.8 level miles, past the shallow
and reed-lined **Olaine Lake**, until you come
to a junction where the two trails split.
Bear left (west) on the Shadow Lake Trail,
soon climbing about 700ft to the outflow
of **Shadow Lake** (no camping permitted at
Shadow Lake), and meeting the John Muir
Trail (JMT) at 1.9 miles. Tracing the north
shore of Shadow Creek, split west from the
JMT after 0.9 miles, continuing another 2.3
miles to 9300ft **Ediza Lake**. The lake is spectacularly framed by the snow-topped Ritter
Range, Banner Peak and Mt Ritter. Camping is not permitted on the south side of the
lake or in the west side meadows.

DAY 2: EDIZA LAKE TO THOUSAND
ISLAND LAKE
4–5 hours, 7.4 miles

Retrace your steps back to the JMT, and prepare to follow it north through a string of
jewel-named lakes, also reaching the highest point of the hike. From 9000ft, ascend
steadily through forest cover until the trail
emerges on a granite ridgetop (10,130ft)
overlooking Garnet Lake, with sweeping
views of Mt Ritter, Banner Peak and Mt
Davis. Descend to **Garnet Lake**, passing
briefly along the south shore, and cross a
wooden footbridge over its outlet, 2.5 miles
from the JMT junction with the trail to
Ediza Lake. The trail turns west and briefly
follows the north shore of the lake, then
turns north and zigzags up the very rocky

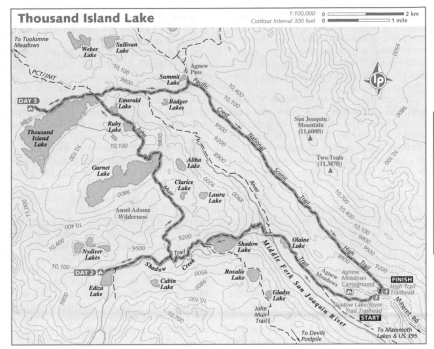

slope to the ridgetop above (10,160ft). The trail drops down and then passes along the east shore of **Ruby Lake** and then the west shore of **Emerald Lake**. The island-speckled **Thousand Island Lake** soon comes into sight below, and this viewpoint is perhaps the best perch to survey its beauty. Descend to the lake, crossing a footbridge over its outlet and intersecting with the Pacific Crest Trail (PCT). Turn left (west) at this point, tracing the far (north) side of the lake for approximately half of a mile to find a campsite. You must camp at least a quarter-mile from the outflow area.

DAY 3: THOUSAND ISLAND LAKE TO AGNEW MEADOWS
4–5 hours, 9.7 miles

Return to the junction of the JMT and the PCT, and follow the PCT (also known as the High Trail here) along the outlet (the headwaters of the Middle Fork of the San Joaquin River). Ascend briefly along a granite outcrop to a junction with the River Trail, and stay on the PCT as it passes the shallow grassy Badger Lakes and then two

trails leading to Agnew Pass. At the second pass trail, you're now 2.6 miles from the day's starting point, and at 9720ft, the highest point of the day. For the next 6.6 miles, the PCT traverses the west side of a ridge, with spectacular sightlines of Shadow Lake to the west, and the unmistakable **Two Teats** formation marking the eastern ridge. With a final 560ft descent via tight switchbacks, the trail returns to Agnew Meadows, about a half-mile east of the parking lot where you began.

DEVILS POSTPILE NATIONAL MONUMENT

Like a stack of warped organ pipes, the Devils Postpile National Monument is one of the strangest rock formations you might ever see. The 60ft, multisided columns of blue-gray basalt are the most conspicuous and interesting evidence of the area's volcanic activity. The accordionlike columns first took shape about 10,000 years ago, when lava, which flowed through Mammoth Pass, cooled and fractured vertically. A glacier came through later, giving them their cracked, shiny surface and causing several to snap off, forming the pile of broken posts at the base. Don't miss the view from above, where the distinct hexagonal honeycomb design is particularly visible, and the pattern could be mistaken for garden paving stones.

Carved from the Ansel Adam Wilderness, the monument is 10 miles west past the ski area. The road there is generally open from June to October, and between 7am and 7pm (until early September), you can only get there on foot or aboard a shuttle (adult/child $7/4), unless you are camping in one of the seven USFS campgrounds. The shuttle departs every 30 minutes daily between those times from the Gondola Building outside the ski area's Main Lodge. Outside of those times, you can drive in, though you'll still need to pay if it's staffed when you enter or exit. Disabled visitors may drive in anytime, but are not exempt from the fees.

The shuttle bus stops at campgrounds, viewpoints and the **Devils Postpile Ranger Station** (☎ 934-2289; www.nps.gov/depo; ☷ 9am-5pm). From here, hike about 1.5 miles to the columns or 2.5 miles through fire-ravaged forest to the true-to-its-title **Rainbow Falls**, a 101ft sheet cascade and prism of mist formed by the Middle Fork of the San Joaquin River. Daily ranger-guided walks to the columns leave from the station at 11am. The shuttle's last stop is at the **Reds Meadow Resort** (☎ 934-2345, 800-292-7758; www.redsmeadow.com), with a café, general store, pack station and backcountry resupply. The entire one-way trip from the ski/bike area takes about 45 minutes.

BISHOP

☎ 760 / pop 3600 / elev 4140ft

The second-largest town in the Eastern Sierra, Bishop is about two hours from Yosemite's east gate. The old part of town features classic Western Americana, with covered sidewalks, 1950s neon signs, and hunting and fishing stores aplenty. Its unpretentious appearance stands in stark contrast to the wonderland of nature surrounding it.

The earliest inhabitants of the Owens Valley were Paiute and Shoshone Native Americans, who today live on four reservations; the largest is the Bishop Indian Reservation. White settlers came on the scene in the 1860s and began raising cattle to sell to nearby mining settlements.

A major recreation hub, Bishop offers access to excellent fishing in nearby lakes, climbing in the Buttermilks just west of town, and hiking in the John Muir Wilderness via Bishop Creek Canyon and the Rock Creek drainage. It's a nice place to visit year-round, but unless you like crowds, you may want to skip Memorial Day weekend, when some 40,000 people descend on the town to celebrate **Mule Days** (☎ 872-4263; www.muledays.org), featuring mule parades, mule races and a mule rodeo.

Bishop also serves as the northernmost gateway to the Owens Valley, a once fertile agricultural region reduced to a desertlike wasteland. Since the early 20th century, water from the Owens River has been siphoned off by the Los Angeles Aqueduct. The 100-sq-mile Owens Lake was sapped dry, leading to decades of toxic dust storms and the loss of important wetlands for migratory birds. Some environmental mitigation and restoration is now in place, but the area is still in recovery mode.

Orientation & Information

Bishop Area Chamber of Commerce & Visitors Bureau (☎ 873-8405, 888-395-3952; www.bishopvisitor.com; 690 N Main St; ☷ 10am-4:30pm Mon-Fri, to 4pm Sat & Sun)

Bishop Library (☎ 873-5115; 210 Academy; ☷ 10am-6pm Mon, Wed & Fri, noon-8pm Tue & Thu, 10am-1pm Sat) Free internet access.

Public Lands Information Center (☎ 873-2500; www.fs.fed.us/r5/inyo; 798 N Main St; ☷ 8am-5pm summer, 8am-4:30pm Mon-Fri rest of year)

Spellbinder Books (☎ 873-4511; 124 S Main St; ☷ 9am-6pm Mon-Fri, 10am-6pm Sat, 10am-4pm Sun) The only full-service bookstore in Owens Valley, specializing in nonfiction, California and Sierra history. Cute adjoining café as well.

Sights

Off Hwy 6, 4.5 miles northeast of town, the **Laws Railroad Museum & Historical Site** (☎ 873-5950; www.lawsmuseum.org; Silver Canyon Rd; requested donation $5; ☷ 10am-4pm) is the last remaining station (and a bit of track) from the narrow-gauge Carson and Colorado railway line. Dozens of historic buildings from the region have been reassembled here with period artifacts to create a time-capsule village.

Mountain Light Photography (☎ 873-7700; www.mountainlight.com; 106 S Main St; ☻ 10am-6pm Sun-Thu, to 8pm Fri & Sat) features the stunning outdoor images of the late Galen Rowell. His work bursts with color, and the High Sierra photographs are some of the best in existence.

Activities

Keough's Hot Springs (☎ 872-4670; www.keoughshotsprings.com; adult/child $8/6; ☻ 11am-7pm Wed-Mon Sep-May, 9am-8pm Mon-Thu, 9am-9pm Fri & Sat, 9am-7pm Sun Jun-Aug), built in 1919, has swimming in two developed spring-fed pools (temperatures are 89°F and 104°F) and space for camping on the grounds. To reach it, drive 7 miles south on Hwy 395 to Keough Hot Springs Rd (on the west side), and then go 1 mile.

Like your soaks a bit more rugged? A number of natural hot-springs pools are nearby, with one set near the resort. From Hwy 395, go just half a mile on Keough Hot Springs Rd, and then turn right onto a paved road near a power line. At another quarter-mile, pools of various temperatures are on both sides of the road. Jump in and admire the sensational White Mountain views.

The Owens River Gorge, 9 miles north of town on the east side of Hwy 395, offers excellent rock climbing, as do the Buttermilk Hills, west of town on either side of Hwy 168; the latter are terrific for bouldering, as are the aptly named Happy Boulders nearby.

Some of the friendly staff at **Wilson's Eastside Sports** (☎ 873-7520; 224 N Main St; ☻ 9am-9pm summer, 9am-6pm Mon-Fri, 9am-9pm Sat & Sun rest of year) are experienced climbers with good route suggestions; the shop rents equipment and sells maps and guidebooks. The folks at **Sierra Mountain Center** (☎ 873-8526; www.sierramountaincenter.com; 174 W Line St) consider themselves Sierra backcountry experts and offer year-round instruction and guided ascents in the Eastern Sierra. They also book a wide range of climbing, hiking, mountaineering, backcountry-skiing and other activity-specific trips.

A short drive west via Hwy 168 takes you to **Bishop Creek Canyon Recreation Area**, a High Sierra alpine playground with pine forests, lakes and streams. Further west the road forks, the south fork ending at pretty **South Lake**, surrounded by jagged peaks. Many trails depart from the lake's trailhead, heading up to Bishop Pass and countless lakes in the John Muir Wilderness. There are several campgrounds in the area.

The north fork ends at sparkling **Lake Sabrina**, encircled by craggy peaks of the Sierra Crest. Sabrina is gorgeous, especially in fall when the trees turn golden. A ribbon of a trail winds along the north shore, leading to a small waterfall (about 2 miles away) and passing several good spots to swim, if you can stomach the cold. Nearby is the much smaller **North Lake**. Both lakes make excellent stops for fishing. **Lake Sabrina Boat Landing** (☎ 873-7425) rents boats with or without motors for $24 to $48 per half-day, and there's a little café with a sun-splashed deck for a postactivity cold beer.

Sleeping

For a scenic night, stretch out your sleeping bag beneath the stars. Eleven nice **USFS campgrounds** (www.fs.fed.us/r5/inyo; sites $) lie along high-elevation Bishop Creek, 9 miles west of town via Hwy 168, all of them surrounded by trees and close to fishing and hiking. All but one are first-come, first-served.

Brown's Town (☎ 873-8522; www.brownscampgrounds.com; sites $) A little closer to civilization, this nicely shaded campground is 1 mile south of town, just off Hwy 395. It has 150 grassy RV and tent sites, hot showers, laundry and other amenities.

Chalfant House (☎ 872-1790, 800-641-2996; www.chalfanthouse.com; 213 Academy; r $$; 🖳) Lace curtains and Victorian accents swirl through the six rooms of this restored historic home. Originally built by the editor and publisher of Owens Valley's first newspaper, some of the rooms are named after Chalfant family members.

our pick **Joseph House Inn Bed & Breakfast** (☎ 872-3389; www.josephhouseinn.com; 376 W Yaney St; r $$$; ☻ closed Jan; 🐾 🖳) A beautiful, restored ranch-style home, it has a patio overlooking a tranquil 3-acre garden, and five nicely furnished rooms, some with fireplaces and all with TV and VCR. Guests enjoy a complimentary gourmet breakfast and afternoon wine and cheese.

Eating & Drinking

Looney Bean (☎ 872-2326; 399 N Main St; pastries $; ☻ 6am-8pm Sun & Mon-Thu, to 10pm Fri & Sat; 🖳) The combination of really fine coffee, a

AROUND YOSEMITE

comfortable modern space and the free wi-fi guarantee the popularity of this central café. It carries some organic brews, and lots of tasty scones and pastries for snacking.

Erick Schat's Bakkery (☎ 873-7156; 763 N Main St; sandwiches $; ⏰ 6am-6pm Sat-Thu, to 7pm Fri) A much-hyped tourist mecca filled to the rafters with racks of fresh bread, the bakery has been making its signature shepherd bread and other baked goodies since 1938. The bakery also features a popular sandwich bar and espresso drinks.

India Palace (☎ 873-7000; 787 N Main St; dishes $-$$; ⏰ lunch & dinner Wed-Mon) Indian food! Forgot you were missing it, didn't you? A rare treat in these parts, India Palace has the *sag paneer* and chicken korma you've been craving. Load up on meat and vegetarian dishes at the all-you-can-eat lunch buffet.

Whiskey Creek (☎ 873-7174; 524 N Main St; mains $$-$$$; ⏰ 7:30am-10pm) In summertime, take your pick between the somewhat saccharine country dining room of floral curtains and captain's chairs or the mist-sprayed patio. The menu has comfort food like meatloaf and pork chops, and a smattering of seafood and pastas.

Getting There & Away

Inyo Mono Transit (☎ 872-1901, 800-922-1930; www.inyocounty.us/transit/transit.htm) operates a weekday CREST bus service between Bishop and Lone Pine ($4) three times daily on weekdays and on the first Saturday of the month. Commuter buses run to Mammoth ($3.50) Monday through Saturday and to Reno ($28) three times a week. Reservations are recommended.

ANCIENT BRISTLECONE PINE FOREST

For amazing high-altitude views, take the hour-long drive to the **Ancient Bristlecone Pine Forest** (☎ 760-873-2500; www.fs.fed.us/r5/inyo; ⏰ mid-May–mid-Nov). Perched above 10,000ft in the White Mountains, these gnarled, picturesque trees are the planet's oldest living things, some dating back 4000 years. To get there from Bishop, drive 15 miles south to Big Pine, then head east on Hwy 168 another 12 miles to the marked turnoff. The 10-mile windy road, usually open from late May to October, is paved to the top, where you'll find hikes of varying lengths and a visitor center that opens June 1. Halfway up the road at 8500ft is a nice primitive **campground** (sites by donation).

Sequoia & Kings Canyon National Parks

With a cleft deeper than the Grand Canyon and a forest harboring the largest tree in the world, Sequoia & Kings Canyon National Parks dazzle with superlatives. Throw in opportunities for cave spelunking, rock climbing and backcountry hiking through granite-carved Sierra landscapes and you have all the ingredients for one of the best parks in the country.

Larger than Yosemite yet overshadowed by that park's eye-candy Valley, Sequoia & Kings Canyon receives less than half as many visitors as its iconic neighbor to the north. It's an effortless place to find solitude, even with five-star geological highlights and hulking giant sequoias within easy reach.

In 1890, prodded into action by George Stewart, the ardent editor of the Visalia *Delta*, Congress created Sequoia National Park, the second national park in the country (Yellowstone was the first). Soon after, the Grant Grove of giant sequoias became General Grant National Park, and that tiny parcel was absorbed by Kings Canyon National Park when it was established in 1940. To further protect vulnerable sequoia groves, more than 327,000 acres of land in the Sequoia National Forest was designated as the Giant Sequoia National Monument in 2000. The two contiguous parks are administered together as one unit, with a section of the Giant Sequoia National Monument gouging into them like a bite in a round cookie.

The parks total 865,257 acres, with a length of 66 miles from north to south and a roomy girth 36 miles across at their widest point. Of that, 83% is designated wilderness and 850 miles of trails await your footsteps.

HIGHLIGHTS

- Backpacking through the marmot-guarded alpine lakes of **Mineral King** (p222)
- Eyeing high peaks and sequoia treetops from **Buck Rock Lookout** (p222)
- Ducking through a maze of toothy stalactites at **Crystal Cave** (p221)
- Hoofing it up the precipitous granite dome of **Moro Rock** (p220)
- Lazing away a sun-splashed afternoon on the shore of **Hume Lake** (p225)

FAST FACTS

- **Total area of Sequoia & Kings Canyon National Parks** 1352 sq miles (865,257 acres)

- **Elevation of Grant Grove (Kings Canyon)** 6600ft

- **Elevation of Foothills (Sequoia)** 2500ft

- **Average high/low temperature in Grant Grove in July** 76°/51°F (24.5°/10.5°C)

- **Average high/low temperature in Foothills in July** 97°/68°F (36°/20°C)

When You Arrive

Both park entrances are open year-round, though some facilities and roads (including those to Mineral King, Cedar Grove and the Moro Rock–Crescent Meadow Rd) are closed in winter. For information on park-entrance fees and passes, see p23.

The *Guide* is the parks' newspaper, which you receive on entry. It's published four to five times a year, with information on seasonal activities, camping and special programs.

Orientation

The parks are only accessible by car from the west, and no roads cross the Sierra range. On Hwy 180, Big Stump is the northernmost entrance station, located in Kings Canyon. The highway continues northeast (where it becomes known as the Kings Canyon Scenic Byway), running from Grant Grove through the Giant Sequoia National Monument area of the **Sequoia National Forest** (☎ 559-338-2251; www.fs.fed.us/r5/sequoia), and then descending into the Cedar Grove section of Kings Canyon.

Further south in Sequoia, the other main access point is the Ash Mountain Entrance on Hwy 198. Most of the park's star attractions are conveniently lined up along the Generals Hwy, the main road that starts here and continues north to Grant Grove Village, traversing both parks. Tourist activity concentrates in the Giant Forest area and in the Lodgepole Village, which has the most facilities, including a year-round campground. In the town of Three Rivers, just south of the park's Ash Mountain Entrance, the windy road to the remote Mineral King region veers east from Hwy 198.

Sequoia & Kings Canyon lie about 100 miles south of Yosemite, though it takes two to three hours to make the drive. From Grant Grove, go west on Hwy 180 to Fresno and then north on Hwy 41 to Wawona.

Information

For 24-hour recorded information, including winter road conditions, call ☎ 559-565-3341; the comprehensive park website is www.nps.gov/seki.

BOOKSTORES

Books and maps can be purchased at park visitor centers as well as at the Giant Forest Museum. Lodgepole and Grant Grove have the most extensive offerings.

INTERNET ACCESS

Free wireless internet access is available at the Cedar Grove, Grant Grove and Wuksachi village areas. There are no computer terminals available within the parks.

POST

Grant Grove (🕙 9am-4:15pm Mon-Fri, 10am-12:15pm Sat)
Lodgepole (🕙 8am-1pm & 2-4pm Mon-Fri)

MONEY

ATMs attentively await your bank card at Lodgepole, Grant Grove, Cedar Grove and the Stony Creek market. There is no foreign currency exchange available.

TELEPHONE

Don't waste your time trying to find cellphone coverage – there isn't any. Pay phones can be found at all village areas and visitor centers and at some campgrounds.

SEQUOIA & KINGS CANYON TELEPHONE NUMBERS

The area code for all telephone numbers within Sequoia & Kings Canyon is ☎ 559. All numbers contain the prefix 565 (ie, ☎ 559-565-4436), so you only really have to remember the last four digits. Locals often give telephone numbers by their last four digits only.

SEQUOIA & KINGS CANYON IN...

One Day

Start the day at the **Foothills Visitor Center** (p221) and scoop up late-afternoon tour tickets for Crystal Cave. Head north on Generals Hwy, with a stop to skip through **Tunnel Rock** (p221) and another to see the Native American pictographs at **Hospital Rock** (p221). At Giant Forest, crane your neck at the supersize **General Sherman Tree** (p220), then leave your car and jump on the park shuttle for an easy hike at luxuriant **Crescent Meadow** (p226). Another quick shuttle stop, then puff and pant to the dizzying panoramic heights of **Moro Rock** (p220). Reunite with your vehicle and make your way to the chilly wonderland of **Crystal Cave** (p221).

Two Days

Continue on from Day One and explore to the north, starting with the mammoth sequoia grove surrounding the **General Grant Tree** (p223). Bump over a dirt road to **Converse Basin Grove** (p225) and take a wistful hike to the lonely Boole Tree. Descending into Kings Canyon, pull over at **Junction View** (p224) to marvel at mountain peaks and the deep, deep canyon. Take a tour of ethereal **Boyden Cavern** (p224) and then feel the refreshing waves of spray from **Roaring River Falls** (p224). Stroll alongside the river and gaze up at granite crests from verdant **Zumwalt Meadow** (p227). Last but not least, cool off with a swim at **Muir Rock** (p224).

Four Days

Grab your pack and head south for the high country. Drive the scenic and tortuous road into **Mineral King** (p222) and test your lung power as you climb avalanche-cleansed granite bowls to deep blue alpine lakes.

VISITOR & WILDERNESS CENTERS

Cedar Grove Visitor Center (☎ 559-565-3793; ☺ 9am-5pm late May–early Sep) The wilderness permit office is 6 miles east at Roads End.

Foothills Visitor Center (☎ 559-565-3135; ☺ 8am-6pm Jun-Aug, to 4:30pm Sep-May) One mile north of Ash Mountain Entrance.

Kings Canyon Park Visitor Center (☎ 559-565-4307; ☺ 8am-8pm summer, 9am-4:30pm winter) In Grant Grove, with exhibits on wildlife habitats and a nice introductory movie on Kings Canyon – all titled in English and Spanish.

Lodgepole Visitor Center (☎ visitor center 559-565-4436, wilderness permits 559-565-4408; ☺ 7am-6pm late May–Aug, 7am-5pm Sep, 8am-4:30pm Oct, closed Nov–mid-May) Maps, information, exhibits, Crystal Cave tickets and wilderness permits (open 7am to 11am and noon to 3:45pm).

Mineral King Ranger Station (☎ 559-565-3768; ☺ 8am-4pm Jun–mid-Sep) This station is 24 miles east of Generals Hwy. Self-issue wilderness permits are available when the office is closed in the fall and before road closure; park-entrance fee must be paid elsewhere.

USFS Hume Lake District Office (☎ 559-338-2251; 35860 E Kings Canyon Rd, Dunlap; ☺ 8am-4:30pm Mon-Fri) Information, maps and permits for the Sequoia National Forest.

Park Rules & Regulations

It probably won't come as a surprise that the parks don't let visitors climb giant sequoias, though you may not know that hitchhiking is allowed, as long as it's done safely.

FOOD STORAGE

Bear boxes (p279) must be used in developed areas. In day-use areas where they are not provided, food must be stored inside the trunk. In vehicles without trunks, food should be placed inside as low as possible and covered so it is not visible. In most wilderness areas, park-approved bear-resistant containers must be used unless a backcountry food-storage locker is available. See p269 for tips on bear interactions.

CAMPFIRES

Fires are generally permitted in the backcountry, with some exceptions. In Kings Canyon, no fires are permitted in Redwood Canyon or above 10,000ft. Sequoia prohibits fires above 9000ft in the Kaweah River drainage and above 11,200ft in the Kern River drainage area.

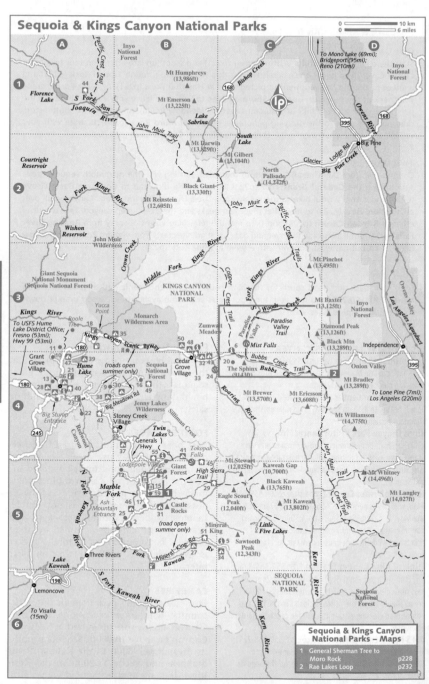

Sequoia & Kings Canyon National Parks

SEQUOIA & KINGS CANYON NATIONAL PARKS

Sequoia & Kings Canyon National Parks – Maps

| 1 | General Sherman Tree to Moro Rock | p228 |
| 2 | Rae Lakes Loop | p232 |

WILDERNESS CAMPING & PERMITS

Overnight backcountry camping requires a wilderness permit, which may be subject to trail quotas. See Backcountry Hikes (p230) for more information.

Getting Around

In 2007 Sequoia National Park debuted a new summertime shuttle system. From the Giant Forest Museum, two routes connect Wuksachi Lodge, Lodgepole, the Sherman Tree and its upper parking lot, Moro Rock and Crescent Meadow. Buses are frequent; schedules are posted at stops. For info on the shuttle from Visalia to Sequoia National Park, see p263.

For drivers, the box below shows average times between sites in and around the parks.

DRIVING TIMES BETWEEN SITES

From/to	Driving time (hr)
Fresno-Grant Grove	1½
Grant Grove-Cedar Grove	1
Grant Grove-Lodgepole	1
Foothills-Lodgepole	1
Lodgepole-Crystal Cave parking lot	1
Hwy 198-end of Mineral King Rd	1½
Visalia-Foothills	1

Gas is not available in either park, but it is sold at Kings Canyon Lodge and Hume Lake, both private facilities on USFS land north of Grant Grove, and at the Stony Creek Village (between Grant Grove and Lodgepole) from spring through fall.

SIGHTS

SEQUOIA NATIONAL PARK
Lodgepole & Wuksachi Village

Lodgepole Village is the main hub of Sequoia. A large visitor center (see p217) has exhibits on park history, including the Buffalo soldiers (see boxed text, p82) and the region's competing land uses from Native American dominion until the present. There's an especially thought-provoking mural about the interdependence of species, and a movie, *Bears of Sequoia*, is screened upon request. A wilderness permit desk offers backcountry information and rents out bear canisters

The village also encompasses a market, two places to eat, coin showers and a Laundromat, all of which are open from April until October, as well as a post office (somewhat hidden behind the visitor center), and an adjacent year-round campground.

The nearby Wuksachi Village contains the parks' poshest hotel and restaurant, both of which stay open throughout the year.

TWO IN ONE

Although administered as a single body, Sequoia & Kings Canyon National Parks are two national parks: Sequoia National Park and Kings Canyon National Park. 'Kings Canyon,' however, can also refer specifically to the eponymous canyon itself. The two parks together are commonly referred to as 'SEKI.'

Giant Forest

The top destination in the parks, this area was named by John Muir in 1875. Encompassing an amazing concentration of ancient giant sequoias, at one point over 300 buildings, including campgrounds and a lodge, encroached upon the sequoias' delicate root systems. Recognizing this adverse impact, in 1997 the park began to remove structures and resite parking lots. It's also introduced a superconvenient and frequent visitor shuttle, significantly cutting traffic congestion and reducing the potential harm to these majestic trees.

GENERAL SHERMAN TREE

By volume the largest living tree on earth, the massive General Sherman Tree rockets 275ft into the sky and *waaay* out of the camera frame. Pay your respects via a short descent from the Wolverton Rd parking lot, or join the **Congress Trail**, a paved 2-mile pathway that takes in General Sherman and other notable named trees, including the see-through **Telescope Tree**. To lose the crowds, set off on the 5-mile **Trail of the Sequoias**, which puts you into the heart of the forest.

A handy hint: if the steep walk back up from the grove doesn't thrill you, catch the shuttle from the lower parking lot (disabled parking only) near the General Sherman tree and ride it back to the main parking area.

GIANT FOREST MUSEUM

A fun primer in sequoia ecology, the pint-sized **Giant Forest Museum** (☎ 559-565-4480; admission free; ☺ 9am-7pm summer, to 6pm spring & fall, to 4pm winter) will entertain both kids and adults. Hands-on exhibits teach about the life stages of these big trees, their seeds and the fire cycle that releases them. To see this info in action, stroll the interpretive **Big Trees Trail** (see p226), which starts right outside. There's also a small bookstore.

BEETLE ROCK EDUCATION CENTER

Bugs, bones and artificial animal scat are just some of the cool things kids get to play with at the **Beetle Rock Education Center** (admission free; ☺ 10am-4pm summer; ⚠). A bright and cheerful cabin with activity stations galore, it's run by the Sequoia Natural History Association and is appropriate for ages three to 15 (all children must have a parent or adult to supervise them). Inquisitive kiddos can scan bugs with digital microscopes, touch a taxidermied bobcat, put on puppet shows and paint ecology posters. Tents are set up for inside play, and there are binoculars out back for spotting animals. At 1:30pm each day, it has free one-hour activity walks.

MORO ROCK

Yosemite has Half Dome, and Sequoia's iconic granite dome is the impressive Moro Rock (also see p226). A steep quarter-mile staircase climbs 300ft to the top for mind-boggling views of the Great Western Divide, a chain of mountains running north to south through the center of Sequoia National Park, splitting the watersheds of the Kaweah River to the west and the Kern River to the east. From this vantage point, you might even be lucky and see bears in the distance below. Historic photos at the trailhead base show the original wooden staircase, erected 1917. Regardless of the sharp grade, you'll be grateful that the current stairs – built in 1931 – are carved into the rock and have sturdy handrails.

From Giant Forest, the trailhead is 2 miles up slim and twisty Moro Rock–Crescent Meadow Rd; the park shuttle stops right beside it.

CRESENT MEADOW

A lush green expanse buffered by a forest of firs and sequoia, John Muir gushed that beautiful Crescent Meadow was the 'gem of the Sierra.' High grass and striking summer wildflowers make for a leisurely loop hike (p226), and a good opportunity to spot bears foraging for food. Several short hikes start from here, including trails to **Tharp's Log**, where the area's first white settler,

SEQUOIA & KINGS CANYON NATIONAL PARKS

Hale Tharp, spent summers in a fallen tree, and **Squatters' Cabin**, an 1880s log cabin (see boxed text, p245). The meadow environment is fragile, so keep on trails or fallen logs to view it.

The meadow is 3 miles down Moro Rock–Crescent Meadow Rd and best accessed by park shuttle; the road closes to car traffic in winter.

CRYSTAL CAVE

Discovered in 1918 by two fishermen, **Crystal Cave** (☎ 559-565-3759; www.sequoiahistory.org; Crystal Cave Rd; adult/child/senior $11/6/10; ☯ tours 10:30am-4:30pm mid-May–Oct) was carved by an underground river and has formations estimated to be 10,000 years old. Stalactites hang like daggers from the ceiling, and milky white marble formations take the shape of ethereal curtains, domes, columns and shields.

To see the cave, you must buy a ticket for a 45-minute tour that covers a half-mile of chambers (the cave passage winds on for 3½ miles), though longer tours ($19) and all-day, off-trail spelunking explorations ($130) are also available. Tickets are *only* sold at the Lodgepole and Foothills visitor centers from 8am to 4pm and *not* at the cave. Weekend tours can fill up, so buy them early in the day or a day or so in advance. From Lodgepole, allow about one hour to get to the cave entrance, which is a half-mile walk from the parking lot at the end of a twisty 7-mile road. From Foothills, give yourself 1½ to two hours. The turnoff is about 3 miles south of the Giant Forest. Bring along a sweater or light jacket.

Foothills

From the Ash Mountain Entrance in Three Rivers, the Generals Hwy ascends steeply through this southern section of Sequoia

---

GETTING AWAY FROM IT ALL

July and August are the busiest months in Sequoia & Kings Canyon, but it never gets anywhere near as saturated as Yosemite Valley. Late spring before Memorial Day (the last weekend in May) and the weeks after Memorial Day weekend until the July 4 holiday are very quiet, and the two weeks after Labor Day are gorgeous and gloriously unpeopled.

National Park. With an average elevation of about 2000ft, the Foothills are much drier and warmer than the rest of the park, and wildflowers begin to bloom in January. Hiking here is best in spring, when the air is still cool and wildflowers peak for a colorful show. Summers are buggy and muggy, but fall again brings moderate temperatures and lush foliage. Swimming holes abound along the Marble Fork of the Kaweah River, especially near Potwisha Campground. Be careful, though – the currents can be deadly, especially when the river is swollen with spring runoff.

FOOTHILLS VISITOR CENTER

This small visitor center (p217) has exhibits on park history and ecology, with a focus on the Foothills ecosystem. Maps and books can be purchased at its bookstore.

TUNNEL ROCK

In 1938 no one anticipated the development of monster SUVs. About 1.5 miles north of the Ash Mountain Visitor Center, a sizable flat granite boulder on the west side of the road caps a tunnel dug by the Civilian Conservation Corps. Until the road was widened in 1997, this narrow passageway was the only route through. It's closed to modern-day vehicles, which would have a tough time squeezing through side by side, but pedestrians can stroll under its constricted arch.

HOSPITAL ROCK

The Potwisha people, a subgroup of the Monache (also known as the Western Mono), lived in this area until the early 1900s, relying primarily on acorn meal. When the first white visitor, Hale Tharp (see opposite), befriended them in 1858, the site was home to about 500 people and had been inhabited for approximately five centuries. Diseases introduced by white settlers in Three Rivers soon killed many of the villagers, and within a decade the site was abandoned. Red pictographs and grinding holes still grace the Hospital Rock picnic area.

Generals Highway

Between the parks, the Generals Hwy bridges sections of the Giant Sequoia National Monument and the Monarch Wilderness (both part of the Sequoia National

Forest). A few businesses are right off the road, and the paved Big Meadows Rd (Forest Service road 14S11) burrows east into the Giant Sequoia National Monument near the Jennie Lakes Wilderness, a popular backpacking area.

STONY CREEK VILLAGE
A seasonal outpost, the Stony Creek Village has a 24-hour gas station (with credit card), ATM, pay phones, coin laundry and fee showers, the small Stony Creek Lodge (p241), a tiny market and a pizza parlor (p243). Everything closes from mid-October until mid-April, including the gas station. Two USFS campgrounds are located less than a mile south.

MONTECITO LAKE RESORT
Four miles north of Stony Creek, this resort (p242) is an active year-round lodge and popular summer family camp. It has been in business for more than 60 years, with summer water sports that revolve around a small private lake, and cross-country ski trails in wintertime.

BUCK ROCK LOOKOUT
Built in 1923, the active **Buck Rock Lookout** (www.buckrock.org; 9:30am-6pm Jul-Oct) is one of the finest restored watchtowers you could ever hope to visit. Staffed in fire season, 172 stairs lead to a dollhouse-sized wooden cab on a dramatic 8500ft granite rise. To reach it from Generals Hwy, go about 1 mile north of the Montecito Lake Resort and then east onto Big Meadows Rd (Forest Service road 14S11). At approximately 2.5 miles, turn

north on the signed dirt road (Forest Service road 14S11) and follow signs another 3 miles to the lookout parking area. Opening hours are approximate, so check online before you make the trek.

To find other Sequoia NF lookouts, go to www.fs.fed.us/r5/sequoia /lookouts/look outs.html.

Mineral King
A scenic, subalpine valley at 7500ft, Mineral King is Sequoia's backpacking mecca and is a good place to find solitude. Gorgeous and gigantic, Mineral King is a glacially sculpted valley ringed by massive mountains, including the jagged 12,343ft Sawtooth Peak. Hiking anywhere from here involves a steep climb out of the valley along strenuous trails, and you'll be starting at 7500ft, so be aware of the altitude, even on short hikes. Enjoyable day hikes go to Crystal, Monarch, Mosquito and Eagle Lakes. For long trips, locals recommend the Little Five Lakes and, further along the High Sierra Trail, Kaweah Gap, surrounded by the sawtooth Black Kaweah, Mt Stewart and Eagle Scout Peak – all above 12,000ft.

From the 1860s to 1890s, Mineral King witnessed heavy silver mining and lumber activity. There are still remnants of old shafts and stamp mills around, though it takes some exploring to find them. A contentious proposal by the Walt Disney Corporation to develop the area into a massive ski resort was thwarted when Congress annexed it to the Sequoia National Park in 1978.

EAGLE EYES

Kathryn Allison, USFS Fire Lookout, Buck Rock

What's your favorite thing about being a fire lookout?
I love watching eagles and falcons as they catch the thermals. Sunrise is my favorite time of day because of all the colors, and the weather changes how it looks every day. I also feel like I'm carrying on a tradition. Lea Dotters was the first female lookout here – she started on D-Day.

What's it like to be here during lightning storms?
Loud and very bright, and literally hair-raising. My dog hates it – she crawls under the bed. So far the lightning rod has protected me, but there are amazing buzzes before it hits, and I've seen blue St Elmo's fire right outside.

What's your view from the lookout?
Let's see, Tehipite Dome, the top of Spanish Mountain, the Great Western Divide, the Middle Fork of the Kings River, the John Muir Wilderness...

TASTY CAR PARTS

You've locked the doors and rolled up the windows. All food and scented stuff has been removed. So why is your car still at risk? Marmots – Mineral King is swarming with hungry yellow-bellied marmots, and what's under your hood is what's for dinner.

In spring and early summer, many of Mineral King's bold and oddly epicurean marmots have come out of hibernation and anxiously await parked cars at the Mineral King trailheads. Besides gourmet items like sweaty clothing, they love to feast on radiator hoses, belts and wiring of vehicles in order to get the salt they crave. They can chew through brake lines and completely disable your car.

Marmot-proofing one's vehicle has become a local art form. Some folks swear by wrapping the engine block in chicken wire, while others swaddle the entire undercarriage with an enormous tarp so it's like a vehicular diaper.

And check under the hood before you drive off. Some marmots have ended up hitching as far as southern California before they were discovered, still munching away.

The area is reached via Mineral King Rd, which heads east from Hwy 198 between the Ash Mountain Entrance and the town of Three Rivers. Open from November 1 until the Friday of Memorial Day weekend, it's a cruelly twisting, steep and narrow 25-mile road that you will not forget. Plan to stay at least one night in the region – only masochists will want to do this drive twice in one day.

Mineral King has two first-come, first-served campgrounds and a ranger station (see p217), all towards the end of the road. About 21 miles in, the Silver City Mountain Resort (p241) is a small camp-style enclave with lodging, a restaurant and tiny market (p241).

The website of the **Mineral King Preservation Society** (www.mineralking.org) has all kinds of info on the area, including the historic mining cabins.

KINGS CANYON NATIONAL PARK

Kings Canyon National Park is divided into two areas – Grant Grove and Cedar Grove – and linked by Hwy 180, which makes a dramatic descent into Kings Canyon along the South Fork of the Kings River. The canyon itself, plunging 8200ft, is the deepest in the contiguous 48 US states.

The stunning backcountry makes the canyon a favorite place among serious hikers and climbers. The road to Cedar Grove closes in winter, usually from mid-November until late April, although it may open as far as Yucca Point by the beginning of April.

Grant Grove
GRANT GROVE VILLAGE

The year-round Grant Grove Village is the main hub of Kings Canyon National Park. A visitor center (see p217) has interesting exhibits on preservation and wildlife habitats, and continuously screens a movie overview of the park. The 'Discovery Room' has independent activities for children. In addition to a number of lodge and cabin accommodations and two restaurants, there's a decent-sized market, free wi-fi and a post office. ATMs are located inside the village lobby and the market, and a few phone booths are located outside. The closest gas is at Stony Creek (opposite).

GENERAL GRANT GROVE

The magnificence of this sequoia grove was recognized in 1890 when Congress designated it General Grant National Park. Decades later that tiny parcel was absorbed into the new Kings Canyon National Park, established in 1940.

The paved half-mile **General Grant Tree Trail** (p226) is an interpretive walk that visits a number of mature sequoias, including the 27-story **General Grant Tree**. This giant holds triple honors as the world's third-largest living tree, a memorial to US soldiers killed in war and as the nation's Christmas tree. The nearby **Fallen Monarch**, a massive, fire-hollowed trunk that you can walk through, has been a cabin, hotel, saloon, and stables for US Cavalry horses. Daily ranger-led walks go to the General Grant Tree in summer.

SEQUOIA & KINGS CANYON NATIONAL PARKS

PANORAMIC POINT

For a breathtaking view, head up 2.3 miles on supersteep Panoramic Point Rd (trailers and RVs not recommended). Precipitous canyons and the snowcapped peaks of the Great Western Divide unfold below you. Snow closes the road to vehicles, when it becomes a cross-country ski and snowshoe route.

REDWOOD MOUNTAIN GROVE

Over 15,000 sequoias cluster in this corner of the park, south of Grant Grove Village, in Redwood Canyon, making it the world's largest grove. Relatively inaccessible, this area lets you enjoy the majesty of the giants away from the crowds on several moderate-to-strenuous trails. The trailhead is at the end of a 2-mile bumpy dirt road across from the Hume Lake/Quail Flat sign on Generals Hwy, about 6 miles south of the village.

Cedar Grove

North of Grant Grove, the Kings Canyon Scenic Byway (Hwy 180) drops 2000ft to Cedar Grove. The drive takes about an hour and ranks among the most magnificent in any national park, including Yosemite. Views from the road into the valley are spectacular, with roaring rivers, rugged peaks and steep granite cliffs jostling for your attention.

Cedar Grove Village

At the bottom of Kings Canyon, this commercial area consists of a market, restaurant, lodge, showers, laundry and a small visitor center (see p217). There's also an ATM. The road is usually open from late April through October or November, but most services don't start until late May.

KNAPP'S CABIN

During the Roaring 20s, a wealthy businessman named George Knapp built this simple wood-shingled cabin to store gear for extravagant fishing and camping excursions. A short walk leads to the semihidden riverview building, the oldest in Cedar Grove.

ROARING RIVER FALLS

One of the park's most accessible waterfalls, a five-minute walk on a paved trail leads to 40ft spillway falls gushing into a granite bowl. Even in dry years, the strength of the cascade doesn't disappoint. Look for the parking lot and trailhead on the south side of the road.

ZUMWALT MEADOW

A verdant green meadow bordered by river and granite canyon, it's an easy and mostly shaded loop hike (see p227) with phenomenal views. If you have time for just one walk, this loop gives you a quick snapshot of the park's beauty.

MUIR ROCK

On Sierra Club field trips to Kings Canyon, John Muir would often give talks on this large flat river boulder, a short walk from Roads End. The rock now bears his name, and the lazy river setting explodes with gleeful swimmers in summer.

ROADS END

Six miles east of Cedar Grove Village, Roads End is just that, with overnight parking, and a seasonal ranger kiosk that issues wilderness permits and rents bear canisters. A major trailhead, hikes starting here head out to all points of the Sierra; it's also the closest park trailhead to both the Pacific Crest Trail and the John Muir Trail.

Kings Canyon Scenic Byway

This 30-mile rollercoaster road descends through Giant Sequoia National Monument, connecting Grant Grove and Cedar Grove. It ranks among the most dazzling in all of California, serpentining past chiseled rock walls: some tinged by green moss and red iron minerals, others decorated by waterfalls. Eventually the road runs parallel with the gushing Kings River, its thunderous roar ricocheting off granite cliffs soaring as high as 8000ft. Turnouts provide superb views, most notably at **Yucca Point** and **Junction View**.

The privately owned **Kings Canyon Lodge** (8am-7pm Apr-Nov) has last-chance gas before you enter Cedar Grove, but sky-high prices and downright surly service make this a last-ditch option only.

BOYDEN CAVERN

Walk up a steep paved grade to the entrance of this **cave** (209-736-2708, 866-762-2837; www .caverntours.com; adult/child $11/6; mid-Apr–mid-Nov, tours 10am-5pm Jun-Sep, 11am-4pm Apr-May & Oct-Nov) and a tour of these fantastical formations. While the rooms are smaller and the interiors less eye-popping than Crystal Cave (p221) in Sequoia National Park, they are very beautiful, and unlike the very-visited Crystal Cave, you can show up here without making advance reservations.

HUME LAKE

This 87-acre lake was originally constructed as a mill pond, when it fueled a huge log flume that whisked sequoias from Converse Basin to a mill more than 70 miles away. There's a popular USFS campground (p240) on one side; and on the other, the private Hume Lake Christian Camp development has groceries, 24-hour gas (with credit card) and a snack bar.

CONVERSE BASIN GROVE

One of the most tragic stories of Sequoia & Kings Canyon, the Converse Basin Grove once contained the world's largest grove of mature sequoias. It is now an unsettling sequoia cemetery. From the late 1800s until the early 1900s, the entire privately owned grove was felled by lumber companies. A financial boondoggle, in part because of high transportation costs, the trees ravaged in this grove were not even suitable for lumber, and many shattered when they hit the ground. Most of the salvageable wood ended up as fence posts and matches.

The only survivor left is a colossus called the **Boole Tree**. The eighth-largest known giant sequoia, it's ironically named for the lumber mill's foreman, and for reasons unknown it was left to live. A 2.5-mile loop hike reaches it from the road. On the road in, stop at Stump Meadow to see the oversized remains of 19th-century logging.

Off a road a bit further south, the tall **Chicago Stump** is all that's left of the once-mighty 3200-year-old General Noble tree. The 285ft giant was cut into sections and transported to the 1893 World's Fair in Chicago to demonstrate the unbelievable scale of the newly discovered sequoia trees. They had one thing right – no one believed it was real. Dubious viewers soon nicknamed it the 'California hoax.' From Hwy 180, it's 2 miles to the trailhead and then an easy half-mile loop walk.

The roads to both Boole Tree and the Chicago Stump are unpaved, and the turnoff signs are hard to spot if you're heading west. The road to the Chicago Stump Trailhead is next to a stone marker at a four-way intersection about 2 miles north of Grant Grove Village. The last quarter-

mile is somewhat steep; consider parking in the turnout just before the descent if it's muddy or you don't have 4WD. The road to the Boole Tree turnoff is 1.25 miles further north; the trailhead is 2.5 miles in.

HIKING

The Sequoia Natural History Association publishes an excellent series of graded trail maps ($3.50 each) covering Cedar Grove, Grant Grove, Giant Forest, Lodgepole and the Mineral King areas; they are vital for day hikers. For a description of the hiking difficulty scale, see the boxed text, p39.

EASY HIKES
Sequoia National Park

These gentle hikes feature scenic waterfalls, subalpine meadows, granite domes and, of course, some fine giant sequoias.

TOKOPAH FALLS

Duration 2 hours
Distance 3.4-mile round-trip
Difficulty easy; elevation change +500ft
Start/Finish Lodgepole campground, Tokopah Falls Trailhead
Nearest Town/Facilities Lodgepole Village, 0.5 miles
Transport private
Summary Stroll along the river to one of the parks' largest and most scenic waterfalls. Starting from the campground, it's a convenient trip for Lodgepole campers, and is popular with groups and families.

From the parking area just inside the campground entrance station, cross the bridge to the opposite side of the Marble Fork of the Kaweah River. The entire hike runs alongside the river, with exceptional views of glacier-carved canyon and good opportunities to see pika, marmots and deer. As you near the falls, the severe 1800ft granite face of the Watchtower looms to the south.

At 1200ft high, the **Tokopah Falls** doesn't free fall but rather bounces off the granite canyon cliffs with all the sound and passion it can muster, especially when the snowpack melts and gushes in early summer. Return along the same route.

CRESCENT MEADOW LOOP

Duration 5 hours
Distance 1-mile round-trip
Difficulty easy; elevation change +75ft
Start/Finish Crescent Meadow parking lot/shuttle stop
Nearest Town/Facilities Giant Forest Museum, 3 miles
Transport shuttle
Summary A beautiful and easily reached subalpine meadow ringed by a canopy of firs and sequoias. Summer wildflowers turn up the color, and bears often graze nearby.

From the trailhead, stroll in either direction around the half-mile-long meadow loop. Downed logs are handy steps to peer over the high grass, but don't let your footfalls crunch and compact the meadow itself. Listen for the rustling of wildlife, and if you're quiet you may hear black bears ripping apart logs as they look for insects. At the northern end of the meadow, you can poke your head inside and look up the hollow fire-scarred **Chimney Tree**.

MORO ROCK

Duration 30 minutes
Distance 0.5-mile round-trip
Difficulty easy–moderate; elevation change +300ft
Start/Finish Moro Rock parking lot (shuttle stop)
Nearest Town/Facilities Giant Forest Museum, 2 miles
Transport shuttle
Summary A short quick ascent to the tippy-top of an iconic granite dome – the panoramic view is worth every ounce of effort. Feast your eyes on amazing peaks and the foothills ever-so-far below.

To scan the park's peaks, you'll be hard-pressed to find an easier or more rewarding short hike. Almost 400 steps shoot up over a quarter-mile to a railed-in corridor on its spine. You do *not* want to be here during a lightning storm. From the summit you're staring down at the Middle Fork of the Kaweah River, across to Sawtooth Peak (12,343ft) south in the Mineral King region,

and the toward the peaks of the Great Western Divide to the east, including the spike of Black Kaweah (13,765ft). Near sunset, the monolith-like crags of Castle Rocks (9180ft) to the southeast cast dramatic shadows.

BIG TREES TRAIL

Duration 1 hour
Distance 1.2-mile round-trip
Difficulty easy; elevation change +80ft
Start/Finish Giant Forest Museum
Nearest Town/Facilities Giant Forest Museum, 0.2 miles
Transport shuttle
Summary A paved trail circling a lush meadow surrounded by giant sequoias, this walk shows off examples of some the parks' best natural features, all visible within one small area.

Starting from the 'Trail Center' next to the museum, follow the path that loops pretty **Round Meadow**. Giant sequoias edge the border, and interpretive panels give the lowdown on sequoia ecology, explaining why areas such as this support these monster trees. The wildflowers peak in summer, giving the meadow amazing bursts of color. This is one of the park's fully accessible trails; starting from the dedicated handicapped parking lot shortens the overall trail length to half a mile.

Kings Canyon National Park

A fine stand of giant sequoias and an interpretive trail through a beautiful meadow are on the menu here.

GENERAL GRANT TREE TRAIL

Duration 30 minutes
Distance 0.5-mile round-trip
Difficulty easy; elevation gain +30ft
Start/Finish General Grant Grove parking lot
Nearest Town/Facilities Grant Grove Visitor Center, 1 mile
Transport private
Summary A short, paved, self-guided interpretive loop through one of the parks' most extraordinary giant sequoia groves. The General Grant Tree is the third-largest tree in the world.

To the east of the parking lot, you can see the cheerfully named tree cluster of **Happy**

Family. At the trailhead, bear right and begin a counter-clockwise loop. Most of the monster sequoias in this grove are named for US states, and the first you come across is the **Pennsylvania Tree**. Just beyond is the **Robert E Lee Tree**, which, like the grove itself, is another Civil War–era namesake. What looks like submerged logs in front of it are actually its exposed roots – the accumulated damage from years of visitors' footsteps.

Past the Lee Tree is the **Fallen Monarch**, a toppled log so big that its hollow core has been used as housing, a hotel and saloon and then as horse stables. Walk through a mix of young sequoias and other conifers, including sugar pine and white fir, until you reach the impressive **General Grant Tree**.

Further on is the one-room **Gamlin Pioneer Cabin**, built from sugar pine in 1872 by the first white settlers in this area. To see another good view of the Grant Tree, detour right here from the main loop and bear up and around to the left. The path leads to a peaceful overlook called **North Grant View** and, unlike the rest of the trail, there's rarely anyone here to share the scenery.

The **California Tree** has had some coddling. Struck by lightning in 1967, the top incinerated and fire simmered inside until the park service grew concerned that burning branches would hurt visitors. A nimble park employee strung a rope between two adjacent trees and extinguished the blaze with a hose.

Amble on until you reach the parking area.

ZUMWALT MEADOW

Duration 1 hour
Distance 1.5-mile round-trip
Difficulty easy; elevation gain +50ft
Start/Finish Zumwalt Meadow parking lot
Nearest Town/Facilities water and restrooms, Roads End, 1.5 miles
Transport private
Summary An extremely scenic and flat loop around a gorgeous meadow, this is a fine choice for families. The quiet mixed forest trail traces a section of the Kings River, and flaunts knockout canyon wall views.

Zumwalt Meadow has been outfitted as an interpretive trail, but you need to buy an accompanying pamphlet ($1.50) for the descriptions of the numbered signposts. If the self-service box at the trailhead has run out, pick one up at the Roads End permit office.

From the parking area, walk parallel to the river then across a suspension bridge spanning the South Fork of the Kings River. Behind you to the north is a view of 8717ft North Dome, with a sheer cliff drop of over 3600ft, equal to Yosemite's El Capitan. At the junction, go right, beginning a counter-clockwise loop through a forest of big-leaf maple, dogwood, incense cedars, black oak, white fir and ponderosa pines. A swath of stumps are the remnants of an avalanche that steamrolled part of the forest after heavy snowfall in 1968 and 1969, opening up the area to more sunlight. To the southeast are the granite half-mile-high cliffs of Grand Sentinel. The trail ascends and continues over a talus slope with great views of the green meadow and the high area cliffs. Stop number 11 points out the geological feature of dikes, the white seams seen in granite boulders. Continue left at the Roads End sign and follow the Kings River bank back through ferns and a carpet of soft pine needles.

DAY HIKES
Sequoia National Park

These more testing routes take you to booming waterfalls and massive sequoias, with the potential for bear sightings along the way.

MARBLE FALLS

Duration 3–4 hours
Distance 7.8-mile round-trip
Difficulty moderate–demanding; elevation change +2000ft
Start/Finish Potwisha campground, Marble Falls Trailhead
Nearest Town/Facilities Potwisha campground
Transport private
Summary A lower elevation hike following the curves of chaparral-blanketed hills, it parallels a river canyon to a thundering cascade. Prime time is March through May, when the wildflowers are blooming and the heat is still mild.

Because of the low elevation and hot summer temperatures, this is a good spring

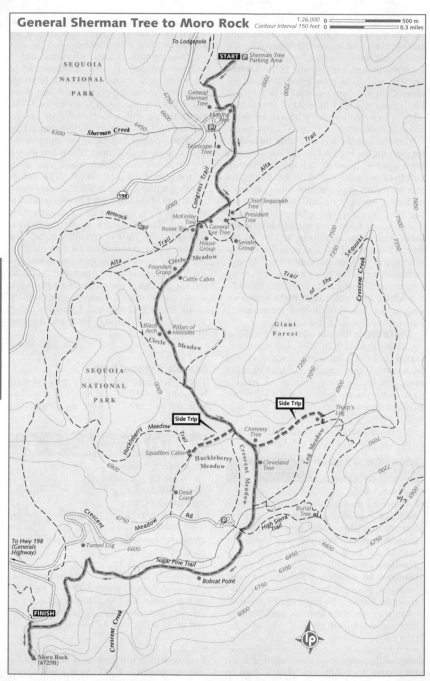

General Sherman Tree to Moro Rock

1:26,000
Contour Interval 150 feet

0 ⎯⎯⎯⎯⎯ 500 m
0 ⎯⎯⎯⎯⎯ 0.3 miles

To Lodgepole

START P Sherman Tree Parking Area

SEQUOIA NATIONAL PARK

General Sherman Tree

Leaning Tree P

Sherman Creek

Telescope Tree

6300
6450
6600
6750
7050
7100

Rimrock Trail

198

Congress Trail

McKinley Tree
Room Tree
General Tree
Lee Tree
House Group
Founders Group
Cattle Cabin

Chief Sequoyah Tree
President Tree
Senate Group

Alta Trail

Circle Meadow

Alta Trail

Black Arch
Pillars of Hercules
Circle Meadow

SEQUOIA NATIONAL PARK

Giant Forest

Trail of the Sequoias

Crescent Creek

7650
7600
7500
7350
7300
7200
7050
7000

Side Trip

Huckleberry Meadow Trail

Squatters Cabin

Side Trip

Chimney Tree

Cleveland Tree

Tharp's Log

Log Meadow

Burial Tree

Crescent Meadow

Huckleberry Meadow

Dead Giant

Crescent Meadow Rd

P

High Sierra Trail

6900
6750
6600

To Hwy 198 (Generals Highway)

Tunnel Log

Sugar Pine Trail

Bobcat Point

6450
6300
6150
6000

FINISH

Moro Rock (6725ft)

Crescent Creek

IP

season hike. Summer visitors should start in the early morning. Park near campsite number 14 and follow the dirt road to a concrete ditch. Look for a sign to the trail, which begins steeply to the right. The beginning of the hike is the most challenging, with a quick ascent via switchbacks. Watch for poison oak, which can be found in this first section.

Past the switchbacks, tree cover gives way to scrubby chaparral and the trail continues north along the eastern side of **Deep Canyon**, with views of the Marble Fork of the Kaweah River. The path crosses several streams and ducks into wooded areas, and then veers towards the river and the booming falls, dead-ending in a heap of boulders.

Retrace your steps to return.

GENERAL SHERMAN TREE TO MORO ROCK

Duration 2½–4 hours
Distance 6 miles one way
Difficulty moderate; elevation change +300ft (at Moro Rock)
Start main (upper) Sherman Tree parking area
Finish Moro Rock parking lot
Nearest Town/Facilities Giant Forest Museum, 3.5 miles
Transport shuttle
Summary A deviation from the popular Congress Trail, this mostly flat one-way hike takes in huge sequoias, gorgeous green meadows and the pinnacle of Moro Rock. Expect stretches of blissful solitude and potential bear sightings.

From the main parking lot/upper shuttle stop for the General Sherman Tree, the paved trail quickly descends through towering sequoias as it heads towards the General Sherman Tree. From an overlook on the way down, you have the best view of the **General Sherman Tree**. Go left onto the well-marked Congress Trail, bearing right at a junction, and then quickly jog left, following a sign for the McKinley Tree. At a five-way junction by the **McKinley Tree**, continue straight on the dirt trail towards **Cattle Cabin**. Pass the hollow-bottom **Room Tree** and the pretty cluster of the **Founders Group**, walking through tufts of ferns and corn lilies. Approaching the bright green

strip of 'C'-shaped **Circle Meadow**, there are no more crowds, and all you can hear is the wind and the birds. Trace the meadow and you'll come to another well-named tree group, the **Pillars of Hercules**. Stand between them and look up for a heroic view; you'll notice that only one is still alive. The trail then goes through the huge charred maw of the **Black Arch** tree.

At a four-way intersection, lush **Crescent Meadow** comes into view. Go left at the junction to continue or make a 0.6-mile round-trip detour to the Squatters' Cabin by going right on the trail marked 'Huckleberry Meadow.' At less than half a mile is the hollow-bodied **Chimney Tree**, and another detour opportunity to visit the tree house of **Tharps Log**. Continue right (south) along Crescent Meadow, walking its length on a trail that is now paved.

In less than a half-mile, join a spectacular segment of the High Sierra Trail, going right (west) and taking in marvelous ridge views. Stop at the **Bobcat Point** overlook to take in the Great Western Divide and Kaweah Canyon. In a quarter-mile, cross **Crescent Creek**, bypassing a use trail to the water for the more defined Sugar Pine Trail above. Go left and follow it for 0.9 miles to **Moro Rock**. Climb your final prize for some of the best views in the parks, and return to the starting point via park shuttle.

Kings Canyon National Park

Try this walk for views of a huge waterfall with the pay-off of a cooling swim on the way back.

MIST FALLS

Duration 3–5 hours
Distance 9.5-mile round-trip
Difficulty moderate; elevation change +600ft
Start/Finish Roads End permit office; Mist Falls-Paradise Valley Trailhead
Nearest Town/Facilities water and restrooms, Roads End permit office
Transport private
Summary A longish walk without significant ascent shows off the beauty of Kings Canyon.

The trail begins just past the Roads End permit office, soon crossing a footbridge over Copper Creek. Travel through sparse cedar and pine forest and low areas of ferns and reeds until a well-marked three-way junction. Turn left (north) and begin a gradual climb that runs parallel to powerful cataracts in the boulder-saturated Kings River.

Sandy stone–framed stairs lead to a granite knob overlook, with wide southern views of Avalanche Peak and the oddly pointed Sphinx (9143ft) behind you. Follow the cairn piles up the rock face and continue briefly through shady forest to **Mist Falls**, one of the largest waterfalls in the parks.

Returning, retrace your steps until the three-way junction 2 miles from Roads End. Instead of heading back on the trail to Roads End, bear left and cross the bridge over the Kings River, briefly joining the Bubbs Creek Trail. After less than a quarter-mile, turn right onto the Kanawyer Loop Trail, which is mostly flat and less used. The tree canopy opens up to show sprawling talus slopes and southern canyon walls. Pass a large boulder curiously inscribed 'W.B. 1912' and rejoin the river. After the **Muir Rock** swimming hole, crossing the red bridge back to the opposite shore. Most people jump in at Muir Rock, but the sandy beach here sees few swimmers and is wonderful for a quick cool down. Continue right to the Roads End parking area.

BACKCOUNTRY HIKES

With 850 miles of marked trails, the parks are a backpacking heaven. Cedar Grove and Mineral King offer the best backcountry access, while the Jenny Lakes Wilderness Area (accessible from the Big Meadows Trailhead near Big Meadows Campground) boasts pristine meadows and lakes at lower elevations. Trails usually open by mid-May. Bear-proof food canisters, which are sometimes mandatory, can be rented at the parks' visitor centers ($5 per trip) and markets.

Wilderness permits are required for all overnight trips and are available at visitor centers and ranger stations. There's a $15 wilderness camping fee per group during the quota season from late May through late September, and free self-issue permits can be obtained at the visitor center closest to the trailhead outside that period. If you want to reserve ahead in season, requests must be received two weeks in advance of the trip date, beginning in March of that year. Each trail sets aside a third of its available permits for first-come, first-served walk-ups; they become available at 1pm *the day before*. Permit applications can be downloaded from the park **website** (www.nps .gov/seki/planyourvisit/wilderness_permits.htm). Fax or mail your request to **Wilderness Permit Reservations** (☎ 559-565-3766; fax 559-565-4239; Sequoia & Kings Canyon NP, 47050 Generals Hwy #60, Three Rivers, CA 93271).

Sequoia National Park

Shoulder your backpack and head for alpine lakes and meadows, with marmots aplenty.

MONARCH LAKES

Duration 2 days
Distance 8.4-mile round-trip
Difficulty moderate–demanding; elevation change +2580ft
Start/Finish Sawtooth-Monarch parking lot, Sawtooth Trailhead
Nearest Town/Facilities Mineral King Ranger Station, 1 mile
Transport private
Summary An excellent out-and-back high-country trip to two alpine lakes at the base of jagged Sawtooth Peak. New backpackers will appreciate that it's not very long or back-breakingly steep. A marmot-lover's paradise!

Steepish stairs start this higher-altitude trek, and at the junction with the Timber Gap trail a quarter-mile in, you can see the end of Mineral King Rd and snow-brushed peaks to the south. Continue straight, following the marker for Sawtooth Pass. Corn lilies and paintbrush speckle grassy **Groundhog Meadow**, named for the prolific whistling marmots that seem to scramble everywhere you look during this hike. Just before leaving the meadow to cross Monarch Creek, glance up to the left to appreciate a small burbling waterfall.

On the far bank of the creek, a shady wooded spot is the perfect place to have lunch. From here, begin ascending a stretch of loose and lazy switchbacks with goosebump views. It's a slow and steady climb through red fir forest that won't leave you too winded, though the altitude can get bothersome the higher you climb. Bold deer and the occasional grouse can be seen on the hillsides. The trail crosses into the **Chihuahua Bowl**, a basin named after a booming mining region of Mexico.

After flipping to the opposite side of the ridgeline, at a little over 3 miles there's a signed junction for the Crystal Lake Trail, which takes a hard and steep right. Bear left and continue straight instead. The tree line wavers and fades away, opening up gorgeous views of the Monarch Creek canyon, Timber Gap and the peaks of the Great Western Divide. The distinctive pitch of 12,343ft Sawtooth Peak is visible ahead. A walk through a large talus field and some easy stream crossings bring you to **Lower Monarch Lake** at 10,400ft, and the round top of Mineral Peak points up directly south. There are a number of established campsites by Lower Monarch Lake, as well as backcountry food lockers. The trail stops here, but **Upper Monarch Lake** can be reached another quarter-mile up to the southeast. When you are ready, retrace your steps to return.

Those looking for a challenging cross-country hike can use the lake as a base to reach scree-covered **Sawtooth Pass**. It's 1.3 miles further on and another 1200ft up; ask rangers at Mineral King for route recommendations.

THE BACK DOOR TO MT WHITNEY

If you don't want the hassle of getting a permit for the Mt Whitney Trail, or just want something different, consider walking there from Sequoia & Kings Canyon. It takes about four to six days from Crescent Meadow via the High Sierra Trail to the John Muir Trail, with no Whitney Zone permit (see p248) required. The two regulations you need to follow within the Whitney area? You gotta pack out your poop (free 'WAG bags' are available at Crabtree), and you are required to use a bear canister.

One-way hikers can use one of the many hiker shuttle services:

High Sierra Transportation (☎ 760-872-1111; www.highsierratransportation.com) In Bishop.

Sequoia Sightseeing Tours (☎ 559-561-4189; www.sequoiatours.com) In Three Rivers.

CRESCENT MEADOW TO BEARPAW MEADOW

Duration 2 days
Distance 22-mile round-trip
Difficulty moderate–demanding; elevation change +1100ft
Start/Finish Crescent Meadow parking lot/ shuttle stop; High Sierra Trailhead
Nearest Town/Facilities Giant Forest Museum, 3 miles
Transport shuttle
Summary Departing from a grove of giant sequoias, on this trail you can get a small taste of a route that continues on to cross the Sierras, with wonderful views of the Great Western Divide.

From the trailhead at Crescent Meadow (6700ft), the High Sierra Trail commences as an undulating traverse high along the forested north side of the canyon of the **Kaweah River's Middle Fork**. Crossing numerous streams, many with pleasant campsites, the wildflower-trimmed trail passes in and out of mixed forest and unfolds with a continuing panorama of the Kaweah Basin and the mountains of the Great Western Divide. The first handful of miles are exposed and hot, so an early start is recommended, especially in summer. A wee bit under a mile from the trailhead is the first highlight, the **Eagle View lookout** point, an excellent vantage point from which to see Moro Rock, to the west, and Castle Rocks, across the canyon. The trail then goes over sections of **Panther Creek** and soon after crossing **Mehrton Creek** at 5.5 miles, it passes a spur trail leading north to the Alta Trail and continues to a bridge over **Buck Creek**. From there it ascends via switchbacks to **Bearpaw Meadow** (7800ft) and intersects a trail leading north to Elizabeth Pass and descending south to **Little Bearpaw and Redwood Meadows**. Campsites are a few yards ahead and south of the trail in the forest.

A seasonal ranger station and the Bearpaw High Sierra Camp (p241) are on either side of the trail a short distance ahead. A number of good day hikes continue on from Bearpaw Meadow, as well as a multi-day trek to Mt Whitney. Return along the same route.

SEQUOIA & KINGS CANYON NATIONAL PARKS

SEQUOIA & KINGS CANYON NATIONAL PARKS

Rae Lakes Loop

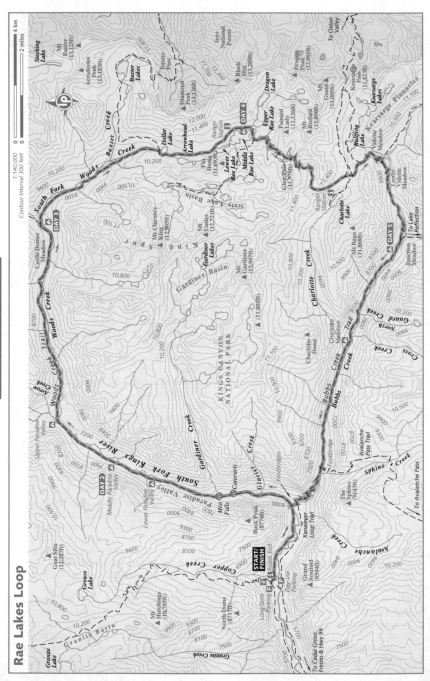

Kings Canyon National Park

This varied, five-day loop showcases some of the best features of the park.

RAE LAKES LOOP

Duration 5 days
Distance 41.5-mile round-trip
Difficulty demanding; elevation change +6943ft
Start/Finish Roads End permit office, Mist Falls-Paradise Valley Trailhead
Nearest Town/Facilities water and restrooms, Roads End permit office
Transport private
Summary The best loop hike in Kings Canyon tours gorgeous forests and meadows, crosses one pass and skirts a chain of jewel-like lakes beneath the Sierra crest in the heart of the Kings Canyon high country.

DAY 1: ROADS END TO MIDDLE PARADISE VALLEY
4–4½ hours, 7.6 miles

See the Mist Falls hike, p229, for a description of the 4.6-mile trail from Roads End to **Mist Falls**. A series of short switchbacks takes you to the top of these falls, and beyond them, a larger and longer set of rocky switchbacks leads you up and into forest above the river. The trail levels out and enters **Paradise Valley**, one hour from the falls. The South Fork of the Kings River flows through forest and meadows, inviting you five minutes further to the first campsites at **Lower Paradise Valley** (6586ft), 1.1 miles beyond Mist Falls. Continue up the beautiful valley, along the river and through fir forest, 1.1 miles further to the ponderosa – and sugar-pine-shaded campsites at **Middle Paradise Valley** (6619ft). It has a nice beach and is typically less crowded than Lower Paradise Valley, with more open views.

DAY 2: MIDDLE PARADISE VALLEY TO WOODS CREEK
4–4½ hours, 7.8 miles

Just beyond the campsite, pass through an open avalanche-cleared area and ascend near the cascading river, passing ponderosa pines, white firs and incense cedars. The trail ascends gradually before dropping back down along the river in a dense forest to **Upper Paradise Valley** (6876ft), at the confluence of the South Fork of the Kings River and Woods Creek, 2.2 miles from Middle Paradise Valley.

Cross a massive log spanning the river, and head south a couple of minutes along the river's true left (east) bank and cross a tiny log footbridge. The trail turns southeast, passing some large sugar pines, and begins a steady ascent up dusty switchbacks on an open slope. Crossing the shoulder of a granite ridge, you enter the forested canyon above Woods Creek.

The trail traverses east, ascending gently, high above rushing Woods Creek. The trail gradually draws near the creek and continues up the forested valley. Ascending an open, manzanita-covered slope amid small granite boulders, the dusty trail rises to a gated fence (8113ft), two hours from the river crossing.

Pass through the gate and descend to the open avalanche-formed **Castle Dome Meadow** beneath the spectacular, polished white granite of the **Castle Domes**. Cross the meadow and re-enter a pine forest. The views of the Castle Domes get better and better as you continue. Climb some stone steps and pass through a gate, going down along Woods Creek to a signed junction with the John Muir Trail.

Turn right (east) onto the southbound John Muir Trail and cross Woods Creek on a large wooden-planked steel suspension bridge. Two campsites (8492ft) are on the south side of Woods Creek; one near the trail and the other downstream a short distance.

DAY 3: WOODS CREEK TO MIDDLE RAE LAKE
3½–4 hours, 5.8 miles

Heading south, the trail rolls easily on open slopes along the west side of South Fork Woods Creek, with good views back of Castle Domes and the granite high country above the confluence. Forty-five minutes from the campsite, cross a side stream that descends from a lake northeast of Mt Clarence King and continue upvalley. Water cascades through granite bedrock, and the trail rises over granite to descend into a small, lodgepole-lined meadow, where you cross a small wooden footbridge.

Cross the stream that cascades over a cleft in the rock as it drains Sixty Lake Basin. This is a good place to stop for water. Beyond the stream, pass through a gated fence. Foxtail pines dot the dry slope above the trail as you continue up to small **Dollar Lake** (10,240ft), which is 2½ hours (3.7 miles) from the Woods Creek crossing.

Near the north end of Dollar Lake, a faint trail branches east, leading to **Baxter Pass** (12,270ft). The striking view of Fin Dome (11,693ft) above Dollar Lake sets the theme of mountain splendor that typifies Rae Lakes. Skirting Dollar Lake's west shore, continue up and arrive at the larger **Arrowhead Lake** (10,300ft).

Crossing the outlet, follow along Arrowhead Lake's east side, with fine views of Fin Dome. Moving away from the lake, the trail ascends gradually to large and beautiful **Lower Rae Lake**. The trail rolls gently through, crossing several small side streams and passing the signed spur trail to the usually unoccupied Rae Lakes ranger station. Continue to the signed turnoff for the campsites above the eastern shore of **Middle Rae Lake** (10,550ft) and descend toward the clear azure lake.

DAY 4: MIDDLE RAE LAKE TO JUNCTION MEADOW
5–5½ hours, 9.9 miles

Return to the John Muir Trail and turn right (south). The trail soon turns southwest across the isthmus separating Middle and Upper Rae Lakes. Walk along the northern shore of **Upper Rae Lake**, where the view of Fin Dome remains marvelous. Cross the connector stream between the lakes and come to a signboard for the Rae Lakes area, where the faint trail to Sixty Lake Basin heads northwest (right), leaving the John Muir Trail.

At this junction, stay on the John Muir Trail, which continues south (left). Ascend well-graded switchbacks above the west side of Upper Rae Lake. Above, more switchbacks take you up a talus slope to a tarn-filled basin, from where Glen Pass is visible ahead on the dark, rocky ridgeline. The trail passes nine small mountain lakes, which glisten in the barren cirque to the west. Turning southwest, you ascend above another aquamarine lake east of the trail, then make a series of switchbacks up talus, with dramatic views back to the north, to narrow **Glen Pass** (11,978ft), 2 miles from the Sixty Lake Basin junction. In the distance to the southwest are massive Mt Brewer (13,570ft), with its snowy northeast face,

and other peaks along the Great Western Divide and Kings-Kern Divide. Mt Bago (11,868ft) is the distinctive reddish peak in the foreground.

Glen Pass is a narrow ridge topped with black rock and ranging in width from 10ft to 20ft. Traverse southwest one to two minutes along the length of this saddle to start your descent. Gravelly but well-graded switchbacks take you down on a steep scree slope toward the pothole tarn at the tree line 15 minutes below. A few whitebark pines grow along its southern shore. Get water here, for the next reliable water is not until the outlet of Bullfrog Lake several miles ahead.

Head down the narrow canyon, passing above a snow-fed, talus-lined pool until the trail swings south. Twenty minutes from the pothole tarn, you have a view of charming Charlotte Lake and remarkable Charlotte Dome. The trail then contours high above Charlotte Lake. Passing an eastbound trail to Kearsarge Pass 2.1 miles from Glen Pass, the trail arrives after 0.2 miles at a sandy four-way junction. The west (right) fork leads to Charlotte Lake and the northeast (left) fork is another trail to Kearsarge Pass.

Continuing straight (south), you catch a glimpse of distant **Forester Pass**, the highest pass on the John Muir Trail, at the head of Bubbs Creek as you cross a low rise and begin to descend. Fifteen minutes (0.7 miles) from the four-way junction, reach the junction with the trail heading northeast (left) to Bullfrog Lake and Kearsarge Lakes. The scenic descent south twice crosses the outlet from Bullfrog Lake to reach **Lower Vidette Meadow** (9480ft) in 30 minutes (1.5 miles).

Leaving the John Muir Trail, turn right (southwest) and follow the trail down Bubbs Creek past campsites along the forested edge of Lower Vidette Meadow. Descending west along tumbling Bubbs Creek, the trail crosses several side streams and a large rock slide, then finds shade beneath some large, red firs. Beneath soaring granite walls on either side of the canyon, the trail drops steadily down to the now narrow and rushing Bubbs Creek. Passing a large waterfall, your descent continues a short distance to aspen-filled **Junction Meadow** (8080ft), 2.9 miles from Lower Vidette Meadow.

Pass the signed junction with the trail to East Lake and Lake Reflection. Continue five minutes to grassy campsites.

DAY 5: JUNCTION MEADOW TO ROADS END
5–5½ hours, 10.4 miles

From the west end of Junction Meadow, the trail continues downvalley. Granite walls tower on both sides, and as you descend toward Charlotte Creek, the superb climbing area of Charlotte Dome is to the north.

Pass **Charlotte Meadow**, beneath white firs just east of Charlotte Creek, 3.8 miles from Junction Meadow. Crossing Charlotte Creek, the trail continues west, 3 miles down Bubbs Creek to Sphinx Creek (6240ft), where the trail to Avalanche Pass crosses Bubbs Creek on a wooden footbridge.

The Bubbs Creek Trail descends steeply on hot, open switchbacks, providing sweeping views into Kings Canyon and of the granite pinnacle of the Sphinx (9143ft) towering above Bubbs Creek. Reaching the valley floor, the trail crosses braided Bubbs Creek over four separate wooden footbridges in close succession and continues across the steel Bailey bridge spanning the South Fork of the Kings River. Just beyond the bridge is the junction of the Bubbs Creek Trail with the Paradise Valley Trail, 1.7 miles from Sphinx Creek. From here, retrace your steps from Day 1 over level ground, 1.9 miles back to Roads End (5036ft).

DRIVING

Experience the park on four wheels via an exciting ascent to Mineral King or a shuttle ride through some of the top attractions.

MINERAL KING RD

Duration 1.5 hours
Distance 25 miles one way
Start Hwy 198
Finish Sawtooth-Monarch parking lot
Nearest Town/Facilities Three Rivers, 6 miles
Transport private
Summary Steel your nerves and take your time, because this madcap road will test your mettle. Skirting the canyon of the Kaweah River's East Fork, this roller-coaster ride of sharp turns ascends to 7500ft.

In Three Rivers, 3 miles south of the Ash Mountain Entrance, take a deep breath and turn off Hwy 198 onto well-signed Mineral King Rd. On your right you'll start to see long sections of **water flume** cutting a sharp line across the hillside. The metal flume you see now was erected in 1947, replacing the original sequoia structure from 1899, which brought hydroelectric power to this remote region. Approximately 9 miles in, look for a cluster of small **natural pools** carved into a smooth granite surface next to the road. The holes are just large enough to fit two people, and on a hot summer day, there's nothing better than being in the cool water.

The park boundary resumes at **Lookout Point**, where there are pullovers and good canyon views. Occasionally you'll see water troughs to the side of the road; they were built for horses pulling stagecoaches – the original users of this road in the 1800s. Some sections of the road are narrow and unpaved, but the grade is never too difficult – just remember that uphill vehicles have the right of way. Across from the Atwell Mill Ranger Residence is a large **steam engine**, a remnant of an old lumber mill used by the Kaweah colonists (see the boxed text, p245) after they lost their claims in Giant Forest. Your final destination is just past the ranger station, where Mineral King Valley unfolds and the high country beckons with unique granite peaks.

Spend the night at one of the campgrounds or at the Silver City Mountain Resort – you really don't want to weave your back the same day.

MORO ROCK–CRESCENT MEADOW RD

Duration 1 hour (with some pull-over time)
Distance 6-mile round-trip
Start/Finish Giant Forest Museum
Nearest Town/Facilities Giant Forest Museum
Transport shuttle
Summary A narrow, windy and sometimes pockmarked road leads to a number of the park's most popular attractions. Moro Rock and Crescent Meadow demand detours, and interesting sequoias line the way.

The park is talking about closing this road to private vehicles in the summer, in which case you can take the shuttle. But why wait? Take the shuttle anyway! Trailers and RVs are strongly discouraged from using this road, and it closes to cars in winter.

From the shuttle bus parking area at the Giant Forest Museum, the Moro Rock–Crescent Meadow Rd swoops into the southwestern section of the Giant Forest. About a mile in you'll find the **Auto Log**, a hefty sequoia that fell in 1917. To give early visitors a sense of scale, a flat section was carved onto its top and the tree was used as part of the road. You can't drive on it anymore, but you can walk on it and imagine.

Turn into the small parking area (we told you to take the shuttle!) to see the pale granite dome of **Moro Rock**. Continuing on, the mesmerizing flamelike roots of the **Buttress Tree** face the road. Without warning, the 2300-year-old tree collapsed in 1959. On the opposite side of the road just a bit further is the **Parker Group**, named for the 8-person family of a former park superintendent.

The renown of Yosemite's Wawona Tunnel Tree often prompted visitors to inquire about Sequoia's drive-through tree, but it didn't have one. So when a 275ft sequoia bit the dust and went splat across the road in 1937, the park took advantage of this gift and promptly cut a passageway for cars. This **Tunnel Log** has an 8ft by 17ft opening, which larger vehicles can skirt using an adjacent bypass.

The road ends at the periphery of **Crescent Meadow**, a lush lawn of deep green. Return as you arrived.

OTHER ACTIVITIES

SWIMMING

The parks have excellent swimming spots, but take note: drownings in both the Kings and Kaweah Rivers are the leading cause of death in the park. In Kings Canyon, Muir Rock (p224) is the favored swimming hole, and in the Giant Sequoia National Monument, Hume Lake (p225) is dreamy on a hot day. There are a number of sheltered river nooks along the Kings Canyon Scenic Byway between Yucca Point and Boyden Cave, but never go in if you see white water.

HORSEBACK RIDING

In Kings Canyon, the **Cedar Grove Pack Station** (☎ summer 559-565-3464, winter 559-337-2314; ☼ spring-Oct) is open when snowfall permits,

with day rides available until its main backcountry business gets busy, which is usually about mid-July. Half-day rides are $65, all-day rambles are $100 and hourly rates start at $30. It also does walk and lead rides for little kids for $10. For backcountry trips, stock rentals are $80 per day and double if you need someone to ride it. Just a quarter-mile north of Grant Grove Village, **Grant Grove Stables** (☎ 335-9292; ☼ 8am-6pm May-Sep) leads one- and two-hour trail rides near the General Grant Grove and to the Sequoia Lake Overlook at comparable rates.

In Giant Sequoia National Monument, the **Horse Corral Pack Station** (☎ 559-565-3404; www.horsecorralpackers.com) also has trail rides, including an all-day excursion to Mitchell Peak ($185, including lunch).

ROCK CLIMBING

Sequoia & Kings Canyon have tons of excellent rock-climbing options, though many of the best require a long hike in. The most spectacular is an 1800ft granite wall in the Valhalla Cirque called the Angel Wings, nicknamed 'an alpine El Capitan' by the renowned climber and photographer Galen Rowell. Other more accessible Sequoia locations include Moro Rock, Little Baldy and Hospital Rock. In Kings Canyon, the Bubbs Creek Trail has good multipitch climbs at Charlito Dome and Charlotte Dome, just before Charlotte Creek.

SPELUNKING

The caves in Sequoia & Kings Canyon are so extensive that the parks could have been designated on the basis of the cave systems alone. Of all the California caves more than a mile long, half of them are here, as well as Lilburn Cave – at 17 surveyed miles it's the longest known cave in the state. New caves are constantly being discovered, like the Ursa Minor in August 2006, and new species of troglobites (animals that live in dark caves) have recently been identified in Crystal Cave, including an eyeless insect and a tiny pseudoscorpion.

Boyden Cavern (p224) and Crystal Cave (p221) are the only developed caves open to the public, and the latter has 'Wild Cave Tours' for those who want to do some serious shimmying and exploring.

FISHING

The rivers, lakes and creeks found here are an angler's paradise, and tackle is sold at park market areas. Kings Canyon's Lewis Creek, Bubbs Creek and the Motor Nature Trail (River Rd in Cedar Grove) are popular spots, as is Hume Lake (p225), where the Forest Service stocks trout. A fishing license, which can be obtained at park markets, is required for those 16 and older. The visitor centers can provide you with a copy of the complete park regulations.

WINTER ACTIVITIES

Winter is a special time to visit Sequoia and Kings Canyon National Parks. A thick blanket of snow drapes over trees and meadows, the pace of activity slows and a hush falls over the roads and trails. Note that snow often closes Generals Hwy between Grant Grove and Giant Forest and that tire chains may be required at any time. For up-to-date road conditions call ☎ 559-565-3341 or check www.nps .gov/seki.

Snowshoeing and **cross-country skiing** are both hugely popular activities, with about 40 miles of marked but ungroomed trails crisscrossing the Grant Grove and Giant Forest areas, and trail maps are available at the visitor centers. The tree-marked trails connect with more in the Giant Sequoia National Monument and the 50 miles of groomed terrain maintained by the private **Montecito Lake Resort** (day pass incl lunch $30); see p242. Winter road closures make excellent for excellent cross-country skiing at Panoramic Point Rd, Big Meadows Rd and Moro Rock – Crescent Meadow Rd, and there are also snow-play areas at Big Stump and Colombine in Grant Grove and at Wolverton in Giant Forest.

Equipment rentals are available at Grant Grove Village, the Wuksachi Lodge, the Wolverton hut (on weekends) and the Montecito Lake Resort. On Saturdays and holidays, rangers lead free two-hour **snowshoe walks** from Wuksachi Lodge and Grant Grove. Free snowshoe use is included, and you can reserve a place at any visitor center or phone ☎ 559-565-4480 (Wuksachi) or ☎ 559-565-4307 (Grant Grove).

And those not intimidated by a steep 6-mile trek can spend the night at the rustic Pear Lake Ski Hut (p240).

SLEEPING

CAMPING

NPS campgrounds are all first-come, first-served, with the exception of Lodgepole and Dorst Creek. Sites come with bear-proof boxes, tables and fire pits; most have flush toilets. The seasonal campgrounds start opening around May and close in September or October, depending on the weather that year. With developed campgrounds, nightly fees revolve around the availability of water. Primitive sites (no potable water) are generally free, and the most expensive sites are those with taps and flush toilets. Free dispersed camping is possible in the Giant Sequoia National Monument; pick up details and a fire permit from a visitor center or ranger station. Reservable campsites in both the parks and Sequoia National Forest can be booked through www.recreation.gov or by calling ☎ 877-444-6777.

Sequoia National Park
LODGEPOLE & WUKSACHI VILLAGE

The only reservable campsites in the Sequoia & Kings Canyon parks are located here. They're large and tend to shoehorn you in, have the best amenities (in summertime) and the ursine companions act the most entitled. Coin-operated showers are available at the Lodgepole Village from April through October (the village closes in winter).

Lodgepole Campground (sites $; ☯ year-round) Situated on the Marble Fork of the Kaweah River, this is the park's biggest and busiest campground, with 214 spots and not a lot of wiggle room between them. It stays open year-round, and the main reason it gets so much action is because it is reservable from late May until early October. If you want a central and surefire location in summer, this is your place; if you want serenity and space, journey on. Some people bring bikes and ride them to the village area, just watch out for the RV nouveau-renters.

Dorst Creek Campground (sites $; ☯ Jul-Aug) Of the 204 sites at the park's second-largest campground, some are definitely better than others. The quieter back sites are for tents only, and the front loops can get jam-packed with RVs. It's often possible to find a spot here, even when Lodgepole is full.

SEQUOIA & KINGS CANYON CAMPGROUNDS

Campground	Location	No of sites	Elevation	Open (approx)	Reservations required?
Atwell Mill	Mineral King	21	6540ft	late May-Oct	no
Azalea	Grant Grove	110	6500ft	year-round	no
Big Meadow	Giant Sequoia NM	40	7600ft	late May–mid-Nov	no
Buckeye Flat	Ash Mountain/Foothills	28	2820ft	Apr-Sep	no
Canyon View	Cedar Grove	23	4600ft	late May–early Oct	no
Cold Springs	Mineral King	40	7504ft	late May-Oct	no
Convict Flat	Giant Sequoia NM	5	4000ft	late May–mid-Nov	no
Crystal Springs	Grant Grove	50	6500ft	mid-May–mid-Sep	no
Dorst Creek	Lodgepole	204	6720ft	Jul-Aug	yes
Hume Lake	Giant Sequoia NM	74	5200ft	late May–mid-Nov	yes
Lodgepole	Lodgepole	214	6720ft	year-round	late May-early Oct
Moraine	Cedar Grove	120	4600ft	summer	no
Potwisha	Foothills	42	2080ft	year-round	no
Princess	Giant Sequoia NM	90	5900ft	late May–mid-Nov	yes
Sentinel	Cedar Grove	82	4600ft	late May-early Oct	no
Sheep Creek	Cedar Grove	111	4600ft	late Apr–mid-Nov	no
Stony Creek	Giant Sequoia NM	49	6400ft	late May–mid-Nov	May-Sep
Sunset	Grant Grove	157	6500ft	late May–early Oct	no
Upper Stony Creek	Giant Sequoia NM	18	6400ft	late May–mid-Nov	no

All campgrounds have: bear boxes, parking, picnic tables, fire pits and trash receptacles.

 Drinking water   Flush toilets   Ranger Station   Wheelchair Accessible   Dogs Allowed (On Leash)   Grocery Store Nearby

ASH MOUNTAIN/FOOTHILLS

At an average elevation of 2500ft, the two area campgrounds are very hot and dry in summer, when they are often packed with groups and sometimes veer on the rowdy side. **Potwisha Campground** (sites $; year-round) has 42 sites plus some nice swimming spots in the nearby Marble Fork of the Kaweah River, and **Buckeye Flat Campground** (sites $; Apr-Sep) has 28 sites and sits in a canyon down a windy road off-limits to RVs and trailers. Both have decent tree shade.

MINERAL KING

Two first-come, first served campgrounds sit near the end of Mineral King Rd. Note that the water taps are turned off in mid-October (so the pipes don't freeze), and

Facilities	Description	Page
	Heavy forest canopy; well-spaced sites; tent only	below
	Surrounded by evergreens; a quarter-mile walk to sequoia grove	240
	Creekside campsites off Big Meadow Rd	240
	In open stand of oaks; hot and sometimes rowdy; tent only	opposite
	Shady sites, some with canyon ridge views; used as overflow; tent only	240
	Close to ranger station; pretty creekside setting; tent only	below
	Secluded and primitive sites near Yucca Point; tree-sheltered views of cliffs	240
	Sites are wooded, well spaced and generally very quiet; smallest campground in Grant Grove area	240
	Sprawling campground; spots usually available; quieter tent-only sites in back	237
	Lakeside hot spot; popular with families and anglers	240
	Busiest campground and fills up quickly in summer; closely packed sites; some features available in summer only	237
	Large, well-spaced and shaded; used as overflow only	240
	Hot in summer, but no snow in winter	opposite
	Convenient to Kings Canyon Scenic Byway; nicely wooded sites	240
	Centrally located next to village area; fills up the fastest	240
	Pretty creekside loops; not as crowded as Sentinel	240
	Comfortable wooded sites, including some right on creek	240
	Largest campground in Grant Grove; nightly campfire programs in summer	240
	Primitive and mostly quiet sites near Stony Creek Village	240

 Payphone   RV Dump Station

SEQUOIA & KINGS CANYON NATIONAL PARKS

the campgrounds are free for the remaining two weeks.

Cold Springs Campground (sites $; late May-Oct) It's a haul, but so worth it. Just a quarter-mile from the ranger station, this 40-site campground has a peaceful creekside location with ridge views and a gorgeous forest setting of conifers and aspen, and ranger programs in the summer. If you spend the night here at 7500ft, you'll be well on your way to acclimatizing for high-altitude wanderings. Cold Springs often fills up on summer weekends, and you can call the ranger station on Friday afternoon to see whether they still have sites available.

Atwell Mill Campground (sites $; late May-Oct;) A bit smaller, Atwell Mill has 21 quiet sites scattered under sky-obscuring forest canopy. It's located near the East Fork of the Kaweah River in a logged sequoia grove. Getting a site here is rarely a problem, even on weekends.

Kings Canyon National Park
CEDAR GROVE
The Cedar Grove area contains four pleasant seasonal campgrounds clustered near the visitor center and village. The market sells token for the showers (located in the washroom across the parking lot), one of which is wheelchair accessible.

Sentinel Campground (sites $; late May–Oct) This 82-site place is the busiest and most centrally located campground, though it can a bit buggy. If you want to unzip your sleeping bag in the morning and be within staggering distance of hot showers and a cooked breakfast, aim here.

Sheep Creek Campground (sites $; late Apr–mid-Nov) A quarter-mile west of Sentinel, the 111-site has pretty creekside loops. Since Cedar Grove is a bit of a trek, you can guarantee getting a site somewhere unless you roll in very late.

Overflow sites open when needed:

Canyon View Campground (sites $; late May–early Oct) Fair amount of shade; 23 sites, some with canyon ridge views; tents only.

Moraine Campground (sites $; summer;) Well-spaced sites (120); some are fully accessible.

GRANT GROVE
Showers are available from 11am to 4pm near the village cabins; pay at the lodging registration desk. The park concessionaire manages all the noncamping options.

Azalea Campground (sites $; year-round) With nice facilities and pretty stands of evergreens, this 110-site campground stays open year-round. From the campground, it's just a quarter–mile walk to a sequoia grove.

Crystal Springs Campground (sites $; mid-May–mid-Sep) Containing just 50 sites (14 are for groups), Crystal Springs is the smallest campground in the Grant Grove area, and it's usually overlooked in favor of the bigger ones. Sites are wooded, well-spaced and generally very quiet.

Sunset Campground (sites $; late May–early Oct) The largest camping area here, it has 157 decent sites and nightly campfire programs in summer.

Giant Sequoia National Monument
This section of the Sequoia National Forest boasts developed campgrounds aplenty, as well as opportunities for dispersed free camping. All campgrounds are open from approximately the end of May through mid-November, or whenever snow closes the roads.

Hume Lake Campground (sites $) A very popular and reservable lakeside campground, it has 74 uncrowded and shaded campsites, a handful with lake views.

Stony Creek Campground (sites $) Off the Generals Hwy near northern Sequoia National Park, this 49-site, reservable and spacious campground is especially well-liked by families.

Upper Stony Creek Campground (sites $) Across the street, this 18-site, primitive and unpaved campground is blissfully undervisited and quiet. Keep an eye out for the very smart and persistent marauder bears that flit between them.

If you come in late or can't find a site anywhere, Big Meadow Rd is the best place to go for dispersed camping. Other campgrounds of note include the following:

Big Meadow Campground (free) Forty creekside campsites off Big Meadow Rd (paved Forest Service road 14S11).

Convict Flat Campground (sites $) Five secluded and primitive sites near Yucca Point with tree-sheltered views of cliffs dappled with huge yucca plants.

Princess Campground (sites $) Close to the Kings Canyon Scenic Byway, with evocative sequoia stumps at the registration area; 90 reservable sites.

LODGING
Sequoia National Park
LODGEPOLE & WUKSACHI VILLAGE
Pear Lake Ski Hut (☎ 559-565-3759; www.sequoia history.org/pearlake/pearlake.htm; bunk per person $; mid-Dec–Apr) In winter, cross-country skiers with reservations can stay in one of the 10 bunks at this 1940s-era pine and granite building run by the Sequoia Natural History Association. You'll be oh-so-glad to see it after the strenuous 6-mile cross-country ski or snowshoe trek from Wolverton Meadow. Reservations are assigned by a lottery in November. Call or check the website for details.

Wuksachi Lodge (☎ 559-565-4070, 866-807-3598; www.visitsequoia.com; r $$$;) Built in 1999 when the hotel complex at Giant Forest was closed, the Wuksachi is the most upscale lodging and dining option in the parks. The wood-paneled atrium has an inviting stone fireplace and forest views, and spacious rooms with oak furniture have a southwestern feel.

MINERAL KING

Silver City Mountain Resort (☎ summer 559-561-3223, winter 805-461-3223; www.silvercityresort.com; $$, cabins with/without bathroom $$$/$$, chalets $$$-$$$$; ☾ late May-early Oct; ♿ ♿) The only food and lodging option anywhere near these parts, this rustic family-run and family-friendly place has everything from cute and cozy 1950s-era cabins to large new holiday chalets. There's a Ping-Pong table, play structure with swings, and nearby ponds to splash around in – and kids love it. Resources are limited, so all guests must bring their own linens and towels. Most of the cabins don't have electricity, and the property's generator shuts off at 10pm. However, nonguests can buy showers.

Kings Canyon National Park
CEDAR GROVE

Cedar Grove Lodge (☎ 335-5500, ext 300; www.sequoia-kingscanyon.com; r $$; ☾ summer only, front desk 7am-9pm; 🖳) The only indoor sleeping option in the canyon, it offers 21 motel-meets-lodge accommodations, some with kitchenettes. Decor isn't a strong point – the hallways tend toward dingy, the basic bathrooms are cramped and the bedspreads scream frumpy. Try to score one of the three ground-floor rooms with shady furnished patios that have spiffy river views. All the rooms have phones but no TVs. The check-in desk is just inside the market, and they suggest reserving rooms at least a month in advance.

GRANT GROVE

Grant Grove Cabins (☎ 559-335-5500, 866-522-6966; www.sequoia-kingscanyon.com; cabins $$; ☾ year-round; ♿) Set amid colossal sugar pines, 50-some cabins range from the decrepit tent-top shacks in 'Tent City' (open summer only) to the rustic yet comfortable heated duplexes (a few of which are wheelchair accessible) with electricity and private bathrooms. For loud lovebirds, number 9 is the lone hard-sided cabin with a queen bed and no attached neighbors. Nicknamed the 'Honeymoon Cabin,' it tends to be booked solid. The heated cabins are the only ones open year-round.

John Muir Lodge (☎ 559-335-5500, 866-522-6966; www.sequoia-kingscanyon.com; r $$$; ♿) An atmospheric wooden building lined with historic old black-and-white photographs, this newish year-round hotel is a comfortable place to lay your head and still feel like you're in the forest. Wide porches have wooden rocking chairs, and the homespun rooms contain rough-hewn wood furniture with bark trim, rustic wood headboards and patchwork bedspreads. The log-and-branch coat hooks are a supercute touch. Naturally, it has the requisite big stone fireplace you can cozy up to on chilly nights, as well as a handy stash of board games.

Giant Sequoia National Monument

Stony Creek Lodge (☎ 559-335-5500, 866-522-6966; www.sequoia-kingscanyon.com; r $$; ☾ mid-May–mid-Oct; ♿ 🖳) A small homey wood and stone lodge with 11 rooms and standard motel bathrooms, this low-key option is very accommodating to families. Rooms are small, but they always have rollaways available to fit everyone in. Folksy patchwork bed coverings and emerald green carpeting break out of the generic motel mold. When evenings are nippy, they light a fire in the high-beamed foyer.

Muir Trail Lodge (☎ 209-966-3195; www.muirtrail ranch.com; ⊗ Jun-Sep; tent cabin or log cabin per person incl all meals $$-$$$) A popular hike-in high camp and backpackers resupply about a mile from the Pacific Crest and John Muir Trails. Stay in a log cabin or tent cabin and they will whip up all your meals. Guests must stay for a minimum of one week in summer high season, but overnighters are accepted in spring and fall. There are never more than 20 people staying on the property – which generates its own electricity – and it has horses available for rides. Last but not least: it has hot springs!

Montecito Lake Resort (☎ 559-565-3388, 800-227-9900; www.mslodge.com; 8000 Generals Hwy; lodge r & cabins incl meals $$$, 6-person suite incl meals $$$$; 🖵 🖫 👪 👶) Operated by the same woman since 1946, this beautiful mountain-view property changed hands in 2007 and was being renovated at the time of research. During the summer, it's booked as a family vacation camp every night but Saturday (and a few Fridays), so kiddies always rule the roost. Water activities are a huge draw – besides a pool and hot tub, there's a small private lake with waterskiing and sailing. In winter, room rates include use of ski equipment. Rates year-round include buffet meals and selected activities. Nonguests can pay for the dinner buffet ($$$).

Sequoia High Sierra Camp (☎ 866-654-2877; www.sequoiahighcamp.com; room per person without bath incl all meals $$$$; ⊗ mid-Jun–early Oct) How far would you go (and how much would you pony up) for gourmet meals and comfy beds in the high country? At this luxury tent-cabin oasis, guests hike in 1 mile (or 10 miles for the purists) to reach a spectacular 8200ft forest aerie, where they're feted with freshly baked cookies and ice water. Opened in 2006, this pricey off-the-grid and all-inclusive resort is nirvana for active, sociable people who don't think 'luxury camping' is an oxymoron. A rare plot of private land in the thick of the Sequoia National Forest, it's a great base for hiking, and the camp does a twice-weekly shuttle from Cedar Grove for one-way hikes to Kings Canyon. Younger children are not encouraged because of nearby drop-offs.

EATING

SEQUOIA NATIONAL PARK
Lodgepole & Wuksachi Village

Wuksachi Lodge (☎ 559-565-4070, 866-807-3598; www .visitsequoia.com; ⊗ 7-10am, 11:30am-2:30pm & 5-10pm; breakfast & lunch $, dinner mains $$$-$$$$; 👶) The dining room here has a breakfast buffet and soup and salad lunch fare, but dinners are all-out extravagant, with mains like seared mahi-mahi, BBQ tri-tip or filet mignon. Seriously decadent desserts like chocolate mousse and ice-cream sundaes top it off.

Wolverton Meadows BBQ (dinner adult/child $$$/$; ⊗ mid-Jun–Aug) This is an outdoor evening picnic and ranger program; buy tickets at Wuksachi Lodge or the Lodgepole Market.

In the Lodgepole Village complex, open April through October, there are a few different food options. The **Lodgepole Market** (☎ 559-565-3301; ⊗ 8am-8pm) is the park's most extensive, with all kinds of groceries, camping supplies and souvenirs. A fast food **snack bar** (⊗ 8am-7:45pm; mains $) slings burgers and grilled sandwiches and dishes up full breakfasts. For lunch or an early dinner, the **Watchtower Deli** (⊗ 11am-6pm; sandwiches $) is a tad more gourmet and healthy, with focaccia sandwiches and prepared deli salads.

SEQUOIA NATIONAL FOREST CABIN RENTALS

For a somewhat rustic overnight without a tent, a number of restored 1930s **Forest Service cabins** (☎ 559-338-2251; www.fs.fed .us/r5/sequoia/recreation/rec_rentals.html; cabins $$) are available as recreational rentals, and two of these nifty buildings are located near the parks. Big Meadow Guard Station sits at 7600ft and is open from mid-June through mid-October. It sleeps six, and though you need to bring your own bedding, there's hot water and electricity. The year-round Camp 4½ Cabin has two bedrooms and generator- and propane-fueled appliances. It's at 1112ft and can sleep up to 12 people.

Mineral King

Silver City Mountain Resort (☎ summer 561-322, winter 805-461-3223; www.silvercityresort.com; mains $; ☯ 8am-8pm Thu-Mon) serves delicious home-made pies and simple fare on wooden picnic tables under the trees. It's located 3 miles west of the ranger station.

KINGS CANYON NATIONAL PARK

Cedar Grove

Cedar Grove Market (☯ 7am-9pm May-Oct) is the hub of the small village complex, hawking foodstuffs and all the silly stuff you forgot to pack. More of a snack bar, the adjacent restaurant (open for breakfast, lunch and dinner mains) has unexciting grill food and sandwiches for order at the counter.

Grant Grove

Pizza parlor (pizzas $; ☯ 2-10pm Thu-Tue summer, variable hours winter) Not expensive and quite fun, this casual eatery is hidden off the back porch of the main restaurant. It has fantastic crisp-crust pies and a decent salad bar, and shows nonstop movies in a cozy room adorned with old-time snow-sports paraphernalia. Though it shares kitchen facilities with the restaurant, it insists on serving everything on throwaway paper plates with plastic cutlery.

Grant Grove Restaurant (mains $-$$$; ☯ 7-10:30am, 11am-2pm, 6-9pm year-round; ♿) More of a diner, this is where most visitors chow down, and there can be a wait at times. There's a breakfast buffet, lunch sandwiches and filling full dinners. Vegetarians can always find at least one non-rabbit-food option, and children get their own menu as well.

Grant Grove Market (☯ 8am-9pm summer, 9am-6pm winter) At one end of the village, the good-sized market has firewood and camping supplies, with a small selection of fruits and veggies for sale along with packaged food. Caffeine junkies line up for espresso at the coffee cart (open 7:45am to 3:30pm in summer) in the central courtyard area.

GIANT SEQUOIA NATIONAL MONUMENT

The Stony Creek Village has a small **market** (☯ 7am-8pm Sun-Thu, 7am-9pm Fri & Sat), and a **pizzeria** (pizzas $; ☯ 11am-2pm & 4:30-8pm Mon-Fri, to 9pm Sat, to 8pm Sun). The market sells tokens for the laundry facility and functional but filthy showers.

AROUND SEQUOIA & KINGS CANYON NATIONAL PARKS

Entering the parks from the south, Hwy 198 passes through the city of Visalia and the resort town of Three Rivers, which borders Sequoia National Park. To the north, Hwy 180 accesses Kings Canyon, but no sizable towns are located along the way from Fresno. From the eastern flank, routes from Lone Pine and Onion Valley allow backpackers to set off into remote wilderness areas.

SOUTHERN ROUTE

Visalia

☎ 559 / pop 100,600 / elev 331ft

Plopped right in the middle of the warm Central Valley, Visalia is the main southern gateway to the parks, and the last sizable population center along the way to Foothills. The downtown area is pleasantly walkable, though the summer heat will have you scouting for shade. Some residential areas have gorgeous restored homes from the late 1800s, and a few are now lovely B&Bs.

A couple of useful places for stocking up include **Big 5 Sporting Goods** (☎ 625-5934; 1430 S Mooney Blvd), which has camping supplies, and **Visalia Farmers Market** (Sequoia Mall parking lot, 3303 S Mooney Blvd; ☯ 7-11am Sat) for fresh produce year-round.

ORIENTATION & INFORMATION

Hwy 198 runs through the middle of town; Main St is the major commercial strip.

Tulare County Library (☎ 733-6954; 200 W Oak Ave; ☯ 10am-8pm Mon-Thu, to 5pm Sat) Free internet.

Visalia Convention & Visitors Bureau (☎ 334-0141; www.visitvisalia.org)

Visalia Towne Trolley (☎ 713-4950; www.ridevcc .com; ☯ Mon-Sat) Free transportation plying the downtown area.

SLEEPING

Lamp Liter Motel (☎ 732-4511, 800-662-6692; www .lampliter.net; 3300 W Mineral King Ave; ▨ ▢ ▨ ♿) It could be a run-of-the-mill two-story courtyard motel, but this excellent family-owned establishment is delightfully nonchain. The 100 spotlessly clean rooms and four opulent cottages are furnished in warm tones, with overstuffed upholstered chairs and sliding glass doors facing the pool. The grounds are impeccably landscaped, and it's a stop on the Sequoia–Visalia shuttle route.

Spalding House (☎ 739-7877; www.thespaldinghouse.com; r incl full breakfast $$; ☒ ☐ ☖) Built by lumber baron WR Spalding, the 1901 Colonial Revival home sits on one of Visalia's grandest residential blocks. It's such a classy and comfortable B&B, you'll feel like a house guest at a private mansion. The three sumptuous guest suites have private sitting rooms and gorgeous details, like mosaic sinks and stained-glass ceiling in the Aviary Suite and the children's sleigh bed in the Cutler Room. Downstairs, the deep red wallpaper, formal library and 1923 Steinway piano are pure atmosphere.

Ben Maddox House (☎ 739-0721, 800-401-9800; www.benmaddoxhouse.com; 601 N Encina St; r incl full breakfast $$-$$$; ☒ ☐ ☖) A 1876 home with high ceilings and every electric amenity you could think of, the four guest rooms have DVD players and most have kitchenettes. Mature fruit trees enliven a lovely back garden, and a large patio room with a separate entrance is a good choice for families with small children.

EATING & DRINKING

Watson's Veggie Garden (☎ 635-7355; 615 W Main St; mains $; ☽ 10am-4pm Mon-Fri) A real live vegetarian deli! Get spoiled for choice with five varieties of veggie burgers, Mediterranean nibbles or healthily stuffed wraps.

Brewbakers (☎ 627-2739; 219 E Main St; mains $; ☽ 11:30am-10pm) The most popular brewpub in town, Brewbakers beckons the thirsty with awesome beer, like their popular Sequoia Red and a heavy black Possum Porter, and house-made sodas. A lengthy menu includes grill items, pizza and pasta, and unexpected gems like a blackened salmon caesar salad.

our pick **Vintage Press** (☎ 733-3033; 216 N Willis St; lunch $-$$, dinner mains $$$-$$$$$; ☽ 11:30am-2pm & 5:30-10pm Mon-Sat, 10am-2pm & 5-9pm Sun) Popular with the corporate crowd and ladies-who-lunch, this is a wonderful marriage of fine food and impeccable surroundings, without pretension. The Savoy dining room is an Art Deco temple of etched glass, but the Rose Room – with vintage French posters, white table cloths, bright palm-clustered window booths and antique wooden saloon fittings – is a matchless time capsule. The wild mushroom puff-pastry appetizer never leaves the menu; other seasonal choices include a cognac-seasoned chicken mousseline and a roasted stuffed baby pumpkin.

ENTERTAINMENT

Visalia Fox Theater (☎ 625-1369; www.foxvisalia.org; 300 W Main St) Built in 1929, it has an impressive East Indian temple-themed interior and puts on intermittent movie screenings and music events. Truly stunning – they just don't make 'em like this anymore.

GETTING THERE & AWAY

The **Sequoia Shuttle** (☎ 877-287-4453; www.sequoiashuttle.com; round-trip $10; ☽ late May-early Sep) debuted in 2007, and it's a great round-trip deal that takes just two hours to get to the park and includes the park fee. Advance reservations are required, and it's okay to park your car at the Holiday Inn (one of its stops) for a few days. **Amtrak** (☎ 800-872-7245; www.amtrak.com) trains on the San Joaquin line connect to Visalia via motor coach from Hanford.

Three Rivers
☎ 559 / pop 2250 / elev 830ft

Right on the border with Sequoia National Park and named for the nearby convergence of three forks of the Kaweah River, Three Rivers is a friendly small town populated by retirees and artsy newcomers.

ORIENTATION & INFORMATION

Just west of the park, Hwy 198 becomes Sierra Dr.

3 Rivers Cyber Café (☎ 561-4165; 41763 Sierra Dr; ☽ 10am-6pm Mon-Fri, 11am-5pm Sat, shorter hours winter) More of a business center, with internet terminals and wi-fi.

Kaweah Commonwealth (www.kaweahcommonwealth.com) The local weekly newspaper and a good source of information and area history, it prides itself as 'a journal for those who labor and think.'

Sierra Foothills Chamber of Commerce (☎ 561-3300, 877-530-3300; www.threerivers.com; 42268 Sierra Dr; ☽ 10am-4pm Mon-Fri, 11am-3pm Sat & Sun) Shares space with the town museum, and has maps and information on local lodgings and restaurants.

SIGHTS & ACTIVITIES

The one-room **Kaweah Post Office**, founded by the utopian Kaweah Co-Operative Colony (see the boxed text, below), is the oldest still-operating post office in the US. Look for the beautiful wooden building 3 miles north on North Fork Dr. The **Three Rivers Historical Museum** (☎ 561-2707; www.threerivers .com/trhs.htm; 42268 Sierra Dr; admission free; ☯ 10am-4pm Mon-Fri, 11am-3pm Sat & Sun) has an excellent collection of local ranching, mining and domestic artifacts, as well as an archive of historical photographs and newspaper clippings.

Want to slough off the heat in summertime? **Kaweah White Water Adventures** (☎ 561-1000, 800-229-8658; www.kaweah-whitewater .com; 42323 Sierra Dr) organizes rafting trips on the Kaweah River, and just west of town on Lake Kaweah, the pools amid big boulders at the **Slick Rock Recreation Area** make perfect swim spots.

SLEEPING

Three Rivers has a healthy number of accommodations and good eating options. Lodgings may not have phones or TVs. If you just want a place to camp and couldn't find a spot in the park, there are a number of unexciting RV parks in town that will let you pitch a tent for the night; some are right on the river.

Buckeye Tree Lodge (☎ 561-5900; www.buckeye treelodge.com; r/cottages $$/$$$; ☒ ◻ ☒) Sit out on your grassy back patio or balcony perch and watch the river ease through a maze of boulders. Modern white-brick motel rooms, some with kitchenettes, feel airy and bright.

Sequoia Village Inn (☎ 561-3652; www.sequoia villageinn.com; 45971 Sierra Dr; cottages $$-$$$$; ☒ ◻ ☒) Across the street from the Buckeye and owned by the same family, these 10 pretty modern cottages, many with full kitchens, border the park and are great for

---

THE KAWEAH CO-OPERATIVE COLONY

A few years before Sequoia National Park was created, an idealistic organization of union workers, skilled craftspeople and economic progressives settled in the southern Sierra Nevada around Three Rivers. Using a law that authorized inexpensive land sales, the group planned a utopian community based on cooperative assets and collective land ownership, and in 1886 approximately 160 members settled in the pristine foothills below Giant Forest. They applied for land grants and got to work setting up a logging business, confident that they would receive title to this available land.

To realize their timber venture, the most pressing and daunting task was the construction of a thoroughfare to Giant Forest. As the colonists toiled on the road, local citizens got wind of their unusually large land filing and grew concerned. During this period of history, it was not uncommon for railroads and other corporations to fraudulently purchase huge tracts of land and quietly expand their monopolies. George Stewart, the editor of the Visalia *Delta* newspaper, had led a 10 year campaign for Congress to protect the giant sequoias, and he put in motion an inquiry into the claim. Ironically, the colony was suspected of the economic motives it abhorred.

The back-breaking road work dragged on for three years, but the Kaweah Co-Operative Commonwealth Company steamed ahead to implement its socialist ideals. They developed a currency based on contributed labor. They organized a school, farmed the land and set up a post office. What's now called the General Sherman Tree was then known as the Karl Marx Tree.

In the summer of 1890, the road had been built to the edge of the mature groves and sequoia logging began with the use of a portable sawmill. The local population no longer harbored suspicions about the settlement, and an initial government report supported their intentions. But within months, Stewart's victory became the colony's undoing. Sequoia National Park was created, an act that shielded sequoias from destruction. The Kaweah settlement sat squarely inside it; their claims and sweat equity were now worthless.

Besides the descendants of this economic experiment, a number of relics remain from its heyday. The most accessible is the Kaweah Post Office, just north of Three Rivers. In Sequoia National Park, the 'Squatters' Cabin' adjacent to Crescent Meadow is another legacy of their failed attempts at land ownership among the giant sequoias. And the Old Colony Mill Rd, a rough 11.5-mile stretch from Crystal Cave Rd, is the difficult passage they forged.

groups or families. Most have decks and BBQs, and the largest can sleep 12.

Lake Elowin Resort (☎ 561-3460; www.lake-elowin.com; 43840 Dineley Dr; cabins $$-$$$; 🌣 🚤) The aging sign on the main road might make you think the place folded up decades ago, but it makes this secluded and lushly landscaped camp feel more like a real find. Popular with families, it offers swimming in its private lake, free canoes to paddle and well-stocked kitchens or kitchenettes in every cabin.

EATING & DRINKING

ourpick **We Three Bakery & Restaurant** (☎ 561-4761; 43368 Sierra Dr; mains $; 🕑 7am-2:30pm Wed-Mon; 🖳) Tasty pastries, chunky French toast and good coffee lure in the breakfast crowd, and hot and cold sandwiches on blindingly bright Fiestaware make it a fun lunch spot as well. A few vegetarian options grace the menu, including a tofu scramble, and summer diners can chow down outside under a shady oak patio.

Sierra Subs & Salads ☎ 561-4810; 41717 Sierra Dr; mains $; 🕑 7am-8pm) Primarily a take-out place (outdoor seating is available), it has a good choice of fresh breads for regionally inspired sandwiches like the Potwisha Portabella and the Tokopah Turkey. The deli salads have a creative mix of ingredients, and if you're staying somewhere with a kitchen, it makes good take-and-bake pizzas.

River View Restaurant & Lounge (☎ 561-2211; 42323 Sierra Dr; mains $-$$; 🕑 11am-10pm Sun-Thu, 11am-11pm Fri & Sat) With a large back patio that practically sits on top of the river and weekend nights packed with local live music, this casual eatery and bar is a hot spot any time of the day. Burgers, hot sandwiches and stone-baked pizza hit the spot, and the full dinners of Santa Fe chicken or sirloin steak are good and filling. The bar ceiling is plastered with $1 bills, and the drinks keep coming until about 2am.

Gateway Restaurant & Lodge (☎ 561-4133; www.gateway-sequoia.com; 45978 Sierra Dr; lunch $$, dinner $$-$$$$; 🕑 11am-9pm Mon-Fri, 9am-9pm Sat, 8am-9pm Sun) The most upscale restaurant in town, the Gateway has indoor and outdoor dining areas with dynamite river views and well-prepared meals. Lunch is mostly burgers and sandwiches, but dinner goes gourmet with dishes like chicken masala and trout almandine. There's also a full bar. The lodge (rooms $$, two-bedroom cabin $$$$) has five institutional cinder-block motel rooms, but rooms 6 and 7 are in a different league, with sweeping river-view decks and tons more space.

GETTING THERE & AWAY

Sequoia Shuttle (☎ 877-287-4453; www.sequoiashuttle.com; $10 round-trip; 🕑 late May-early Sep) offers summer transport to Visalia and Sequoia National Park; advance reservations required.

EASTERN ROUTE
Lone Pine
☎ 760 / pop 1700 / elev 3700ft

The last stop on the way up to the Mt Whitney Trailhead, Lone Pine is also a convenient stopover for drivers on Hwy 395, and those traveling to and from Death Valley. The town was once a popular set location for movie Westerns.

MANZANAR NATIONAL HISTORIC SITE

On Hwy 395, 9 miles north of Lone Pine, look for a wooden guard tower marking one of the country's most important and disturbing national historical sites, **Manzanar** (☎ 878-2194 www.nps.gov/manz; admission free; 🕑 interpretive center 9am-4:30pm Nov-Apr, 8:30am-5pm May-Oct). From 1942 to 1945, barbed wire and machine gun–mounted towers ringed a dusty square mile of the Owens Valley, housing 11,000 Japanese-American internees at the Manzanar War Relocation Center. During WWII President Franklin D Roosevelt authorized the internment of all Japanese-Americans living on the West Coast. This supposedly precautionary step against espionage included American citizens and young children – anyone of Japanese heritage.

Visitors can do a self-guided auto tour of this former concentration camp, and an excellent interpretive center tells the stories of the families who languished here yet built a vibrant community. The last Saturday of April, former internees make an annual pilgrimage to honor family members who died here, keeping alive the memory of this national tragedy.

DRIVING IS FOR WIMPS

In eastern California, the highest and lowest points in the continental US are a mere 135 miles apart by road, and about 30 years ago someone came up with a preposterous idea: why not run a race between them? The **Badwater Ultramarathon** (www.badwater.com) was born, and it now draws masochists from around the world. Over 60 hours, runners attempt a nonstop course that knows no match. Starting from the 120°F heat of Death Valley at 280ft below sea level, participants conquer three mountain ranges for a whopping 13,000ft of ascent and 4700ft of cumulative descent. The finish line is at Whitney Portal, but many of these crazed souls continue on for a summit of 14,496ft Mt Whitney. It gets even more insane. Some runners summit and then run *back* to the starting point, just for the hell of it. The race takes place in July, and you can cheer on the knots of weary and bedraggled runners or sign up to be one yourself.

ORIENTATION & INFORMATION

Hwy 395 turns into Main St within the town limits.

Eastern Sierra InterAgency Visitor Center (☎ 876-6222; cnr Hwy 395 & SR 136; www.fs.fed.us/r5/inyo; ⏱ 8am-5pm, to 6pm summer) Both a visitor center and a ranger station, this is the one-stop shop for wilderness permits, regional recreation information and Mt Whitney permits.

Inyo County Library (☎ 876-5031; cnr Bush & Washington Sts) Internet access.

Lone Pine Sporting Goods (☎ 876-5365; 220 S Main St; ⏱ mid-Feb–mid-Dec) This place has camping gear and maps.

SIGHTS & ACTIVITIES

To get a sense of the local history, the **Museum of Lone Pine Film History** (☎ 876-9909; www .lonepinefilmhistorymuseum.org; 701 S Main St; admission free; ⏱ 10am-4pm, closed Tue) contains exhibits of Western movie paraphernalia and includes a small theater. Downtown, the tiny **Southern Inyo Museum** (☎ 876-5052; 127 W Bush St; admission free; ⏱ 9am-4pm Thu-Sat) has a cool collection of regional artifacts.

Located on Whitney Portal Rd, the warm colors and rounded contours of the **Alabama Hills** stand in stark contrast to the jagged snowy Sierras just behind. The setting for countless ride-’em-out movies and the popular *Lone Ranger* TV series, the stunning orange rock formations are a beautiful place to experience sunrise or sunset. A number of graceful rock arches are within easy hiking distance of the roads.

SLEEPING & EATING

Tuttle Creek (www.blm.gov/ca/st/en/fo/bishop/camping /tuttle.html; Horseshoe Meadow Rd; sites $; ⏱ Mar-Oct) Off the Whitney Portal Rd, this first-come,

first-served campground has primitive sites with panoramic ‘pinch-me!’ views of the Sierras, White Mountains and the rosy Alabama Hills.

Dow Villa Motel (☎ 876-5521, 800-824-9317; www .dowvillamotel.com; 310 S Main St; r $$; 🅿 🖵 🐕 🅰) Centrally located with lots of amenities, this is the best place to stay in Lone Pine itself. While the small but inexpensive rooms in the ‘historic hotel’ building are nothing special, the modern and larger motel-annex rooms have a splash of color, kitchenettes, comfy furniture and lots of mountain light.

High Sierra Café (☎ 876-5796; 446 S Main St; mains $; ⏱ 24hr) Refuel after Whitney with a big plate of fried chicken or pork chops, or get a sandwich to eat on the l-o-n-g way up. Need some quick comfort food? Breakfast’s served around the clock.

Seasons (☎ 876-8927; 206 N Main St; mains $$$; ⏱ 5-9pm daily Apr-Oct, 5-9pm Tue-Sat Nov-Mar) Another place that hits the spot with hungry hikers, Seasons has everything you fantasized about the last time you choked down freeze-dried rations. Sautéed trout, roasted duck, filet mignon and plates of carb-replenishing pasta will revitalize your appetite, and nice and naughty desserts will leave you purring.

Stock up on groceries and grab a newspaper at **Joseph's Bi-Rite** (☎ 876-4378; 119 S Main St; ⏱ 8am-9pm May-Oct, to 8pm Nov-Apr), the town supermarket.

GETTING THERE & AWAY

Inyo Mono Transit (☎ 872-1901, 800-922-1930; www .inyocounty.us/transit/transit.htm) operates a weekday CREST bus service three times a day to Bishop ($4), with an additional service on the first Saturday of the month.

BUSY HIGHWAY TO THE HEAVENS

The biggest obstacle to reaching the top of Mt Whitney is obtaining the wilderness permit ($15), which is required for all overnight trips and for day hikes past Lone Pine Lake (about 3 miles from the trailhead). A quota system limits daily access to 60 overnight and 100 day-hikers from May 1 through November 1. Because of the *huge* demand to do this hike, permits are awarded in a lottery. Mail your application in during February (a February postmark is required) to: Mt Whitney Lottery, Wilderness Permit Office, 351 Pacu Lane, Suite 200, Bishop, CA 93514. Check www.fs.fed.us/r5/inyo/recreation/wild/mtwhitney.shtml for full details and application forms.

Lottery losers, don't despair! You can always summit via the back door route (see the boxed text, p231) from Sequoia & Kings Canyon trailheads

---

Mt Whitney

Mt Whitney (14,496ft), the tallest point in the continental US and the southern terminus of the John Muir Trail, sits smack on the eastern border of Sequoia National Park. The mystique of Mt Whitney captures the imagination, and bagging its superlative summit becomes an obsession for many.

The main summit trail leaves from Whitney Portal, about 13 miles west of Lone Pine via the Whitney Portal Rd (closed in winter), and it climbs some 6000ft over 11 miles. It's a superstrenuous, really, *really* long walk that'll wear out even experienced mountaineers, but doesn't require technical skills if attempted in summer or early fall. Earlier or later in the season, you'll likely need an ice axe and crampons.

Toilets are no longer available on the trail, much to the relief of the workers who had to service them. Hikers must now pack out their human waste, and free 'WAG bags' are available when you pick up your permit. Pack a few extra plastic bags just in case you need them.

Many people in good physical condition make it to the top, although only superbly conditioned, previously acclimatized hikers should attempt this as a day hike. Breathing becomes difficult at these elevations and altitude sickness is a common problem. Rangers recommend spending a night or two camping at the trailhead and another at one of the two camps along the route: **Outpost Camp** at 3.5 miles or **Trail Camp** at 6 miles up the trail.

When considering an ascent, do your homework. A recommended guide is *Climbing Mt Whitney* by Walt Wheelock and Wynne Benti. Before setting out, call or stop by the Eastern Sierra InterAgency Visitor Center (p247) in Lone Pine to get the latest scoop about weather and trail conditions. An excellent website with up-to-date info and tips for first-timers is the Whitney Portal Store message board at www.whit neyportalstore.com.

For a sampling of the Whitney trail, you can day hike as far as Lone Pine Lake (3 miles) without a permit.

Directory

ACCOMMODATIONS

Accommodations options in both Yosemite and Sequoia & Kings Canyon National Parks run the gamut from basic to bourgeois. You can shack up in rustic tent cabins in both parks, sleep in comfort at one of the lodges within or around the parks or go totally overboard staying somewhere like Yosemite's famous Ahwahnee Hotel. And, of course, you can camp.

Most campgrounds, many lodges and some B&Bs close during the winter season (generally October through March, April or May), but you'll find something open in and around both national parks year-round. If an accommodations option or campground is open only part of the year, we've included its opening hours following the '🕑' sign.

Pricing

Throughout this book, you can easily identify how much a place charges by where it falls in the list of options and by the number of dollar signs it receives. Accommodations are listed in order of least expensive to most expensive. All sleeping options are classified as '$' (meaning budget, or less than $50); '$$' (midrange, or $50 to $149); '$$$' (top end, or $150 to $249) or '$$$$' (deluxe, or $250 and up).

Budget choices range from campgrounds to tent cabins and cheap motels found along the gateway routes into the park. Midrange accommodations are generally (though not always) comfortable hotel-type places, some lodges and B&Bs. At the upper end of the midrange spectrum, you can expect good beds, hot water and private bathrooms as a bare minimum. Basic tent cabins fall into the lower end of the midrange spectrum during the summer high season.

PRACTICALITIES

- Major US newspapers are available from coin-op newspaper boxes in Yosemite and Sequoia & Kings Canyon.

- The National Weather Service broadcasts regular NOAA Weather Radio updates (frequency 162.450MHz) from its Yosemite tower.

- Local FM and AM radio stations can be picked up within Yosemite Valley.

- US domestic electrical current is 110V, 60Hz (same as Canada).

- For information on telephone, electric and internet systems throughout the world, see www .kropla.com.

- The USA uses the imperial system of weights and measures; road signs are in miles.

- To convert between metric and imperial, see the inside back cover.

At a top-end joint, you can generally expect solid service, comfy beds, private bathroom, hot water, spacious accommodations and, depending on the place, amenities like cable TV (except at most places within the parks), telephone and room service. Staying at deluxe accommodations pretty much guarantees spectacular service and amenities all the way around.

Reservations

If you want to stay within either park, make a reservation no matter what time of the year you plan to visit. Anyone hoping to sleep in Yosemite during the peak months of May through September should reserve *far* in advance (see the boxed texts, p161 & p166). However, if you don't have a reservation, don't write off your trip – you might get lucky, especially if you're camping in May, early June or September and you turn up before noon. For information on reservations within Sequoia & Kings Canyon, see the boxed text, p241.

B&Bs

There are no bed and breakfasts per se in the national parks. But they are easily found in towns along the gateway routes into the parks. B&Bs generally start around $150 and offer intimate accommodations, usually in an old house or small historical building. Service is always personal (often by the owners themselves), and breakfasts are generally wholesome and filling.

Camping
TYPES OF CAMPGROUNDS

There are several types of campgrounds in and around Yosemite and Sequoia & Kings Canyon. Most are designated for car camping, meaning you pull up, unload your car and pitch your tent. Some are walk-in campgrounds, meaning you have to park your vehicle in a designated lot and carry your camping equipment and supplies to the campsite. Camp 4 in Yosemite is walk-in; in Sequoia & Kings Canyon, Cold Creek and Lodgepole campgrounds offer a combination of walk-in and car camping sites. The advantage of walk-in sites is the lack of cars and RVs, which makes for a more 'natural' experience. Nearly all car camping and walk-in sites within the parks have fire pits, picnic benches, bear boxes and a nearby rest-

room. No campgrounds in Yosemite have showers. In Sequoia & Kings Canyon, all campgrounds except Buckeye Flat, Potwisha and South Fork have showers. For a breakdown of campground services see the boxed texts, p162 and p239.

Yosemite has three backpacker campgrounds to accommodate people heading into or out of the backcountry. You must have a wilderness permit to stay in these. There are no backpacker campgrounds in Sequoia & Kings Canyon National Parks.

INSIDE THE PARKS

All campgrounds inside the national parks are operated by the **National Park Service** (NPS; www.nps.gov). There are 13 different campgrounds in **Yosemite** (www.www.nps.gov/yose) and 14 within **Sequoia & Kings Canyon** (www.nps.gov/seki). Four Yosemite campgrounds are open all year: Upper Pines, Camp 4, Wawona and Hodgdon Meadow. In Sequoia & Kings Canyon, Lodgepole, Azalea, Potwisha and South Fork stay open year-round.

Camping inside the parks offers the distinct advantage of putting you closest to what you came up to see. You likely won't have to drive to the trailhead nor (and this pertains primarily to Yosemite) face the day-parking nightmare that day-trippers face. On the other hand, park campgrounds generally fill up the fastest.

OUTSIDE THE PARKS

Campgrounds outside the national parks are either privately owned or operated by the **US Forest Service** (USFS; www.fs.fed.us). Campgrounds at lower elevations are open year-round, while upper-elevation campgrounds usually open only seasonally. The advantage of staying outside the park is that you'll likely pay a little less (though the amount is generally negligible) and reservations are often easier to make closer to the date you wish to camp. Although not covered in this book, there are many free car-accessible campgrounds within the national forests surrounding the parks, though they generally lie at the end of long dirt roads and don't offer access to the parks.

RESERVATIONS

Make reservations for all NPS campgrounds through the federally operated **Recreation .gov** (☎ toll free 877-444-6777, international 518-885-

3639; www.recreation.gov). Of the 13 NPS campgrounds within Yosemite, six are considered reservation only. This title is slightly misleading, however, since you can drive into the park and 'make a reservation' for that night on the spot (see the boxed text, p161), provided, of course, there are sites available. In summer, there rarely are.

FIRST-COME, FIRST-SERVED

Some campgrounds, both within and around the parks, operate on a first-come, first-served basis. For folks without reservations (especially those heading to Yosemite), these generally offer the only hope. The key to scoring a first-come, first-served campsite is arriving between 8am and noon. Arrive too early and the previous night's guests haven't yet left; too late and sites are full of new campers.

In Yosemite, seven campgrounds (see the boxed text, p161) operate on a first-come, first-served basis. In Sequoia & Kings Canyon 12 of the 14 campgrounds are first-come, first served.

Even in the heat of summer, getting a first-come, first-served campsite isn't that difficult if you arrive early enough. The park recommends 9am, but on weekdays you'll probably be fine before noon. The method is simple: drive or walk around the campground loops until you see an unoccupied site – that means no tents, equipment or hired bodyguards there to hold it, and no receipt hanging from the site's little signpost. If it's free, take it, because if you're too picky it might be gone the next time you drive by. Remember that check-out time is not until noon at most campgrounds, so late risers may not clear out until close to lunchtime. Take a look at the check-out date printed on the campsite receipt for some guidance. And be patient.

Once you have claimed a site, head back to the campground entrance and follow instructions listed there for paying and properly displaying your receipt. Pay for as many days as you expect to stay; and if you extend your stay, just pay again in the morning before check-out time.

WILDERNESS CAMPING

Also called 'backcountry camping' or 'dispersed camping,' wilderness camping is just what it sounds like: camping in the wilderness. Provided you meet certain requirements (see the boxed text, p137), you can camp wherever you want. Along popular trails there are often established wilderness campsites; in heavily visited areas (such as Little Yosemite Valley) pit toilets minimize camper impact. Although sleeping in an established campsite might not seem your idea of wilderness camping, doing so helps minimize impact on other areas.

Hostels

There are very few hostels in the area. In fact, we know of one: the Yosemite Bug Rustic Mountain Resort (p177), located on Hwy 140, just outside of Yosemite National Park, is a hostel-cum-lodge.

Hotels

Most hotels are found outside the parks. Two exceptions are the Wawona Hotel (p167) and the famous Ahwahnee Hotel (p166), both in Yosemite.

Lodges

The word 'lodge' usually connotes an eye-catching, stately structure with stone fireplaces, beamed ceilings and rustic but well-kept rooms. Lodges in and around the parks often fit the stereotype, but they can actually be anything from a 200-plus room place with standard motel-type rooms (like the Yosemite Lodge; p166) to traditional places like the warmly welcoming Evergreen Lodge (p167) near Hetch Hetchy, the classic Tamarack Lodge & Resort (p208) in Mammoth Lakes or the historic John Muir Lodge (p241) in Sequoia & Kings Canyon. Most lodges offer choices of rooms in the main lodge (which sometimes have shared bathrooms) or cabins (with private bathrooms). Rates at places like this can start as low as $70 off-season and climb as high as $400 for a cabin in July and August. The latter may seem high, but when you consider that cabins can hold up to several families, the price seems more manageable.

Tent Cabins

Tent cabins are a sort of in-between option: not quite camping, not quite a hotel. Generally, these consist of cement walls with canvas roofs, and amenities mean a light bulb, an electrical outlet and cots. Bedding

DIRECTORY

usually costs extra, so you're better off (and more comfortable) bringing your own. All parks have tent cabins. Sleeping up to four (sometimes more) and costing anywhere from $50 off-season to $80 in summer, they're an affordable alternative to lodges. If you're staying in a tent cabin in spring or winter, remember that they lack heating and get very cold.

ACTIVITIES

Whether you want to dangle from the side of a granite cliff, whiz down snowy slopes, fish for brown trout or throw the whole family in a rubber raft and float down the Merced River, Yosemite and Sequoia & Kings Canyon National Parks offer endless fun in the great outdoors. For a complete rundown of all you can do in the parks, see p38.

BUSINESS HOURS

Businesses and services maintain opening hours based on a wide range of factors: some close for the winter, and 'winter' can begin and end on different dates each year. Others stay open year-round, but maintain shorter hours in winter and their longest hours in summer. But there are some standards. Specific opening hours are provided for establishments and services throughout this book only when they differ significantly from the following standard hours or when they open only seasonally. We've also included opening hours for most information offices and, because they're hard to pin down, entertainment venues. Note that even when opening hours are listed, they're still subject to change based on weather, demand and budgetary constraints.

- Cafés and restaurants generally serve breakfast from 7am to 10:30am, lunch from 11am to 2:30pm and dinner from about 5pm to 9pm.
- Bars are usually open from about 5pm to 2am.
- Shops and services are open from about 9:30am to 5:30pm, and they usually stay open during lunch.

CLIMATE CHARTS

The parks have something different to offer in every season. See p23 for guidance on planning your trip.

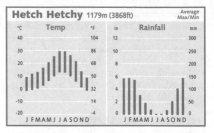

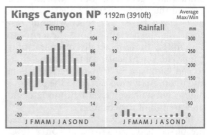

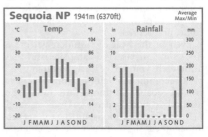

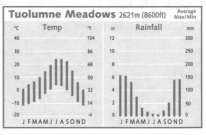

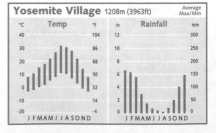

COURSES

Both parks and surrounding areas offer a wide range of learning opportunities, from fun family-style nature walks to photography excursions and college-credit courses. For information on climbing, wilderness and other activity-related courses, see p38. For kid-specific courses, such as Yosemite's Junior Ranger program, see p59.

Yosemite

In Yosemite Village, the Art Activity Center (p100) offers free, informal art classes covering a different medium each week. You can join free photography walks offered through the park service or through the Ansel Adams Gallery (p99). Park rangers and naturalists lead a plethora of educational walks and gatherings throughout the park, but especially in Yosemite Valley and Tuolumne. For more information and schedules, check the free publication *Yosemite Today*, or stop by one of the visitor centers (p92). Group sizes are generally limited to about 15 people, either on a first-come, first-served basis or by reservation, depending on the program.

For those who want to plunge deeper, there are lots of options. You can study everything from bats to basketry through the **Yosemite Association** (☎ 209-379-2321; www.yosemite .org), which offers a vast array of well-regarded seminars through its Yosemite Outdoor Adventures program. These classes are college-level educational opportunities for adults and, in some specific cases, teenagers 16 and up. Hiking is often involved, so participants need to be able to handle varying degrees of physical activity. Day classes include everything from snowshoe jaunts at Badger Pass to 'Map and Compass for Beginners.' Longer trips involve overnights, including wildflower explorations, beginner backpackers' trips, rafting excursions on the Merced River and outdoor-survival classes for women. You can also attend writing, drawing, photography and natural-history seminars. There are even college-level art and photography classes that may be taken for UC Berkeley credit. Prices run from $75 for a single-day course to around $400 for multiday courses. Sign up online, by telephone or by mailing in the form provided on the website.

The **Yosemite Institute** (☎ 209-379-9511; www .yni.org/yi) is a private nonprofit group that has run its own educational programs in partnership with park since 1971. Trips, which are available for learners of all ages, combine hiking with environmental education. The institute operates cabins in the Valley as well as a center on Tioga Rd near Crane Flat.

Astronomy buffs and budding stargazers will likely dig the evening Stars Over Yosemite programs. Free programs take place weekly (usually on Saturday night) at the amphitheater at Glacier Point, and the talks on constellations and stars are often accompanied by free telescope viewing courtesy of various California astronomy clubs, who volunteer their time. 'Starry Skies' programs also happen in the Valley at Yosemite Lodge and Curry Village, though these usually involve a reservation and a modest fee; sign up at the tour desk at Yosemite Lodge. You can also go to a 'Starry Skies' program at Wawona (sign up at the Wawona Hotel); those in Tuolumne Meadows should check the campfire program for a special ranger talk on stars.

Sequoia & Kings Canyon

The **Sequoia Natural History Association** (☎ 559-565-3759; www.sequoiahistory.org) is another superb educational resource, offering a number of classes through its 'Sequoia Field Institute Edventure' seminars.

TIPS FOR TEACHERS

Educational and scientific groups who want to study in Yosemite can get their entrance fees waived if they apply in advance and provide the proper documentation. The trip must be for educational purposes, not simply recreation. For details, contact the **Yosemite Fees Office** (☎ 209-372-0207) or check the Yosemite website at www.nps .gov/yose/trip/waivers.htm.

Both Yosemite and Sequoia & Kings Canyon National Parks run field-trip programs specifically for teachers who wish to bring their students to study in the parks. Teachers can contact **Yosemite's education office** (☎ 209-375-9505) or the **Sequoia & Kings Canyon Education Coordinator** (☎ 559-565-4303). Also check the 'For Teachers' sections of the **Yosemite** (www.nps.gov/yose) and **Sequoia & Kings Canyon** (www.nps.gov/seki) websites.

DIRECTORY

Outside the Parks

Established in 1978 to preserve Mono Lake, the **Mono Lake Committee** (☎ 760-647-6386; www .monolake.org) offers very affordable and highly respected programs and seminars with the goal of educating people about the unique lake and its surroundings.

DISCOUNT CARDS

Under its newly titled 'America the Beautiful' passes, the National Parks service offers the lifetime Senior Pass (formerly known as the Golden Age Passport) for $10, an outstanding deal. The pass allows the cardholder, who must be at least 62 years old, and three accompanying adults free entry to all US national parks and federal recreation areas, plus deep discounts on some campgrounds and services.

The parks offer no student or youth discount cards. Children under 16 enter the parks free of charge with a paying adult. For information on free park passes for travelers with disabilities, as well as annual park passes available to the general public, see p23.

FESTIVALS & EVENTS

Local festivals can provide great impetus for a trip to Yosemite or Sequoia & Kings Canyon, as well as to towns around the parks. Events like the wildly popular Bracebridge Dinner at the Ahwahnee Hotel or the Strawberry Music Festival at Camp Mather, just outside the park, draw huge crowds across great distances. Needless to say, tickets go quickly for the most popular events, so always check availability as early as possible. For a list of the area's biggest festivals and events, see p25. Events of predominantly local significance are covered in their destination sections throughout the book.

FOOD
Restaurants

Throughout this book, eating options are qualified by dollar signs to make an establishment's affordability (or lack thereof) easily recognizable. Budget options – that is, places where main courses cost less than $10 – get one '$'. At a midrange joint ($$), you'll pay $10 to $16 for a main course. At restaurants falling into our top-end category ($$$), expect to pay $17 to $25 for a main course. At deluxe restaurants ($$$$)

you'll pay over $25 – and damn it, it better be good. By 'mains' (used in Eating sections) we mean main courses (entrées).

Inside Yosemite, you'll find everything from sandwich shops and pizza joints to the fancy sit-down restaurants in the Ahwahnee and Wawona Hotels. Although pricey, the latter generally serve delicious meals. As for the other options, the food is generally only mediocre. In Sequoia & Kings Canyon, most restaurants are part of lodges or the local stores and food is generally good. The best food is found outside the parks (see the boxed text, p181).

A few places in the parks are open year-round, though in most cases hours are reduced during winter. For more on business hours, see p252.

Self-Catering

Small grocery stores inside both parks stock items such as cooking oil, canned foods, ice, beer and other staples as well as the usual junk food, but you're better off bringing everything from home, lest you be charged top dollar. If you can't plan that far ahead, stop en route – it'll still cost less than inside the park. Nearly all campsites have fire pits (over which you can grill your food if you bring a grill), and most have picnic tables.

Bear-Proof Lockers

All campsites, most trailheads and many parking lots have bear-proof metal storage boxes. You are required by law to store *all* your food (including canned goods, beverages and coolers) and all scented products (toothpaste, shampoo, sunscreen etc) in these boxes at all times. Never leave food unattended in your car, especially in Yosemite, whether you're taking a multiday backpacking trip or just spending a few hours meandering through the museum. It may seem like a hassle to put your picnic lunch in a locker, but having a bear break your window, ransack your car and tear up your upholstery is even more of a hassle. What's more, you can be fined for leaving anything in your car (or in your bike's panniers). Most importantly, this helps keep bears from becoming 'problems,' which can mean a bad end for the bear. Backcountry hikers must use bear-proof canisters; for more information, see p137.

HOLIDAYS

The parks (and the areas surrounding the parks) are at their absolute busiest during the summertime school-holiday period, which runs roughly from mid-June through August. During this period, *everything* is packed, and reservations are a must. July and August are peak times. For the best times to visit, see p23. The greatest numbers of visitors also hit the parks during the following public and/or school holidays:

New Year's Day January 1
Martin Luther King Jr Day Third Monday in January
Presidents' Day Third Monday in February
Easter A Friday through Sunday in March or April
***Spring Break** Two weeks around Easter
***Summer Break** Mid-June to early September
***Memorial Day** Last Monday in September
***Independence Day** July 4
***Labor Day** First Monday in September
Columbus Day Second Monday in October
Veterans' Day November 11
Thanksgiving Day Fourth Thursday in November
Christmas December 25
***Christmas/Holiday Break** School holiday running from mid-November through around January 5

Holidays marked with an asterisk (*) are extremely popular times for people to hit the parks; expect traffic and make reservations.

INSURANCE

If you're traveling very far to get here (and especially if you're flying), it's a good idea to get some travel insurance. Although most travel-insurance policies won't cover your $1500 digital Canon camera ($500 is usually the max on a single piece of electronic equipment), they will cover baggage theft, trip cancellation and, most importantly, medical emergency. When choosing a policy, read the fine print; some policies will not cover 'extreme' activities, which could include anything from river rafting to rock climbing. Domestic rental and homeowners insurance policies often cover theft while you're on the road. Look into it.

Worldwide travel insurance is available at www.lonelyplanet.com/travel_services, and you can buy, extend and make a claim online anytime – even if you're already on the road. For auto insurance, see p264; for health insurance, see p268.

INTERNATIONAL VISITORS
Entering the Country

Entering the United States is straightforward – provided your documents are in order and you can cope with the US-VISIT biometric entry procedures. Under these procedures, everyone (except US and Canadian citizens) is photographed and has their fingerprints digitally scanned upon entering the United States.

For up-to-date information on travel to the United States, as well as current procedures, visit the websites of the **US Department of State** (www.travel.state.gov) and the **US Customs and Border Protection** (www.cbp.gov). It is highly recommended that you check and confirm all entry requirements with a US consulate in your home country.

PASSPORTS & VISAS

Citizens of Visa Waiver Program (VWP) countries can enter the United States as tourists for up to 90 days without obtaining a visa. There are 27 VWP countries, including Australia, France, Germany, New Zealand, Spain and the UK. For a complete list, see the Department of State website. Citizens of VWP countries must have a valid passport, however, and this is where it gets confusing. If your passport was issued before October 26, 2005, it must be a machine-readable passport (MRP). If your passport was issued on or after October 26, 2005, it must be an MRP, *and* its data page must have a digital photograph. If your passport was issued on or after October 26, 2006, it must be an e-Passport, meaning it has a computer chip (containing all your personal information) embedded in the back cover. That said, there is generally no need to get a new passport until your current one expires.

INTERNET ACCESS

Public internet access – sometimes free, sometimes extremely expensive – is available at a few places in the parks. For Yosemite, see p90; for Sequoia & Kings Canyon, see p216. Most hotels and B&Bs offer wireless internet for folks carrying laptops. If you're camping and have your laptop, it's worth taking it into hotel lobbies to see if you can jump an unsecured wireless connection.

LOST & FOUND

There are two numbers to call if you lose or find an item in Yosemite. For anything left or recovered in restaurants, hotels, gift shops or on buses, call **DNC Lost & Found** (☎ 209-372-4357). For items astray elsewhere, call the **NPS** (☎ 209-379-1001). If you're still in the Valley, you can also just go to the information desk at the Yosemite Valley Visitor Center (p92), where rangers keep a stash of things found. The park service will ship most items to their owners free of charge.

In Sequoia & Kings Canyon, each visitor center (p217) maintains its own lost and found.

MONEY

Prices in this book are quoted in US dollars ($). For a general idea of what things cost, see p23.

If you're arriving from abroad and need to change money, do so at the airport when you arrive or at an exchange bureau or bank in a major city. It is nearly impossible to exchange money in most small towns throughout the Sierras, and no one within the parks accepts or exchanges foreign currency.

Major credit cards (Visa, MasterCard, Amex) are widely accepted throughout the region and are often required as deposits when renting a car or reserving a hotel room. Traveler's checks (in US dollars) are a good way to carry a large amount of money that is replaceable in the event of loss or theft. That said, the easiest way to obtain cash throughout much of the area is with an ATM card. Nearly every small town has an ATM, and there are even ATMs inside Yosemite and Sequoia & Kings Canyon.

POST

Nearly every town around the national parks has a post office. Yosemite National Park has five (see p92) and Sequoia & Kings Canyon National Parks has two (p216). Sending a postcard domestically costs $0.26 to $0.41, depending on its size. The international rate averages $0.90. A letter costs $0.41 domestically and about $1.80 internationally.

SOLO TRAVELERS

Aside from the fact that you usually end up paying more for camping and lodging (with no one to split it with), there is generally no problem traveling alone in the region. However, solo women travelers should consider a few things before setting out; for more, see p258.

TELEPHONE

In all three national parks, you'll find pay phones at every developed location, including Yosemite Village, Curry Village, Tuolumne Meadows, Wawona and most campgrounds in Yosemite; and at Cedar Grove, Lodgepole, Ash Mountain and Mineral King in Sequoia & Kings Canyon.

With patchy cell-phone reception everywhere in the Sierra foothills, you'd never guess that there's excellent reception in parts of Yosemite Valley – but only in parts. Generally, the more open the area, the better the reception. Once you ascend out of the valley, reception often gets even better. (It's fantastic at the top of Nevada Fall!) In Tuolumne, there's usually reception in the Wilderness Center parking lot. Cell-phone reception is spotty to nonexistent in Wawona. In Sequoia & Kings Canyon, forget it.

When breaking out that cell phone, consider the reality of noise pollution. Hearing someone's cell phone ring in a neighboring campsite or at scenic lookout is annoying at best, while being subjected to a loud and lengthy phone conversation is grounds for a pine-coning.

For up-to-date information on the changing world of international cell-phone technology (including world phones, GSM, quad-band phones and all that fun stuff), check out www.kropla.com.

For emergency numbers, see the inside back cover.

TIME

From November to mid-March, California is on Pacific Standard Time, which is eight hours behind Coordinated Universal Time (UTC or Greenwich Mean Time). At 2am on the second Sunday in March, clocks are set forward one hour to Pacific Daylight Time (aka daylight saving time). On the first Sunday in November clocks revert to Pacific Standard Time. So, when it's noon in July in Yosemite, it's 2pm in New York, 7pm in London and 5am the following day in Sydney or Auckland. When it's noon in December in Yosemite, it's 3pm in New York.

TOURIST INFORMATION

Rather than lacking information on Yosemite and Sequoia & Kings Canyon (and California in general), you'll probably find there's *too much* information out there. Begin your internet research at the source by checking out the websites listed on p27. For rock-solid information on California, browse the state-funded **California Tourism** (☎ 800-462-2543; www.visitcalifornia.com) website or call the information line.

Tourist information offices (known as visitor centers) are found throughout Yosemite (see p92) and Sequoia & Kings Canyon (p217), and in nearly every town in the Sierras. For information on everything from road conditions and wilderness permits to employment opportunities and lodging, call the **Yosemite National Park Phone Menu** (☎ 209-372-0200), which will connect you to just about anything you want. For local tourist offices consult specific town sections throughout this book.

Other useful sources for areas around the national parks include:

Inyo National Forest (☎ 760-873-2400; www.r5.fs
.fed.us/inyo)

Sierra National Forest (☎ 559-297-0706; www.r5.fs
.fed.us/sierra)

Stanislaus National Forest (☎ 209-532-3671; www
.r5.fs.fed.us/sierra)

Tuolumne County Visitors Center (☎ 209-533-
4420; www.thegreatunfenced.com)

Yosemite Sierra Visitors Bureau (☎ 559-683-4636;
www.yosemitethisyear.com)

TOURS

Organizations such as the Yosemite Association and the Sequoia Natural History Association (see Courses, p253) offer multiday courses and seminars that are great alternatives to tours. However, you generally have to get to the parks on your own. For information on shuttle services and buses to the parks, see p262.

DNC (☎ 209-372-4386, 209-372-1240, 559-252-4848; www.yosemitepark.com), Yosemite's main concessionaire, runs the Valley's traditional tram tours, which include a wheelchair-accessible two-hour Valley Floor Tour, an all-day Grand Tour, a Big Trees Tram Tour to Mariposa Grove, and a Moonlight Tour. It also offers tours to Tuolumne Meadows and Glacier Point. Reservations can be made online, by telephone, at the Curry Village registration desk, at the Yosemite Lodge tour desk (inside the lobby) or by dialing extension ☎ 1240 from any park courtesy phone. Prices start around $25/20/15 for adults/seniors/children for the Valley Floor Tour and top out around $65/60/35 for the Grand Tour.

Numerous companies run generic bus tours to Yosemite, only to whiz you around the Valley beneath the barrage of amplified narration before shuttling you back to your starting point. For something different, try one of the following companies, which cater to more adventurous souls and allow for more time off the bus.

Backpacker-friendly **Green Tortoise** (☎ 415-956-7500, 800-867-8647; www.greentortoise.com; 494 Broadway, San Francisco, CA 94133) runs two-day (about $170) and three-day (about $230) trips to Yosemite from San Francisco that are more adventure travel than standard bus tour: travelers sleep in the converted bus or in campgrounds, cook collectively and choose among activities like hiking, swimming or just hanging out (and there's always some great hanging out). Prices (which change annually) include most meals and the park entry fee.

Using biodiesel vans to transport its generally fun-loving clients, San Francisco-based **Incredible Adventures** (☎ 415-751-7791, 800-777-8464; www.incadventures.com) runs all sorts of tours to Yosemite, from one-day sightseeing tours ($95) to three-day camping tours, to six-day 'backpack and raft' tours. Park entry fees and most meals are included, though some help with food prep is required. It's a far cry from your average tour company, and it provides all cooking and camping gear except sleeping bags.

Yosemite Bug Rustic Mountain Resort (p177) offers multiday backpacking tours throughout Yosemite through its **Yosemite Bug Bus** (☎ 866-826-7108; www.yosemitebugbus.com) operation. The bus picks up passengers at hotels and hostels in San Francisco, stops at the Bug hostel (just outside the park) and continues into the Yosemite on whichever guided trek you've joined.

Located just outside the Hetch Hetchy park entrance, Evergreen Lodge (p167) leads fly-fishing trips, GPS instructional tours, guided biking and hiking trips, rafting excursions and more.

Yosemite Sightseeing Tours (☎ 559-568-8687; www.yosemitetours.com) operates bus tours year-round from Oakhurst, Fish Camp and Bass Lake, all south of the park along Hwy 41. The 'Deluxe Summer Tour' lasts over nine hours (and runs about $75 per person, less for teens, free for children), taking in Yosemite Valley, Glacier Point and Mariposa Grove. Winter tours are shorter. The company also offers natural-history and hiking tours.

TRAVELERS WITH DISABILITIES

Both national parks publish an accessibility brochure (available at park entrances and visitor centers) and all parks have an accessibility coordinator. Both are excellent sources of information on everything from hotels and campgrounds to visitor sites and ranger-led activities. If you need to make arrangements in advance, call any park visitor center or contact the coordinator prior to your arrival.

To obtain Yosemite's accessibility brochure online, visit the National Park Service website at www.nps.gov/yose/planyourvisit /accessibility.htm. For NPS information on Sequoia & Kings Canyon visit www.nps .gov/seki/planyourvisit/accessibility.htm.

The shuttle buses in Yosemite all have wheelchair lifts and tie-downs (as does the shuttle that runs between Yosemite Valley and Tuolumne), and the drivers can assist disabled passengers on and off. Lower Pines Campground in Yosemite Valley has campsites suitable for wheelchairs, as well as power outlets for charging electric wheelchairs. All lodging options within Yosemite have wheelchair-accessible rooms.

The **Yosemite Lodge Bike Stand** (☎ 209-372-1208) and the **Curry Village Rental Stand** (☎ 209-372-8319) both have one wheelchair for rent ($7.50/11 per hour/day); in other words, get there early if you need one. Many sites within Yosemite Valley, including the base of Yosemite Falls, are wheelchair accessible; for a complete and detailed list, download the accessibility brochure.

For hearing-impaired visitors, a ranger may be available during summer months for American Sign Language (ASL) interpretation during park-led walks and talks. For information, contact the one of the visitor centers or call ☎ 209-372-4726 (TTY). For paid tours, ASL interpretation can be arranged through the **Yosemite Lodge tour desk** (☎ 209-372-1240).

Based in Mammoth Lakes, the nonprofit organization **Disabled Sports Eastern Sierra** (☎ 760-934-0791; www.disabledsportseasternsierra.org) offers a variety of educational opportunities for disabled travelers, including skiing and climbing courses. For more information, see the boxed text, p205.

Easy Access to National Parks: The Sierra Club Guide for People with Disabilities, by Wendy Roth and Michael Tompane, is a carefully researched guide for intrepid travelers with physical limitations. Published in 1992, it's not fully up-to-date but is still quite useful. It's available used for under $10 (shop around) online.

VOLUNTEERING

Besides helping the national parks, volunteering is a great way to see a side of Yosemite and Sequoia & Kings Canyon that most tourists never do. For more information, see p56.

WOMEN TRAVELERS

Women traveling solo or in groups in the national parks rarely experience any problems. Sexism on the trail is a pretty rare thing and, especially within the parks, women regularly hike alone. In national forest areas outside the park, where you'll find hunters, off-roaders and fishermen (ie large groups of beer-swilling males), women may feel less comfortable, and justifiably so.

Many women feel reluctant about solo overnight backpacking. Although the *fear* of spending the night alone in the wilderness is obviously a different beast for women than it is for men, women are generally just as safe. See the boxed text, p46, for one woman's solo experience on the Pacific Crest Trail.

The notion that a menstruating woman attracts bears is a myth. However, used tampons and pads should be sealed up and stored in a bear-proof food canister or poop tube, just like anything else that's scented.

If you're nervous about hiking alone, ranger-led hikes and group excursions in the parks offer a great way to take to the trail and push yourself further than you normally might. Another approach – and this is true for anyone hiking alone – is sticking to busy trails and building your confidence for more remote trips.

When it comes to climbing, women have proven themselves equally capable (and often more so) on rock than their male counterparts, so respect is usually shown in both directions. One only has to think of Lynn Hill, the first person to free-climb the Nose route on El Capitan.

There are some good books out there to help prepare for a trip. Check out Thalia Zepatos' *Adventures in Good Company: The Complete Guide to Women's Tours and Outdoor Trips* and Adrienne Hall's *Backpacking: A Woman's Guide*.

WORK

Nearly everyone employed inside the parks is employed either by the National Park Service or by park concessionaires. Most employment opportunities within the parks are seasonal – roughly Memorial Day (the last Monday in May) through Labor Day (the first Monday in September) – although the occasional year-round job does come up. Applications are almost always due at least six months in advance.

Yosemite's chief concessionaire is **DNC Parks & Resorts at Yosemite, Inc** (DNC; ☎ 209-372-1236; www.yosemitepark.com), which runs nearly all of the park's lodges, restaurants, shops, tours, shuttle buses and recreation centers. During the summer, DNC employs about 1800 people, so it's by far your best bet if you're eager to nab a job inside the park. For a list of jobs available through DNC, visit the 'Employment Opportunities' section of the DNC website (under 'About Us'). If you're already in the Valley and are struck by the need to stay and work, drop by the Human Resources department in the DNC administration offices in Yosemite Village. DNC occasionally hires people on the spot if they're short staffed. International visitors are eligible for employment with DNC through **Intrax International** (www.intraxworktravel.com).

The main concessionaire at Sequoia & Kings Canyon National Parks is **Sequoia-Kings Canyon Park Service Company** (☎ 559-335-5500, ext 302; www.sequoia-kingscanyon.com), which employs about 80 people during summer.

Most jobs through the National Park Service are part of the **NPS Seasonal Employment Program** (☎ 877-554-4550; www.sep.nps.gov), which hires park rangers, park guides and visitor assistants. All vacancies are posted online. To browse the occasional year-round jobs that surface, visit www.usajobs.gov or the jobs section of the **NPS website** (http://home.nps.gov/applications/digest/usajobs.cfm). Only US citizens are eligible for NPS employment.

Transportation

CONTENTS

GETTING THERE & AWAY

Most visitors to the parks come by car. It's definitely the easiest option, but others do exist. There is no direct plane or train service, though connections by bus are available to Yosemite and Sequoia National Parks (not to Kings Canyon). For further information on transportation *within* Yosemite National Park, see p94; for Sequoia & Kings Canyon National Parks, see p219.

Flights, tours and rail tickets can be booked online at www.lonelyplanet.com /travel_services.

AIR

The headaches associated with air travel both within the United States and throughout the world have grown exponentially since 9/11, but you can keep them to a minimum with a little pretrip research. The **Transport Security Administration** (www.tsa.gov) offers comprehensive, up-to-date information on all US federal security requirements, including carry-on regulations and what to expect when traveling with children or if you have a disability.

Airports

Several major international airports lie between three and five hours' driving time from Yosemite and Sequoia & Kings Can-

yon. The nearest to both parks are in San Francisco, Oakland and San Jose (all about 200/250 miles from Yosemite/Sequoia & Kings Canyon), Sacramento (180/250 miles), Las Vegas (350/400 miles) and Los Angeles (315/230 miles).

The closest international airport to Yosemite and Kings Canyon & Sequoia National Parks is **Fresno-Yosemite International Airport** (☎ 559-621-4500; www.flyfresno.org), which is about only 90 miles southwest of Yosemite and 60 miles west of Sequoia & Kings Canyon. There are no *direct* international flights to Fresno, however; all flights are via nearby international airports.

The following international airports are the most convenient for domestic flights as well.

Los Angeles International (airport code LAX; ☎ 310-646-5252; www.lawa.org)

McCarran International (LAS; ☎ 702-261-5211; www.mccarran.com) In Las Vegas.

Oakland International (OAK; ☎ 510-563-3300; www .flyoakland.com) Just east of San Francisco.

Sacramento International (SMF; ☎ 916-929-5411; www.sacairports.org)

San Francisco International (SFO; ☎ 650-821-8211; www.flysfo.com)

San Jose International (SJC; ☎ 408-277-4759; www .sjc.org)

Reno-Tahoe International (RNO; ☎ 775-328-6870; www.renoairport.com)

Airlines
US AIRLINES
AirTran Airways (airline code FL; ☎ 800-247-8726; www.airtran.com; hub Atlanta)

THINGS CHANGE...

The information in this chapter is particularly vulnerable to change. Check directly with the airline or a travel agent to make sure you understand how a fare (and ticket you may buy) works and be aware of the security requirements for international travel. Shop carefully. The details given in this chapter should be regarded as pointers and are not a substitute for your own careful, up-to-date research.

TRANSPORTATION

CLIMATE CHANGE & TRAVEL

Climate change is a serious threat to the ecosystems that humans rely upon, and air travel is the fastest-growing contributor to the problem. Lonely Planet regards travel, overall, as a global benefit, but believes we all have a responsibility to limit our personal impact on global warming.

Flying & Climate Change

Pretty much every form of motorized travel generates CO_2 (the main cause of human-induced climate change) but planes are far and away the worst offenders, not just because of the sheer distances they allow us to travel, but also because they release greenhouse gases high into the atmosphere. The statistics are frightening: two people taking a return flight between Europe and the US will contribute as much to climate change as an average household's gas and electricity consumption over a whole year.

Carbon Offset Schemes

Climatecare.org and other websites use 'carbon calculators' that allow travelers to offset the level of greenhouse gases they are responsible for with financial contributions to sustainable travel schemes that reduce global warming, including projects in Honduras, Kazakhstan and Uganda.

Lonely Planet, together with Rough Guides and other concerned partners in the travel industry, support the carbon offset scheme run by climatecare.org. Lonely Planet offsets all of its staff and author travel.

For more information check out our website: www.lonelyplanet.com.

Alaska Airlines/Horizon Air (AS/QX; ☎ 800-426-0333; www.alaskaair.com; hub Seattle)

American Airlines (AA; ☎ 800-433-7300; www.aa.com; hub Dallas-Fort Worth)

ATA (TZ; ☎ 800-435-9282; www.ata.com; hub Midway Chicago)

Continental (CO; ☎ 800-525-0280; www.continental.com; hub Houston)

Delta (DL; ☎ 800-221-1212; www.delta.com; hub Atlanta)

Frontier (F9; ☎ 800-432-1359; www.frontierairlines.com; hub Denver)

Jet Blue (B6; ☎ 800-538-2583; www.jetblue.com; hub JFK, New York)

Midwest Airlines (YX; ☎ 800-452-2022; www.midwestairlines.com; hub Milwaukee)

Northwest Airlines (NW; ☎ 800-225-2525; www.nwa.com; hub Minneapolis-St Paul)

Southwest (WN; ☎ 800-435-9792; www.southwest.com; hub Love Field, Dallas)

United (UA; ☎ 800-241-6522; www.united.com; hub Chicago O'Hare)

US Airways/America West (US/HP; ☎ 800-428-4322; www.usairways.com; hubs Charlotte, Philadelphia, Phoenix)

INTERNATIONAL AIRLINES

Aer Lingus (EI; ☎ 800-474-7424; www.aerlingus.com; hub Dublin)

Aeromexico (AM; ☎ 800-237-6639; www.aeromexico.com; hub Mexico City)

Air Canada (AC; ☎ 888-247-2262; www.aircanada.com; hub Pearson, Toronto)

Air France (AF; ☎ 800-237-2747; www.airfrance.com; hub Charles de Gaulle, Paris)

Air New Zealand (NZ; ☎ 800262-1234; www.airnewzealand.com; hub Auckland)

Alitalia (AZ; ☎ 800 223-5730; www.alitalia.com; hubs Fiumicino, Rome; Malpensa, Milan)

ANA (NH; ☎ 800-235-9262; www.fly-ana.com; hub Narita, Tokyo)

Asiana (OZ; ☎ 800-227-4262; flyasiana.com; hub Incheon, Seoul)

British Airways (BA; ☎ 800-247-9297; www.britishairways.com; hub Heathrow, London)

Cathay Pacific (CX; ☎ 800-228-4297; www.cathaypacific.com; hub Hong Kong)

Iberia (IB; ☎ 800-772-4642; www.iberia.com; hub Barajas, Madrid)

Japan Airlines (JL; ☎ 800-525-3663; www.ar.jal.com; hub Narita, Tokyo)

KLM (KL; ☎ 800-374-7747; www.klm.com; hub Schiphol, Amsterdam)

Lufthansa (LH; ☎ 800-645-3880; www.lufthansa.com; hub Frankfurt)

Mexicana (MX; ☎ 800-531-7921; www.mexicana.com; hub Mexico City)

Qantas (QF; ☎ 800-227-4500; www.qantas.com; hub Sydney)

Singapore Airlines (SQ; ☎ 800-742-3333; www.singaporeair.com; hub Changi, Singapore)

TRANSPORTATION

Virgin Atlantic (VS; ☎ 800-862-8621; www.virgin-at
lantic.com; hubs Heathrow, London; Gatwick, London)
WestJet (WS; ☎ 888-937-8538; www.westjet.com; hub
Calgary)

BICYCLE

Cycling is a great way to get to the national
parks, but it's not an excursion for the novice
peddler. Roads are narrow, grades are steep
and summer temperatures can climb well
over 90°F. Altitude presents another challenge
if you're considering a ride to Tuolumne or
elsewhere in the high country. That said, numerous people see both parks by bike every
year and never have any problems.

Better World Club (☎ 866-238-1137; www.bett
erworldclub.com) offers emergency roadside assistance for cyclists for an annual membership fee of about $40. If you plan to bring
your bike from abroad, be sure to check
up on current baggage requirements; some
airlines charge up to $100 *each way* for a
bicycle. For more information on cycling
within Yosemite National Park, see p149.

BUS

Buses are the only forms of public transportation into the parks. While bussing it may
seem like a hassle, it usually ends up saving
you money in the long run and, in Yosemite,
the headache of dealing with summer traffic.
Once you're in Yosemite Valley, you can get
around on the free shuttle (see p95).

Getting around Sequoia & Kings Canyon
is a little trickier. First, you need to get to
one of the hub cities for the park you're
heading to: Merced (p175) for Yosemite;
Visalia (p243) for Sequoia & Kings Canyon. **Greyhound** (☎ 800-229-9424; www.greyhound
.com) buses run to both cities from nearly
every major city in the United States. Both
cities also have Amtrak train stations (see
p265). Once you're in Merced or Visalia,
you get the local bus to the parks.

For information on organized tours to
Yosemite and Sequoia & Kings Canyon,
see p257.

To/From Yosemite National Park

From the Central Valley town of Merced,
the **Yosemite Area Regional Transportation
System** (YARTS; ☎ 209-388-9589, 877-989-2787;
www.yarts.com) runs buses along Hwy 140
into Yosemite Valley. The 3¼-hour ride
costs $25 (round trip) and includes the
park entry fee (a $20 value in itself).
Children under 12 and seniors (over 62)
pay $18 for the round-trip ticket. The
route originates from the **Merced Transpo
Center & Greyhound Terminal** (16th St btwn N &
0 Sts) and buses stop at Merced's Amtrak
station before heading to Yosemite. Buses
depart daily at 7am, 8:45am, 10:30am
and 5:15pm, except in winter, when the
5:15pm bus goes only as far as the Bug
Hostel in Midpines.

ROUTES INTO THE PARKS

Yosemite National Park
Yosemite operates three entrance stations on the west side of the Sierra Nevada: the South Entrance on Hwy 41 (Wawona Rd) north of Fresno – convenient from southern California; the Arch
Rock Entrance on Hwy 140 (El Portal Rd) east of Merced – convenient from northern California
but closed to vehicles over 28ft; and the Big Oak Flat Entrance on Hwy 120 W (Big Oak Flat Rd)
east of Manteca – the quickest route from the Bay Area. Roads are generally kept open all year,
though in winter (usually November to April), drivers may be required to carry tire chains.

The Tioga Pass Entrance, along Hwy 120 E (Tioga Rd) on the east side of the park, is open
from about June to October, depending on when the snow is cleared. From Tioga Pass, drivers
connect with Hwy 395 and points such as Reno and Death Valley National Park.

Sequoia & Kings Canyon National Parks
The two routes into Sequoia & Kings Canyon approach from the west, departing Hwy 99 from
Fresno or Visalia. From Visalia, Hwy 198 leads 46 miles east into Sequoia National Park. From
Fresno, Hwy 180 east leads 57 miles east to Kings Canyon. The two roads are connected by the
Generals Hwy, inside Sequoia. There is no access to either park from the east, and no internal
roads between the parks.

Reservations for YARTS buses are not required, but it's best to obtain tickets before boarding. You can purchase tickets from area motels, the California Welcome Center in Merced, the visitor center in Mariposa and the Yosemite Bug Lodge & Hostel in Midpines. Bus drivers also sell tickets. Inbound buses from Merced stop at Yosemite Lodge, the Valley Visitor Center, the Ahwahnee Hotel and Curry Village.

Another option, if you're shacked up at a San Francisco hotel or hostel, is the Yosemite Bug Bus (p257), which will pick you up and take you as far as the Yosemite Bug Rustic Mountain Resort (p177) for $60.

YARTS also offers round-trip bus service between Yosemite Valley and Mammoth Lakes once daily in July and August, and on Saturday and Sunday only in May, June and September. The bus departs Mammoth at 7am and Yosemite Valley at 5pm, stopping at June Lake, Lee Vining, Tuolumne Meadows, White Wolf and Crane Flat. It will stop anywhere en route upon request.

To/From Sequoia & Kings Canyon National Parks

From the San Joaquin Valley town of Visalia, the 16-person **Sequoia Shuttle** (☎ 877-287-4453; www.sequoiashuttle.com) runs to Sequoia & Kings Canyon National Parks during summer (Memorial Day to Labor Day), stopping in Three Rivers and other towns en route. The $10 round-trip fare includes the park entry fee. The service began in 2007 and will be piloted through 2009. The plan is to make the shuttle permanent if the pilot is successful. Call or check the website for updated information.

CAR & MOTORCYCLE

Driving is by far the most popular way to get to and around both national parks. In Yosemite, this means battles with traffic, smog and sometimes frustrating battles for parking spaces – woes of the urban world that, sadly, are inescapable here during peak summer months. There are two alternatives: one is to arrive in the Valley early, park in the day parking lot near Curry Village and take advantage of the excellent free shuttle system that operates in Yosemite Valley, Tuolumne Meadows and Mariposa Grove. The other, which makes little logistical sense for day-trippers, is to park in a town along Hwy 140 (outside the park)

and take the YARTS bus (see opposite) into the park. Traffic problems are generally nonexistent in Sequoia & Kings Canyon.

Yosemite lies about four hours from San Francisco and about six hours from Los Angeles. Sequoia & Kings Canyon National Parks lie four to five hours from Los Angeles (depending on which entrance you choose) and 4½ to 5½ hours from San Francisco.

Automobile Associations

California's main automobile association is the **California State Automobile Association** (CSAA; ☎ 800-922-8228, 24hr roadside assistance 800-874-7562; www.csaa.com), a division of the nationwide **American Automobile Association** (AAA; www.aaa .com). Recently, an alternative to AAA has sprung up: the **Better World Club** (☎ 866-238-1137; www.betterworldclub.com), which offers similar services and donates 1% of its revenue to environmental clean-up and advocacy.

Driver's License

Non-California residents can drive in California for up to a year using their home-state driver's license. Non-US residents can legally drive in the United States with only their home driver's license and passport, but proffering an international driver's license (in the event you get pulled over) can make things easier on everyone. Most car-rental companies do not require an international driver's license, but their representatives claim that having one makes the rental process easier.

Rental

Renting a car in California is a straightforward procedure, provided you're 25 years of age, have a valid driver's license, a credit card and, if you're a nonresident, a passport. Rentals are available at all the airports listed earlier as well as at offices in major cities and the larger cities en route to the parks. The following car-rental companies maintain branches at major airports and throughout California:

Alamo (☎ 800-327-9633; www.alamo.com)
Avis (☎ 800-331-1212; www.avis.com)
Budget (☎ 800-527-0700; www.budget.com)
Dollar (☎ 800-800-4000; www.dollar.com)
Enterprise (☎ 800-325-8007; www.enterprise.com)
Fox (☎ 800-225-4369; www.foxrentacar.com)
Hertz (☎ 800-654-3131; www.hertz.com)
National (☎ 800-227-7368; www.nationalcar.com)
Thrifty (☎ 800-367-2277; www.thrifty.com)

TRANSPORTATION

Should you wish to join the legions of folks touring the parks in motor homes, you can rent one through **El Monte** (www.elmonterv.com) or **Cruise America** (www.cruiseamerica.com).

Insurance

Anyone driving in California is required to have a minimum of $35,000 in liability insurance, and they must carry proof of that insurance in the car at all times. If you're driving a rental, you might already be insured through a credit card or through your own auto-insurance policy (be sure to check both); if not, you can purchase liability insurance upon rental of the car. This rarely adds more than $10 per day to the rental rate. If you're driving a friend's car,

you'll be insured under their policy (assuming they have one). If you plan to purchase a car for the trip, there are heaps of insurance options available online.

Road Rules

Californians drive on the right-hand side of the road. Unless signed otherwise, it's legal to make a right turn on a red light after coming to a complete stop. Distances and speed limits are shown on road signs in miles (not kilometers). If you're stuck behind a slow driver on a two-lane highway, you can pass them on the left-hand side, provided the center line is broken (not solid yellow). For a complete list of California road rules, see the *California Driver Hand-*

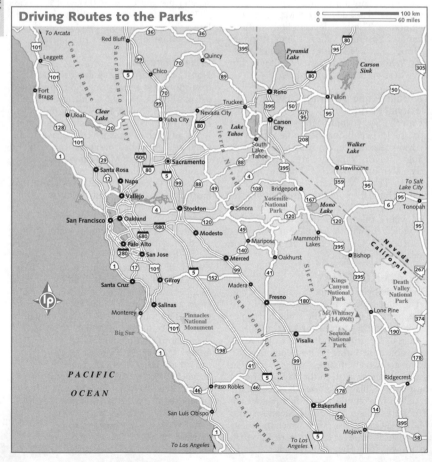

Driving Routes to the Parks

Road Distances (miles)

	Kings Canyon National Park	Las Vegas	Los Angeles	Mammoth Lakes	New York City	Portland	San Francisco	Seattle	Sequoia National Park	Yosemite Valley
Kings Canyon National Park	---									
Las Vegas	450	---								
Los Angeles	273	270	---							
Mammoth Lakes	272	272	309	---						
New York City	2958	2520	2810	2710	---					
Portland	834	1052	1040	741	2895	---				
San Francisco	272	570	385	260	2905	635	---			
Seattle	1010	1125	1135	915	2850	175	810	---		
Sequoia National Park	59	415	240	268	2920	832	270	1005	---	
Yosemite Valley	177	405	312	130	2785	745	188	914	176	---

book at the website of the **California Department of Motor Vehicles** (DMV; www.dmv.ca.gov); it's under 'Publications.'

TRAIN

No trains serve the parks directly. However, **Amtrak** (☎ 800-872-7245; www.amtrak.com) offers daily service to the transport hubs of Merced (for Yosemite) and Visalia (for Sequoia & Kings Canyon), where bus service is available into the parks. In Merced, you transfer directly to the YARTS buses, a leg of the ticket you can pay for when you purchase your Amtrak ticket. When you do it this way, the park entry is included in the fare, and you're guaranteed your seat on the YARTS bus is automatically reserved.

For Sequoia & Kings Canyon, it's slightly more complicated because you have to get off the train in the town of Hanford (20 miles west of Visalia), where an Amtrak bus picks you up and takes you to Visalia. There, you transfer to the Sequoia Shuttle (summer only), which is a non-Amtrak affiliated service.

From most major airports, the first leg of Amtrak service is often by bus to the nearest train station. The earlier you book your Amtrak ticket, the cheaper the fare. Updated fares are posted online.

GETTING AROUND

The vast majority of visitors get around the parks by car. It's the most convenient way to get around Sequoia & Kings Canyon National Parks, as well as around the greater Yosemite National Park area. However, due to traffic, it can be extremely frustrating in the Yosemite Valley during peak summer season. It is then that the other options become increasingly attractive.

BICYCLE

As countless repeat visitors to Yosemite National Park can tell you, the easiest way to get around Yosemite Valley is by bike. Cycling outside of Yosemite Valley is another story altogether. Should you wish to visit somewhere like Tuolumne Meadows by bike,

TRANSPORTATION

you'd better have your peddling legs on, because it's a steep climb up a narrow road in thin air. This is when peddling Yosemite National Park becomes an adventure only for the experienced cyclist on a proper bike. If you're staying at Sequoia's Lodgepole campground, a bike can be a decent way to get back and forth to the village.

All trails within the national parks are off-limits to mountain bikes. For off-road adventures of this sort you'll have to head somewhere like Mammoth or Bear Valley. For information on bike rentals in Yosemite, see p149. Also see Cycling (p47) and Mountain Biking (p48).

BUS

Yosemite has a surprisingly good public-transportation system (see p95), making it easy to get around Yosemite Valley and relatively easy to get anywhere along Tioga Rd and even as far as Mammoth Lakes. For information on the latter, see p195.

Sequoia National Park has two shuttle routes (p219) within the park, but Kings Canyon has none. There is no public transportation *between* any of the parks.

CAR & MOTORCYCLE

Most folks visiting the parks get around inside them just as they got to them – by car.

Fuel & Spare Parts

Fuel and spare parts get cheaper as you move further from the parks (until you hit the San Francisco Bay Area, where they skyrocket again), so do your best to gas up before you get near the parks. The nearest place to Yosemite Valley for fuel is in El Portal, about 14 miles west of Yosemite Village along Hwy 140. There are no gas stations in Sequoia & Kings Canyon; the nearest gas stations are at Kings Canyon Lodge, Stony Creek Lodge (both open mid-April to mid-October only) and Hume Lake. Also see the Getting Around sections for Yosemite (p94) and Sequoia & Kings Canyon (p219).

Road Conditions

Both parks are accessible year-round, and almost all roads within the parks are paved. In Yosemite, there are some unpaved roads, such as those to campgrounds at Tamarack Flat and Yosemite Creek. These roads are

---

RVS & TRAILERS

For the most part, all three parks are RV- and trailer-friendly. Consider the following if you're visiting Yosemite National Park:

- There are no electrical hookups.

- No vehicles over 28ft are allowed past the detour around the rockslide on Hwy 140, 10 miles west of the Arch Rock Entrance. At publication time, widening the road was still at least a few years off.

- Vehicles over 40ft are not allowed on the Mariposa Grove Rd nor in Yosemite Valley. The same road is closed to vehicles over 23ft between 6am and 9pm daily (when the free shuttle operates).

- The potholed dirt roads down to Yosemite Creek and Tamarack Flat campgrounds are notorious RV/trailer traps. RVs over 24ft are not recommended for these campgrounds, nor for Porcupine Flat or White Wolf.

- Yosemite's only year-round dump station is in Yosemite Valley near the Upper Pines Campground. In summer, there are also stations in Wawona and Tuolumne Meadows.

The following applies to Sequoia & Kings Canyon National Parks.

- No RVs or trailers are permitted on Mineral King Rd.

- Vehicles over 22ft are not recommended on Crystal Cave Rd, at Panoramic Point or on the Moro Rock–Crescent Meadow road between Potwisha and the Giant Forest Museum.

In Yosemite, generators can only be used in campgrounds between 7am and 7pm, but only sparingly. Generator hours vary at Sequoia & Kings Canyon, but they exist.

WINTER DRIVING CONDITIONS

Winter is a splendid time to explore Yosemite and Sequoia & Kings Canyon. Crowds are thinner and the snowy magic is unforgettable. But snow and ice present hazards and road closures that summer drivers never face. If you're driving anywhere in the Sierras during winter, you should carry tire chains unless your vehicle is equipped with snow tires or has four- or all-wheel drive.

During winter months (or unseasonably early or late snows) motorists will encounter 'chain controls' on many mountain roads; continuing past these without snow tires or four- or all-wheel drive is illegal. Unless you're properly equipped, your only option is to buy or rent chains on the spot or turn back. If you plan drive to the parks when there's any chance of snow, the easiest solution is to bring your own chains, as renting or purchasing at or near chain controls is expensive. Even if you bring your own chains, you don't have to get out of the car and put them on yourselves; there are invariably people along the roadside who will do this for you for a modest fee, and save your knuckles in the process. If you plan to put your chains on yourself, be absolutely certain to bring a pair of gloves; purchasing a pair of cheap leather gardening gloves and storing them permanently in the chain box is a good idea.

If you're exploring the parks during winter, another smart precaution is packing emergency food and water and a sleeping bag (whether you plan to camp or not) for each person in the car. If you're on a country road and get stuck or lose control and slide off the road, assistance could be hours or days away. Having provisions and warmth in the car can literally save your life.

Snow closes Yosemite's Tioga Rd (Hwy 120 east of Crane Flat) all winter long. In Sequoia & Kings Canyon, the Kings Canyon Scenic Byway (ie the road to Cedar Grove) and the Generals Hwy both close periodically in winter due to snow. Mineral King Rd, in Sequoia, closes November 1 to late May.

---

manageable in an ordinary passenger vehicle, but forget it if you're pulling a long trailer or driving a large RV. Outside the parks lies an endless network of fire and forest-service roads, many leading to remote campgrounds and lakes. While many of these roads are drivable with a standard-clearance vehicle, they'll definitely beat the hell out of your shocks and your car. In other words, you're better off with above-average clearance and heavy-duty shocks and tires should you wish to explore these roads.

For current road conditions for highways throughout California, call the **Caltrans Highway Information Network** (☎ 800-427-7623; www.dot.ca.gov/hq/roadinfo/) or check the website. For road information within Yosemite park, call ☎ 209-372-0200. For Sequoia & Kings Canyon, call ☎ 559-565-3341 (ext 941).

Road Hazards

Speeding motorists represent one of the parks' principal road hazards. Not only does speeding put humans in danger, but it also endangers park wildlife. Many animals, including bear and deer, are hit by motorists every year. Not only does plowing into one of these mean a bad ending for the animal, the odds are it will total your car and seriously injure or kill you and your passengers. On a slightly more mundane level, small animals such as squirrels, foxes and chipmunks regularly dart across roads, and most people's natural reaction is to swerve to avoid hitting the little critter; nothing could be more dangerous. If a small animal dashes in front of your car, slow down if you can do so safely, or wince and keep driving. Snow and ice are extreme road hazards (see the boxed text, above).

HITCHHIKING

Hitchhiking is never entirely safe anywhere in the world, and we don't recommend it. While it's technically illegal within the parks, it is quite common – hitching in Yosemite is sometimes necessary to get to or from a trailhead before or after a hike. Outside the parks, hitchhiking is legal, but can be difficult due to the fact that hitchers are generally viewed with suspicion. If you're trying to get home from Yosemite, Camp 4 (p162) is a good place to try to line up a ride; check the bulletin board there for rides offered and needed. For loads of information on hitchhiking and ride-sharing, check out **Digihitch** (www.digihitch.com).

TRANSPORTATION

Health & Safety

Keeping healthy while on vacation in a national park depends on your predeparture preparations, your daily health care while traveling and how you handle any medical problems that develop. While the potential problems can seem quite frightening, in reality few visitors experience anything worse that a skinned knee. The sections that follow cover worst-case scenarios, which can be avoided or dealt with if you are properly prepared.

BEFORE YOU GO

INSURANCE
It's a good idea to review the terms of your health-insurance policy before your trip; some policies don't cover injuries sustained as a result of dangerous activities, which can include such pursuits as rock climbing or mountaineering. You may also want to double-check that emergency medical care, as well as emergency evacuation to your home country (if you're not from the US), is covered by your policy.

MEDICAL CHECKLIST
- acetaminophen (Tylenol) or aspirin
- adhesive or paper tape
- antibacterial ointment for cuts and abrasions
- antihistamines (for hay fever and allergic reactions)
- anti-inflammatory drugs (eg ibuprofen)
- bandages, gauze, gauze rolls
- DEET-containing insect repellent for the skin
- moleskin (for blisters)
- pocketknife
- scissors, safety pins, tweezers
- steroid cream or cortisone (for poison ivy and other allergic rashes)
- sun block
- thermometer

INTERNET RESOURCES
Yosemite National Park – Your Safety (www.nps.gov/yose/planyourvisit/yoursafety.htm) Safety recommendations for Yosemite visitors.
Sequoia & Kings Canyon National Park – Your Safety (www.nps.gov/seki/planyourvisit/yoursafety.htm) Safety tips for visitors to Sequoia & Kings Canyon.
WMI – Curriculum Updates (www.nols.edu/wmi/curriculum_updates) Wilderness medicine information and helpful articles.

FURTHER READING
Backcountry First Aid and Extended Care (Buck Tilton, Falcon, 2007) An inexpensive pocket-sized wilderness survival manual.
NOLS Wilderness Medicine (Tod Schimelpfenig, National Outdoor Leadership School, 2006) A comprehensive curriculum to wilderness first aid, emphasizing teamwork and communication skills.

IN THE PARKS

The parks are not immune from crime – and it's no wonder, considering that they see millions of visitors each year. However, the majority of crimes are small-time theft, vandalism and public drunkenness.

Car break-ins are more often the work of opportunistic bears than burglars. The chances are your car will be fine if parked for the day or even longer, but it's wise to ask at the nearest visitor center or ranger station about known problems at your trailhead, especially if you're heading out for several days. Carry your money and valuables with you. If you do leave anything in the car, put it in the trunk or other enclosed area. When possible, avoid leaving your vehicle at an isolated trailhead and instead park in a more heavily used parking area within reasonable walking distance. Better yet, use shuttle buses or arrange a carpool. Park your vehicle facing in, so the trunk or rear access door remains visible. Never hide your vehicle's keys in, under or near the vehicle.

Poison oak and summer mosquitoes are two of the more trying natural annoyances in the parks. Poison oak can be found at elevations below 6000ft, so pay attention to the shrubbery on low-elevation hikes.

MEDICAL SERVICES & EMERGENCIES

For emergencies, call ☎ 911.

Yosemite area

The **Yosemite Medical Clinic** (Map p93; ☎ 209-372-4637) and **Yosemite Dental Clinic** (Map p93; ☎ 209-372-4200) are in Yosemite Valley, on the Ahwahnee Hotel road near Yosemite Village. Hours vary, but emergency care is available around the clock.

The hospitals nearest to Yosemite include the **John C Fremont Hospital and Clinic** (☎ 209-966-3631; 5189 Hospital Rd) in Mariposa, **Tuolumne General Hospital** (☎ 209-533-7100; 101 Hospital Rd) in Sonora and **Doctors Medical Center** (☎ 209-578-1211; 1441 Florida Ave) in Modesto, the largest facility in the region.

Sequoia & Kings Canyon area

Emergency first aid is available at all ranger stations. The major trauma center in the region is **University Medical Center** (☎ 559-459-4000; 445 S Cedar Ave) in Fresno, which has 24-hour emergency care. Closer to the parks, **Sierra Kings Hospital** (☎ 559-638-8155; 372 W Cypress) in Reedley is 24-hour but only handles minor injuries, and further south, **Kaweah Delta Hospital** (☎ 559-624-2000; 400 W Mineral King) in Visalia has 24-hour emergency services.

TRAVELERS DIARRHEA
Amoebic Dysentery

While a change of water, food or climate may give travelers a case of the runs, serious diarrhea caused by contaminated water is an increasing problem in heavily used backcountry areas. If diarrhea does hit you, however, fluid replacement is the mainstay of management. Weak black tea with a little sugar; soda water; or soft drink allowed to go flat and 50% diluted with water are all

good. With severe diarrhea, a rehydrating solution is necessary to replace minerals and salts. Commercially available oral rehydration salts (ORS) are very useful. You should stick to a bland diet as you recover.

Gut-paralyzing drugs such as diphenoxylate or loperamide can be used to bring relief from the symptoms, although they do not actually cure the problem.

Giardiasis

If you drink snowmelt, stream, lake or groundwater in the park, you risk coming into contact with the waterborne parasite *Giardia lamblia*, which causes giardiasis, an intestinal disease marked by chronic diarrhea, abdominal cramps, bloating, fatigue and weight loss. Symptoms may take a week or so to manifest. Though not usually dangerous, it is unpleasant and requires treatment with antibiotics.

As a rule, don't drink any naturally occurring water without boiling it for several minutes, filtering it with a Giardia-rated water filter, or treating it with an iodine-based purifier. Also refrain from brushing your teeth or doing dishes with untreated water.

ENVIRONMENTAL HAZARDS
Altitude

In the thinner atmosphere of the High Sierra, lack of oxygen may cause headaches, nausea, nosebleeds, shortness of breath, physical weakness and other symptoms. These can lead to serious consequences, especially if combined with heat exhaustion, sunburn or hypothermia. Most people adjust to altitude within a few hours or days. In mild cases of altitude sickness, everyday painkillers such as aspirin may relieve discomfort. If symptoms persist, descend to lower elevations.

Bears

Bears are active day and night throughout the Sierra Nevada and are especially prevalent in the parks, thanks in large part to the presence of humans and the enticing smells we bring with us. Only black bears live in California. To many visitors, bears represent a mix of the fascinating and the frightening. It's not often we get to see such powerful, majestic animals in the wild – at the same time, many of us would just as soon not see one while in the park.

HEALTH & SAFETY

Bears elsewhere often flee at the sight, sound or smell of people. Sadly, many park bears do the exact opposite and are notorious for regularly breaking into vehicles and raiding campgrounds and backcountry campsites in search of food. Though the bears rarely charge visitors, having one traipse through your campsite or make off with your food or backpack can leave you quite unnerved.

To keep the bears at bay, the parks insists that you remove *all* scented items from your car, including any food, trash (scour the car for those empty potato - chip bags and soda cans) and products such as gum, toothpaste, soap and sunscreen. It's best, too, to cover anything in your car that even looks like a cooler or food. Place the items in bear canisters – large metal storage lockers found in most major parking lots, every park campsite and a few popular backcountry campgrounds. In the national parks, failure to use bear boxes often results in a fine (rangers do nightly campground and parking-lot monitoring in summer) – not to mention the possibility of your car windows being shattered and upholstery ravaged by a hungry beast. Elsewhere in the Sierra, you'll find bear boxes at national-park trailheads and the most troublesome United States Forests Service (USFS) trailheads.

So what's the big deal if a bear nabs a little human food? Well, it could mean the eventual death of the bear. Bears that associate people with food become increasingly bold about approaching people, to the point where the bears become dangerously aggressive. Once a bear becomes a serial campground bandit, or begins charging visitors, rangers are obligated to kill it. Please do not contribute to the death of one of these beautiful, intelligent animals – a fed bear is a dead bear.

At campsites, think of the bear box as your refrigerator – keep it shut and latched if you are not actively using it. With padded feet, bears can stealthily appear out of nowhere and leave you no time to lock things up. There are plentiful tales of distracted cooks turning around to discover extra dinner guests. Prepare evening meals well before dusk and wash dishes immediately after eating. If a bear does enter your campsite, make lots of noise – yell, clap your hands, bang pots – and try to look big by raising your arms and opening your jacket. More than likely the bear will wander off. Whatever you do, don't corner the bear – give it room to escape. And never, ever get between a mother bear and her cubs.

Backpackers without a park-approved bear-resistant food container must usually rent one unless they are overnighting in one of the rare backcountry campgrounds that has a bear locker. Containers are available at wilderness centers, visitor centers and stores throughout the parks. If confronted by a bear, don't drop your backpack – that's probably just what the bear wants, and it will only lead to more problems for other people (and, ultimately, the bear). Never run from a bear, either. You'll only trigger its instinct to chase, and you cannot outrun a bear.

You can and should fight back if a black bear attacks you. Use any means available – throw rocks and sticks or hit it with your gear. Fortunately, however, it's extremely

---

BEAR FEEDINGS

To this day, there is hardly a park visitor who does not consider a bear sighting to be part of the requisite experience. In the early years, bears and many other animals were valued as food and for their warm pelts. Though a grizzly adorns the state flag, the ferocious species was hunted to statewide extinction by 1922, but after hunting was banned in the park, the population of the peaceable black bear swelled.

However, the garbage generated by tourists has created a new and ill-adapted caste of bear. During the early 20th century, Yosemite dumped its garbage onto theatrically lit bear-feeding platforms for the entertainment of Valley tourists, who came each night to photograph the bears. The practice came to an end in the early 1940s, though by then the camp bears had become highly dependent on the easy pickings and went on to perfect their skills at raiding campgrounds and breaking into locked automobiles. The re-education of visitors is now a high park priority, so do your part to keep bears wild.

WHAT TO DO IF YOU ENCOUNTER A BEAR

Bears entering developed areas in search of human food should be treated differently to bears spotted in their natural environment, and how you should react to a bear varies according to the location.

Be Loud in the Campground

- Do not drop your food and run.
- Make sure all food and scented items are stored properly.
- Gather others together and wave your arms so you look intimidating.
- Make lots of noise by banging pots and pans and yelling.
- Do not attempt to retrieve food from a bear, or to surround it.

Be Deferential on the Trail

- Do not run or drop your pack.
- Stay together (especially if you're walking with small children).
- Give the bear lots of room (300ft or more).
- Never get between a mother and her cubs.
- Don't linger too long.

rare for a bear to make an unprovoked attack on a human.

Also check out www.sierrawildbear.gov, which has everything you've ever wanted to know about black bears, plus a detailed map showing wilderness food-storage requirements for the entire Sierra Nevada.

Bites & Stings
SNAKES
Snakes frequent areas below 5000ft, so keep your eyes on the trails and don't stick your hands into places you can't see. Rattlesnakes usually give warning of their presence and backing away from them (slowly!) usually prevents confrontation. Their bites are seldom fatal and only one in three adult rattlers actually injects venom when it bites (younger ones are more prone to inject venom, as they haven't learned self-discipline!).

If bitten, place a light, constricting bandage above the bite, keep the wounded part below the level of the heart and move it as little as possible. Administer CPR if breathing stops. Stay calm and get to a medical facility as soon as possible. Bring the dead snake for identification if you can, but don't risk being bitten again. The use of tourniquets and sucking out the poison are now comprehensively discredited.

TICKS & MOSQUITOES
Much of the Sierra teems with annoying mosquitoes, especially in June and July. You're most likely to run across them anywhere there's standing water. If you're susceptible, bring lots of insect repellent and wear long-sleeved shirts and long pants. Backpackers should bring a lightweight tent or mosquito net for protection.

Present in brush, forest and grassland, ticks may carry Lyme disease or relapsing fever (borelliosis), which are transmitted by bite. Early symptoms of both diseases are similar to the flu: chills, high fever, headache, digestive problems and general aches. Check your clothes, hair and skin after hiking, and your sleeping bag if it has been out beneath trees.

Cold
HYPOTHERMIA
Temperatures in the mountains can quickly drop from balmy to below freezing. A sudden downpour and high winds can also rapidly lower your body temperature. If possible, avoid traveling alone; partners are better able to avoid hypothermia. If you must travel alone, especially when hiking, be sure someone knows both your route and your schedule.

HEALTH & SAFETY

WALKING ON THE WILD SIDE

Before embarking on a walking trip, consider the following points to ensure a safe and enjoyable experience:

- Pay any fees and possess any permits required by local authorities.
- Be sure you are healthy and feel comfortable walking for a sustained period.
- Obtain reliable information about physical and environmental conditions along your intended route (eg from park authorities).
- Be aware of local laws, regulations and etiquette about wildlife and the environment.
- Walk only in regions, and on trails, within your realm of experience.
- Be aware that weather conditions and terrain vary significantly from one region, or even from one trail/track, to another. Seasonal changes can significantly alter any trail. These differences influence the way walkers dress and the equipment they carry.
- Ask before you set out about the environmental characteristics that can affect your walk and how local, experienced walkers deal with these considerations.

Seek shelter when bad weather is unavoidable. Woolen clothing and synthetics, which retain warmth even when wet, are superior to cottons. A quality sleeping bag is a worthwhile investment, although down loses much of its insulating properties when wet. Carry high-energy, easily digestible snacks like chocolate or dried fruit.

Symptoms of hypothermia include shivering, loss of coordination, slurred speech and disorientation or confusion. These can be accompanied by exhaustion, numbness (particularly in toes and fingers), irrational or violent behavior, lethargy, dizzy spells, muscle cramps and bursts of energy. To treat early stages of hypothermia, get victims out of the wind or rain, remove any wet clothing and replace it with dry, warm clothing. Give them hot liquids – not alcohol – and high-calorie, easily digestible food. In advanced stages, it may be necessary to place victims in warm sleeping bags and get in with them. If possible, place them near a fire or in a warm (not hot) bath. Do not rub a victim's skin.

FROSTBITE

This refers to the freezing of extremities, including fingers, toes and nose. Signs and symptoms of frostbite include a whitish or waxy cast to the skin, or even crystals on the surface, plus itching, numbness and pain. Warm the affected areas by immersion in warm (not hot) water or with blankets or clothes, only until the skin becomes flushed. Frostbitten parts should not be rubbed. Pain and swelling are inevitable. Blisters should not be broken. Get medical attention right away.

SNOW BLINDNESS

This is a temporary, painful condition resulting from sunburn of the surface of the eye (cornea). It usually occurs when someone walks on snow without sunglasses. Treatment is to relieve the pain – cold cloths on closed eyelids may help. Antibiotic and anesthetic eye drops are not necessary. The condition usually resolves itself within a few days, and there are no long-term consequences.

Heat

DEHYDRATION & HEAT EXHAUSTION

Dehydration is a potentially dangerous and generally preventable condition caused by excessive fluid loss. Sweating and inadequate fluid intake are among the commonest causes in hikers. It's easy to forget how much fluid you are losing via perspiration while you are trekking, particularly if a strong breeze is drying your skin quickly. You should always maintain a good fluid intake – a minimum of three to four quarts a day is recommended. The first symptoms are weakness, thirst and passing small amounts of very concentrated urine. This may progress to drowsiness, dizziness or fainting on standing up and, finally, coma.

Dehydration and salt deficiency can cause heat exhaustion. Salt deficiency is characterized by fatigue, lethargy, headaches, giddiness and muscle cramps. Salt tablets are overkill – just adding extra salt to your food is probably sufficient. Sports drink powders like Gatorade are also effective.

HEATSTROKE

This is a serious, occasionally fatal condition that occurs if the body's heat-regulating mechanism breaks down and the body temperature rises to dangerous levels. Long, continuous periods of exposure to high temperatures and insufficient fluids can leave you vulnerable to heatstroke.

The symptoms are feeling unwell, not sweating very much (or at all) and a high body temperature (102°F to 106°F or 39°C to 41°C). Where sweating has ceased, the skin becomes flushed and red. Severe, throbbing headaches and lack of coordination will also occur, and the sufferer may be confused or aggressive. Eventually the victim will become delirious or convulse. Hospitalization is essential, but in the interim get victims out of the sun, remove their clothing, cover them with a wet sheet or towel and then fan continually. Give fluids if they are conscious.

SUNBURN

You face a greater risk from sun exposure when hiking in high elevations. Sunburn is possible on hazy or cloudy days and even when it snows. Use sunscreen and lip moisturizer with UV-A and UV-B protection and an SPF of 30 or greater. Reapply it throughout the day. Wear a wide-brimmed hat and sunglasses and consider tying a bandanna around your neck for extra protection.

Cliffs & Waterfalls

Smooth granite beside the area's many rivers, streams and waterfalls is often slippery, even when dry. Tumbling over a waterfall is almost certain to be fatal. Approach any waterfall with caution and, above all, don't get into the water. If you slip, the current will drag you over the fall. Despite warning signs in several languages and protective railings in many places on Yosemite's Mist Trail, many people have died after wading above its waterfalls.

Use caution, too, when hiking to and around Yosemite's Glacier Point, Taft Point, Dewey Point and other precarious viewpoints. Some of these overlooks have railings, but plenty of others don't.

Storms

Changeable weather, a given in the mountains, presents a small yet inherent risk. Before starting your hike – especially if you're heading to the top of an exposed peak or dome – check the forecast at a visitor center or ranger station, which post daily weather reports on bulletin boards. Regardless of the forecast, if you're planning a long hike carry rain gear and be prepared for the worst. The pocket guide *Reading Weather: Where Will You Be When the Storm Hits?* by meteorologist Jim Woodmency explains how to anticipate storms by understanding clouds and weather patterns.

SAFE HIKING
Crossing Streams

You may have to ford a river or stream swollen with snowmelt that is fast-flowing enough to be a potential risk. Before stepping out from the bank, ease one arm out of the shoulder strap of your pack and unclip the belt buckle – should you lose your balance and be swept downstream it will be easier to slip out of your backpack. If linking hands with others, grasp at the wrist – this gives a tighter grip than a handhold. If you're fording alone, plant a stick or your hiking poles upstream to give you greater stability and help you to lean against the

HEALTH & SAFETY

BE PREPARED, BE REALISTIC

Never head out thinking that if you get in a tight spot, you can merely whip out a cell phone and summon a helicopter. Besides phone coverage being spotty in the Sierra Nevada, it is irresponsible to knowingly put yourself and potential rescuers at risk, straining limited resources.

With the extra challenge of thin air and heightened exposure, doing an 8-mile hike or 20-mile bike ride becomes a whole different beast in the mountains. So even if you're extremely fit, always keep the elevation factor in mind. Go easy on your body for the first couple of days so you can acclimatize properly.

current. Use them to feel the way forward and walk side-on to the direction of flow so that your body presents less of an obstacle to the rushing water.

Lightning

If a storm brews, avoid exposed areas such as Yosemite's Half Dome or Sequoia's Moro Rock. Lightning has a penchant for crests, lone trees, small depressions, gullies, caves and cabin entrances, as well as wet ground. If you are caught out in the open, try to curl up as tightly as possible with your feet together and keep a layer of insulation (such as your backpack) between you and the ground. Place metal objects such as metal-frame backpacks and hiking poles away from you.

Rescue & Evacuation

If someone in your group is injured or falls ill and can't move, leave somebody with them while one or more others go for help. If there are only two of you, leave the injured person with as much warm clothing, food and water as it's sensible to spare, plus a whistle and flashlight. Mark the position with something conspicuous – an orange bivvy bag or perhaps a large stone cross on the ground.

SAFE BIKING

Mountain biking and trail riding are prohibited in the parks, so unless you're riding the Yosemite Valley Loops bicycle paths, you must stick to paved roads shared with cars. Consequently, traffic is the biggest danger to cyclists. Though cyclists under 18 must wear a bike helmet, every cyclist should wear one regardless of age. On busier roads such as Yosemite's Tioga Rd or Sequoia's Generals Hwy, early mornings are the best time to avoid heavy traffic or drivers in a hurry to get somewhere.

If you're going on a longer ride, plan ahead. Stay sufficiently hydrated, and bring a patch kit and pump so you won't get stranded with a flat.

Clothing & Equipment

CONTENTS

Heading to Yosemite National Park or Sequoia & Kings Canyon National Parks for the first time? If you plan to backpack, keep in mind that you'll be shouldering everything for a few days, so a comfortable pack weight is crucial. Pare down to the essentials, and make sure that what you bring isn't unnecessarily bulky. Having a clean shirt every morning is nowhere near as important as how your back feels at the end of the day. That said, use a checklist to ensure that all the important stuff makes it in there (see our sample checklist on p278). It doesn't matter how light your stove is if you forget to bring a way to ignite it.

CLOTHING
Layering
A secret of comfortable walking is to wear several layers of light clothing, which you can easily take off or put on as you warm up or cool down. Most hikers use three main layers: a base layer next to the skin, an insulating layer and an outer, shell layer for protection from wind, rain and snow.

For the upper body, the base layer is typically a shirt of synthetic material such as polypropylene, with its ability to wick moisture away from the body and reduce chilling. The insulating layer retains heat next to your body, and is often a windproof synthetic fleece or down jacket. The outer shell should be a waterproof jacket that also protects against cold winds.

For the lower body, the layers generally consist of either shorts or loose-fitting pants; polypropylene 'long-john' underwear; and waterproof rain pants (choose a pair with slits for pocket access and long leg zippers so that you can pull them on and off over your boots).

Waterproof Shells
The ideal specifications are a breathable, waterproof fabric (Gore-Tex is a popular choice), a hood that is roomy enough to cover headwear but still allows peripheral vision, a capacious map pocket and a heavy-gauge zipper protected by a storm flap. If heavy rain is unlikely, a poncho is a good lightweight option.

Footwear, Socks & Gaiters
Sneakers or walking shoes are fine over easy terrain, but for more difficult trails and across rocks and scree, the ankle support

ROUTE FINDING

While accurate, our maps are not perfect. Inaccuracies in altitudes are commonly caused by air-temperature anomalies (for more information on this subject, see Altimeter, p277). Natural features such as river confluences and mountain peaks are in their true position, but sometimes the location of villages and trails is not always so. This may be because a village is spread over a hillside, or the size of the map does not allow for detail of the trail's twists and turns. However, by using several basic route-finding techniques, you will have few problems following our descriptions:

- Be aware of whether the trail should be climbing or descending.
- Check the north-point arrow on the map and determine the general direction of the trail.
- Time your progress over a known distance and calculate the speed at which you travel in the given terrain. From then on, you can determine with reasonable accuracy how far you have traveled.
- Watch the path – look for boot prints and other signs of previous passage.

NAVIGATION EQUIPMENT

Maps & Compass

Carry a good map of the area you are hiking in (see Maps, p26), and know how to read it. Before setting off, ensure that you understand the contours and map symbols, plus the main ridge and river systems in the area. Familiarize yourself with the true north–south directions and the general direction in which you are heading. On the trail, try to identify major landforms, eg mountain ranges, and locate them on your map. This will give you a better grasp of the region's geography.

Buy a compass and learn how to use it. The attraction of magnetic north varies in different parts of the world, so compasses need to be balanced accordingly. Compass manufacturers have divided the world into five zones. Make sure your compass is balanced for your destination zone. There are also 'universal' compasses on the market that can be used anywhere in the world.

How to Use a Compass

This is a very basic introduction to using a compass and will only be of assistance if you are proficient in map reading. For simplicity, it doesn't take magnetic variation into account. Before using a compass we recommend you obtain further instruction.

Reading a Compass

Hold the compass flat in the palm of your hand. Rotate the bezel so the red end of the needle points to the N on the bezel. The bearing is read from the dash under the bezel.

1	Base plate
2	Direction of travel arrow
3	Dash
4	Bezel
5	Meridian lines
6	Needle
7	Red end
8	N (north point)

Orienting the Map

To orient the map so that it aligns with the ground, place the compass flat on the map. Rotate the map until the needle is parallel with the map's north–south grid lines and the red end is pointing to north on the map. You can now identify features around you by aligning them with labeled features on the map.

Taking a Bearing from the Map

Draw a line on the map between your start and end points. Place the edge of the compass on this line with the direction of travel arrow pointing towards your destination. Rotate the bezel until the meridian lines are parallel with the north–south grid lines on the map and the N points to north on the map. Read the bearing from the dash.

Following a Bearing

Rotate the bezel so that the intended bearing is in line with the dash. Place the compass flat in the palm of your hand and rotate the base plate until the red end points to N on the bezel. The direction of travel arrow will now point in the direction you need to walk.

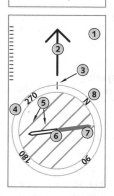

offered by boots is invaluable. Nonslip soles (such as Vibram) provide the best grip. Buy boots in warm conditions or go for a walk before trying them on, so that your feet can expand slightly as they would on a walk. Most hikers carry a pair of sandals or flip-flops to wear at night or at rest stops. Sandals are also useful when fording waterways.

Hiking socks should be free of ridged seams in the toes and heels. For longer hikes, synthetics wick away moisture better than cotton and wool, and help to avoid blisters. Also consider wearing longer socks for protecting your ankles from scratches and bug bites.

If you will be hiking through snow, deep mud or scratchy vegetation, gaiters will protect your legs and help to keep your socks dry. The best are made of strong fabric, with a robust zip protected by a flap, and secure easily around the foot. Gaiters are an especially good idea if you'll be walking through mushy Sierra melt-off in the spring.

Determining your Bearing

Rotate the bezel so the red end points to the N. Place the compass flat in the palm of your hand and rotate the base plate until the direction of travel arrow points in the direction in which you have been walking. Read your bearing from the dash.

Global Positioning System

Originally developed by the US Department of Defense, the Global Positioning System (GPS) is a network of more than 20 earth-orbiting satellites that continually beam encoded signals back to earth. Small, computer-driven devices (GPS receivers) can decode these signals to give users an extremely accurate reading of their location – to within 15m, anywhere on the planet, any time, in almost any weather. The cheapest hand-held GPS receivers now cost less than $100 (although these may not have a built-in averaging system that minimizes signal errors). Other important factors to consider when buying a GPS receiver are its weight and battery life.

Remember that a GPS receiver is of little use to hikers unless used with an accurate topographical map. The receiver simply gives your position, which you must then locate on the local map. GPS receivers will only work properly in the open. The signals from a crucial satellite may be blocked (or bounce off rock or water) directly below high cliffs, near large bodies of water or in dense tree cover and give inaccurate readings. GPS receivers are more vulnerable to breakdowns (including dead batteries) than the humble magnetic compass – a low-technology device that has served navigators faithfully for centuries – so don't rely on them entirely for your navigational needs.

Altimeter

Altimeters determine altitude by measuring air pressure. Because pressure is affected by temperature, altimeters are calibrated to take lower temperatures at higher altitudes into account. However, discrepancies can still occur, especially in unsettled weather, so it's wise to take a few precautions when using your altimeter.

- Reset your altimeter regularly at known elevations such as spot heights and passes. Do not take spot heights from villages where there may be a large difference in elevation from one end of the settlement to another.

- Use your altimeter in conjunction with other navigation techniques to fix your position. For instance, taking a back bearing to a known peak or river confluence, determining the general direction of the track and obtaining your elevation will usually give you a pretty good fix on your position.

Altimeters are also barometers and are useful for indicating changing weather conditions. If the altimeter shows increasing elevation while you are not climbing, it means the air pressure is dropping and a low-pressure weather system may be approaching.

EQUIPMENT
Backpacks & Daypacks

For day hikes, a daypack (1800 to 2450 cu inches, or 30L to 40L) will usually suffice, but for multiday hikes you will need a backpack of between 2750 and 5500 cu inches (45L and 90L) capacity. A good backpack should be made of strong fabric, a lightweight internal or external frame and an adjustable, well-padded harness that evenly distributes weight (internal frames distribute weight better than external, so are more popular). If you can, try several out in the store, with weights inside to give you a sense of the comfort levels. Even if the manufacturer claims your pack is waterproof, use heavy-duty liners or a pack cover.

Tents

A three-season tent will fulfill the requirements of most hikers. The floor and the outer shell, or fly, should have taped or sealed seams and covered zips to stop leaks. Most hikers find tents of around 4.4lb to 6.6lb (2kg to

CHECKLIST

This list is a general guide to the things you might take on a walk or hike. Your list will vary depending on the kind of walking or hiking you want to do, whether you're camping or planning on staying in hostels or B&Bs, and on the terrain, weather conditions and time of year.

Clothing

☐ boots and spare laces
☐ gaiters
☐ hat (warm), scarf and gloves
☐ jacket (waterproof)
☐ rain pants (waterproof)
☐ sneakers, sandals or flip-flops
☐ shorts and trousers or skirt
☐ socks and underwear
☐ sun hat
☐ sweater or fleece jacket
☐ thermal underwear
☐ T-shirt and long-sleeved shirt with collar

Equipment

☐ backpack with liner or cover (waterproof)
☐ first-aid kit*
☐ food and snacks (high energy) and one day's emergency supplies
☐ insect repellent
☐ map, compass and guidebook
☐ map case or clip-seal plastic bags
☐ pocketknife
☐ sunglasses
☐ sunscreen and lip balm
☐ survival bag or blanket
☐ toilet paper and trowel
☐ flashlight or headlamp, spare batteries and bulb
☐ water container
☐ whistle

Overnight Hikes

☐ cooking, eating and drinking utensils
☐ dishwashing items
☐ matches and lighter
☐ sewing/repair kit
☐ sleeping bag and bag liner/inner sheet
☐ sleeping mat (and if inflatable, patch kit)
☐ spare cord
☐ stove and fuel
☐ tent, pegs, poles and ropes
☐ toiletries
☐ towel
☐ water filter, purification tablets or drops
☐ bear canister

Optional Items

☐ altimeter
☐ binoculars
☐ camera, film/charger and batteries
☐ candle
☐ emergency distress beacon
☐ GPS receiver
☐ groundsheet
☐ cell phone**
☐ mosquito net
☐ notebook and pen
☐ bathing suit
☐ walking/hiking/trekking poles
☐ watch

*see the Medical Checklist (p268)   **see Telephone (p256)

3kg) a comfortable carrying weight. Dome- and tunnel-shaped tents handle windy conditions better than flat-sided tents. Devoted acolytes of ultralight can ditch the tent and opt for using the fly and footprint (ground tarp) option available with some tent sets.

Sleeping Bag & Mat

Down fillings are warmer than synthetic for the same weight and bulk, but unlike synthetic fillings do not retain warmth when wet. Mummy bags are the best shape for weight and warmth. The given figure (eg

10°F/-12°C) is the coldest temperature at which a person should feel comfortable in the bag (although the ratings are notoriously laughable and unreliable).

An inner sheet helps keep your sleeping bag clean, as well as adding an insulating layer. Silk 'inners' are lightest, but they also come in cotton or polypropylene.

Self-inflating sleeping mats work like a thin air cushion between you and the ground, and also insulate you from the cold. Foam mats are a low-cost, but less comfortable, alternative.

Stoves & Fuel

Fuel stoves fall roughly into four categories: propane, multifuel, methylated spirits (ethyl alcohol) and butane gas. Bulky car camping stoves run on propane canisters, the configuration most commonly used by visitors in developed campgrounds. This fuel is inexpensive and available everywhere, including many gas stations. Multifuel stoves are small, efficient and ideal for places where a reliable fuel supply is difficult to find. However, they tend to be sooty and require frequent maintenance. Stoves running on methylated spirits are slower and less efficient, but are safe, clean and easy to use. Butane gas stoves are clean and reliable, but can be slow, and the gas canisters can be awkward to carry and a potential litter problem. Propane and butane performamance decreases in below-freezing temps.

Bear Canisters

Most backcountry hikes require a bear-resistant container for storing food and toiletries. If you have your own, confirm that your model is approved for that area (bears have learned how to open some). The popular Garcia canisters, made locally in Visalia, can be rented in the parks and at nearby USFS ranger stations. New canisters cost anywhere from $70 for a standard Garcia canister to $275 for an ultralight Wild Ideas expedition model, meaning that renting can be a great option.

BUYING & RENTING LOCALLY

Renting equipment is a good way to go if you've never tried an activity. Why sink money into equipment that might live in a closet forever after? That said, rentals aren't that cheap if you plan to use something for more than a weekend. A tent rental may be only $15 per day, but an inexpensive or secondhand tent can be $100 or so.

Yosemite has a number of excellent stores that sell or rent camping supplies and backpacking and climbing gear (see p38). Sequoia & Kings Canyon only has odds and ends at the park village areas, so your best nearby option is the Fresno **REI** (☎ 559-261-4168; 7810 N Blackstone Ave), which sells and rents tents, sleeping bags, backpacks and stoves. In Lone Pine, close to Mt Whitney, **Elevation** (☎ 760-876-4560; 125 N Main St) rents crampons and some climbing gear.

CLOTHING & EQUIPMENT

Glossary

AAA – American Automobile Club of America; usually called 'triple-A'

backcountry – anywhere more than a couple of hundred yards from roads, boardwalks or other park infrastructure
basalt – a hard, dense and very common volcanic rock; solidified lava
BLM – Bureau of Land Management

concessionaire – private business or service provider permitted to operate inside the parks by the park service

GPS – Global Positioning System; an electronic, satellite-based network that allows for the calculation of position and elevation using a hand-held receiver/decoder

hookup – facility at a campsite for giving an RV water and/or electricity

KOA – Kampgrounds of America; a private chain of campgrounds throughout the USA

Labor Day – national holiday that falls on the first Monday in September

Memorial Day – national holiday that falls on the last Monday in May

NPS – National Park Service

out-and-back – hike backtracking to its starting point from its destination
outfitter – business supplying guides, equipment and/or transport for fishing, canoeing, hiking, rafting or horseback trips

RV – recreational vehicle; also called a motor home or camper

saddle – low place in a ridge
shuttle hike – a destination hike where it is necessary to leave a vehicle at both trailheads

talus – slope of rock boulders or debris
tufa – a porous rock formed as a deposit from springs or streams

USFS – United States Forest Service, which manages the nation's system of national forests
USGS – United States Geological Survey; the national cartographic organization

YARTS – Yosemite Area Regional Transport System

Behind the Scenes

THIS BOOK

This 2nd edition of *Yosemite, Sequoia & Kings Canyon National Parks* was researched and written by Danny Palmerlee, Beth Kohn and David Lukas. *Yosemite National Park 1* was written by Kurt Wolff, Amy Marr, David Lukas and Cheryl Koehler. This guidebook was commissioned in Lonely Planet's Oakland office, and produced by the following:

Commissioning Editor Heather Dickson
Coordinating Editors Pete Cruttenden, Charlotte Orr
Coordinating Cartographer Andrew Smith
Coordinating Layout Designer Paul Iacono
Senior Editors Helen Christinis, Sasha Baskett
Managing Cartographer Alison Lyall
Managing Layout Designer Adam McCrow
Cover Designer Amy Stephens
Color Designer David Kemp
Project Manager Eoin Dunlevy

Thanks to Sam Benson, Jennifer Garrett, Suki Gear, Chris Girdler, Michelle Glynn, Brice Gosnell, James Hardy, Laura Jane, Lisa Knights, Adriana Mammarella, Raphael Richards, Glenn van der Knijff, Celia Wood

THANKS
DANNY PALMERLEE

I dedicate my portion of this book to my daughter, Nadine Sabri Palmerlee, who may never know the patience her mother showed while her dad ran around the Sierras researching this book, before and after she was born. And, of course, to Aimee, for everything. Huge hugs to Ellen and Mick for joining me on hikes and keeping me fired up. Thanks to my coauthor, Beth Kohn, and my commissioning editor, Heather Dickson, for their patience amidst my endless barrage of emails and questions. Suki, thanks for the cameo! In Yosemite, many thanks to Adrienne Freeman, Scott Gediman, Bonnie Gisel, Kenny Karst, Dave Bengston and Glenn Crosby. Thanks also to the previous authors of this book – Kurt Wolff, Amy Marr, David Lukas and Cheryl Koehler – whose work forms the bedrock of this edition. Finally, thanks to all the hikers I met on the trail, both for their conversations and their inspiration.

BETH KOHN

Thanks to all the helpful rangers and interpretive staff in Yosemite, Kings Canyon and Sequoia and

---

THE LONELY PLANET STORY

Fresh from an epic journey across Europe, Asia and Australia in 1972, Tony and Maureen Wheeler sat at their kitchen table stapling together notes. The first Lonely Planet guidebook, Across Asia on the Cheap, was born.

Travelers snapped up the guides. Inspired by their success, the Wheelers began publishing books to Southeast Asia, India and beyond. Demand was prodigious, and the Wheelers expanded the business rapidly to keep up. Over the years, Lonely Planet extended its coverage to every country and into the virtual world via lonelyplanet.com and the Thorn Tree message board.

As Lonely Planet became a globally loved brand, Tony and Maureen received several offers for the company. But it wasn't until 2007 that they found a partner whom they trusted to remain true to the company's principles of traveling widely, treading lightly and giving sustainably. In October of that year, BBC Worldwide acquired a 75% share in the company, pledging to uphold Lonely Planet's commitment to independent travel, trustworthy advice and editorial independence.

Today, Lonely Planet has offices in Melbourne, London and Oakland, with over 500 staff members and 300 authors. Tony and Maureen are still actively involved with Lonely Planet. They're traveling more often than ever, and they're devoting their spare time to charitable projects. And the company is still driven by the philosophy of *Across Asia on the Cheap*: 'All you've got to do is decide to go and the hardest part is over. So go!'

the surrounding national forests, especially Sierra Willoughby in Yosemite and Carey Goldstein in Sequoia & Kings Canyon. Dillon Dutton and Jennifer Gorospe get special over-the-fold billing for more favors than I can think of, and Julia Brashares gets props for keeping me company on my favorite backcountry hike. Suki Gear stepped in with advice when we needed her, and Sam Benson was (and still is) my SEKI superstar. Biggest thanks go to Heather Dickson for putting me to work in the parks all summer, and Danny Palmerlee for keeping me giggling over the keyboard. As always, love and bowls of soup to Claude Moller.

OUR READERS

Many thanks to the travelers who used the last edition and wrote to us with helpful hints, useful advice and interesting anecdotes:

Rosanna D'Costa, Daniel Jarzemsky, Elizabeth Rothman, Brian Tiernan

ACKNOWLEDGMENTS

Many thanks to the following for the use of their content:

Internal photographs p5 by Randy Lloyd/Flickr; p8 Brian King/Flickr; p10 Paige Falk/Alamy; p12 Lars Jensen/Flickr; p12 Dolan Halbrook/Flickr; p13 Barbara Kalister; p14 John Lens/Alamy; p15 Beth Kohn. All other photographs by Lonely Planet Images, and by Neil Wilson p3; John Elk III p4 (#1), p5 (#3), p6 (#2), p11 (#4); Thomas Winz p4 (#2), p13 (#3); John Mock p5 (#6), p6 (#4), p7 (#1), p10 (#5); Cheyenne L Rouse p7 (#3); Richard Cummins p7 (#7), p9 (#3), p15 (#4); Woods Wheatcroft p8 (#2); Wes Walker p9 (#4); Mark Newman p14 (#3); Andrew Peacock p15 (#5); Emily Riddell p16.

All images are the copyright of the photographers unless otherwise indicated. Many of the images in this guide are available for licensing from Lonely Planet Images: www.lonelyplanet images.com.

Index

See also separate subindex for Hikes (p292).

INDEX

INDEX

HIKES

000 Map pages
000 Photograph pages

INDEX

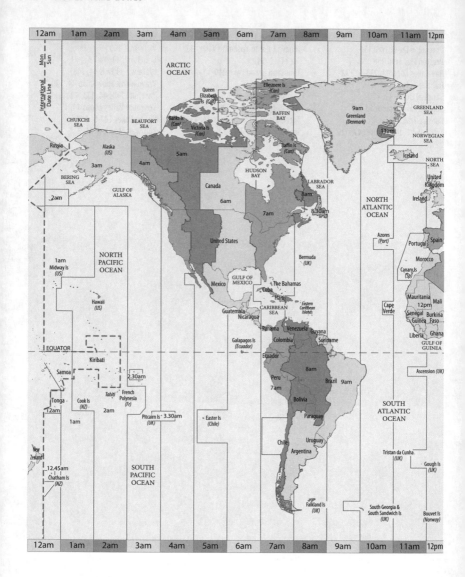

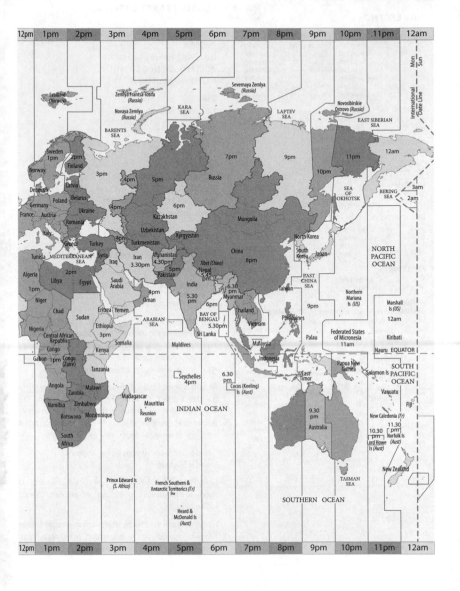

MAP LEGEND

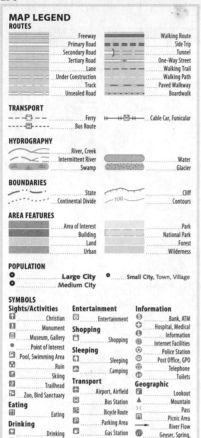

ROUTES
- Freeway
- Primary Road
- Secondary Road
- Tertiary Road
- Lane
- Under Construction
- Track
- Unsealed Road
- Walking Route
- Side Trip
- Tunnel
- One-Way Street
- Walking Trail
- Walking Path
- Paved Walkway
- Boardwalk

TRANSPORT
- Ferry
- Bus Route
- Cable Car, Funicular

HYDROGRAPHY
- River, Creek
- Intermittent River
- Swamp
- Water
- Glacier

BOUNDARIES
- State
- Continental Divide
- Cliff
- Contours

AREA FEATURES
- Area of Interest
- Building
- Land
- Urban
- Park
- National Park
- Forest
- Wilderness

POPULATION
- ● Large City
- ● Medium City
- ○ Small City, Town, Village

SYMBOLS

Sights/Activities
- Christian
- Monument
- Museum, Gallery
- Point of Interest
- Pool, Swimming Area
- Ruin
- Skiing
- Trailhead
- Zoo, Bird Sanctuary

Eating
- Eating

Drinking
- Drinking
- Café

Entertainment
- Entertainment

Shopping
- Shopping

Sleeping
- Sleeping
- Camping

Transport
- Airport, Airfield
- Bus Station
- Bicycle Route
- Parking Area
- Gas Station
- Taxi Rank

Information
- Bank, ATM
- Hospital, Medical
- Information
- Internet Facilities
- Police Station
- Post Office, GPO
- Telephone
- Toilets

Geographic
- Lookout
- Mountain
- Pass
- Picnic Area
- River Flow
- Geyser, Spring, Waterfall

LONELY PLANET OFFICES

Australia
Head Office
Locked Bag 1, Footscray, Victoria 3011
☎ 03 8379 8000, fax 03 8379 8111
talk2us@lonelyplanet.com.au

USA
150 Linden St, Oakland, CA 94607
☎ 510 893 8555, toll free 800 275 8555
fax 510 893 8572
info@lonelyplanet.com

UK
2nd Floor, 186 City Road,
London ECV1 2NT
☎ 020 7106 2100, fax 020 7106 2101
go@lonelyplanet.co.uk

Published by Lonely Planet Publications Pty Ltd
ABN 36 005 607 983